G000127245

The Adversity Formula:
Inspirational Lessons from History
By
Steven Mason
ISBN:978-1-8382223-5-2

Published By: -

i2i Publishing. Manchester.

www.i2ipublishing.co.uk

In praise of The Adversity Formula

'What a great idea for a book and superbly executed. There's so much to learn from and so much to be inspired by, packed into this volume'.

Daniel Finkelstein, Award-winning Journalist, Associate Editor and Political Columnist - *The Times*

'This is a spirited case for the role of great men and women in shaping the world. Whether in politics or golf or on the stage, Steven Mason seeks to draw out the common threads: the attitudes, habits and qualities that allow inspirational figures not just to survive misfortune but to profit from it ...'

Sir Graham Brady, MP, Chairman - 1922 Committee

'The Adversity Formula: Inspirational Lessons from History is motivational. Steven Mason has shared the personal challenges that many icons from the world of politics, sports and entertainment have faced along with the resilience they demonstrated in ways for all of us to relate to, learn and live by'.

Janet Fanaki, Host - The RESILIENT PEOPLE podcast, resilientpeople.ca

'Steven Mason has managed to capture every nuance of Muhammad Ali's remarkable life in a single chapter and it's a fascinating read. I was privileged to have spent ten years - from 1971 to 1981 - going around the world with Ali, covering all his major fights. His name will always be prominent in any history of the twentieth century.

Mason must have had difficulty in deciding where to place him in his book. Ali could also have fitted comfortably among 'The Humanists', 'The Entrepreneurs', 'The Politicians' and 'The Entertainers', such was his mesmerising influence on mankind'.

Colin Hart, Boxing Columnist - *The Sun*

'Delighted that Steven Mason has chosen Ella Fitzgerald to figure among his subjects as an inspirational lesson from history in overcoming adversity. In her own quiet and understated way, Ella epitomised the American Dream, literally starting with nothing as a homeless waif, she ended her life in Beverley Hills luxury in an America riven with racial prejudice — it's an object lesson we can all learn from'.

Professor Stuart Nicholson. Author - *Ella Fitzgerald: A Biography Of The First Lady Of Jazz*

'Steven Mason has compiled some fascinating portraits of some of the most inspirational figures of the past century, who overcame adversity despite overwhelming odds. We all have limiting beliefs and this book will help you to shed yours, by witnessing the limits of the human resolve.'

Rabbi Chaim Miller, Author - *Turning Judaism Outward: A Biography of the Rebbe, Rabbi Menachem Mendel Schneerson*

'Like never before, we would be wise to listen to the figures talking to us through Steven Mason. They remind us that adversity is not only nothing new, it's a requisite of the human experience'.

Julie Des Jardins, Historian of American women and gender. Author - *The Madame Curie Complex: The Hidden History of Women in Science*

'Mason's emphasis on adversity as a catalyst for positive change is a good addition to the literature on self-improvement'.

Robin Gerber, Best-Selling Author, Speaker and Historian. Author - *Leadership the Eleanor Roosevelt Way*

'An essential resource for anyone looking to improve their own performance. This book demonstrates that looking back at our role models' reaction to adversity, helps prepare us for any challenges that lie ahead'.

Tania Friedlander, Certified Leadership & Development Coach for Fortune 500 employees

'Thomas Paine wrote, "These are the times that try men's souls." In order to get through contemporary trying times, I highly recommend Steve Mason's 'The Adversity Formula' that delivers the message of fortitude, persistence, and enlightenment'.

Marlene Wagman-Geller, Author - *Women of Means: Fascinating Biographies of Royals, Heiresses, Eccentrics and Other Poor Little Rich Girls*

'In these trying times of the Covid-19 pandemic, most of us need reassurance that brighter days lie ahead. Steven Mason shows us the way forward in this remarkable work that focuses on the biographies of thirty notable figures. Coming from diverse backgrounds and fields, these individuals overcame almost unbelievable adversity to both triumph in their own pursuits - whether in business, sports, entertainment, politics, or war - and make the world a better place for others. Drawing on the life experiences of figures as different as Eleanor Roosevelt, Muhammad Ali, Nelson Mandela, Katharine Graham, Margaret Thatcher and Ella Fitzgerald, Mason provides an inspiring message that adversity can serve as a challenge rather than a defeat.

The book provides much-needed inspiration during a period of global uncertainty on many fronts - medical, political, and cultural - leaving the reader with a renewed appreciation of the human potential'.

Maurine H. Beasley, Ph.D., Professor Emerita, University of Maryland, College Park, US. Author - *Eleanor Roosevelt, Transformative First Lady*

'A thought-provoking read, particularly in these most challenging times, of how to cope with and ultimately triumph over adversity'.

Jim White, Columnist - Telegraph Media Group. Author *- Manchester United: The Biography*

Dedicated to the memory of my Grandfather, Walter Levy, whose triumph over adversity is as great as any of the stories you will read within this book.

Acknowledgments

There is so much more to writing a book than I could ever have imagined. Whilst the project begins alone, with hour upon hour of independent work, I quickly learnt that the publication process is more about teamwork than individual effort.

Along the way, I have come to learn much about friendship, selflessness, family and the powers of positivity and encouragement.

Within these pages, we will discover how the personal success of our chosen personalities was, in no small part, down to the support and effort of people behind the scenes. With that in mind, I would like to thank several people who made this a far less daunting experience than had first appeared.

My first thanks must go to Lionel Ross, the owner and publisher at i2ipublishing.co.uk, who supported the project from the outset. His feedback upon reading the initial draft chapters was positive enough to give me the confidence to attempt to turn a simple idea into a book. His sage counsel was invaluable throughout the process.

I must also express sincere thanks to my editor, Mark Cripps for helping turn this first-time author's manuscript into a fully-fledged book. A first-class editor, his patient and calm approach was the perfect counterweight to my own unique style of working. I greatly appreciate his foresight and continuous encouragement.

Thanks, are also due to Dino Caruana for patiently listening to my ideas and feedback, before coming up with an excellent cover design.

Several people from a range of backgrounds made themselves available to help with reviewing the text and providing quotes in praise of the book.

Having read over the manuscript for what seemed like the hundredth time, I needed a fresh pair of eyes to help with the final proofread. Janinne Bracha Shor enthusiastically did just that and I thank her for undertaking that challenging job.

It was a great honour to receive feedback from one of my favourite writers, Daniel Finkelstein.

Likewise, Sir Graham Brady took the time out of an extremely busy schedule to review and comment on the manuscript. I am grateful to both for their generosity of spirit.

Colin Hart, the veteran boxing writer, spent years traveling the world, covering Muhammad Ali's fights. It was only natural that I approached him for his feedback on that particular chapter. I was truly humbled by his positive response to the contents of the chapter.

Janet Fanaki is the founder and lead content creator of *Resilient People,* which was set up after the tragic death of her husband. Having spent a lot of time researching individuals who demonstrated tremendous resilience, I was honoured when she agreed to take a look and comment on the impact the book could have on those dealing with major life challenges.

I have known Jim White, the excellent *Daily Telegraph* columnist and author of *Manchester United: The Biography,* for some time and am appreciative of the time he spent reviewing the chapters on the various sports stars.

Rabbi Chaim Miller has written one of the best books ever produced on the life of Rabbi Menachem Mendel Schneerson, the Lubavitcher Rebbe. I have long admired his writing style and greatly appreciate the kind words he provided on the book.

Julie Des Jardins is a fantastic historian and author of four critically acclaimed books, including one featuring Marie Curie. The encouragement and support of such a seasoned author meant a lot to this first-time author.

Robin Gerber is another excellent historian and best-selling author, having produced a wonderful book on Eleanor Roosevelt. She agreed to provide her comments prior to publication.

Maurine H. Beasley is another historian who I approached to review the Eleanor Roosevelt and Katharine Graham chapters. I was bowled over by her enthusiasm for the project as a whole and the time she spent reviewing the manuscript.

It also meant a lot to get words of encouragement from Marlene Wagman-Geller, who has written the fantastic book: *Women of Means: The Fascinating Biographies of Royals, Heiresses, Eccentrics and Other Poor Little Rich Girls*.

Professor Stuart Nicholson, the noted Jazz writer and biographer, took time out of his busy schedule to clarify a number of relating to the life of Ella Fitzgerald. His input was greatly valued.

Thank you to tennis historian and author, Joel Drucker for his assistance and feedback in relation to the chapter on Althea Gibson.

Last, but certainly not least, I was privileged to strike up correspondence with Tania Friedlander, an inspirational leadership and development coach to top executives. Her words of support are also greatly appreciated.

Several members of my family provided tremendous support for my endeavours and all deserve my thanks.

Firstly, my parents, Tony and Hilary Mason, have been a constant source of support and encouragement. In the context of this book, I would like to thank my father for sharing his thoughts and anecdotes on some of the personalities featured within, namely Winston Churchill and Margaret Thatcher. His own interest in history and reading made him an obvious choice to turn to for the proofread of the final manuscript.

Secondly, my children, Eliana, Yoni, Benny, Ariel and Akiva, have all contributed in their own way. Having children with a love of learning made it possible to obtain valuable feedback at the dinner table. In the case of both Helen Keller and Rosa Parks, I must confess that it was my children who, in their various school projects, brought these two remarkable women's lives to my attention. As well as being the most important people in my life, they allowed me the space to work in a quiet environment, which was no mean feat during regular lockdowns.

Finally, I cannot adequately express enough just how grateful I am for the support of my wife, Dina. An avid reader herself, she assisted with regular proofreading as well as providing feedback and support throughout. Juggling her roles as a dedicated teacher, mother, wife, and regular volunteer provided me with the inspiration to emulate what she does best, which is helping others in need.

13

Contents

Prologue

Adversity Overload

A worldwide pandemic and more

The Covid-19 pandemic, which overwhelmed the world in 2020, resulted in global disruption not seen since the end of the Second World War. Wherever you were, whatever your age, gender, profession, or social class, you will have been affected in some way by the rapid spread of the virus and the ensuing disruption that followed.

The pandemic managed to seep into every nook and cranny of our lives, disrupting daily routines and changing lives forever. Phrases such as 'flattening the curve' and 'social distancing' became the new normal. The virus continued its spread across the world, with millions of confirmed cases and over one million related deaths. At the time of writing, whilst a vaccine has been approved in the UK and is being developed at record pace in other countries, there is no guarantee it will work. Disruption is expected to continue for some time.

Giant industries and corporations, previously considered to be infallible, ground to a halt and in some cases, collapsed. Restaurants, shops, entertainment venues, sporting arenas and places of worship closed indefinitely. The airline industry teetered on the brink of bankruptcy as flights dropped ninety per cent in April 2020.

A report from the Institute for Fiscal Studies spoke of, 'a debate starting on whether the adverse health effects of a recession may have a greater impact than the deaths caused by the pandemic itself'.

To add to the undercurrent of insecurity, global events caused further significant disruption at a time when least desired. The death of George Floyd in police custody in the United States sparked widespread protests in some cases, rioting and civil unrest, across the globe. Then, in early August, a huge blast in a Beirut warehouse holding over two-thousand tonnes of ammonium nitrate led to the deaths of over two-hundred people, injuries to over six thousand people and left nearly three-hundred thousand people homeless. It was estimated that the blast in the Lebanese capital was one-twentieth that of the nuclear bomb dropped on Hiroshima. In every corner of the globe, adversity was widespread. An overload of adversity appeared to be hitting the world all at once.

Definition and effects of adversity

Whilst Covid-19 may be the most significant challenge many of us have faced, it is certainly not the first, nor will it be our last setback. If Benjamin Franklin had time to think again before uttering his famous quote, a third component, adversity, might well rank alongside death and taxation, as the only certainties in life.

But the term adversity can mean different things to different people. Using one dictionary definition of adversity, it is, 'a noun - a difficult or unlucky situation or event'. Other definitions speak about misfortune and calamity. On balance, most people would likely agree that the term adversity comes to define a scenario where normal life is affected and disrupted in a significant and yet negative manner.

The effect of adversity can be far reaching, resulting from unexpected bereavement, a traumatic accident, illness, disability, or a marital breakdown. Alternatively, it may arrive in more transient forms such as an exam failure, job loss, or sporting defeat. Sometimes it creeps up, unexpectedly, whilst at other times, it forms part of a chronic situation.

For those of a certain age, our only choice has been to learn on the job, so to speak, when working out how to react when adversity strikes. For something so central to our lives, it is astonishing how little adversity was spoken about in our education up to recent times. For many of us, our schooling in how to deal with adversity has come after a difficult event, when in hindsight, it would have been more beneficial to learn vital skills before facing such challenges.

Fortunately, for today's youngsters, mental health and emotional well-being education forms an integral part of today's UK school curriculum. Key Stages 3 and 4 include promotion of emotional wellbeing and healthy coping strategies. Older students are taught about developing 'digital resilience' in the context of online pressures and most significantly, reframing negative thinking.

The Oklahoma Standard shows up good and bad

Adversity has always brought out the best or worst in people. I first became aware of a phenomenon called 'The Oklahoma Standard', when studying the aftermath of the 1995 Oklahoma City bombings.

After the devastating terror attack, which claimed one-hundred and sixty-eight lives, the local community responded in an unprecedented manner. Residents, acting on their own initiative, brought food to rescue workers and donated their own time, skills, supplies and even blood. The outpouring of compassion and help was so remarkable, it became known simply as 'The Oklahoma Standard'. It was poignant to note that as the twenty-fifth anniversary of that terrible event was marked, communities across the world invoked their own version of the standard.

Here in the UK, after the arrival of Covid-19, the remarkable sum of over twenty-million pounds was raised by the British public and distributed to National Health Service (NHS) charities. Spearheaded by an inspirational centurion, the late Captain Sir Tom Moore, thousands were inspired to support the doctors, nurses and other healthcare workers battling on the front line.

Conversely, there were heart-breaking stories. Heartless thieves stole eighty-thousand PPE face masks destined for the NHS and front-line workers. Domestic abuse killings doubled over a twenty-one-day period in the lockdown and a national abuse helpline received forty-nine per cent more calls than usual.

Adversity clearly presents us with opportunities; some pass with flying colours, whilst others buckle under the pressure. Indeed, whatever a person's circumstances may be, as we shall see, it is often not what they experience, but how they deal with their challenges, that shapes the outcome. In fact, experience has taught many of us that it is always better to be proactive, rather than reactive, when coming to terms with adversity.

Adversity as an opportunity

During the last major economic crisis in 2008, data showed that periods of adversity encourage invention. The Kauffman Index of Entrepreneurial Activity revealed that the rate of new-business creation was higher during the deepest part of the 2009 recession than it had been in the fourteen previous years. We are already seeing a changing marketplace and astute businessmen and women have been quick to spot gaps in the market.

From my own point of view, the writing of this book would simply never have been possible. Even if the idea to write a book would have developed in my head, it is likely that a combination of a new-born baby, childcare demands, school rotas and a social life would have put paid to the project early on. The invisible straightjacket imposed by lockdown forcing me to stay in my home with all other normal activities curtailed, turned into a positive experience for me.

Many well-known people from the past have spoken positively about adversity, rather than viewing it in an exclusively negative light. Former British Prime Minister, Benjamin Disraeli said, 'there is no education like adversity'. Another former Prime Minister, Israel's Golda Meir reinforced this view saying, 'you'll never find a better sparring partner than adversity'.

Terry Waite – A positive view of a negative situation

A fascinating example of how adversity can be dealt with and perceived in a positive way, can be learnt from the experiences of Terry Waite, in a story which captivated me as a child. As a humanitarian and envoy for the Church of England, Waite travelled to Lebanon in 1987 to try to secure the release of four hostages held by Hezbollah. Accused of being a CIA agent, he was kidnapped and held captive for nearly five years, or one thousand, seven-hundred and sixty-three days to be precise. Held in solitary confinement, Waite spent most of his time blindfolded and chained to a radiator.

At the outset of the pandemic, with a period of lockdown looming, Waite's wisdom was much in demand. Media outlets across the world rushed to interview one of the world's foremost authorities on isolation.

Waite was adamant that whilst the type of adversity we are currently confronted with can be difficult, 'out of it, something creative and quite unexpected can emerge'. Recalling those dark days in Lebanon, he recounted, 'I remember telling myself that though severely restricted, I still had life. I had to learn how to live one day at a time and live that day as fully as possible. I had no opportunity for physical exercise but could exercise my brain, so I began to write in my head'.

Waite's words show the capacity for finding meaning in adversity. There is the remarkable resilience that people display amidst a crisis. There is the chance to return to a simpler life, rediscover community and the opportunity to summon up reserves of strength we never knew existed within us.

In dealing with major adversity by anyone's standards, perhaps Waite summed up his view of adversity best with the words, 'hard it certainly is, but suffering need not destroy'.

Covid-19 and the question of how to cope

Like most people, I experienced a range of differing emotions during this difficult period in 2020. The early days dealing with the lockdown caused by the virus, were filled with fear, dread, lethargy and growing frustration at being kept from my usual routine.

Cabin fever struck early on and I found myself spiralling towards a dark place. With no football, cricket, or other activities that I usually partake in, a twelve-week lockdown seemed like a painfully long time.

I began to see several people in my neighbourhood fall victim to the dreadful condition. By the end of May, I had attended one socially distanced and sparsely attended funeral and watched several more on Zoom - truly sobering experiences.

Fortunately, I still had my job, but even that created its challenges. My new home office was a gloomy windowless basement in my house. Apart from devising an exercise programme, binging on documentaries and reading, I knew I had to find a way to keep my mind active. I had to shake off this image of a twelve-week calendar in my head, in which I was agonizingly marking off one day at a time, as if I were in some sort of mental prison.

Faith and adversity

While contemplating my own approach to dealing with the situation created by Covid-19, it struck me that in fact, I had long grappled with the subject of finding meaning in adversity. As a practicing Jew, I was taught that the point of life was to learn and grow from challenges. The Torah teaches us that man has the capability to withstand any challenge, however difficult. Not only that, but every such challenge is for our ultimate good.

Rabbi Yoseph Kahanov, an emissary of the Lubavitcher Rebbe, featured in Chapter Eleven, makes the point succinctly in comments which resonated deeply with me. He said, 'a spiritual mentor of mine put it rather bluntly: "You want tranquillity? Visit the cemetery; among the dead it is very peaceful. Among the living there is strife and disorder."'

Adversity in my family

From a family perspective, I had an early grounding in stories of resilience and positivity. As a young child, I heard tales of my own grandfather, Walter Levy's wartime experience of real captivity. If not for his positive attitude, determination, and resilience in the face of adversity, I would not be here today.

Upon the outbreak of the Second World War, along with his regiment, he was sent to the Far East to fight in that particularly unforgiving theatre of war. Badly equipped for the terrain, surrender to the Japanese Army soon followed.

Unfortunately, I never really had a chance to speak to him about his experiences as he died shortly before my thirteenth birthday. However, part of his story featured in Martin Sugarman's 2014 book, *Under the Heel of Bushido*.

'On the twenty-ninth of November 1942, they docked at Moji in Japan, where they spent three years in Fukuoka 4B Camp ... Of two-hundred and fifty men, one-hundred and sixty died within six months, mainly because the Japanese deliberately refused to supply simple remedies such as saline or glucose for the many dysentery cases ... Walter Levy of Glasgow, stole drugs from the Japanese M1 room, at great risk to his own life, but saving many other lives'. The book goes on to explain the desperate conditions in which the men were held. Despite a mumps epidemic in 1944, malnourishment, regular beatings, harsh labour and a solitary, dirty bath for forty men to soak in once a week, he somehow managed to survive. Re-reading the account of his challenges helped me re-evaluate my own circumstances.

Suddenly, life did not appear to be so difficult.

An idea for a book formed

In 2001, I graduated in International History and Politics. I had long been fascinated in society, events and people from the past and what we might learn from all that experience. As a combined effect of my family history, my faith and my academic interests, I realised that my fascination with inspirational stories could be used to help others.

Viktor Frankl, the subject of Chapter One, talks about having meaning in adversity. This project gave me that meaning. I soon began to see that every successful person I had ever admired had overcome their own fascinating tales of hardship.

I had an idea that passing on thought-provoking anecdotes in the face of adversity via a vlog might help and inspire family and friends during this difficult time. Maybe, by sharing, I might help others find purpose in challenging times too if I sought out those whose experience of adversity could be a lesson for others? Indeed, I found that sharing my vlogs on social media gave me a renewed sense of purpose.

So, each night, I began to research the lives of the well-known and in some cases, the less well-known, people who I had admired, seeking out those who I felt had experienced a significant amount of adversity in their lives. Invariably, I ended up going to bed late, feeling moved and excited by the stories I would be telling the next day. Friends spoke of listening to hardships and gaining a new perspective on the current situation. I was asked to keep sharing my wisdom, although it was not my wisdom I was sharing, but the experiences, responses and coping strategies of the people I had researched. It was then that I decided to expand the project beyond the scope of my family and friends and put my findings into writing.

The most challenging aspect has been to narrow down my search to thirty people. I could have picked so many more to feature. But after much consideration, I decided to limit the book to thirty, as this number allowed me to provide a good selection of people from a range of categories across society.

I have tried to include a broad range of personalities from diverse backgrounds: scientists, entrepreneurs, humanitarians, politicians, entertainers, sports stars and war heroes. I believe there is something in here for everyone.

How to deal with adversity

One quote had a strong effect on me throughout. Another former British Prime Minister, Margaret Thatcher, used to say to those around her, 'don't tell me what ... tell me how'. What Thatcher wanted to know was not simply what had happened, but what possible actions might be taken in any given situation.

This approach became my constant navigational tool during the writing of this book. I wanted to show how the people I had selected dealt with the adversity that they were faced with. I say this, in part, because, the reader, still needs some background biographical information on each of the people featured within the book.

On the one hand, this book is most certainly not a biographical work. It will not give you every detail of each life covered. You will need to engage in further reading for that. However, it is about trying to understand how each of the individuals featured overcame adversity to the extent that it assisted them in their lives and can assist us in ours.

Each chapter focuses on one individual, with a short biography summarising what they experienced in their individual life. For example, many readers will know what Nelson Mandela endured during his twenty-seven subsequent years in prison. But few will know how Mandela dealt with his incarceration. So, my main aim has been to show how Mandela and the other people featured, overcame the significant adversity experienced in their life. Hopefully, these examples might be applicable to those who read the book.

I felt that the purpose of the book was best served by writing about those who have completed their journey in life.

Those that are still alive are likely to face many more challenges. Therefore, their story is not complete.

With each selected person, I aimed to identify five key characteristics that helped them in their fight against the adversity they experienced. This book has taught me that there may be no single recipe for tackling adversity. However, as I delved into the lives of these thirty remarkable people, I noted a striking number of similarities in the factors which I picked out for each individual.

In the conclusion, I summarise my findings and offer readers a seven-point point plan for tackling life's challenges. This is presented as 'The Adversity Formula', the title of this book. I believe that this formula offers a powerful tool for readers in handling adversity in their lives. I hope you will find the formula helpful in dealing with life's challenges as they present themselves to you.

The book is the result of much background reading and research. While I considered putting reference numbers and footnotes on the pages of the book, ultimately, I decided that a detailed bibliography at the end of the book, would be more useful for readers who wanted to take further their interest in any of the book's subjects or themes. I have made the bibliography as extensive as possible but would be happy for any reader to contact me about any aspect of the text or the bibliography.

Facing adversity – You are not alone
Whatever you may be going through in life, it is guaranteed that someone will have experienced something similar before. As King Solomon said, 'what has been done will be done again; there is nothing new under the sun'.

I hope you find an affinity with some of the people profiled in this book. That will be for you to decide. But who better to try to emulate than those who succeeded despite their challenges? Whatever your situation, whether you are a student, an aspiring entrepreneur, lawyer, political leader, father, mother, husband, or wife, you will be able to learn many valuable lessons from those featured inside. I hope those who share my interest in self-development and in history will enjoy the journey on which we are about to embark.

I feel privileged to have researched and studied the lives of those featured in the book. Researching how they overcame adversity and presenting my findings in this book, has helped me immensely. My hope is that, in some way, it will also help you. American novelist, James Ray Allan once said, 'adversity does not build character - it reveals it'. I hope I am successful in revealing the character of the people I have selected in the pages that follow and I hope you will form a better and a more positive understanding of yourself and how to deal with the adversity in your life by reading this book.

The Scientists

Chapter One

Viktor Frankl

Everything can be taken from a man but one thing, the last
of the human freedoms, to choose one's attitude in any
given set of circumstances

Viktor Frankl was a prominent Jewish psychiatrist and neurologist, who survived several of the Nazi concentration camps during the Holocaust. It is no coincidence that Frankl's profile features at the outset of this book. Frankl became one of the most influential thinkers of the twentieth century after he developed the theory of healing through meaning, which became known as logotherapy.

Using his own experiences, as prisoner number 119104, amidst the horrors of the Theresienstadt concentration camp, he developed a method that focuses on discovering the meaning of life for every person. As well as helping him to move forward from his own tragedies, Frankl's therapeutic methods have been applied successfully by psychologists worldwide to treat a countless number of patients.

Frankl had previously studied medicine at the University of Vienna, specialising in neurology and psychiatry, with a focus on depression and suicide. Whilst still a medical student, he had been active in setting up special youth centres to address the high number of teen suicides that occurred at report card time. The programme was a success. By the end of 1931, not a single Viennese student had committed suicide.

In 1937, he began his private practice. However, after the German Anschluss (unification) with Austria, his working practices as a Jewish doctor were severely curtailed and he was forced to close his clinic.

In 1940, Frankl became head of the Neurological department of the Rothschild Hospital. At great personal risk, he deliberately misdiagnosed mentally ill patients to ensure they were saved from the Nazis' Euthanasia programme. Despite obtaining an immigration visa to the United States, Frankl decided against emigration, taking the difficult decision to remain in Austria to care for his elderly parents.

In 1942, Frankl married a nurse, Tilly, who worked at his hospital. Jews were forbidden from having children even if they were married and Tilly was forced to sacrifice the child she was carrying. Soon after, the couple were arrested, along with Frankl's parents and deported to the Terezin Ghetto, north of Prague. In 1944, after deportation to Auschwitz, Frankl's mother and brother were killed, whilst his wife later perished in the Bergen-Belsen camp.

At Auschwitz, Dr Joseph Mengele selected him for the left queue, leading to the gas chambers. However, Frankl saw a few of his colleagues in the right queue and switched to that line behind Mengele's back. Little did he know at the time, but it was a decision that saved his life.

Frankl spent three years experiencing the horrors of the Holocaust in four different concentration camps, including Dachau. Despite the tragic losses encountered during the war, Frankl was able to use his professional skills to provide psychological assistance to fellow inmates, as well as using the time to conduct further research into his own theories.

In April 1945, as the war ended, Frankl returned to Vienna, where he learned of the death of his beloved mother, brother and wife. Determined to carry on with life, he went on to become the director of the Vienna Neurological Polyclinic.

Over the course of nine days in 1946, he wrote, *Man's Search for Meaning,* a renowned memoir based on the lessons he learnt in the camps. The book has been described as one of the ten most influential ever published in the United States. A prolific author, he went on to write over forty books published in over fifty languages.

Despite the loss of a young wife, parents and brother, Frankl was able to find the inner strength to propose an inspiring and positive view of the human psyche that dissented heavily from the accepted theories of the era.

How was Frankl able to survive such extreme adversity and formulate his theories?

Find meaning in adversity

A reason for living was at the heart of Frankl's approach. He once said, 'life is never made unbearable by circumstances, but only by lack of meaning and purpose'. Indeed, Frankl held that, 'life holds meaning under any conditions, even the most miserable ones'. His personal experiences in the camps taught him that those who found meaning and gave away their last piece of bread, were even more resilient than those who were physically fit, but in a state of despair. The theory espouses the view that in the worst suffering, it is possible to find purpose and attain personal growth, thus diminishing one's suffering. If not, then Frankl believed it to be inevitable that people in the camps would despair and eventually perish.

The theory became known as the Third Viennese School of Psychotherapy, which contrasted greatly with the views expounded by contemporaries, Sigmund Freud and Alfred Adler. Frankl argued that Freud had been wrong to think that pleasure was a person's main goal in life. Moreover, Adler's theory that the pursuit of power was man's primary drive was also disputed. According to Frankl, even in the worst of situations, all a person really needs is meaning.

According to logotherapy, meaning can be discovered through three different sources:
1. Within one's work.
2. Through one's love for others.
3. By remaining strong in the most challenging of circumstances.

To accentuate his point, Frankl told of a meeting with an elderly general practitioner who was struggling with severe depression after the death of his wife.

In his consultation, Frankl asked, "What would have happened, Doctor, if you had died first and your wife would have had to survive you?"

"Oh," the doctor said, "For her, this would have been terrible; how she would have suffered!"

Whereupon Frankl replied, "You see, Doctor, such a suffering has been spared her, and it was you who have spared her this suffering."

What makes Frankl's theory so unique is the fact it was not developed in the corridors of academia, but rather, out in the field: in places of indescribable suffering. Embracing the meaning in one's difficulties is certainly not an easy task. It takes time, practice and considerable introspection. Yet, it is possible.

Frankl concluded that there is no one answer to the meaning of life. Each person is forced to answer this question for themselves. Such a profound question is likely to trouble us even more when we see suffering and death across our society. Frankl believed that one does not need to meditate on a mountain top to figure out the meaning of life. Our life itself will reveal what is expected of us. Accordingly, 'life ultimately means taking the responsibility to find the right answer to its problems and to fulfil the tasks which it constantly sets for each individual'.

The theory becomes even more persuasive when one considers how meaning, or a lack of it, affects athletes upon retirement. According to Freud, they should surely have enough resources to indulge in the pleasures that will maintain their happiness. Yet, research has shown that many retired athletes feel an emptiness in their lives, caused by a lack of meaning, which inevitably leads to domestic and emotional instability.

Frankl's theory has been embraced by those in the most desperate of situations. By mid-August 2015, Oliver Sacks, the British neurologist was aware of the terminal nature of his cancer. Nevertheless, writing in *The New York Times*, he demonstrated that suffering had allowed him a deeper sense of meaning in life. 'I feel intensely alive and I hope in the time that remains to deepen my friendships, to say farewell to those I love, to write more, to travel if I have the strength, to achieve new levels of understanding and insight'.

Frankl taught that meaning brings considerable depth to life and affords a new perspective of one's difficulties.

Make your attitude shape your response

It wasn't the particulars of your situation that was important to Frankl but rather how you viewed and then acted upon them. He was adamant, that even amidst the horrors of the death camps, 'the one thing you can't take away from me is the way I choose to respond to what you do to me'.

On his first evening in Auschwitz, Frankl made the conscious decision not to commit suicide. The Nazis could take away all his possessions, even his loved ones, but they had no power to take away his responses to their cruel actions. Despite the desperate situation in which he found himself, this realisation was truly liberating to him.

Frankl's view was that people have choices in difficult times. Do they share what they have, be it food or provisions in short supply? Or do they selfishly hoard valuable commodities at the expense of others who may need them?

'In concentration camps ... we watched and witnessed some of our comrades behave like swine while others behaved like saints. Man has both potentialities within himself ...'

The theory applies as much today as it does to some of history's most serious humanitarian disasters. The Covid-19 crisis inspired people to volunteer both time and resources to assist those less fortunate in these difficult times. To behave in this manner is, as Frankl would say, 'to remain brave, dignified and unselfish'.

In the camps, Frankl worked on his own attitude by repeatedly distancing himself from the ongoing reality. Having been forced to march, in freezing temperatures, a man next to

Frankl whispered, 'if our wives could see us now. I do hope they are better off in their camps'.

At that point, Frankl no longer felt the icy water at his feet. Instead, in his mind's eye, he saw his wife Tilly smile and look at him with encouragement. He had no idea whether she was even alive, but he spent the rest of the day visualizing himself talking to Tilly. In the worst of moments, Frankl claimed that he felt the power of love for the first time.

Such a remarkable attitude shows the powers of choice that we have. There is so much in our lives that we cannot control and will never be able to control. Frankl showed that what matters is not necessarily the hand we have been dealt, however dire, but our attitude whilst playing that hand. As he concluded, 'when we are no longer able to change a situation, we are challenged to change ourselves'.

If Frankl had lived through today's pandemic, he would undoubtedly state that these times afford us the perfect opportunity to work on our attitude. Accordingly, he may even have questioned whether it is healthy to ingest every newspaper, radio and television soundbite, which inevitably focus on disaster and impending catastrophe. Or do we remain positive and focus on what we can, and are able to do in the situation?

Caryn Sullivan, an award-winning author and inspirational speaker, accentuates this point, 'faced with adversity, we can be bitter, or we can be better. It's a choice.'

Focus on future goals

Having an objective to aim for was another fundamental component of Frankl's methodology. He once said, invoking the words of Friedrich Nietzsche, the German philosopher and writer, 'he who has a 'why' to live for can bear with almost any 'how''.

In his work counselling other inmates, Frankl found that the most important element in helping people was to teach them to retain a future goal.

In the camps, he came to see that those inmates who, 'were oriented toward the future, toward a meaning waiting to be fulfilled', were more likely to survive. When a prisoner gave up hope, they quickly succumbed. He was adamant that he owed his own survival to his determination to reconstruct a manuscript he had written before being sent to the camps - a book he later called *The Doctor and the Soul*. The manuscript had been slipped into a pocket sewn between the lining and the outer fabric of his coat. Unfortunately, it was lost when he was stripped of his clothing at Auschwitz. Despite this devastating loss, he maintained hope that it would be published after the war.

Frankl acknowledged that the Nazis sought to cut the prisoners off from the goals that had formerly given them meaning in life. Those who survived saw their predicament in the camp as a temporary existence. 'A man who let himself decline because he could not see any future goal, found himself occupied with retrospective thoughts, tended to turn inward and eventually, found everything pointless. They would then give up, fall sick and die'. Frankl was determined to avoid this scenario. On a wintry day in Poland, he was marching through a field with a group of prisoners, dressed only in light clothing and suffering from malnutrition and mistreatment. He started to cough. The cough caused him to fall to his knees. A guard came over and began to beat him with a club and told him that he would be left to die if he did not get up. Frankl felt like giving up. Suddenly, he imagined himself in post-war Vienna delivering a magnificent lecture. He no longer saw himself as deathly sick in the field and was able to summon up the strength to continue the march and return to his bunk. All this was possible because of his motivation to give a brilliant lecture in the future to a standing ovation.

Use dereflection whenever possible
Shifting the focus away from one's self was an integral part of a healthy approach to life and realising life's opportunities.

Frankl stated, 'the more one forgets himself — by giving himself to a cause to serve or another person to love — the more human he is and the more he actualizes himself'.

Frankl observed that people tend to become preoccupied on their problems and goals. In other words, they become hyper-focused on themselves. Over-focusing or dwelling on a problem or a symptom can often make matters worse or cause a compulsive tendency towards self-observation.

A sportsman or sportswoman can often make technical deficiencies worse by overthinking. Dwelling on one's flaws can be counterproductive and will only increase stress. The simple answer, according to Frankl's logotherapy, is to focus attention on something or someone else. In other words, ignore what is bothering you.

Dereflection encourages a patient to observe something new in a situation so that they may let go of old observations and ways of doing things. When we get locked into our own thought patterns and focus on the negativity that is around us, we lose sight of the good in our life. By learning to perform dereflection and shift our attention from that which is bothering us to a more positive outlet, we gain new insights into solving the original problem.

The technique involves redirecting attention away from the worrying thoughts or a challenging situation towards something more meaningful. By moving attention away from fears and focusing on what meaningful things there are in our lives, a person can transcend their situation.

Too often, people become discouraged when they believe that long held ambitions have become unattainable. Instead of feeling despair, Frankl encouraged people to accept their situation and change their thoughts and focus on the present, for example, a hobby or the needs of other people.

Acceptance does not have to mean giving up on your ambitions. Rather, the practise often results in accomplishment of the original goal. The act of taking a step back and being present allows you to determine what actions are needed for a successful outcome. It is far better to give yourself a break, reframe your situation and focus on a plan of action than fall into despair through excessive pressure.

In present times, this appears to be increasingly timely advice. Researchers from King's College, London found that a significant proportion of the public have experienced changes to their sleep patterns since the UK government announced its lockdown measures to stop the spread of the coronavirus on the twenty-third of March 2020. There is no doubt that the effects of the pandemic have caused people to worry about significant elements of their own life, be it health or economic uncertainty.

Whilst it is understandable that uncertainty causes excessive worry, by focusing attention on the needs of others, such as assisting the vulnerable and the elderly, a person is able to take the focus off themselves, dealing with the here and now and not worrying about events that remain outside of their control.

Let happiness ensue
To Frankl, happiness was a by-product of a meaningful life, rather than something that could be directly obtained. He cautioned that, 'it is the very pursuit of happiness that thwarts happiness'.

In April 1984, on a trip to America, Frankl spoke before a packed audience of nine-hundred people at the Washington Hebrew Congregation. He bemoaned the fact that Western, and specifically, modern, American culture had created the illusion that happiness could be directly sought. 'You're always forced, even ordered, to feel joy, be happy and experience pleasure. This is precisely what obviates the possibility to enjoy oneself'.

Perhaps it is because life has become so comfortable that people have been sold the idea that happiness is a commodity, which can be bought like anything else. If this was possible, then the global population suffering from depression would not have reached two-hundred and sixty-four million people. Americans spent eleven billion dollars in 2008 on self-improvement books, CDs, seminars, coaching and stress-management programmes, that is 13.6% more than they spent back in 2005, according to Marketdata Enterprises. It is likely that many of the purchasers were seeking a happier life.

Frankl lamented, 'ever more people today have the means to live, but no meaning to live for'. Frankl taught that life does not owe us pleasure. If it did, why would so many successful and prosperous people be so miserable. Good mental health does not come to those who demand happiness but to those who find meaning in their daily life; happiness is simply a product of their meaningful life. 'It must ensue', noted Frankl, 'it cannot be pursued'.

It is certainly no failing on anyone's part to want to be happy. In Frankl's eyes, though, if you chase it, you will likely have little peace. 'It (happiness) is an unintended side-effect of living for a cause greater than oneself', he noted. 'It will only happen by not caring about it'.

Today's generation tends to be so focused on this elusive goal to the point that people have become completely absorbed by it, resulting in emptiness and depression. Against the backdrop of Covid-19, this pursuit appears to be even more fleeting.

Eleanor Roosevelt, whose life will be discussed in greater depth in Chapter Six, concurred with Frankl's view that to search out happiness is essentially futile. She stated that, 'happiness is not a goal; it is a by-product. Paradoxically, the one sure way not to be happy is deliberately to map out a way of life in which one would please oneself completely and exclusively'.

Alex Pattakos is recognised as a world leading authority on applying Viktor Frankl's system of logotherapy. He believes that more and more people are rebelling against this so-called search for happiness, acknowledging that the search has not provided them with the inner peace they thought it would bring.

Instead, he teaches three core lessons based on logotherapy:

1. Connect meaningfully with others.
2. Engage with deeper purpose.
3. Embrace life with attitude.

To let happiness just happen seems an astonishingly simple exercise, yet wholly alien to present conditioning. In difficult times, focusing on meaningful activities, instead of pursuing happiness as an end, can help overcome many challenges.

'What man really wants', according to Frankl, 'is ultimately, not happiness, but a reason to be happy. As soon as a reason for happiness is given, happiness ensues'.

Chapter Two

Marie Curie

Life is not easy for any of us. But what of that? We must have perseverance and above all confidence in ourselves

Marie Curie is best known for her research on radioactivity which contributed towards the earliest treatments for cancer. Curie became the first woman to win a Nobel prize and is the only person to win the prize in two separate scientific fields. The story of how she was able to achieve so much, in the face of considerable adversity, is a truly inspirational one.

Her prior accomplishments in her adopted home of France were no less impressive; she became the first woman in France to earn a PhD in Physics in 1903, the first woman professor at the Sorbonne University and in 1995, long after her death, she became the first woman to be entombed, on her own merit, in the Pantheon.

Born Marie Sklodowska in Russian-controlled Warsaw in 1867, her family had suffered financial loss and discrimination through her father's support for Poland's national uprisings. Marie's life was further affected by the death of her mother when she was aged just ten.

Discriminatory practices operated in Poland which forbade women attending university. In 1891, she left Poland for Paris, enrolling at the Sorbonne University to study mathematics and physics. She paid her way initially, by cleaning glassware in university labs and was so poor that she was forced to ration her food.

It was at the Sorbonne that she met Pierre Currie, a professor of physics, whom she married in 1895. The Curies worked together investigating radioactivity. In 1898, the pair announced the discovery of two new chemical elements, polonium and radium. The two went on to share the 1903

Nobel Prize for physics with A. Henri Becquerel. Even then, it was only on the insistence of Pierre, that Marie had instigated the research, that the committee were persuaded to include Marie in the prize along with her two male counterparts.

Three years later, Pierre Curie was tragically killed in an accident on a Paris street. Despite her devastation, Marie responded by immersing herself in her work. Instead of taking a widow's pension, she became head of her husband's laboratory and the first woman lecturer at the Sorbonne. She was awarded a second Nobel prize in chemistry in 1911 for isolating pure radium.

During the First World War, she helped develop the use of X-rays in medicine. Curie personally helped equip and operate more than twenty ambulances (known as 'Petits Curies'). Numerous field hospitals were established, complete with primitive X-ray machines to assist doctors with the location and removal of shrapnel and bullets from wounded soldiers. In 1921, President Harding of the United States, on behalf of the women of America, presented her with one gram of radium in recognition of her service to science.

After the war, Marie continued her work as a teacher and researcher and received many awards and prizes. When Curie died of leukaemia, aged sixty-six in 1934, her death was mourned throughout the world. It is a sad irony that her illness was likely contracted after years of exposure to radiation. *The New York Times* called her a, 'martyr to science', who 'contributed more to the general welfare of mankind', as a 'modest, self-effacing woman'.

Her legacy continues to this day. Numerous research institutions have been named after her, including the Pierre and Marie Curie University in Paris. Curie also permitted the use of her name when the Marie Curie Hospital in London was opened in 1930. It was staffed entirely by women to treat female cancer patients using radiology.

She is recognized throughout the world not only for her ground-breaking research but also for having boldly broken many gender barriers during her lifetime.

In Poland, her family suffered under an oppressive Russian regime. In France she was regarded with suspicion as a foreigner and of course, as a woman operating in a decidedly male world. How did Marie Curie manage to triumph over adversity when the odds were stacked so heavily against her?

Be willing to sacrifice

An altruistic approach was at the heart of Marie Curie's scientific one. She once confirmed, 'physicists always publish their research completely. If our discovery has a commercial future that is an accident by which we must not profit'.

After discovering radium in 1898, Pierre and Marie Curie could have cashed in on their findings and made a fortune. After all, factories began to emerge across the United States, not only to supply the scientific community but also to enable the substance to be marketed for alternative uses. The product became widely used in dubious treatments and potions, ranging from soap to chocolate bars. Other scientists and chemical companies processed radium, then sold it to for military research and cancer treatment at one-hundred thousand dollars per gram. Money was there to be made but the Curies declined all invitations to take out a patent on the techniques to extract radium.

Instead, as part of their passion for science, Marie and Pierre shared their discovery as well as their methods of extraction. Whilst never regretting the decision, because financial gain was never on their mind, Marie later paid the commercial price for her decision. By 1920, she could not even afford to buy a gram of the very substance she discovered, to continue her research.

Marie Curie never regretted revealing her discovery. 'Radium is an element, it belongs to the people, it was not to enrich anyone', she told American journalist, Marie Mattingly

Meloney on a trip to the United States in 1921 who confirmed, 'to make money from it would have been against the scientific spirit in which she operated'.

This was entirely in keeping with the modest way in which the couple had worked. For years, the couple toiled in a cold and damp shed, with poor ventilation, which was situated next to the Departments of Physics and Chemistry. If nothing else, this was an environment totally unsuited for scientific discovery, let alone one in which respected academics should be working. German chemist, Wilhelm Ostwald, visited the couple and wrote that the lab resembled, 'a cross between a stable and a potato shed, and if I had not seen the worktable and items of chemical apparatus, I would have thought that I was been played a practical joke'. Both Curies were afflicted by burns and fatigue that were likely caused by repeated exposures to high doses of radiation.

Perhaps the only benefit Marie ever received from her work came on the twentieth of May 1921, when American President Harding presented to Marie that gram of radium as a gift of the people of the United States, which had been purchased for one-hundred thousand dollars. Even then, it was only natural that she would use this gift towards her continued research for the benefit of humanity.

Upon the outbreak of the First World War, Marie put all her work on hold to assist the allied forces. Together with her seventeen-year-old daughter, Irene, she visited the Belgian front-line hospitals and examined patients. Not only did Curie personally instruct and supervise young women in the operation of the X-ray equipment, but she even drove an X-ray ambulance, despite the inherent dangers at the front line.

Whether it is sacrificing free time, spending time away from family or leaving a comfortable job to fulfil the ambition of working for yourself, it often requires sacrifice. Marie Curie showed that to achieve one's objectives, a person must truly be willing to make sacrifices. In her case, the sacrifices were physically dangerous, but the principle remains relevant to everyone's journey in life.

Nurture your passion

An intense enthusiasm and love for her subject was at the core of Marie Curie's work. 'I am among those who think that science has great beauty', she once said.

On the twenty-sixth of July 1895, Pierre and Marie were married in a civil ceremony in Sceaux, France. Instead of a traditional wedding dress, Marie chose a dark blue dress. She later explained, 'I have no dress except the one I wear every day. If you are going to be kind enough to give me one, please let it be practical and dark so that I can put it on afterwards to go to the laboratory'.

The lengths that Curie would go to study were evidenced even on her wedding day when she was unable to stop thinking about her passion for her work. It was a passion that had been nurtured at the illegal night school she attended with her sister, Bronya, in Warsaw. Women were forbidden from attending Warsaw University. In an act of defiance, Marie and her sister met up with other Polish women who wanted to learn, meeting in informal settings at the so called 'Flying Universities'. To avoid detection from the Russian authorities, classes were held in ever changing locations. It was there that Maria discovered she had a talent for maths, physics and chemistry.

The most striking aspect of Curie's life was her persistent devotion to her research. Personal or physical hardships were no deterrent. She had to fight for many years to obtain a faculty position at the Sorbonne and space in which she could conduct her work. That, 'miserable, old shed,' as she called it, was the place in which the couple passed the best and happiest years of their life.

Lots of people are looking to find their passion in life. The truth is that, in the words of American author, Mark Manson: 'If you need to look for what you're passionate about, then you're probably not passionate about it at all. If (like Marie Curie) you are passionate about something, it will already feel be an ingrained part of your life'.

Whilst the education Marie Curie received at the underground Flying University was no match for the curriculum at one of the mainstream universities, it was there that she developed a taste for academic research and received a basic introduction to scientific concepts that lit an everlasting fire inside her.

'To my great joy, I was able, for the first time in my life, to find access to a laboratory … the first trial confirmed in me the taste for experimental research in the fields of physics and chemistry'.

Seek a partner who complements you

A stable and loving relationship underpinned Curie's success and led to a positive working environment. 'My husband and I were so closely united by our affection and our common work that we passed nearly all of our time together', she stated.

Marie Sklodowska was introduced to Pierre Curie by Polish physicist and professor, Count Józef Wierusz-Kowalski, who had invited her to stay when she moved to France. On her first meeting with Pierre, Marie recalled, 'I was struck by the open expression of his face and by the slight suggestion of detachment in his whole attitude. His speech, rather slow and deliberate, his simplicity, and his smile, at once grave and youthful, inspired confidence'.

They say that opposites attract and in the case of Pierre and Marie, this appeared to be true. Marie was a much more aggressive personality than Pierre, whilst her future husband enjoyed a low-key existence, with no interest in competition. The two complimented each other perfectly and it is doubtful whether either would have accomplished what he or she did without the other.

Helene Langevin-Joliot, the pair's granddaughter, described Marie and Pierre's collaboration. 'It is difficult to imagine personalities more different: Pierre was as dreamy as Marie was organised, so they complemented each other very well', she said.

Pierre was already a highly respected industrial scientist and inventor who, in 1880, had jointly discovered piezoelectricity with his brother, Jacques. He was also particularly skilled in designing scientific instruments and had a comprehensive knowledge of physics. His readiness to suspend his own research on crystal growth and link up with Marie in her studies of radioactivity was of tremendous benefit to Marie. In an age of male dominance and antipathy to women, Pierre was able to open doors for Marie to leading professors, which enhanced Marie's scientific knowledge.

Marie and Pierre decided to hunt for the new element they suspected might be present in pitchblende. By the end of 1898, after processing tons of the substance, they announced the discovery of two new chemical elements, polonium, and radium, in a paper read to the French Academy of Sciences. Together, they came up with a new word for the sensation they had witnessed: Radioactivity.

Tragically, their life together came to an end in 1906, when Pierre was killed after being hit by a horse-drawn carriage in the street. The two remain known as the most iconic couple in science, forging a partnership both inside and outside of the laboratory.

Pierre and Marie overcame their scientific challenges because of their common vision. Whilst the two had different skills, they shared the same vision. By his nature, Pierre was happy for Marie to gain the limelight whilst Marie was thrilled to receive the guidance and experience of her more experienced spouse.

Find your inner strength
Everything in life, even the unpalatable, had to be faced according to Marie Curie. 'Nothing in life is to be feared, it is only to be understood.' In November 1910, she put herself

forward as a candidate for the vacant seat for a physicist in the French Academy of Sciences. Despite having worked as a scientist in France for the best part of a decade, Curie had to contend with more than just sexism. There had been a marked increase in anti-Semitism and anti-foreign sentiment in the years preceding the First World War. The right-wing press seized on false rumours that Curie was, in fact, Jewish. Two weeks before the academy was about to select its candidate, a nationalistic newspaper, *L'Action Française*, published an attack on Marie whilst other papers followed, with some claiming it was Pierre who had done all the hard work for the couple. When the final tally was counted in January 1911, Marie lost to her rival by two votes.

1911 also marked the year which has come to be known as her *annus horribilis* or horrible year. It was revealed that Curie was involved in a relationship with physicist Paul Langevin, a married man, albeit one who was estranged from his wife. Once again, the press tore her reputation to shreds and played on her foreign origins. False reports again began to surface about alleged Jewish ancestry with some reporters claiming the home of a good Frenchwoman, 'had been wrecked by a Jewish foreigner'. Other newspapers even went as far to suggest her husband had committed suicide five years earlier. On her return home from a conference in France, she found angry French citizens stood outside her home, with some throwing stones. 'Get the foreign woman out', they chanted.

Some good news finally seemed to have arrived that November in the form of a telegram from the Nobel committee announcing that its chemistry prize would go to Curie for her work with radium and polonium.

However, the Nobel committee was concerned with the rumours of the affair and an impending court date was set to implicate Curie in divorce proceedings. Curie was discouraged from travelling to Stockholm to accept the award. The scientist, Svante Arrhenius, who sat on the Nobel committee, went as far as writing to her, urging her not to come and accept the prize until she had cleared her name.

With her reputation under attack, Curie had to summon her inner strength to stand up to her critics. Accompanied by her sister, Bronya and daughter, Irene, she travelled to Stockholm to give her Nobel lecture on the eleventh of December. The lecture was a show of defiance against those who claimed the work had not been her own. She spoke assertively of her hypothesis that radioactivity was an atomic property, but without detracting from Pierre's valuable contribution.

It may have been her most challenging year, but 1911 was the year in which Marie Curie showed her steel in standing up defiantly against xenophobia, anti-Semitism, sexism, false accusations and attempts to discredit her work.

What is most impressive about the life of the rejuvenated scientist was the fact that she accomplished so much despite recurrent bouts of depression. The death of Marie's mother at a young age had an enormous impact on her, triggering a life-long battle with the depression. Anyone who has had to confront the heaviness of depression will know how difficult a journey that can be. Yet, she found the inner strength, not only to stand up to her tormenters but to change the world of science forever.

Adopt a patient approach
Taking the long road to achieving success was essential for a research scientist like Marie Curie. Confirming that commitment, she emphasised, 'I was taught that the way of progress was neither swift nor easy.'

Starting in 1898, Curie began the task of isolating radium to prove its existence beyond doubt. It was both invigorating and arduous work. 'Sometimes, I had to spend a whole day mixing a boiling mass with a heavy iron rod nearly as large as myself. I would be broken with fatigue at the day's end'. Batch by batch, in a giant iron cauldron, she stirred her stew of pitchblende mixed with chemicals. Other days, she performed a delicate technique called fractional crystallization to obtain pure substances.

Those years certainly brought their fair share of frustration, but as Curie said, they did not keep her down for long, for 'the feeling of discouragement that naturally occurred, did not last long and gave way to renewed activity'.

Finally, in 1902, Curie announced she had successfully isolated one decigram of radium. It had taken her almost four years of painstaking work to produce the rigorous proof that was needed to demonstrate that radium was a new element.

Whether seeking weight loss, or business success, everyone wants to see instant results. Unfortunately, they very rarely arrive that quickly. Rabbi Menachem Mendel Levin wrote in his book *Heshbon HaNefesh*, (which translates as *An Accounting of the Soul*), 'woe to the pampered man or woman who has never been trained to be patient. Either today or in the future, he is destined to sip from the cup of affliction'.

Whist we are living in challenging times, if anything, we can look positively on this time as one which is providing us with a crash course in patience. Like Marie Curie, if we choose to be patient, we can come out of the other side, as more grateful and humble people.

Chapter Three

Albert Einstein

Adversity introduces a man to himself

Mention the name Albert Einstein and the first word that usually comes to mind is genius. It is often surprising to many people that the man named *Time* magazine's 'Person of the Twentieth Century', experienced his fair share of failure, mockery and disappointment.

Born to a secular Jewish family in Germany, Einstein was the son of a salesman turned engineer. Whilst excelling at physics and mathematics, the young Einstein struggled with grammar and social interaction, causing contemporary psychologists to speculate whether he suffered from dyslexia, dyspraxia, autism, or Asperger's syndrome.

By 1894, having experienced business difficulties, Einstein's father moved the family business to Italy. Albert was left behind in Munich to complete his final year at school. Albert's parents had selected a school which specialised in classical languages and literature but the choice was not well received by their son, who resented the rigid Prussian style of rote learning. An insubordinate and unhappy student, he behaved poorly and longed to leave. In the spring of 1895, without consulting his parents, he left school without obtaining his diploma.

In October 1895, Einstein took the entrance examination for the Swiss Federal Polytechnic in Zurich. Whilst obtaining high marks in mathematics and science, his marks in history and languages were so low that he failed to pass. The contradiction in the personality of Einstein was evident. A self-taught mathematical and physics genius on the one hand; an inflexible, disinterested linguist on the other.

Einstein had, however, impressed enough with his scientific marks. He was advised to enrol in a Swiss secondary school with the prospect of guaranteed admission to the polytechnic the next year.

He spent four years at the polytechnic, receiving a teaching diploma but failed to create enough of an impact to be awarded the assistantship he craved. This was, in part, down to the poor impression he made on his professors. A disorganised and forgetful student, Einstein skipped classes and irritated his teachers with his disrespectful attitude. No one in the polytechnic's teaching faculty would have disagreed with Einstein's schoolteacher, in Munich, Joseph Degenhart, who informed his young student, 'you will never amount to anything'.

For some months, Einstein was unemployed after receiving his diploma. Salvation only came courtesy of a classmate, Marcel Grossman, whose father pulled some strings to get Einstein an interview for a role as an examiner at the Swiss patent office in Bern. The job was not a prestigious one, but coming as it did, in June 1902, it gave him the time to think about the scientific theories that he was working on.

Einstein's personal life was no less challenging. His parents disapproved of his first wife, Mileva Maric. Despite reluctantly providing his consent to the marriage, Einstein's father died soon after, in 1902, disappointed at his son's lack of success. The marriage was not a happy one, with divorce following in 1919.

Einstein was still working at the patent office in 1905, a year which he referred to as his *annus mirabilis*, or miraculous year. In those twelve months, Einstein released five extraordinary papers that established him as the world's leading physicist. It was in one of those papers that Einstein asserted his views on the equivalence of mass and energy, which led to the famous $E = mc^2$.

Einstein's career was beginning to take off. By 1908, he was recognized as a leading scientist and was appointed lecturer at the University of Bern. Prestigious openings at leading universities across Europe became available. In 1922, he was awarded the 1921 Nobel Prize in Physics 'for his services to Theoretical Physics, and especially for his discovery of the law of the photoelectric effect'.

The rise of Nazism in Germany forced him out of Europe in 1933. Together with his second wife Elsa, he moved to New Jersey, where he accepted a position at Princeton University. It was there that Einstein would spend the rest of his life working on a unified field theory. During the Second World War, he worked on navy-based weapons systems and made big monetary donations to the military by auctioning off manuscripts worth millions.

In the last decade of his life, Einstein, withdrew from the spotlight, preferring to stay in Princeton and immerse himself in scientific thought. Einstein died on April 18, 1955, at the age of seventy-six at the University Medical Centre at Princeton.

Without the setbacks suffered early on in his career, it is quite possible that Einstein may not have been able to reach the heights that he later realised. The question that one must ask is how exactly did Einstein move from an unemployed underachiever in 1900, to a respected scientist by 1908?

Undertake everything with curiosity

Einstein believed that an approach built on asking questions was fundamental. 'The important thing is not to stop questioning. Curiosity has its own reason for existence', he said. The Oxford University Dictionary defines curiosity as 'a strong desire to know or learn something' and learning was at the heart of Einstein's method.

An experience occurred when Einstein was a young child that was etched on his mind forever. He was sick in bed one day and his father brought him a compass. He later said that he was so excited as he examined the device that he trembled and grew cold. Einstein's marvel of science had begun.

He continued to demonstrate a passion for science during his teenage years. Tutored by a family friend, Max Talmud, Einstein was given a geometry textbook. After a short time, the twelve-year-old prodigy had completed the book and such was his mathematical genius that Talmud, the medical school student, found himself unable to keep up with the young mastermind.

How did Einstein satisfy his intellectual curiosity? His greatest breakthroughs in science came from *Gedankenexperiment*, or thought experiments, carried out in his mind. He liked to think visually, coming up with experiments in his mind and working them around in his head until he could see the ideas with clarity.

At the age of sixteen, Einstein imagined an experiment that led to the theory of relativity. He envisioned what it might be like to chase a beam of light: Could he keep up with the beam or could he go faster and overtake it?

In 1907, he made a breakthrough in trying to broaden special relativity to include gravity. 'I was sitting in a chair in the patent office at Bern when suddenly, a thought occurred to me', he remembered. 'If a man falls freely, he will not feel his weight'. He later called it, 'the happiest thought in my life'.

Einstein's inquisitiveness was the key to his success. He had hated the rigid, formal education that had been forced on him. Memorising facts did little to arouse his intellectual curiosity. Instead, asking questions and contemplating their answers led him on his voyage of scientific discovery.

Without curiosity, nothing would ever change. Curiosity allows us to ask how we got into a certain predicament in the first place and what can be done to help solve the issue. For Einstein, answers came from his thought experiments. For others, it may come by simply writing things down and analysing what steps can be taken to improve the situation.

Keep things simple

Converting the complex into the simple was the ultimate accolade for Einstein. He stated, 'the definition of genius is taking the complex and making it simple'. Indeed, a lot of people consider Einstein's greatest ability to be his mathematical mind. However, like Steve Jobs, who we shall read about in Chapter Five, it appears that Einstein regarded simplicity as one of the most fundamental principles in his life. 'I soon learned', Einstein said, 'to scent out what was able to lead to fundamentals and to turn aside from everything else, from the multitude of things that clutter up the mind'.

Einstein's thought experiments were essentially simple attempts to come to terms with complicated theories. The essence of the theory of relativity, he said to a newspaper reporter during his first trip to the United States, was 'the logical simplicity with which it explained apparently conflicting facts in the operation of natural law'. His personal philosophy was very much based on straightforwardness. Einstein was once asked why he did not buy shaving cream (he shaved with an ordinary bar of soap). He countered that he could not stand the thought of keeping two kinds of soap when one would do! The thought of using anything extra was absurd to a scientist who calculated energy expenditure in a universe that conserves everything.

In his 1931 book, *The World as I See It*, Einstein said, 'I believe that a simple and unassuming life is good for everybody, physically and mentally'. For that reason, he intended all his non-scientific writings to be clear and direct.

It might sound strange, given Einstein's grasp of complicated theories that go far beyond most people's comprehension, but Einstein hated complexity and loved simplicity, in daily life, as well as in his scientific thinking.

Use your intuition

Einstein was clear about the high regard that he believed intuition held within human conditioning. For him, 'the intuitive mind is a sacred gift and the rational mind is a faithful servant. We have created a society that honours the servant and has forgotten the gift'. Baruch Spinoza, the seventeenth century Dutch philosopher called intuition, 'a superior way of knowing ultimate truth without the use of prior knowledge or reason. With intuition, there is no conscious reasoning. It acts as our own inner GPS, often described as a sixth sense, where we listen to our inner voice and gut feeling.

It may come as another surprise to learn that a scientist like Einstein placed great emphasis on intuition. Science tends to focus on cold hard facts whilst intuition is indefinable, after all. Nevertheless, Einstein was adamant that he never came upon any of his discoveries through rational thinking. Einstein described his intuitive thought processes at a physics conference in Kyoto in 1922, when he indicated that he used images to solve his problems and only found words later.

How did Einstein use his intuition? He first daydreamed about riding on a beam of light that he followed in his mind's eye back to its point of origin. He then spent years formulating the mathematical equations that would turn his daydream into a fully-fledged scientific theory: the theory of relativity.

Einstein was a creative individual, taking breaks from his work to play the violin. Engaging in creative activities was believed to quieten his mind and allow his intuition to speak up. He was also an advocate of, 'combinatory play' - taking seemingly unrelated things outside the realms of science (art, ideas, music, thoughts), and blending them together to come up with new ideas. It has been said that this is how he came up with his most famous equation, $E = mc^2$.

Intuition is an area where Steve Jobs and Albert Einstein would again find common ground. Speaking to his biographer, Walter Isaacson, Jobs said, 'intuition is a very powerful thing … more powerful than intellect'. In his famous 2005 Stanford commencement speech, Jobs credited his instinctive nature as having a major impact on his career. 'You have to trust in something', he said, 'your gut, destiny, life, karma, whatever'.

Just like Einstein and Jobs before us, we can achieve great things by learning to recognise and trust our intuition. Einstein's theory of relativity caused tremendous controversy in the scientific community, but he followed his instinct and stood by his theory, which is now a staple of modern-day physics. 'All great achievements of science must start from intuitive knowledge', Einstein once told a friend. 'At times, I feel certain I am right while not knowing the reason'.

Be flexible with all options

Not getting stuck in a single way of thinking or acting was another fundamental principle for Einstein. 'The measure of intelligence is the ability to change', he confirmed. However, he wasn't always as flexible as he later became. Until 1931, Einstein believed that the universe was static rather than expanding. Previously, Einstein had applied the theory of general relativity to the universe and suggested a universe that was homogenous, static and spatially curved. In 1917, Einstein even inserted a term called the, 'cosmological constant', into his theory of general relativity to force the equations to predict a stationary universe in keeping with physicists' thinking at the time.

Over the years, despite criticism from scientists such as Alexander Friedman and Georges Lemaitre, he refused to modify his view. According to Marcia Bartusiak, a science journalism professor at MIT, the expanding cosmos simply, 'didn't fit with his view of how the universe acted.' However, he was open to listening to evidence from astronomer Edwin Hubble and admitted his error.

In a 1931 report to the Prussian Academy of Sciences, Einstein finally conceded and adopted a model of an expanding universe. In 1932, he teamed up with the Dutch theoretical physicist and astronomer, Willem de Sitter, to propose an eternally expanding universe which became the cosmological model generally accepted until the middle of the 1990s.

Having the good grace to admit such an error, at the same time as being considered one of the world's most pre-eminent scientists would have taken a great deal of humility. But Einstein was not averse to changing his views, if presented with evidence to the contrary.

Einstein was long held to be a pacifist. However, when Hitler came to power in 1933, pragmatism turned Einstein from war resister to warrior. In August 1933, he wrote a letter to *The New York Times* which showed his viewpoint towards war had changed. 'I should not, in the present circumstances, refuse military service, rather I should enter such a service cheerfully in the belief that I would thereby be helping to save European civilization'. In 1939 and 1940, he even sent two letters to President Roosevelt urging him to investigate the possibility of the United States acquiring an atomic bomb.

Flexibility is the ability to respond effectively, with an open mind, to external changes. Life is always evolving; nothing remains the same. Being flexible allows you to adapt to new situations and gives you the ability to modify your views when new information comes to light.

In 1931, Einstein had no problem holding his hands up and owning up to his scientific mistake, later called the cosmological constant, as the 'greatest blunder' of his career.

Work smarter not just harder
Einstein unashamedly adopted working practises that best suited his personality. 'If a cluttered desk is a sign of a cluttered mind, of what, then, is an empty desk a sign?' he once answered, perhaps in response to those who questioned his own unique methods.

After getting a call from a *LIFE* magazine editor telling him that Albert Einstein had died, photographer Ralph Morse snatched his cameras and headed up the highway to Princeton. In an interview with *LIFE* in 2014, Morse recalled that Einstein died at the Princeton Hospital. 'So, I headed there first. But it was chaos with journalists, photographers, onlookers. So, I headed over to Einstein's office at the Institute for Advanced Studies. On the way, I stopped and bought a case of scotch. I knew people might be reluctant to talk, but most people are happy to accept a bottle of booze, instead of money, in exchange for their help. So, I get to the building, find the superintendent, give him a fifth of scotch and like *that*, he opens up the office'.

Morse then took a photo of Einstein's cluttered desk, just as he left it. The photo has become an iconic image, but it belies the fact that Einstein was in fact, fantastically productive and very organised.

Einstein worked ten hours a day, six days a week for years. Like Winston Churchill, who we shall read about in Chapter Sixteen, Einstein's routine was inviolable and unconventional. Quirky it may have been, but the routine afforded him the space to tackle the complex scientific concepts that percolated inside his busy mind.

Indeed, in the early years, when he worked at the Swiss patent office, he found that he could complete a day's work in three or four hours, leaving him time to think about his own work, physics and the complex problems he was trying to solve.

Whilst Einstein demonstrated a tremendous ability to focus on the work for extended periods, productivity did not result solely from working. Einstein's daily walk was sacrosanct. At Princeton University, he would walk the mile and a half journey there and back. The walks were not just about keeping fit. The walks had a trance like effect, emptying the mind to allow that one fresh thought to enter his consciousness.

A superficial look at Einstein's habits may provoke questions about his work ethic. Not many other successful people are reported to have slept for ten hours a day. But Einstein knew that productivity did not reside solely in the four walls of his office.

It was during moments of solitude, whether whilst walking, or playing the violin, that Einstein would discover imaginative answers to challenging problems. As one friend recalled, 'he would often play his violin in his kitchen late at night, improvising melodies while he pondered complicated problems. Then, suddenly in the middle of playing, he would announce excitedly, "I've got it!"'.

Like Einstein, it is about working smarter, not necessarily harder. Taking time out, or ensuring adequate leisure time, may even result in the Eureka moment that you have been waiting for.

Chapter Four

Stephen Hawking

However difficult life may seem, there is always something you can do and succeed at

Widely regarded as one of the greatest minds of his generation, Professor Steven Hawking was a theoretical scientist who made science available to the masses through his books, talks, and television appearances. His life story was depicted in the 2014 film, *The Theory of Everything*.

Remarkably, this was achieved whilst confined to a wheelchair, having spent over half a century afflicted by amyotrophic lateral sclerosis (ALS). His computerised voice expressed his thoughts and in doing so, he smashed through outdated perceptions regarding what could be achieved, despite one's disabilities.

Hawking was born during the Second World War in Britain. His early academic life was unremarkable. He was described as a bright student, but not a particularly exceptional one. During his first year at St. Albans School, he was third from the bottom of his class. Still, there were enough signs of brilliance for one pupil, Basil King, to bet another of Hawking's friends, John McLenahan, a bag of sweets that, 'Stephen will turn out to be unusually capable'.

Hawking arrived at Oxford University on a scholarship at the start of 1959. Aged only seventeen, his first few years at Oxford were unhappy. His chosen subject, mathematics, was not on offer so he was forced to study physics. He felt isolated amongst the older students, whose attitude was a complete contrast to his. 'You were supposed to be brilliant without effort or accept your limitations and obtain a fourth-class degree', he explained. Gradually, he began to feel more comfortable, finding physics, 'ridiculously easy'. Joining the university boat club helped him make more friends and find social acceptance. By 1962, he had graduated with honours in natural science before moving onto Cambridge University and Trinity Hall, where he studied for a PhD in cosmology.

The warning signs regarding his health had been evident in his final year at Oxford. He became clumsier, falling downstairs on one occasion and losing consciousness. Shortly after his twenty-first birthday, he was diagnosed with a form of motor neurone disease, a devastating illness that destroys the nerves that control the body's muscles. Hawking was shaken by the doctor's grim news; he had a maximum of three years to live. How could he go on?

The answer came in the form of his wife, Jane, whom he had met at a party, a year earlier. Their engagement in October 1964, gave him something to live for. The couple had three children. Defying established medical wisdom, he lived for another fifty-five years, remarkable given that only five per cent of people with the illness survive for more than a decade after diagnosis.

In 1985, Hawking caught pneumonia. He was forced to undergo a tracheostomy operation, irreversibly removing his voice. After the operation, he needed round-the-clock nursing care. It was then that he grew close to Elaine Mason, whom he married in 1995.

Hawking's illness never stalled his academic progress or research. Quite the opposite. In 1979, He was named to the distinguished post as Professor of Mathematics at Cambridge University.

Nine years later, Hawking published his signature work, *A Brief History of Time*. Six years in the making, it was described as a layman's guide to cosmology. The book broke new ground on the basic laws governing the universe, including his hypothesis that black holes had a temperature and produce radiation.

The dissemination of science was only one motivating factor for the book but there were also practical considerations.

The financial demands of managing his condition, with the round-the-clock care and expensive equipment, were substantial. He continued his work at Cambridge and in 2001, published a second book, *Universe in a Nutshell*.

He lectured to packed audiences across the world and influenced popular culture through his appearances on popular television shows. The awards quickly followed; a CBE in 1982, the Companion of Honour in 1989 and the US Presidential Medal of Freedom in 2009.

Hawking's influence continues to be felt to this day. During the current pandemic, his family donated his personal ventilator to the Royal Papworth Hospital in Cambridge.

He once wrote that his illness had not stopped him being a success in his work or having a family. 'It shows', he said, 'that one need not lose hope'.

How did Hawking, a man who experienced almost unparalleled suffering, achieve such phenomenal success?

Make your work your purpose
A commitment to work underpinned Hawking's whole approach to life. He once said, 'My goal is simple. It is a complete understanding of the universe, why it is as it is and why it exists at all'. In a 2010 interview with the American journalist Diane Sawyer on *ABC World News*, Sawyer asked Hawking what piece of advice he would give to his children. His answer was simple: 'Never give up work. Work gives you meaning and purpose, and life is empty without it'.

Born on the eighth of January 1942, three-hundred years to the day after the death of the father of modern science, Galileo Galilei, he believed science was his destiny. From an early age, Hawking's curiosity demanded answers to the major scientific questions of the time. That was evident to his mother, who often lay down in the backyard on summer evenings to stare up at the stars. 'Stephen always had a strong sense of wonder. And I could see that the stars would draw him'.

His passion for science was unaffected by his initial diagnosis or worsening health after 1985. He never lost his passion for writing, lecturing, or trying to come to a better understanding of the universe. His life saw him embrace two passions; education and sharing his love of the universe with children. He also advocated strongly for the rights of disabled people.

His workload was always heavy, although he still insisted on leaving time to have fun. In 2007, he became the first quadriplegic to experience weightlessness on board the so-called 'vomit comet', a modified plane specially designed to simulate zero gravity. Determined to keep pushing boundaries, he wanted to encourage interest in space travel and booked a seat on Sir Richard Branson's Virgin Galactic sub-orbital space plane. In his final years, he joined forces with Silicon Valley Philanthropist, Yuri Milner, to search for extra-terrestrial life in space.

It could never be proven whether Stephen Hawking's love of his own work, was a contributing factor in his remarkable longevity. But by refusing to succumb to depression and continuing to work towards greater understanding of the universe, he was, in his own words, able to, 'lead as normal a life as possible, and not think about my condition, or regret the things it prevents me from doing, which are not that many'.

Become an effective communicator

Hawking was acknowledged as a good writer and communicator. *The Guardian's* review of his book, *A Brief History in Time* spoke of, 'a succinct, entertaining and brilliantly lucid book.' Hawking was on a trip to CERN in Geneva in 1985, when he contracted pneumonia. In the hospital, he was put on a ventilator, where his condition was listed as critical. His first wife, Jane, was asked whether she wanted doctors to turn his life support machine off. She refused and insisted he be flown back to Cambridge, where doctors managed to control the infection. The life-saving treatment left him unable to speak, but amazingly, the motor neurone disease sufferer went on to publish the book which brought him worldwide fame.

Hawking had no wish to write a dry book for experts. He told *The Wall Street Journal* in 2013 that he had wanted to write, 'the sort of book that would sell in airport bookstores'. Like so many aspiring authors, Hawking's hopes were initially dashed by a literary agent, who told him there was little chance of that happening. Hawking though, was in the business of defying predictions. By 2018, more than ten million copies had been sold. The first run sold out in the United States in days. It spent one-hundred and forty-seven weeks on *The New York Times'* bestseller list and back in the UK, a record-breaking two-hundred and thirty-seven weeks on *The Times'* bestseller list.

Upon publication, its clarity was highlighted as its strength. The book was described by *The New York Times* as, 'a jaunty and absolutely clear little book', that shared his ideas about the universe, 'with everyone who can read'.

As well as his own innate ability to communicate, Hawking clearly benefited from up-to-date technology that helped make up for mobility and speech difficulties. He used a thumb switch and a blink-switch attached to his glasses to control his computer. Hawking began to use his cheek muscles to communicate following the degradation of nerves in his thumb and in 2014, hailed a new Assistive Context-Aware Toolkit (ACAT) platform developed in partnership with Intel as, 'life changing'.

Professor Stephen Hawking may have lost his voice in 1985, but his ability to communicate complex ideas clearly and effectively lived on until his death in 2018. It is what led Professor Brian Cox, the English physicist, to call him a 'truly brilliant communicator'.

See the funny side
Hawking possessed a brilliant sense of humour. Despite dealing with a major life disability, he always tried to use his

sense of fun. 'People who boast about their IQ are losers,' he responded in his last major television interview at Cambridge University in 2017, when asked about his own IQ by television presenter, Piers Morgan.

As well as being a world-renowned scientist, Hawking was known to have a keen sense of fun and mischief. He embraced his place in popular culture, even appearing on an episode of *The Simpsons* in 1999. Simpsons' fans will recall the memorable night that Homer Simpson was joined at the bar in Moe's Tavern by none other than Stephen Hawking. Having listened to Homer's theory of a, 'donut-shaped universe', the scientist remarked that the theory was certainly interesting. Hawking was thrilled to appear on the show, stating that he 'accepted immediately, because I thought it would be fun. And because *The Simpsons* is the best thing on American television'.

He appeared on the television programme, *The Big Bang Theory* seven times and used his fame for *Comic Relief*, participating in several sketches over the years. In her 2013 biography of Hawking, Kitty Ferguson stated how Hawking enjoyed using his wheelchair to run over the toes of people who annoyed him. At one point, he is alleged to have done so to Prince Charles, at an event to celebrate the Prince's induction into the Royal Society. Ferguson wrote that, 'the Prince was intrigued by Hawking's wheelchair and Hawking, twirling it around to demonstrate its capabilities, carelessly ran over Prince Charles' toes. One of Hawking's regrets in life was not having an opportunity to run over Margaret Thatcher's toes'.

After a talk he delivered at the Sydney Opera House, he was asked by an audience member about the 'cosmological effect of Zayn Malik leaving (the pop group) *One Direction*'. Hawking dryly replied, 'finally, a question about something important'.

Not many people could have coped with the adversity that was sent his way. In a documentary in 2013, Hawking remarked that as well as an active mind, maintaining a sense of humour was vital towards his survival. And what a sense of humour it was. In perhaps his most amusing quip, Hawking told the then British Prime Minister, Theresa May, 'I deal in tough mathematical questions every day, but please don't ask me to help with Brexit'.

When asked what inspired him to keep going, amidst such tremendous suffering, Stephen Hawking simply replied, 'my work and a sense of humour'.

Accept reality

Hawking had an amazingly humble acceptance of situations in life, including his own disability, confirming, 'I don't have much positive to say about motor neurone disease. But it taught me not to pity myself, because others were worse off and to get on with what I still could do. I'm happier now than before I developed the condition.'

In 2004, Hawking was interviewed by *The New York Times* journalist, Deborah Solomon. He grew excited during the interview and spoke of his joy at being able to explain complex science to ordinary people. Solomon was amazed, asking him if he was always so cheerful, Hawking explained that his expectations had been reduced to zero when he was twenty-one. Therefore, 'everything since then has been a bonus'.

Despite Hawking's fortitude, ALS is a particularly cruel illness. A rare neurological disease, it affects voluntary muscle movements such as chewing, walking, and talking. It is progressive, there is no cure and no scientist has managed to find a treatment to reverse or even halt the disease. Before the diagnosis, Hawking claimed he was unfocused and bored with life. Accepting his condition allowed him to begin viewing life with a new sense of perspective. He pursued his career with more vigour, travelled the world and supported causes that would improve the lives of fellow disabled people.

In a 2011 interview with *The New York Times,* he implored others to accept their challenges with a 'can-do', attitude. 'My advice to other disabled people would be, concentrate on things your disability doesn't prevent you doing well, and don't regret the things it interferes with. Don't be disabled in spirit, as well as physically'.

Technology enabled Hawking to continue writing and delivering lectures after his illness of 1985. In Hawking's view, however, technology only made a difference when combined with a positive attitude and acceptance of his situation.

It is certain that Stephen Hawking did not like his condition; it is just that had he not accepted it, he would never have been able to move forward. When a person does not accept their situation, it is often a one-way ticket to a life of depression, anxiety or bitterness.

People naturally gravitate towards Hawking's intelligence as his major strength but what if there has been a misunderstanding of why he was so intelligent. 'Intelligence is the ability to adapt to change', Hawking said at his Oxford University graduation speech. The point is that all the knowledge in the world would have been meaningless if Hawking had not had the wisdom to adapt to and accept his difficult reality.

Never give up hope
Hawking had an ability to always look for the positive, using his scientific knowledge in relation to life's situations. 'Black holes are not as black as they are painted. They are not the eternal prisons they were once thought. Things can get out of a black hole both on the outside and possibly to another universe. So, if you feel you are in a black hole, don't give up — there's a way out', he observed. Hawking used his speech at the Hawking Radiation Conference in Stockholm in 2015, to provide solutions to issues baffling a generation of physicists. Perhaps more significantly, Hawking was again able to draw in a wider audience, receptive to his ability to draw a striking parallel between the black holes and the hopelessness and depression that is prevalent in modern times.

The day before his seventy-sixth birthday, Hawking was invited to deliver the Reith Lecture at the Royal Institute in

London about depression. The scientist told the crowd of four hundred about appreciating his achievements, despite his diagnosis. 'Although it was unfortunate to get motor neurone disease, I have been very fortunate in almost everything else. It's important not to become angry, no matter how difficult life may seem because you can lose all hope if you can't laugh at yourself and life in general'.

Of course, there were dark days but despite his predicament, Hawking rarely allowed self-pity to penetrate his heart. Shortly after his diagnosis, he experienced a period of profound depression, during which he drank and debated whether he should continue with this postgraduate research at Cambridge. With the help of his future wife, Jane, he found the strength to continue. Then came his illness and tracheostomy in 1985, a time in which he admits that he briefly tried to commit suicide by holding his breath. Yet overall, Hawking accepted and even embraced his illness, with no hint of bitterness or sorrow. After all, he had few regrets.

Stephen Hawking, one of the great minds of our time refused to believe there was no hope. 'One has to have a positive attitude and must make the best of the situation that one finds oneself in; if one is physically disabled, one cannot afford to be psychologically disabled as well', he confirmed.

The Entrepreneurs

Chapter Five

Steve Jobs

Life sometimes hits you in the head with a brick. How you respond? That's what matters most

Steve Jobs co-founded Apple in 1976 and transformed the company into the number one brand in the world. In doing so, he rewrote the rules of business. Widely considered as a brilliant visionary, Jobs oversaw the launch of iconic products such as the Apple Mac, the iPod, and the iPhone.

Jobs' path to the top was far from straightforward. His career was littered with product failures, fallouts and setbacks. Jobs later acknowledged that his eventual successes were based on the lessons he acquired from his failures and the hardships that he had to endure.

Given up for adoption by his birth parents in 1957, he had a hard time with formal schooling, mainly due to boredom. Reports also suggested that he was seen by his classmates as somewhat of a loner.

In his high school years, he did, however, take an interest in electronics. At one point, Jobs needed some parts for an electronic counting machine for a class project. He found the phone number of Bill Hewlett of Hewlett-Packard, called him up and chatted for about twenty minutes. He got the parts he needed as well as receiving an invitation for a summer internship at HP.

Jobs never graduated from college, lasting only six months before dropping out. After a few years of soul searching, including a spiritual retreat to India, Jobs joined forces with Steve Wozniak to start a company from his family garage. Within two years, he was worth over one million dollars.

Nevertheless, the problems were only just starting. Despite Apple becoming a publicly traded company in 1980, successive products suffered significant design flaws, resulting in recalls and consumer disappointment. The company's expensive Macintosh struggled to compete in an IBM PC-dominated business world.

Feeling that he needed more experience in the boardroom, Jobs lured John Sculley from PepsiCo. 'Do you want to sell sugared water for the rest of your life? Or do you want to come with me and change the world?' he asked Sculley in his famous pitch.

What seemed like a good idea at the time, soon turned into a nightmare. Sculley believed Jobs was hurting Apple. In the ensuing power struggle, in 1985, the board fired Jobs from his own company. Jobs described feeling like a public failure and regarded the sacking as devastating.

Following his departure, Jobs went on to found NeXT. He formulated plans for a computer dubbed the Cube because of its shape, but it never found a market. At that time, *Forbes* magazine slammed Jobs for being a poor manager who made 'fundamentally wrong decisions'.

Nevertheless, NeXT ended up being an important springboard for recovery. In 1997, a struggling Apple bought its competitor and incorporated some of the technology into Apple products. The deal also brought Jobs back to Apple. By this time, Jobs had founded and achieved significant success with the animation studio, Pixar.

When the prodigal son returned, many felt that Apple was beyond redemption. However, just as he instigated Apple's earlier success, he revitalized the company in the 1990s. The company branched out into music distribution and later entered the phone market with the introduction of the iPhone. Having transformed the fortunes of the company he founded, Steve Jobs died at the age of fifty-six in 2011.

Even though Jobs was a college dropout, a fired tech executive and occasionally unsuccessful businessman, that is not how he is remembered. Instead, we use his Apple products daily, enjoy the iconic films that Pixar produced with our families and fondly remember him as someone who changed the world forever.

How did Steve Jobs manage to embark on such a dramatic career transformation that earned him the title as one of the business world's greatest comeback kids, especially after being fired by the company he set up?

Burn with passion for the task at hand

An intense focus on the topic at hand was essential for Steve Jobs. 'You have to be burning with an idea, or a problem, or a wrong that you want to right. If you're not passionate enough from the start, you'll never stick it out', he emphasised. When he returned to Apple in 1997, the company was haemorrhaging cash. Jobs called a staff meeting and explained the importance of passion at the core of his plan for rescuing the troubled brand. 'Apple is not about making boxes for people to get their jobs done, although we do that well. Apple is about something more. Its core value is that we believe that people with passion can change the world for the better', Jobs told his staff at Apple.

In 1998, Apple introduced the iMac, the all-in-one computer that reinforced the company's turnaround. By January 2010, *Harvard Business Review* had named Steve Jobs the best performing CEO in the world. Even at the end of his life, when Jobs knew he was dying, he had the appetite to begin new projects and 'elicited promises from his friends at Apple to finish them'.

Throughout his entire career, Jobs had a hunger for creating products of the highest quality and this led him to inspire his teams at Apple to create products that broke the mould. Working at Apple was never to be considered just a job for his employees. The work needed to be a crusade, a mission to bring better computer power to people.

In his first spell at Apple, Jobs was able to instil his own passion in the team members with whom he worked. The original Apple Mac development team typically worked ninety hours a week for months at a time. The group even had sweatshirts made up with the words, 'Ninety Hours a Week and Loving it'. Jobs translated his passion for calligraphy into his passion for technology. In his famous commencement speech at Stanford University in 2005, Jobs recalled how dropping out of college left him with time to take a calligraphy class, which later would inform the typography aesthetic of the first Mac.

Jobs had already displayed this passion for perfection at NeXT in 1986. He was determined to build the next generation of the personal computer, a machine so powerful, that it would put Apple to shame. From the elegant logo, designed by Yale art professor, Paul Rand, to the hi-tech factory, Jobs' passion for designing the perfect product was all-consuming. Whilst Jobs never succeeded in this quest, (the product was too expensive for the market) no one questioned his burning passion to, 'right the wrong', that had been committed against him at Apple.

On becoming the majority shareholder at Pixar Animation Studios in 1986, Jobs may not have designed the graphics or created the characters, but he was passionate about creating joyful movies.

What can we take from Steve Jobs' story? As Matthew Weiner, creator of the highly successful television series, *Mad Men* once said, 'you should want it so badly that you don't have a choice'.

Keep it simple

On his return to Apple in 1997, Jobs discovered that the company had been making multiple versions of products to satisfy requests from retailers, including twelve versions of the Macintosh. It was too much. The company had become a jack of all trades and a master of none. 'A zillion and one products' was how Jobs' described Apple's product line. 'Simplicity is the ultimate sophistication', was his firm belief.

According to Walter Isaacson, Jobs' biographer, in the book *Steve Jobs*, he got up and shouted, 'Stop!' in the middle of a product meeting, continuing, 'this is crazy'. Taking a marker, he drew a chart that was to form the basis of Apple's product range for years to come. The simple insight was to help people choose a computer using only two questions - are you an everyday consumer or pro? Do you want portable or desktop? A decision was then taken to dramatically scale down Apple's product line to just a few different products.

Out went peripheral products like scanners. A forty-product range was whittled down to just four. Jobs wanted Apple's engineers to focus on the thirty per cent that was left, or what Jobs called, 'the gems.' Doing this allowed the company to focus on creating excellent products for home and business and saved the company money by stopping superfluous projects.

Did it work? Well consider that in 2000, Apple was worth five billion dollars and facing the threat of bankruptcy. By 2010, the company had a value of one hundred and seventy billion dollars. This was only achieved by building simplicity into every aspect of the company's operations, from design through to strategy.

Jobs' love of simple interfaces was evident from the beginning. In 1975, he returned from India to work at Atari, where together with Apple co-founder, Steve Wozniak, he designed video games. The remit at Atari was to produce games that were simple enough for a stoned freshman to figure them out. Jobs got the remit. The only instructions for the Atari's Star Trek game that he worked on were: '1. Insert quarter. 2. Avoid Klingons'.

In his first spell at Apple, Jobs insisted that Apple's mantra would be simplicity. 'The way we're running the company, the product design, the advertising, it all comes down to this: Let's make it simple: Really simple', he urged his staff.

Jobs' belief in the power of simplicity as a design principle reached its zenith with the three devices he produced in 2001: the iPod, iPhone and iPad. He immersed himself in the design of the original iPod and its interface. 'Simplify!' was his main demand. One of the reasons Apple retains its loyal customer basis to this day is the simplicity of its products and user experience.

Steve Jobs was superb at drilling down to the fundamentals. People are often looking for complicated solutions to their problems, spending significant amounts of time and money searching for solutions. Jobs' belief in the power of simplicity is a lesson to us all. 'Keep it Simple: Really Simple', he said.

Analyse what you have done
Looking inward at the things that happened to you with all their implications on your life was important to Jobs. 'Getting fired from Apple was the best thing that could have ever happened to me. The heaviness of being successful was replaced by the lightness of being a beginner again ... It freed me to enter one of the most creative periods of my life', he said later. Indeed, Jobs used the period after his initial departure from Apple to reassess his life and reflect on where things had gone wrong. He described his sacking as, 'awful tasting medicine, but I guess the patient needed it'. Of course, Jobs did not want to get fired from his own company. But he could not control that. The only thing he could control was how he responded. Instead of running away from Silicon Valley, as he had initially threatened, Jobs bought the animation studio, Pixar and started the computer company, NeXT.

Jobs also learnt from his indiscretions at Apple during his first spell at the company. His early days at Apple were marked by his manipulative, demanding and aggressive behaviour. His impossibly high standards had alienated employees unable to keep up with his demand for perfection.

Having been humiliated at his exit from Apple, Jobs undertook a period of introspection and self-correction. In his words, he decided to start again and this extended to his personal life, when he began efforts to reconcile with his estranged daughter, Lisa. Considered a control freak at Apple, Jobs decided to follow a different strategy at Pixar. Having bought the company in the mid-1990s, it was still working on its first feature film, *Toy Story* and struggling financially. Jobs learned how to be more collaborative and ceded some control to others.

Pamela Kerwin, former vice president at Pixar, commented on the change in Jobs' approach: 'After the first three words out of your mouth, he'd interrupt you and say, "Okay, here's how I see things". It isn't like that anymore. He listens a lot more, and he's more relaxed, more mature'. The perfectionist boss whose behaviour had been so divisive in the past had learned to listen and delegate. By the time he had returned to Apple in the late 1990s, Jobs increasingly focused on spirituality. His adherence to the practise of Zen Buddhism may be another reason for a calmer, kinder countenance.

Jobs was the first to admit that adversity was his greatest teacher. It offered the chance to gain valuable insight and learn from mistakes, so that when his time at Apple came again, he had grown wiser and did things differently.

Allison Linn, in her excellent article, *What Steve Jobs Taught us: It's OK to Fail,* gives us hope that with serious introspection, we too can look inward and make lasting change. 'Jobs is fondly remembered as the poster child for how making mistakes — and even failing — can sometimes end up being the best thing that ever happens to you', she remarked.

Use focus to fine-tune your goal

Jobs adopted a ruthless approach to ideas and activities around him. 'People think focus means saying 'yes' to the thing you've got to focus on. But that's not what it means at all. It means saying 'no' to the hundred other good ideas that there are', was his view.

A famous story from 2006 best illustrates Jobs' obsession with focus. When Mark Parker took over as CEO of Nike in 2006, one of the first things he did was call Jobs seeking his advice. At the time, Nike was struggling. They were failing to fit their digital strategy into the numerous product lines that they sold. Jobs gave Parker a piece of advice in his typically blunt fashion, that literally helped change the fortunes of Nike: 'You make some of the best products in the world. But you also make a lot of crap. Just get rid of the crappy stuff and *focus* on the good stuff'.

When Jobs returned to Apple, it was evident to him that the company lacked a coherent, focused, corporate and product strategy. Turnaround would only be possible, he believed, through laser guided focus. Therefore, Jobs quickly scaled down Apple's three-hundred and fifty products in development to just ten.

Jobs made the difficult decision to end production of Apple's hand-held PDA. Jobs admitted that the decision was unpopular. His view was in the minority and convincing Apple's corporate team to end production was not an easy task. However, under the banner of focus, Jobs reluctantly concluded that the beloved product had to go.

In 2012, with Apple's stock price at an all-time high of over seven-hundred dollars per share, only a dozen products constituted most of Apple's sales. By contrast, Sony, whom Apple had replaced as the leading consumer electronics company, made over two-thousand products, with hardly any leading their categories in either sales or customer satisfaction. Focus produces results.

Jobs took one hundred of the top performing Apple staff members on a retreat each year. On the last day, he would stand in front of a whiteboard and ask, 'What are the ten things we should be doing next?' Jobs would write down the propositions. Eventually, the list was whittled down to ten.

Then Jobs would cut the bottom seven and announce, 'we can only do three'.

In his own life, Jobs ruthlessly filtered out distractions. He had already embraced the practice of meditation and mindfulness in the 1970s. Mindfulness meditation involves sitting quietly, for five or ten minutes, and closely observing one's own breath and the sensations that accompany breathing. The goal is pure awareness without judgment or reflection. Mindfulness has become so popular in the West that software developers have created mindfulness apps available for download.

Jobs used mindfulness meditation to reduce distractions which allowed him to focus on creating unique products. Colleagues and family members would be infuriated as they tried to get him to deal with important issues. Yet Jobs refused to shift his intense focus until he had finished dealing with the problem at hand.

Often, we get distracted by new ideas, projects or business opportunities that appear in front of us. We may have pressure coming at us from different directions. Instead of focusing on the most important task at hand, we become bogged down by the volume of tasks in front of us. Many people lose focus by trying to get involved in areas they simply have no expertise in. This can be a sure-fire way to fail. As Lord Sugar, the British business tycoon stated, 'do not start a business on your own if you haven't had experience in it'.

Collaborate with those around you
Working with and through others to achieve success was essential in Jobs' modus operandi. 'It doesn't make sense to hire smart people and tell them what to do; we hire smart people so they can tell us what to do', he once said. Although Jobs became the face of Apple in the 1980s, he cannot be credited with single-handily building the company. Instead, he focused on the marketing machine, whilst partners, like co-founder Steve Wozniak, took on other more technical roles. Likewise, Jobs did

not create the protype for the iPod or manage the manufacturing process. Jobs provided the vision, guided development, and made many of the key decisions. 'He didn't create anything really, but he created everything', said former CEO, John Sculley, when referring to Jobs' contribution to the original Apple Mac.

Jobs stated in the documentary, *Steve Jobs: The Man in the Machine*, 'I consider the most important job of someone like myself as recruiting'. Once Jobs was satisfied with his team, he worked closely with the team members, delegating tasks but keeping control of the process. Jobs acted as the team director, a referee who rejected or accepted the work of his creative people. Despite his reputation as a notorious micromanager, Jobs maintained an outstanding and stable executive team during his second stint at Apple. More secure in himself, Jobs became comfortable in surrounding himself, and even listening, to strong, opinionated executives who were not afraid to argue with him.

Having been fired by Apple, taking over at Pixar in 1986, Jobs was fortunate to inherit a team with a strong collaborative ethos. 'Watching our collaboration, where we were making ourselves better by working together, I think that fuelled Steve', says John Lasseter, the director of *Toy Story*. 'That was one of the key changes when he went back to Apple. He was willing to be open to the talent of others, to be inspired by and challenged by that talent, but also to inspire them to do amazing things he knew he couldn't do himself'.

On his return, Jobs gave his team huge responsibilities and an abundance of flexibility. Fred Anderson, the CFO, who had been kept on by Jobs stated that his boss did not involve himself in the financial operations of the company. 'It wasn't his strength, and he knew it', he says.

When Jobs introduced the iPhone, he initially refused to allow independent developers to create software for the device. It was only after he listened to his team that he relented and this led to the creation of the App Store, thus securing the iPhone's place in history.

Former Apple retail chief, Ron Johnson, told a group of Stanford MBA students, 'Steve was the best delegator I ever met'.

John Lennon and Paul McCartney became one of the greatest song-writing partnerships in recorded music history. Yet the two men could not have been more different. Paul was known to be meticulous, organised, and polite whilst Lennon was known as disorganised and rebellious. Yet, the two were still able to collaborate in creative partnership. Lennon's first wife, Cynthia, said, 'John needed Paul's persistence and attention-to-detail while Paul needed John's anarchic, lateral thinking'. In writing *Lucy in the Sky with Diamonds*, it is understood that they shared lines back and forth, coming up with ideas and engaging in creative collaboration.

Jobs himself hailed *The Beatles* as his model for business. 'They were four guys who kept each other's kind of negative tendencies in check. They balanced each other and the total was greater than the sum of its parts. That's how I see business: great things in business are never done by one person'.

Collaboration means working cooperatively with others to overcome conflict and build towards a common goal. 'Only I know best', is an unproductive mindset for confronting adversity. After all, your problems will always involve other people.

Chapter Six

Katharine Graham

What I essentially did, was to put one foot in front of the other, shut my eyes and step off the ledge. The surprise was that I landed on my feet

Meryl Streep earned rave reviews for her portrayal of Katharine 'Kay' Graham in Stephen Spielberg's *The Post* in 2017. The film depicted the true story of attempts by journalists at *The Washington Post* to publish the Pentagon Papers, a classified report regarding the twenty-year involvement of the United States government in Vietnam.

Graham's story, whilst inspirational, is not one of rags-to-riches. The joke during the Watergate crisis was that if Graham lost control of *The Post*, she would be down to her last six-hundred million dollars. The significance lay in her role as one of the first female business leaders, a role she reluctantly took on after the suicide of her husband, Phil. Graham went from playing the role of housewife and mother of four children to becoming one of the most powerful women in America, all in the space of a few years. As the only woman in such a prominent role at the time, she suffered from sexism and suggestions from patronising male colleagues that she should leave decision making to them.

Widely known to be shy and reserved, she overcame many challenges to become the first female CEO of a Fortune 500 company after taking the company public in 1971. Prior to this, it was her decision to publish the Pentagon Papers and the earth-shattering coverage of the Watergate scandal that elevated her to national prominence.

She had been born to a wealthy family in New York in 1917. Raised by emotionally and often, physically distant parents, her father was a financier and later, owner of *The*

Washington Post. Due to her parents' work and social commitments, she was all but raised by nannies and tutors. The little time she did spend with her mother was not particularly happy. A difficult woman, Agnus Meyer set impossibly high standards for her daughter.

Working for a short time at a San Francisco newspaper, in 1940, she met and married Phil Graham. The marriage was not a happy one. Whilst charming, Phil suffered from manic depression, alternating between periods of depression and mania. He drank heavily and could be extremely demeaning to his wife.

Graham's father, Eugene Meyer, had entrusted control of the paper to Phil in 1946. Despite her experience in journalism, Eugene favoured Phil over his daughter because, 'no man should be in the position of working for his wife'. The only role left for Graham was, she later wrote, 'doormat wife … tail to his kite'.

By 1962, it was clear that Phil was extremely ill. Phil began telling his friends that he was going to divorce Katharine. After suffering from a bout of mania and indulging in an affair with a young reporter, he returned home and shot himself. His wife found the body.

Advised by her friends to leave the business to be run by others, Graham decided that she owed it to her children to take over. From the time of the company going public in 1971 until she stepped down as chairman in 1993, the annual return to shareholders was 22.3 percent and she became known as the best newspaper executive in the country over the period. The company grew rapidly, to revenues totalling one billion dollars in 1985.

Graham's memoir, *Personal History*, won the Pulitzer Prize in 1998. She died a few years later, in 2001, aged eighty-four. How did Graham, a known introvert, manage to put her self-doubt aside to become known as the toughest guy in the boardroom?

Delegate but have the final say

When Graham took over *The Washington Post*, she suffered from an array of difficulties: not least, the attitude of conceited and patronizing men. Painfully unsure of herself and feeling ill-equipped to run a newspaper, she had been brought up under the mistaken assumption that only men possessed a managerial gene. But that viewpoint was to change and ultimately, Katharine Graham demonstrated that she was the boss. As her close colleague Ben Bradlee said after her death, 'she gave her executives great autonomy, but it was always clear that she was in charge.'

Graham slowly but surely grew in confidence and showed a notable instinct for whom to hire and whom to get rid of from her husband's time as publisher of *The Washington Post*. According to Warren Buffet, her trusted advisor, she understood 'one of the most basic rules of business: to surround yourself with talented people and then nourish them with responsibilities and your gratitude'.

Two years after taking over, she made her best pick, with the hiring of Ben Bradlee as editor. The two made a formidable team. With her backing, he built a staff of reporters and editors and put an emphasis on investigating government with passion. Bradlee's style electrified his staff and invigorated his publisher. At Bradlee's urging, she began investing in creating a dynamic newsroom, ensuring the paper had excellent foreign correspondents.

Whilst Graham insisted that she never wanted to be surprised by what she read in the paper, she believed in leaving most journalistic decisions down to her editors. 'People literally do think that I run downstairs and tell them what to print and what not to print. I mean it's so crazy, it's hard to answer', she said. 'It isn't right for a publisher to tell an editor what to do or not to do. But it is certainly the publisher's responsibility to see that the paper is complete, accurate, fair and as excellent as possible'.

On June 17, 1972, five months before Nixon's re-election, five men were caught breaking into the headquarters of the Democratic National Committee in the Watergate complex. *The Washington Post* started an intense investigation that connected the break-in to the White House. Graham backed Bradlee and his two young investigative reporters, Bob Woodward and Carl Bernstein, in their dogged pursuit of the truth in the Watergate story.

Warren Buffet, considered the most successful investor in the United States, greatly helped Graham in 1971 with obligations to shareholders, teaching her about management and how to make a profit while maintaining editorial quality. 'He literally took me to business school, which was just what I needed', she wrote of her financial mentor. However, when it came to decision making, Graham was quite prepared to have the final say.

Sheila Murray Bethel, in her book, *A New Breed of Leader*, describes meeting Graham and being struck by an intense listening ability, a 'supreme leadership skill', that builds great loyalty amongst followers. A good leader, like Graham, knew that the final decision was their responsibility but they were also unafraid of listening to the views of those around them, before doing so.

Step courageously into uncertainty

'I took a big gulp and said, "Go Ahead. Go Ahead, Go Ahead. Let's go. Let's Publish."' These were the words Katharine Graham uttered at a moment which could have shaped her career, her reputation, even her life, depending on the impact of her decision. In making that choice, Graham had no clue which way the impact of that decision would go.

In June 1971, Katharine Graham had a tough decision to make. *The Washington Post* was in receipt of sections of the Pentagon Papers from a source. The government had requested that the paper cease publication. Printing the papers might be illegal and could ruin *The Washington Post's* reputation if writers got anything wrong.

Bradlee was telling Graham she had to publish whilst her lawyers insisted she should not do so. The lawyers urged Bradlee to wait until the courts decided *The New York Times'* case against publishing part of the papers. It would be far less risky to let *The New York Times* carry the can against the government, they said.

The Washington Post had only been listed on the stock exchange two days before receiving the papers and publication could easily have seen a reduction in its stock price.

Still learning the business, Graham was inspired by the ideal proposed by Bradlee, of finding and telling the truth, come what may. The decision was vindicated when the Supreme Court supported the decision. Graham was emboldened by the courageous stance she had taken and it served as a stepping stone for an even bigger moment; the investigation into the Watergate scandal that ended the presidency of Richard Nixon.

The intimidation by the Nixon administration, in the build up to publication, was intense. When *Post* reporter Carl Bernstein called Nixon's attorney general, John Mitchell, to fact-check his involvement in the scandal, Mitchell said, 'Graham's going to get caught in a big fat wringer if that's published'. During the paper's investigation, Nixon vowed to, 'do a number', on *The Washington Post* and the licenses of two of the company's television stations were challenged.

Yet Graham bravely supported her staff and authorised Bradlee to run stories about Watergate when few other news outlets were willing to do so. In 1974, *The Washington Post* won a Pulitzer for its coverage of the scandal. Graham showed that she was prepared to go to jail rather than disclose the paper's sources and took possession of her reporters' notes to make sure that if anyone were to be jailed, it would be her.

'With her backing, Bradlee forged a staff of reporters and editors and put out a breezy, gutsy paper that investigated government with gusto', wrote *The New York Times*.

In 1975, the company faced a massive strike led by the powerful pressmen's union, which began with strikers setting fire to the printing facility. It appeared for a time that *The Washington Star* might usurp *The Washington Post*, unless the strike was settled. Pickets burned her in effigy, with one sign cruelly stating, 'Phil shot the wrong Graham'.

Graham fought the strike and assembled a skeleton crew that managed to get the paper out for one-hundred and thirty-nine days before the pressmen agreed to accept significant financial concessions.

Such courage was a hallmark of Graham's character even before her role with the paper. She had, after all, survived her husband's mania, depression, alcoholism, infidelity and suicide.

Courageous people, like Katharine Graham, feel fear like anyone else. They simply stand firm and overcame those fears.

Build your confidence

Graham had shown her level of confidence when she responded to suggestions that she replace her late husband by exclaiming, 'Me? That's impossible. I couldn't possibly do it'. Yet her response was in no way connected to her ability, but rather reflected her low opinion of herself. Katharine was summing up a characteristic of her personality which she would have to develop to succeed.

When Allison Pearson of *The Daily Telegraph* asked Graham what she might write for her own epitaph, she declined to answer. 'Here lies Katharine Graham, who finally stopped apologising for herself', suggested Pearson.

It is little wonder that Graham struggled with confidence, having been brought up with a cold, distant mother and having to deal with the erratic behaviour of her criticising husband.

'My mother seemed to undermine so much of what I did, subtly belittling my choices and my activities in light of her greater, more important ones', she wrote. 'As for Phil, at the same time that he was building me up, he was tearing me down'.

After Phil's death, Graham was filled with doubt before taking the role at *The Washington Post*. She told CNN's Larry King, 'I didn't want to run it because I didn't think I could'. 'Of course you can do it … you've just been pushed down so far you don't recognize what you can do', an acquaintance reassured her.

At the outset, things were not easy. Before making speeches, she shook with terror. When she received difficult news, she would break down in tears. Nervous and feeble, she was horrified at the thought of asking a stupid question.

It took a few years for Graham to find the confidence to believe in herself. She learned to stand up for herself in meetings and soon recognised that the paper had been far from perfect in the hands of her husband. Armed with the support of Bradlee and Buffet, she set about making the necessary changes to turn the paper into a leaner outfit, getting rid of the slackers in the newsroom and raiding rival newspapers across the country for their best talent.

During her time, she also ensured that the number of women working at the paper increased and demanded gender equality. In a sales meeting at *Newsweek*, another publication she owned, she was told by a male executive that there was enough trouble without adding more women. Graham reached for an ashtray and threw it across the room, shouting, 'Sexist!' amongst other choice words. Her work on behalf of women led the historian, Arthur Schlesinger, to refer to her as a quiet revolutionary on behalf of all women. Women began to identify with her, both because of her lack of confidence and her determination to overcome it.

Some believe that confidence is something people are born with. Graham showed how the development of confidence is a work in progress and achievable through practice and hard work.

As a quick learner, Graham realised that she had to appear decisive, even if she did not really feel it at the time. 'Her triumphs over her own self-doubts and demons were every bit as impressive as her public triumphs'. Al Hunt of *The Wall Street Journal* remembers his former publisher, Warren Phillips saying of Katharine Graham, 'it was her determination to work on her confidence and her audacious decision making, such as the decision to go to print on the Pentagon Papers and Watergate, that turned her from a doormat wife to journalistic icon'.

Accept mistakes as normal

In her book, *Personal History*, with characteristic honesty, Graham reveals great sorrow for several decisions she made in the wake of her husband's death. She deeply regretted the decision to send her eldest son, Donald, back to his internship at *The New York Times* whilst also sending her two younger sons, Bill and Steve, back to summer camp. She also lamented the fact that she then jetted off to Europe to meet her eldest child and a group of friends for a holiday. 'That decision may have been right for me', she wrote, 'but it was so wrong for Bill and Steve and even for Don — so wrong that I wonder how I could have made it. Up to that time, I had been a fairly present mother'.

Her admission of failure was unusual for someone of her calibre. In the words of David Remnick, of *The New Yorker* magazine, her candid admission was, 'not the sort of moment one could hope to find in the self-examination of Andrew Carnegie or Colonel McCormick, much less of Bill Gates or Rupert Murdoch'.

Yet, it was typical of Graham, who as well as speaking openly about her mistakes, was also adept at learning from them. Graham was a complete novice in management. It was, therefore, predictable that she would make some simple mistakes. The early years were difficult as she found it hard to earn the trust of her colleagues. Graham was happy to point out that, at that time, she was, 'stumbling around, learning and making mistakes'. Indeed, her opinion on how to view mistakes changed into ultimately seeing mistakes in a positive way. 'A mistake is simply another way of doing things,' she would say.

Initially, she though it would be business as usual whilst she could learn on the job. She soon learnt that nothing in life stands still. Her biggest initial mistake may well have been her failure to see her own potential. A few months after her husband's death, she was so ill at ease before attending the company Christmas party that she rehearsed how to say 'Merry Christmas'.

In her early days, at both *Newsweek* and *The Washington Post*, she was often guilty of erratic behaviour and known to turn on people for bizarre reasons such as the fact that she did not like their appearance. She went through several company presidents and editors of *Newsweek*, before making the right choices for those roles.

She acquired several companies early in her career which proved to be bad investments. In 1974, the company bought the *Trenton (N.J.) Times*. In 1981, it was sold to recoup losses. In 1980, a monthly magazine, *Inside Sports* was started. A year later, down twenty million dollars, it too, was sold. Graham learned to apply stricter tests to later purchases.

Occasionally, Graham overstepped the mark and was put in her place by her editor. *Style*, the newspaper's section on culture and lifestyles, was created by Bradlee in 1969 to replace the traditional women's pages in *The Washington Post*. It was the subject of many of what Graham called continuing conversations with her editor. Bradlee answered yet another of her suggestions for it by saying, 'I can't edit this section unless you get your finger out of my eye'. Graham backed off and learned to give her editors the independence they needed.

Early in her reign at the paper, Graham discovered that mistakes were natural. The important thing was to learn from them. Bradlee, her beloved editor, said of Graham, 'You know, she learned the way the rest of us learned, by making mistakes and not being scared of saying so'.

Subdue your ego

In his book, *Ego is the Enemy*, Ryan Holiday, includes the stories of many great individuals, who he claimed reached the highest levels of power and success by conquering their own ego. It is interesting to note that Katharine Graham's profile features prominently in the book.

According to Holiday, the ego is especially prone to show its true colours after the type of tragedy and scandal Graham suffered. If Graham had an ego, at the time of her husband's death, it would have prevented her from accomplishing a fraction of what she did at *The Washington Post*. It would have been easy for Graham to have played the role of victim because of her personal circumstances. The trauma behind her husband's death certainly lent itself to that scenario. Phil Graham was a verbally abusive alcoholic, who was subject to devastating depressions and manias. He had just run off with his mistress and threatened to take his majority share in the Washington Post Company with him.

Instead, Holiday praises Graham, stating that to succeed at *The Washington Post*. 'She did not need swagger or bluster. She needed a sense of right and wrong. To know that it was not about her, it was about preserving her family's legacy. Protecting the paper. Doing her job', he stated.

When Graham was initially belittled in meetings by several cynical male executives, Holiday claims that the ego would have tried to tell her, 'I knew you couldn't do it. Why did you ever try? It claims: This is not worth it. This is not fair. This is somebody else's problem. Why don't you come up with a good excuse and wash your hands of this?'

Everyone has an ego. In moderation, ego can be healthy and used to propel a person towards success and overcome difficulty. It is when the ego takes over, distorting our vision and causing us to act irrationally, that difficulties emerge. Balance is, therefore, the key.

When Katharine Graham published her memoir, *Personal History*, it won the Pulitzer Prize. The committee praised her remarkable frankness in telling her story with, 'no hint of trendy victimization, self-pity or sensationalism'. Humble people like Graham have the tendency to complain less and instead display stoic, resilience. Having worked on her ego, pity was not something she was prepared to listen to. She had already subdued her ego.

Chapter Seven

Ole Kirk Christiansen

Life is a gift, but it's more than just that. Life is a challenge

You may well be unfamiliar with the name, Ole Kirk Christiansen, but you will have heard of his famous invention: LEGO. By 2015, the company, founded nearly ninety years ago in Denmark by Christiansen, had overtaken Mattel to become the world's largest toy company.

To say his route to success was fraught with difficulties, would be something of an understatement. Christiansen himself acknowledged that without the setbacks, difficulties and obstacles that were sent his way, it is very possible that the iconic LEGO brick, would not have seen the light of day.

Christiansen was born in Denmark in 1891, the tenth child of a poor family. Growing up in the remote village of Billund, he began working in a factory before becoming a carpenter. After working in Germany for a few years, he returned to Denmark in 1916, opening his own shop. The business focused on manufacturing stepladders, ironing boards and what came to be known as his speciality, wooden toys. Moderate success followed and by 1924, the young Dane was looking to expand his business.

Disaster number one promptly ensued: Two of his young children were playing with some wood shavings in his workshop, before accidentally setting fire to both the factory and adjoining house. Christiansen responded with determination, almost immediately drawing up plans to build a bigger workshop and family home. To fund the expansion, sacrifice was needed. The growing family moved into one room, so that the others could be rented out.

After the Wall Street crash in 1929, the Great Depression hit Denmark hard and Christiansen's business was not immune from its effects. The family suffered further tragedy in 1932, when Ole Kirk's wife died. Overwhelmed with grief, and struggling to cope with the difficult economic conditions, the company teetered on the brink of bankruptcy and was forced to let most of its staff go.

Having secured a bailout loan from his siblings, Christiansen was able to pick himself up and began a new company, turning his attention to making cheaper wooden household products such as Christmas tree stands and toys.

It soon became clear that toy sales were by far the most profitable. Christiansen had, by now, been joined in the business by his son, Godtfred. Boosted by rising profits and a growing reputation for quality, the company began to focus solely on toy production.

Christiansen wanted a name for the group and in 1934, launched a competition amongst the company's employees to come up with a catchy name. The prize was a bottle of his own homemade wine. Christiansen awarded the prize to himself, as his own choice was head and shoulders above all the other entries. The name he had come up with was LEGO, an abbreviation of the two Danish words, 'leg godt', meaning 'play well'. It also means, 'put together', in Latin.

By the mid-1930s, the company had forty-two different product ranges, which were said to be expensive but well-made and popular. The bestselling wooden duck, whose beak opened and closed when pulled, is now a sought-after collectible.

Christiansen's difficult days seemed a distant memory. That was until 1942, when another fire destroyed the company premises. This time, at least the family home was saved but insurance monies were insufficient to cover the total losses. It was only out a sense of responsibility for his sons and employees that Christiansen was again able to pick himself up and rebuild the factory one more time.

By the end of the Second World War, Christiansen was finding it increasingly difficult to source beechwood, the key raw material for his toys. This period coincided with the company's experimentation with plastics after the arrival of its first plastic-injection moulding machine. As a result, the brave decision was made in 1949, to move LEGO products away from a traditional wooden material in favour of the modern plastic brick: The Automatic Binding Bricks.

By 1953, LEGO owner, Ole Kirk Christiansen, had all but retired and left the company in the hands of son, Godtfred. After enjoying his final years in retirement, Ole Kirk died aged sixty-six in 1958. The modern version of the LEGO building block was patented in 1958, the same year that Ole died. The LEGO story is an inspirational tale for aspiring entrepreneurs and one that was undoubtedly born out of adversity. Rather than marking the end, misfortune simply meant starting again and rebuilding, just like children do every day with Christiansen's legendary LEGO bricks.

Despite his many personal and professional troubles, how did Christiansen find the energy to repeatedly rebuild his company?

Use your faith
His family's deep commitment to their religious faith was at the heart of Christiansen's approach to dealing with life's challenges. He said, 'I am convinced that father's faith in God, which was evident in everything he did, helped carry him through his grief and the difficulties that followed'.

Like many of the residents of sleepy Danish village of Billund, at the time, religion played a central role in the life of the Christiansen family. Christiansen was an active member of the community and lived his life according to basic principles, which to a large degree came from his faith.

He was a frequent attendee at the mission hall in Billund and was heavily involved in the Sunday school as well as in the local YMCA. Christiansen later spoke about his childhood home stating, 'We grew up – all of us – in a modest home but a good home, trusting in the mercy of God'.

Together with his wife, Kristine, he was a leading member of the Church Association for the Inner Mission, which was an evangelical offshoot of the Danish Lutheran Church. Faith, combined with factors such as optimism and determination, helped him survive when times were tough, in both his personal and corporate lives.

How did the LEGO company survive a global depression, repeated fires, and the German invasion of Denmark? Christiansen himself attributed this to his devout faith. 'His faith made him an active man. It gave him the courage and solace that enabled him to take on new responsibilities - and the strength to see a job through despite hardship', stated his son, Godtfred, in a 1982 interview.

Understand the importance of reputation

'Det bedste er ikke for godt'. Only the best is good enough, was a driving mantra for Christiansen. The importance of reputation became a guiding principle for him. Indeed, during the 1930s, when Christiansen's son, Godtfred, joined the family business, he soon learned a valuable lesson from his father about the importance of this principle. Godtfred had just dispatched an order of painted wooden ducks. On his return to the factory, he boasted to his father how he had saved the company money.

"How did you manage that?" asked Ole Kirk Christiansen.

"I gave the ducks just two coats of varnish, not three as we usually do!" Godtfred responded.

The furious father reprimanded his son and told him in no uncertain terms what to do next.

"Fetch those ducks back, give them the last coat of varnish, pack them and return them to the station! AND you'll do it on your own – even if it takes you all night!"

'That taught me a lesson about quality', says Godtfred Kirk Christiansen on a later occasion.

Soon after the incident, Godtfred himself was to carve and display a sign on the factory floor, which spelled out the company message to its half a dozen employees, 'Only the best is worthy'. Christiansen demanded quality at every stage of the process, especially from his own children.

Christiansen had learnt over the years that he was a better toymaker than he was an ironing board maker. He refused to cut corners to save money during toy production. Only the highest quality of birchwood was used during the manufacturing process. In time, his models of cars and animals attracted a following across Denmark and the name LEGO became synonymous with quality craftsmanship.

When plastic came into widespread use after the Second World War, Christiansen kept with the times and began producing plastic toys. It was not until 1958 that the modern-day brick design was developed. The bricks were improved with hollow tubes in their undersides. This added support in the base, enabling much better locking ability and improved versatility.

Only through decades of striving for quality, was the LEGO company able to develop its reputation as a world class brand. As Jorgen. E. Christensen, Quality Director of the LEGO Group, said, 'it is a principle that is in the DNA of the company', a DNA that traces its origins back to its founder, Ole Kirk Christiansen.

Hang in there

When dealing with extreme adversity, Christiansen adopted an attitude summed up by the well-known American president, Franklin D. Roosevelt who said, 'sometimes you just have to hold on at the end. When you get to the end of your rope, tie a knot and hang on'.

By the middle of the 1920s, the Christiansen family, made up of Ole Kirk, his wife and four vibrant young boys, were living comfortably in the tranquil Danish village of Billund. Life was looking good, until a devastating fire of 1924.

It was a quiet Sunday afternoon. The Christiansen family had attended church and both Christiansen and his wife, Kristine, were having an afternoon nap. Two of the younger children, Karl George and Godtfred had crept into the workshop playing quite innocently, when a pile of wood shavings caught fire. Before long, the fire had spread from the workshop to the adjoining family residence. To lose both his work premises and domestic residence in one moment must have been devastating. How did he respond? Christiansen was relieved, thankful that his family had escaped the inferno.

Undaunted, Ole Kirk reacted by drawing up plans to build a bigger workshop and family home. The plans were ambitious, more than this fledgling company could possibly afford. Nevertheless, this was no deterrent.

The worldwide depression was late in coming to Denmark, but when it did arrive, its impact was devastating. Trade declined twenty-four per cent from 1930 to 1932. Christiansen desperately needed to find a way to make a living. As other businesses around him shut, he defiantly pushed ahead with plans to manufacture stepladders and ironing boards as well as his novel product line - wooden toys. Times may have been tough, he reasoned, but children always need toys to play with. Made with high quality birchwood and painted, finished and packaged beautifully, the LEGO company had started to form a reputation for quality and profits rose. LEGO was able to thrive, despite the difficult economic conditions. A 1932 price list showed no less than twenty-eight different designs, including vehicles, airplanes and buses.

On the night of the twenty-second of March 1942, a short circuit caused an electrical fire and the LEGO factory and warehouse burned down. This time, it would take longer for the older and less vibrant Christiansen to pick himself up, but that is exactly what he did. He took out several loans and built a new, larger 2,300-square-metre building on the same grounds as the old workshop. It was the company's first factory designed for assembly line production. By 1944, despite being in the fourth year of a five-year German occupation, the company had taken on its fortieth employee.

Life is full of bumps in the road. Trials come our way and it is easy to feel like quitting. Whether it seems fair or unfair, some people seem to get sent more of these curveballs than others, none more so than the LEGO founder, Ole Kirk Christiansen. Without tenacity and single mindedness, there is no way that he could have survived the devastating personal and professional setbacks that engulfed the family. There may be many factors in determining success but is any as important as just hanging in there when things all around seem to be falling apart?

Many others would have simply let go and moved on after experiencing setbacks of the type experienced by Ole Kirk Christiansen. Luckily, for children around the world, the LEGO founder had the tenacity to just hang in there and keep going.

Think outside the box
Initially Ole Kirk was resistant to change fundamental aspects of his toy business, a view that was echoed in the trade press at the time, which stated that … 'plastics will never take the place of good, solid wooden toys'.

In 1949, The LEGO company began producing plastic bricks, calling them 'Automatic Binding Bricks', upon which the modern LEGO block would be based. The bricks developed in the spirit of traditional wooden blocks that could be stacked upon one another but could be locked together. They had several round studs on top and a hollow rectangular bottom.

Around this time, the Danish toy-trade magazine, *Legetois-Tidende*, visited the company's premises before giving a lukewarm reaction on the company's new plastic product. To be fair to the magazine, this feeling was shared by many retailers and consumers at the time.

In 1947, Ole Kirk received a visit from a salesman from Hull who represented a British machine-tool company that was trying to find new customers for their plastic injection moulding equipment. The new machine, the Windsor SH, did not come cheap. At thirty-thousand DKK, the machine cost more than twice the company's previous year's profits. Against the advice of his trusted advisers, Christiansen bought the machine.

It was not an easy transition for the company. It took time to perfect the plastic products. Although Christiansen had seen the potential for plastic to replace wood in the long term, it proved difficult to persuade customers to change their habits. In the early years, many customers returned the new plastic products, unhappy with the transition from wooden based ones. It took years of trial and error and experimentation before the company succeeded in the plastic market.

In an article in 2014, Dominic Basulto of *The Washington Post* lauded LEGO as one of the most innovative companies in the world. Basulto asked what the keys had been to the company's innovative success? Quite simply, LEGO had been unafraid to experiment with emerging new technologies to extend its brand from the world of physical play to the world of digital play. It is a philosophy that can be traced back to the company's formative years.

Business as usual; carrying on with the same tried and tested methods, does not produce the changes needed during these difficult times. In business, innovation is one of the most important drivers of growth. In any aspect of life, the need to be bold, think outside the box and take risks can be a key driver of positive change.

After the Second World War, Christiansen believed that the world had changed forever. It would take time, but he perceived that consumer demands would also change. One of the most valuable lessons that Christiansen taught was that that thinking outside the box means contemplating different solutions for reaching your goals.

Watch out for blessings in disguise

Taking advantage of what looked like a major problem for his company turned out to be a huge opportunity. 'It was not until the day I told myself, "You'll either have to drop your old craft or put toys out of your head," that I began to see the long-term consequences. And the decision turned out to be the right one', Christiansen stated.

Ole Kirk Christiansen was a talented individual. In a funny kind of way, that turned out to be the thing that had held him back. On the first of February 1916, at the age of twenty-three, he bought the Billund Joinery Company for ten-thousand DKK. The factory made a variety of products including cupboards, chests of drawers, kitchen cabinets and perhaps somewhat morbidly, coffins. Christiansen's products were top grade. No one ever complained about the craftsmanship of the talented young carpenter.

Over time, the business expanded and Christiansen undertook bigger projects, including the building of several farmhouses, agricultural buildings and mission halls. At the start of his career, Christiansen won the contract to build Skjoldberg Church, a project that returned little profit but something he felt was worthwhile, as it served a good purpose. A noble sentiment but not one suited to business success.

Christiansen was a member of the National Association for Danish Enterprise and heavily leant on the organisation for support during the depression. Whilst he had always enjoyed making toys, it had always been more of a hobby than anything else. However, after reading a copy of the members' magazine, he was inspired by an advice column which stated that it made good sense to make toys.

The wider family did not agree with Christiansen's new plan to focus solely on toys. When he asked his brothers and sisters to act as guarantors for a loan of three-thousand DKK for the company, one of them asked if he could find something more useful to do. The episode shows that the toy business was not yet taken seriously but it was one Christiansen had a deep passion for. Indeed, when Christiansen repaid the loan in full in 1939, he regarded it as one of the most important days in his life. Until 1934, LEGO manufactured furniture, and toys, but from that time onwards, the revolutionary owner took the decision to focus on what he did best: toy production. He never looked back.

There are many interesting parallels between the tough times experienced by Ole Kirk Christiansen in depression-hit Denmark and the current Covid-19 pandemic. It is reported that a total of more than 6.5 million jobs could be lost due to the economic fallout of the coronavirus crisis. This is undoubtedly a tragedy for many, but it is important to recognise that others will see this as a chance to escape unfulfilling roles that did little for their self-development. Some of these people will be free to pursue their own passions and in years from now, we will read of success stories that came out of the upheaval.

In his memoirs, Ole Kirk wrote of the difficulties he faced in 1932. 'We could not see what lay ahead. During the summer, we were asked to make toys for Jens W. Olesen, Fredericia and as we had no other work, we looked on it as a gift from God'.

At one stage, Christiansen could not see a way out of his predicament and only ended up following his passion for toymaking because of the lack of other orders to fulfil. The crisis turned out to be a blessing in disguise and one that Ole was extremely grateful for. Sometimes, our greatest challenges are blessings in disguise.

Chapter Eight

Madam C. J. Walker

I got my start by giving myself a start

Madam C. J. Walker's rags-to-riches story was until recently, not widely known. The award-winning Netflix series, *Self-Made*, helped bring the life of this astonishing woman into the public domain.

Nothing in her background suggested that Walker would become the first self-made black millionaire in American history. Her life looked like it was destined to follow a predictable path; one in which discrimination and poverty were never far away. She was, after all, a child bride; a widowed single mother; an abuse victim and two-time divorcee. By the end of her life, Walker had defied the odds, to leave a legacy as an innovative cosmetics entrepreneur who revolutionised black hair care whilst at the same time, using her affluence to fight for equality and civil rights.

Born Sarah Breedlove, in 1867 in Louisiana, she was the daughter of freed slaves who was orphaned by the age of seven. Sent to live with her sister and brother-in-law, she faced abuse at the hands of her sister's husband. Poorly educated, she stated that three months of Sunday school was the sum total of her entire schooling. At the age of fourteen, she married to escape the cruelty of her brother-in-law. By the age of twenty, her first husband had died, leaving her with a two-year-old daughter to care for. Remarrying in her late twenties, she worked as a washerwoman but in 1903, divorced her abusive, unfaithful, second husband.

It was at this time that Walker was hired as a sales agent for Annie Malone, a successful, black, businesswoman who manufactured products that claimed to accelerate hair growth in black women. Although the position did not work out,

Walker used the time wisely, picking up valuable information that she used in her own product lines.

By 1906, she had moved to Denver, Colorado and married for the third time. Her new husband was Charles Walker, a newspaper salesman. Another divorce followed but not before her husband helped the fledgling hair care business take off. The couple travelled around the South promoting her products and giving live demonstrations on the 'Walker Method'. Business was booming and in 1908, they relocated to Pittsburgh, Pennsylvania, where a studio and college were established to train 'hair culturists'. In 1910, Walker transferred her business operations to Indianapolis, where the Madam C. J. Walker Manufacturing Company become hugely successful.

In Indianapolis, the company not only manufactured cosmetics but also trained sales beauticians. 'Walker Agents' became well known throughout the black communities of the United States. In 1913, Walker travelled throughout Latin America and the Caribbean promoting her business and recruiting others to teach unique hair care methods. Walker returned in 1916 and based herself out of New York. Sadly, she died of hypertension, just three years later, aged just fifty-one. At the time of her death, she was said to be the wealthiest black woman in America, leaving behind an impressive legacy of activism and philanthropy.

How did Walker manage to change her life around and produce one of America's most heart-warming success stories?

Value experimentation

'Perseverance is my motto!' summed up C. J. Walker's philosophy in identifying products which would cater for the type of hair that black women had to deal with.

By the time she was nearing her forties, C. J. Walker's hair had begun to fall out. This was due, in part, to years of damage caused by hair-care products as well as her stressful life conditions. Poor nutrition may have been another contributor. Her first role, as a laundress, exposed her hair to harsh lye soap, dirt and hot steam and caused yet more damage to it. Her situation was replicated amongst many black women at the time. Unlike others, Walker was unwilling to wear head scarves to hide her predicament. She wanted to emancipate black women, in more ways than one.

Unfortunately, there were no products on the market to help female hair loss. Chemists had developed lotions, oils and powders but Walker found that many of these items contained ingredients that caused side effects and triggered even more damage.

Walker did what many entrepreneurs have done over time; she experimented until she got it right. She was helped by her brothers' work as barbers in St Louis, which provided her with useful insight into haircare. Additionally, her work as a washerwoman allowed her to learn about the properties of chemicals. The work took time. Initially, she enrolled at Annie Malone's Poro College and later, became an agent for Malone. However, those products remained ineffective on her own hair.

Eventually, Walker managed to develop her own hair growing product. This was after a dream which she described, 'A man appeared to me in a dream and told me what to mix up for my hair. Some of the remedy was grown in Africa, but I sent for it, mixed it up, put it on my scalp, and in a few weeks my hair was coming in faster than it had even fallen out'.

Starting with a few dollars' worth of chemicals, Walker mixed batches of products in her washtub and began selling door-to-door to friends and neighbours. The technique worked, and black women throughout St. Louis began buying her wares with enthusiasm. Walker was soon inspired to produce other beauty supplies like creams and cosmetics, but no product was as popular as 'Walker's Wonderful Hair Grower'. Walker began to share the product with friends, with remarkable success. Had she never experimented, she would certainly not have gotten to the bottom of her own hair troubles or created the products that enriched the lives of so many other women.

All in all, there is no such thing as a failed experiment. Madam C. J. Walker showed that experimentation allows unexpected opportunities to emerge and provide the groundwork for future breakthroughs.

Innovate at all times

Success emerged out of adversity because Madam C. J. Walker was willing to try out something new. 'There would be no hair growing business today had I not started it', she said.

With help from her husband, Walker began placing advertisements in black newspapers and quickly developed a flourishing mail order business. The business was turning over ten dollars per week and according to her husband, had reached its full potential. Luckily, Madame Walker disagreed.

Walker began a sales tour across the Southern states and within a few months, she was making weekly sales of more than thirty dollars. To give an indication of how impressive that was, it was approximately twenty times the weekly earnings of the average black woman worker.

She soon realised there was only so much she could do herself and began to train teams of travelling saleswomen to demonstrate her products before taking orders. A born businesswoman, she had initially promoted her products with free public demonstrations in St Louis, with considerable success. Direct sales methods may be commonplace today, but at the time, they were virtually unheard of.

Furthermore, her willingness to show her own image on her products, was at the time, uncommon; an especially bold move for a black woman in the early 1900s. 'There were so many things that we think we invented or came out of Harvard Business School and this is something that this woman was doing one-hundred years ago', says Nicole Jefferson Asher, one of the writers of the current Netflix show. 'It was her own innate business acumen'.

By the time the company had moved to Indianapolis in 1910, Walker-trained sales beauticians were a regular feature within the black communities of the United States. Her philosophy of, 'cleanliness and loveliness', was innovative and a means of advancing the status of black Americans.

What kind of an employer was Walker? A good one, by all accounts. She arranged conventions for her representatives and a heavily incentivised sales programme served to motivate her agents. According to her biographer and great-granddaughter, A'Lelia Bundles, in her book, *Self-Made: Inspired by the life of Madam C. J. Walker*, whilst other companies such as Avon and Annie Malone's had their merits as pioneers of modern sales methods and commission sales, none proposed what Madam Walker had created, 'a national sales force expressly organized around the principles of corporate responsibility, social betterment and racial justice'.

During her conventions, Walker gave prizes to women who had sold the most products and brought in new sales agents. She also rewarded those who made the largest contributions to charities in their communities. The company vision and employee reward programme sounded more akin to 2020 than 1910.

Personal innovation is the act of making a change in your life with the aim of making your world a better one. Madam C. J. Walker did not settle, as her husband felt she should. Perhaps, that is why he soon became her ex-husband! Like most innovative people, Walker asked the most questions and looked at the most dynamic ways to market herself and her products. The results were simply startling.

Demonstrate relentless energy

What was the secret of Walker's success? According to the lady herself, there was none, except for hard work and determination. 'Don't sit down and wait for the opportunities to come. Get up and make them!' she said. Walker was impatient and eager to succeed. These were traits that were recognisable even before she even thought of her business empire. A widow at twenty years of age, she had an unwavering desire to build a better life for herself and her daughter, Leila. This was a woman who after all, had worked fourteen-hour days for eighteen years as a laundress, earning a meagre $1.50 a day. She still managed to save enough to send her Leila to Knoxville College for the type of education that she had been deprived of herself.

Fast forward two decades to 1916. Her products and business model were already a resounding success, but there was no let-up in her activity. She continued to work with an almost evangelical zeal to promote and improve her business. The business was not, after all, going to grow itself. That April, she had begun what was described as a 'spring sweep' of the South. During April and May she had barnstormed Alabama, Georgia, Tennessee, Kentucky and Indiana, 'juggling invitations to speak at black colleges, fraternal conferences, religious gatherings and prestigious churches'. By the end of the summer, having spent time in New England, she returned South for what she called, 'the last tour of the South', from Florida to Kentucky, from North Carolina to as far west as Texas and Oklahoma.

Once she became a person of means, her energy towards philanthropy was no less energetic. When she learned that the black soldiers in the First World War were not receiving the same level of medical care as the white soldiers, she bought ambulances for the black soldiers.

The Canadian writer, Susy Alexandra, made a great point when she emphasised that very few success stories contrast with Walkers own journey. 'So, there I was, sitting around, doing nothing and the chance of a lifetime fell into my lap' is, according to Alexandre, a phrase rarely heard from any successful entrepreneur. Madam C. J. Walker did not work nine-to-five but rather crossed the continental United States in service of her vision. Author and entrepreneur Tim Ferriss said, 'an entrepreneur isn't someone who owns a business, it's someone who makes things happen'.

Whether it's starting a new business, changing jobs, losing weight, or writing the novel you believe you have in you, unless you dedicate yourself entirely, with the same fervour as Madam C. J. Walker, it is unlikely you will make things happen.

Show true grit

Complete commitment to the cause was at the heart of Walker's method. 'My advice to everyone expecting to go into business is to hit often and hit hard; in other words, strike with all your might,' she once stated, reinforcing this fact.

The Madam C. J. Walker Legacy Center sits on the grounds of the headquarters and manufacturing plant of Madam C. J. Walker Hair Care in Indiana. In 1910, Walker showed her grit by moving the company's base to Indiana, which also happened to be the home of the Klu Klux Klan. At the time, lynching of boys and men was not uncommon. In fact, a black man could by lynched for simply looking at a white woman.

Looking back at all the hardship in her life, it seems clear that without grit, she would not have survived the abusive and failed relationships, bereavements and hardships that occurred in her life.

The sixth child of newly freed slaves, she was brought up in a rundown rural cabin. People are born with different levels of grit, but it is a trait that develops through experience. Walker had plenty of experience in developing that skill. Losing her mother at five, and father at seven would have been a huge blow. Despite desiring an education, she was forced to pick cotton, all whilst having to deal with the cruel abuse suffered at the hands of her brother-in-law. She brought up her daughter single-handedly after the death of her husband when Walker was twenty years old. The only positive in all of this was the courage and bravery which she had built up, having experienced more in twenty years that many do in a lifetime.

As with others in similar situations, adversity became the catalyst for her success.

Michael Matthews is a psychologist who has spent years studying the notion of grit. 'We should never ignore talent', he stated, 'but grit is the flame in which talent grows'. The research shows that, 'to get gritty, you need to be deeply interested in an activity and have fire in your belly to really keep at it'.

The yearning to succeed saw Walker invest ten-thousand dollars out of her own pocket to open the Walker Manufacturing Company, at a time when she struggled to get backers for the factory in Indiana. Undeterred, she became the lone shareholder of the enterprise, which resulted in massive profits. Possessing the grit to keep going after the setbacks in her life is what turned Walker into the success that she was.

Be selfless always

Walker always thought of others as exemplified by what might be termed as her mission statement, 'I am not merely satisfied in making money for myself, for I am endeavouring to provide employment for hundreds of women of my race'.

It was not just in the field of business that Walker showed her passion. At a time when it was dangerous to do so, Walker spoke out against racial injustice. She used her position to advocate for the advancement of black Americans. In 1917, Walker and other Harlem leaders went to the White House to confront President Woodrow Wilson and tell him that black American service in the First World War should guarantee federal support for equal rights. Among other things, the group specifically wanted to have lynching and white mob violence classified as federal crimes. Wilson refused to see them, but Walker continued the fight.

Business was not just about making money for Walker; it was about changing the lives of black women. Financial independence was her message for the eager ear. 'Open your own shop. Secure prosperity and freedom. Many women of all ages who had despaired for years of acquiring success, confronted with the problem of earning a livelihood have mastered the Walker System', she said. Walker saw her products as more than just a way to make money but as a way to help other black women achieve their full potential.

It is remarkable that the innovation Madam C. J. Walker showed was about more than money making. It was a way of helping other black women join her in business when the most they had previously aspired to was being a menial worker at low pay. Walker valued her employees, providing prizes for their profitability while also encouraging charitable giving – inspiring them with a favourite phrase – 'lifting while we climb'.

Although she was uneducated herself, she used much of her wealth to help others receive what she had lacked, establishing scholarships at several black women's schools and colleges as well as making generous donations to the National Association for the Advancement of Colored People (NAACP), the YMCA and various other charitable organizations.

Later in her life, she bought a mansion in Irvington, New York. This home, which is now a national landmark, was a meeting place for NAACP and other black leaders of the day. Her intention behind the building of the lavish mansion was to inspire other black people and show what could be achieved.

In 1919, just prior to dying of hypertension at the age of fifty-one, Madam C. J. Walker revised her will, bequeathing two-thirds of her company's future net profits to charity, as well as one-hundred-thousand dollars to various orphanages, individuals, and educational institutions for youths.

'Madam Walker, as part of the first generation out of slavery, really was inventing the way that she operated in the world', says A'Leila Bundles.

Walker took inspiration from the National Association of Colored Women (NACW) to invent the business model that is known today as direct sales. She admired the NACW's civic-minded organizing and found their networking structure to be the perfect model upon which to model her business. By educating sales agents and creating an institution that supported employees on a local and national level, Walker's business saw great success and allowed for the betterment of her workers. In 1917, Walker held a meeting with two hundred of her sales agents from all over the United States. She awarded prizes to the highest selling saleswomen as well as to those who had given the most to charity.

During the current pandemic, selflessness is as relevant as ever. Countries where there is traditionally more conformity and unity such as Japan, China and South Korea have handled the outbreak in a more effective manner than those countries where individualism and personal liberties are valued more than the collective. Only by working together, selflessly, can nations overcome the pandemic.

The most important asset to any company is its people. The policies employed by Walker were not too dissimilar to those adopted in modern times, with tremendous success. Madam C. J.'s selflessness was not only socially responsible; it made sound business sense. Her business became a collective unit in which the saleswomen become emotionally invested in the success of the company. All in all, a pretty smart move.

Chapter Nine

Colonel Harland Sanders

One has to remember that every failure can be a stepping stone to something better

In 1955, Colonel Harland Sanders reached the landmark age of sixty-five, normally a sign to reduce, rather than increase one's business activities. In the case of Sanders, there was one small problem: he had not had lasting success. Apart from a novel recipe for chicken and a small pension, there was little to show from five decades of toil.

Rather than looking back with resentment, Sanders persisted. The results were impressive: by the time of his death in 1980, KFC had become the world's largest fast-food chicken chain, operating in forty-eight countries worldwide, with two billion dollars of sales annually.

Sanders had a difficult start to life. His father died when he was just five, forcing his mother to support the family through her job at a tomato cannery. The experience did at least allow him to hone his culinary skills as he fed his younger siblings. In 1903, he dropped out of school and moved to southern Indiana to work as a farmhand.

Sanders drifted from job to job, in a nomadic career, that saw several failed business ventures. He was mocked by his first wife as, 'a no-good fellow … who can't hold a job'. Whether it was as a gas station operator, fireman, steamboat pilot or salesman, as hard as he tried, he just could not catch a break. For every high, there were several lows such as his sacking for insubordination from a job selling life insurance in 1916.

In 1930, Sanders' luck seemed to turn. The Shell Oil Company offered him a service station in North Corbin, Kentucky, rent free, in return for paying the company a percentage of sales. He began to cook for travellers who stopped by for fuel. He did not own a restaurant, so customers could only dine on a makeshift table set up in the station. This led him to begin selling meals to families and through this small business, he formulated his famous recipe for fried chicken.

Disaster struck in November 1939, when his restaurant and motel was destroyed in a fire. Sanders picked himself up and had it rebuilt as a motel with a one-hundred and forty-seat restaurant.

Sanders had finalised his secret recipe by 1940, frying his chicken in a pressure fryer rather than in a pan. But timing was never Sanders' strong point. Gas rationing was introduced after the United States entered the war in December 1941. Tourism dried up and Sanders was forced to close his motel.

As long as Sanders still had his secret recipe and his service station-come-restaurant in Kentucky, he would not give up. In 1952, he franchised his recipe to an operator of one of Salt Lake City's largest restaurant operators. Things were looking up. But just when he was beginning to reap the rewards of a difficult life, disaster struck again, landing him penniless and jobless at the age of sixty-five. The federal government's rerouting of a highway drained the area of tourist traffic and drove Sanders out of business. Having rejected an offer of one-hundred and sixty-four thousand dollars for his business in 1953, he was forced to sell the business at auction, at a loss, for seventy-five-thousand dollars in 1956.

Aged sixty-five, Sanders was left with only meagre savings and just over one-hundred dollars a month in social security. He still would not give up. Armed with a few pressure cookers and a bag of seasoning, he hit the road and travelled across the United States looking for potential franchisees. To save money, he often slept in his car. The persistence paid off. By 1963, the Colonel had more than six hundred franchised outlets for his chicken in the United States and Canada, putting him well ahead of the other fried chicken operators.

No stranger to adversity, Colonel Sanders' heart-warming story teaches us many lessons, not least that with the right mindset, a happy ending is always possible.

What qualities helped Sanders keep going to achieve that happy ending?

Work hard

The Colonel was a relentless hard worker. 'No hours, nor amount of labor, nor amount of money would deter me from giving the best that there was in me', he once said.

In an interview speaking about his life, Colonel Sanders returned to the scene of his first job, which he began when he was ten years old. Sanders spoke about an important lesson he was taught about the value of hard work. His mother sent him out to clear ground in the woods for a neighbouring farmer, Charlie Norris. Receiving two dollars a month and room and board, he cleared about an acre of land, but as was common amongst young boys, became easily distracted by nature. 'There were bluebirds and red squirrels and other things that attracted a boy's interest and I didn't clear as much ground as I ought to have cleared'.

The lesson came when he was promptly fired within the first month. 'You're not worth a doggone, boy', a furious Norris screamed at him. Sanders describes returning home, tail between his legs, before handing his two-dollar wage over to his mother and explaining his dismissal. Having received a dressing down from her, Sanders resolved that if he ever got another job, he would prove to his mother that he was worthy of it.

According to his second wife, Claudia Ledington, like many children of single mothers, he worshipped his mother and cringed at the thought of not living up to her piety and philosophy of hard work. Sanders' granddaughter, Cindy Wurster Sjorgen, further added that what is often lost from the feel-good story surrounding Sanders is the fact that he was, 'a hardworking, intelligent man'.

A year later, Sanders set about making amends. He went to work on a farm belonging to a Henry Monk. He ploughed the ground with a team of mules all day and then, despite fatigue, spent the evening milking the cows. According to Josh Ozerky in his book, *Colonel Sanders and the American Dream*, Sanders was up before dawn and worked until ten o'clock in the evening, his hard graft, 'the very picture of the Protestant work ethic back when the Protestant work ethic really meant something'.

Whilst many of his later employers questioned his temperament, few ever accused him of being work-shy. It was a work ethic that stayed with him, into later life, as he travelled the country in his 1946 Ford signing up new franchisees to his chicken recipe.

Thomas Jefferson, one of the founding fathers of America declared that, 'I'm a great believer in luck, and I find the harder I work the more I have of it', a view shared by Sanders, who saw that instead of waiting for things to happen, actions in themselves can lead to further opportunities.

Putting in the hard yards, Sanders eventually made a success of himself. Of course, hard work does not automatically entitle anyone to success, but there can be few success stories where hard work was not a large part of the story. 'Once you get used to it, there's great pleasure in working hard', Sanders later said of his industrious nature.

Go above and beyond

One experience, early in his working life shaped Sanders' view of how to provide service to others and that approach was summed up by the question, 'Anything else I can do for you?'

In 1924, Sanders lost his job as a salesman for Michelin. A chance meeting with the general manager of Standard Oil of Kentucky saw him being asked to run a service station for the company. When Sanders took over, the locals in town were hostile to the new kid on the block. Sanders had to find out how to attract local custom. The first day he ran the station, he only sold three and a half gallons of gas. 'Then I remembered something. When I was travelling around selling tires, one place had given me the kind of service I had never gotten anywhere else. They had wiped my windshield', he recalled.

When a car came into Sanders service station for gasoline, the first thing he did was grab his watering can and head for the radiator. As he went past the window, he cleaned the windshield. He then asked if there was anything else he could do. This type of service was unheard of at the time.

'Whatever it was, I would do it for free. I'd fill a tank with gas, and I'd say, 'Notice your back tire is a little low. If you will pull over to the hose, I'll be glad to fill that tire for you'.

News spread fast about the all-inclusive service Sanders offered. From being shunned by the locals on his first day of trade, the fledgling business ended up turning over twelve-thousand dollars a month, only thirty days later.

Unfortunately, just as Sanders was making his way in the trade, a severe drought hit Kentucky and farmers were unable to pay down their lines of credit he had extended to them at the service station. Before long, the depression hit. In Sanders words, 'the whole country had gone broke'.

It would not be his first failure, but it showed Sanders' ability to add value to his services. It built him a reputation as someone who went above and beyond for his customers. The reputation he built working for Standard Oil stood him in good stead. It was not long before Shell offered him a station rent free, if he relocated to Corbin, Kentucky. It was there that the fledgling KFC business got off the ground. All because for Sanders, nothing was too much trouble.

At his new gas station in Corbin, Sanders managed to sell three times as much gas as his competitors. Not only did it prove that he was a natural salesman, his new approach also showed that going above and beyond customers' expectations was imperative.

Accept that things will take time

Sanders' own experience with success later in life meant that he advocated patience in others. 'Don't quit at age sixty-five, maybe your boat hasn't come in yet, mine hadn't', he said.

To say Sanders had something of a varied CV, is something of an understatement. There were not many successful entrepreneurs who could list, obstetrician, lawyer and life insurance salesman on their resume.

Aspiring to be a lawyer, Sanders studied law by mail at night. His legal career ended in disgrace after a courtroom brawl with his own client ruined his standing. The incident exposed his many flaws. As his biographer, John Ed Pearce wrote, Sanders 'had encountered repeated failure largely through bullheadedness, a lack of self-control, impatience, and a self-righteous lack of diplomacy'. Realising he was not suited to the role, he simply moved on, determined to find something that would result in both personal satisfaction and success. Sanders had no problem admitting when he was not good at a job. In 1922, he took on a role as Secretary at the Chamber of Commerce in Columbus, Indiana. He lasted only a year before admitting to himself that he just was not suited to the role. 'They didn't fire me, but I could see that was going to happen, so I resigned. If you are honest with yourself, you can tell if you're doing a good job or a bad one!' he confirmed, looking back.

What was remarkable, given his chequered past, was the lack of bitterness in his life. Sanders was adamant that, 'a person must not go round feeling sorry for himself'.

It is interesting to note that Sanders saw the value in every one of his experiences. 'You are not starting from nothing but from the point at which you have assimilated the lessons of a lifetime'. Towards the end of his unpublished autobiography, Sanders shared possibly his most valuable piece of advice, one that can be applied not just for business, but for anyone looking for light at the end of the tunnel. 'It takes some of us longer than others to find what we're looking for. But if you are honest in your purpose and you try to render a genuine service and sell the right kind of product, there's no question in the world, you're building something lasting and worthwhile', he advised.

It took time, but at the age of seventy-four, Sanders sold KFC for two-million dollars to a group of investors.

Be a hedgehog not a fox

Knowing your special skill can be the route to success. As Sanders commented, 'it came to me that the one thing I could do was cook. I figured I couldn't do any worse than the people running these places around town'.

In 1930, when Shell Oil offered Sanders the chance to run the service station in North Corbin, Kentucky, the deal was too good to turn down. Sanders was able to operate rent-free in exchange for paying the company a portion of his turnover.

It was in North Corbin that Sanders started out in the restaurant business. He had a rudimentary knowledge of food; nothing too ambitious, instead focusing on meeting the needs of the truckers who exited the highway in search of gas. Initially, fried chicken was not on the menu because it took too long to prepare. As an alternative, Sanders focused on classic Southern offerings such as country ham and steak dishes.

One thing that mattered to Sanders and his customers, was the quality of his food. Talking in his autobiography, he explained, 'because my food was good and because truck drivers tell one another about that, it was a good source of revenue for us'.

Pretty soon, it became clear that the money was in food, not gasoline, so Sanders took the decision to focus his efforts on his restaurant and motel. At the time, motels just did not exist like his, that far east of the Mississippi.

In a review in the *Hotel Monthly* magazine, John Willy, a visiting journalist reviewing the fledgling motel, spoke about having been in one of the rooms. He was astonished that within a few minutes, a waitress came to his door with a tray of coffee, sugar and cream, on the house. Sanders was never one to spread himself thin. He always focused on keeping the menu small but good, giving the best attention and care to what he did best.

When someone tries to be good at everything, there is the danger of spreading themselves too thinly. No one wants to be known as the jack of all trades and a master of none.

In time, Colonel Sanders scaled back his menu to focus primarily on his signature dish of fried chicken. He did so because he realised that was bringing in most of his money. With the help of his new pressure cooker, he perfected his recipe and ensured he was serving up the best fried chicken in the south.

There are a lot of people who try to be all things to everyone and as a result, just end up being average at everything, rather than excelling at what they are good at. In his famous essay, *The Hedgehog and the Fox*, Isaiah Berlin divided the world into hedgehogs and foxes, based upon an ancient Greek parable: 'The fox knows many things, but the hedgehog knows one big thing'.

Berlin argued that the foxes pursue many goals and interests at the same time. As a result, their thinking is scattered and unfocused and as a result, they achieve little. Hedgehogs, on the other hand, focus on a single, central vision, which they then achieve.

Jim Collins, ran with the idea in his 2001 book, *Good to Great*, in which he argued that companies and by extension, people, are more likely succeed if they can identify the one thing that they do best, their 'Hedgehog Concept'.

When KFC began to struggle early in 2020, it decided to go back to basics, resurrecting the values of the Colonel. Modern day company president, Kevin Hochman, said it was not just bringing the Colonel back for marketing purposes but bringing the icon founder's, 'focus on quality back as well, and not taking shortcuts'.

Commit to the trial and error process

A willingness to test new methods helped the Colonel develop his successful formula. He observed, 'by trial and error, I finally arrived at what I felt was the perfect blend to supplement the fragrance of my chicken'.

Whilst Sanders was in receipt of a secret family recipe, he knew that he had to keep up with the times, if he wanted to mass produce his chicken. He invested in several pressure cookers along the way, with mixed results. Chicken sales began to outperform other dishes, but Sanders was always trying to perfect his product. One day he got an order for five-hundred chicken meals, to be eaten on a boat trip.

Sanders had a bright idea. 'These chicken eaters were not my regular customers. They don't even know my chicken. I will try my extra new seasoning element out on them ... I threw two handfuls of it into the flour and stirred it up with the rest of my seasonings. When I fried it up, it was the best chicken I'd ever tasted in my life'.

Thanks to Sanders' willingness to experiment, he had stumbled across the perfect recipe. His ingredients never changed from that day forward.

Two decades on and Sanders was at a crossroads. Should he continue with his own restaurant ventures? Or should he try franchising his products to other restaurateurs? Sanders had already experimented with franchising on a smaller scale in 1952, selling his franchise to Pete Harman.

Fate intervened and by 1955, a federal highway project had begun, starving his business of custom and forcing his North Carolina restaurant to close. By the age of sixty-five, most people are set in their ways and not too keen to experiment.

Sanders was willing to give it a go. After all, what did he have to lose? He sold his properties and travelled the country marketing his concept to restaurant owners. Many said no, but it wasn't long before he had persuaded several independent owners to pay him four cents on each chicken sold as a franchise fee, in exchange for Sanders' recipe and method and the right to advertise using his name and likeness.

Despite the slow initial progress in signing up franchisees, interest in Kentucky Fried Chicken began to grow in the late 1950s and early 1960s. Word had reached other owners of Pete Harman's success. By then, he was doing brisk business at multiple locations. Eventually, franchise applicants became so large in volume that Sanders no longer went out to meet them. Instead, he summoned them to his estate in Shelbyville, Kentucky. Colonel Sanders' business grew exponentially because of a willingness to embrace trial and error.

The Humanitarians

Chapter Ten

Rosa Parks

I knew someone had to take the first step and I made up my mind not to move

Rosa McCauley Parks was born in Alabama, in 1913. Growing up in the segregated South, Parks encountered racial discrimination daily. When her parents separated, Rosa was two years old. She went with her mother to live with her grandparents in Pine Lodge, Alabama. As a child, Parks stated that life was, 'just a matter of survival, of existing from one day to the next'. She remembered going to sleep as a child hearing the Klu Klux Klan roaming the neighbourhood on horseback. She vividly recalled the image of her grandfather guarding the front door with a shotgun whilst on another occasion, she recollected hearing a lynching and being afraid her house would be burnt down.

A feisty young girl, she refused to be cowed by repeated bullying suffered at the hands of local white children. She recalled being threatened by a local boy when she was ten years old, 'picking up a brick and daring him to hit me. He thought the better of it and went away'.

Parks also told of the less physically harmful, but equally damaging prejudice that was endemic in society at the time. She wrote that it took a, 'major mental acrobatic feat', to endure life as a black person at the time. Whilst white students were provided with bus transportation by the local municipality, black students were forced to walk to school. The segregated, one-room school that she attended lacked even basic supplies such as desks. When she was sixteen years old, Parks was forced to drop out of school to care for her grandmother and later, her mother, when she too, became ill.

In 1932, after meeting and marrying Raymond Parks, a barber and civil rights activist, she became involved in attempts to improve the lives of the black community. She supported her husband's campaign to free the 'Scottsboro Boys', who were falsely accused of rape and sentenced to death.

Parks became actively involved in civil rights in her own right by joining the Montgomery chapter of the National Association for the Advancement of Colored People (NAACP) in 1943, serving as the section's youth leader as well as acting as secretary to NAACP president, E. D. Nixon.

The seminal moment in Rosa's life came on the first of December 1955. After a hard day's work at the Montgomery Department Store, Parks boarded the bus for home where she defied the law by refusing to give up her seat to a standing white passenger. She was arrested and sent to trial, sparking the Montgomery bus boycott. The boycott lasted for three-hundred and eighty-one days and ended with a Supreme Court ruling declaring segregation on public transport to be unconstitutional.

Most historians date the beginning of the modern civil rights movement in the United States to the day a little-known seamstress from Montgomery, Rosa Parks, refused to give in to injustice. The bus boycott thrust her into the public arena and turned her into a civil rights icon. Her actions started a chain reaction, which concluded with the 1964 Federal Civil Rights Act, banning racial discrimination in public places. Although widely honoured in later years, she suffered for her defiant act; she lost her job and received numerous threats against her life.

On the fifteenth of September 1996, President Bill Clinton awarded Parks the Presidential Medal of Freedom. The following year, she was awarded the Congressional Gold Medal. *TIME* magazine named Parks on its 1999 list of 'The 20 Most Influential People of the 20th Century'.

How did someone, described as timid and shy manage to shake up America's unjust race laws and become known as the 'mother of the civil rights movement' in the process?

Show defiance

In the end, Rosa Parks had had enough. Commenting on the pivotal moment of her life, she said, 'people always say that I did not give up my seat because I was tired ... the only tired I was, was tired of giving in'.

There appeared nothing unusual on that winter evening in Alabama, when Rosa Parks boarded the bus for her usual commute home. Having taken her seat, the bus began to fill with white passengers. Eventually, the driver noticed that several white passengers were standing in the aisle. In line with protocol, the bus driver stopped the bus and asked four black passengers to give up their seats.

Three of the other black passengers complied with the driver, but Parks refused and remained seated. The driver shouted, "Why don't you stand up?" to which Parks replied, "I don't think I should have to stand up."

The police arrested Parks at the scene and charged her with violation of Chapter Six, Section Eleven, of the Montgomery City Code. She was taken to police headquarters, where, later that night, she was released on bail. Parks was later found guilty of violating a local ordinance and was fined ten dollars, as well as a four-dollar court fee.

Parks' insubordination against the race laws of the time did not begin on that cold winter's evening. In 1943, Parks had boarded the bus, driven by the same driver, James Blake, through the front door. The correct etiquette at the time was for black passengers to pay at the front, exit and re-enter via the rear. Blake demanded that she exit, 'his bus', immediately but Parks refused to move. A brief altercation occurred before Parks finally left. Retribution for the injustice would not come for another twelve years.

In the meantime, in her role as branch secretary of the NAACP, Parks had pressed for desegregation of schools and public spaces and stood up for victims of white brutality and sexual violence. But it was Parks' defiant refusal to give up her seat on a bus that changed race relations in America forever.

Parks, with her strength of character and moral determination was the ideal candidate for civil rights activists to rally around. As one young Montgomery resident said at the time, city officials had, 'messed with the wrong one now'. Parks told Pacifica Radio in April 1956, 'the time had just come when I had been pushed as far as I could stand to be pushed'. Noting later that it was, 'not easy to remain rational and normal mentally in such a setting', she defiantly rejected the absurd rules which black Americans were expected to comply with under segregation.

Parks' defiance allowed a previously little-known minister named Dr Martin Luther King Jr, to gain prominence as a leader of the civil rights movement.

Defiance is a tactic that has been used by many seeking to overturn injustice. President Obama claimed Parks' 'singular act of disobedience, launched a movement'. Her role was so significant that when she met Nelson Mandela after his release from prison, he told her, 'you sustained me while I was in prison all those years'.

It is difficult to fight against what appears to be never-ending misery. Often, despair permeates our soul and we can easily crumble in the face of adversity. Knowing when to stand up, in defiance, may not always result in success. But at the right time and in the right circumstances, it certainly has its place.

If you are struggling to overcome a troublesome trait or a difficult personal situation, remember the defiant approach adopted by Rosa Parks. After all, it may be more tiring to give in, than to allow things to continue as they are.

Respect your beliefs and principles
An awareness of what had gone before was a factor which influenced Rosa Parks' decision to take a stand. As she confirmed, 'When I made that decision, I knew that I had the strength of my ancestors with me'.

There are many who portray Parks' actions in refusing to give up her seat as a spontaneous gesture, coming about after a long, tiring day at work. This view contradicts the evidence that Rosa Parks' actions were actually, many years in the making and a result of deeply held beliefs.

Born Rosa McCauley, her grandparents inculcated religious values in her from an early age. In her autobiography, Parks states, 'every day before supper and before we went to services on Sundays, my grandmother would read the Bible to me and my grandfather would pray. Prayers and the Bible became part of my everyday thoughts and beliefs'.

In adult life, Parks was described as a, 'staunch and active Christian', heavily involved in the African Methodist Episcopal Church. Parks wrote, 'The church was and is, the strength, our refuge and our haven'.

Park credits her faith with removing fear and giving her the courage to stand up to segregation on that fateful day in December 1955. 'I was fortunate God provided me with the strength I needed at the precise time when conditions were ripe for change. I am thankful to him every day that he gave me the strength not to move', she said. Parks always carried her Bible around with her and learned in Bible classes that, 'people should stand up for their rights just as the Children of Israel stood up to the Pharaoh'.

Parks is often portrayed as a simple seamstress, but it is important to remember her long-time social activism and dedication to the cause of social justice. In her choice of husband, she found a soul mate equally committed to overturning the daily injustice experienced by African Americans.

'We had always been taught that this was America, land of the free and home of the brave and we were free people, and I felt that it should be ... in action rather than something that we hear and talk about,' she said.

A few months before the bus incident occurred, she attended a two-week workshop on desegregation and civil disobedience at the Highlander Folk School in Tennessee. She later said that her training at the school helped her take a stand against segregation. Participants were both black and white, and they worked together as equals. Parks spoke of the period as one of the few times in her life when she did not feel any hostility from white people.

It was in the context of this long-term activism that Parks decided to act on that December day in 1955.

Maintaining faith or belief in one's principles in difficult times can be challenging for many. People of faith, like Rosa Parks, inevitably conclude that they have been placed in their current situation for a reason.

What this really means is that whilst one person may not be able to change the world completely, he or she must stand up and do their bit at the time of asking. This is exactly what Rosa Parks did.

Faith guided the early forebears of the civil rights movement, from Rosa Parks to Dr Martin Luther King Jr. Such leaders often realise that their generation alone cannot finish the job. They take the first step and then entrust future generations with finishing what they started. The recent riots and protests in response to the death of George Floyd show that there is some way to go before the work of Rosa Parks is finished.

Work together
Working with others to achieve a combined goal became important to Parks. 'The one thing I appreciated was the fact that when so many others, by the hundreds and thousands, joined in, there was a kind of lifting of a burden from me individually … I was not alone', she said.

Rosa Parks worked alone on the day of the arrest but relied on a much greater network to achieve the bigger aim of taking a stance against discrimination. The very next day, Dr Martin Luther King Jr, the Reverend Ralph Abernathy and a group of other black ministers formed the Montgomery

Improvement Association and called for a boycott of Montgomery's public transit system.

When Parks arrived at the courthouse for trial that morning, she was greeted by a crowd of around five-hundred supporters, who cheered her on. Parks and King were part of large groups of people who worked hard to plan marches, rallies, sit-ins and other activities that were key to the success of the civil rights movement.

The Montgomery black community became united behind these efforts. These networks provided both the moral and collective support necessary to influence these actions for wider effect.

During the boycott, members of the black community (many of whom did not have cars), made their own sacrifices. Many taxi drivers, in camaraderie with the boycotters, began charging black passengers only ten cents per ride. When the city government announced they would prosecute these cab drivers, leaders began a 'private taxi plan' offering coordinated transportation. They risked not only arrest, but police brutality and mob violence.

The boycott was powerful as blacks constituted seventy-five per cent of bus passengers in Montgomery and the boycott lasted for three-hundred and eighty-one days. In November 1956, the District Court ruled that segregation on buses was unconstitutional and the boycott officially ended in triumph.

Over the years that Parks was with the NAACP, she and other activists learnt a great deal about the power of public speaking, mobilizing people and how to win sympathy from the white public.

Everyone may be familiar with the phrase, 'there is no 'I' in team'. It is doubtful whether Rosa Parks would have been able to achieve the same success had she acted alone. She benefitted from the backing of a much larger network of grass roots supporters and other prominent leaders. By working as a collective, they were able to ensure the bus boycott was well-coordinated and resulted in lasting success.

Take risks

Convincing herself that a proposed course of action was the right thing to do was important to Parks, especially where outcomes were uncertain. She stated, 'I have learned over the years that when one's mind is made up, this diminishes fear; knowing what must be done does away with fear'.

Parks had long been a risk taker in pursuit of her ideals. She would not use separate bathrooms that were designated for the black community. She refused to drink from 'colored' water fountains, preferring instead to go without water if that was the only choice. Rosa and Raymond Parks were already involved in organizing Voter League meetings and encouraged their friends and neighbours to register to vote. These meetings were held secretly because of violence aimed at activists.

When Parks appealed her conviction and officially challenged the lawfulness of segregation, she took a big risk. White segregationists retaliated with violence. Black churches were burned with some black citizens even arrested for violating an ancient law prohibiting boycotts. Both she and her husband lost their jobs during the ensuing trial and boycotts.

Parks' husband, Raymond, was forced to quit his job after a rule was established that Rosa could not be spoken about in the workplace. The couple could barely make ends meet. 'She struggled for a good ten years after that arrest', niece, Urana McCauley said.

Faced with death threats during the year long struggle, Parks and her family were forced to leave for a new life in Virginia and then Detroit.

Parks was, 'feisty', according to Carla Hayden, the fourteenth Librarian of Congress. Hayden points out, in the 1950s, in the segregated South and with the threat of physical harm, it took immense courage to fight publicly for civil rights. 'At that point, you get a sense that she was making a conscious decision, that she was going to do what she could to help others. And she was going to take the risk', Hayden says.

Expecting blacks to resist age-old racist laws and traditions meant asking them to risk great harm and to summon an extraordinary amount of personal courage, according to Donna Braden, Curator of Public Life at the Henry Ford Museum of American Innovation. That is exactly what Rosa Parks was prepared to do.

Rosa Parks showed that a seemingly small, but risky act can be the catalyst for great change and revolution. The flapping wings of a butterfly can cause a tornado. Without small acts by individuals willing to take risks, there would likely be few changes in society.

In taking risks, we provide a platform for change to occur. Who knows how long Montgomery's prejudicial race laws would have continued had Rosa Parks done nothing and meekly vacated her seat on that December day in Alabama?

Remain optimistic
Despite experiencing adversity, Parks always tried to remain optimistic, a belief confirmed when she said, 'I did the very best I could to look upon life with optimism and hope and looking forward to a better day'.

After the difficult years which followed the bus boycott, Parks eventually made a new life for herself in Detroit, working tirelessly for the city's civil rights movement. She was an active member of several organizations which worked to end inequality in the city.

By 1980, Parks, now widowed, suffered from financial, personal and health troubles. After her heroic act, local community members and churches had to come together to stop Parks from being evicted from her home. What was notable, however, was the optimism Parks held onto into her later life. Her positive attitude never waned, despite her not inconsequential financial and health troubles.

Parks was equally optimistic about the future of the civil rights movement, despite the many difficulties felt by the black community. She explained her attitude in an interview with

Norman Libman in *The Chicago Tribune* in September 1991, 'I concentrate on what's good. I have to be aware of what isn't good, but not to the extent that I would be discouraged and depressed and feel that all is lost'.

Positivity spread through Parks' life work. Speaking before a group of students in 1986, Parks displayed optimism that good would triumph over evil and there would in fact, be, in time, 'no need for the type of demonstration, the type of struggle that we have had to face over the years'.

It is hard to know how Rosa Parks would have felt after the recent turmoil following the death of George Floyd. However, it is difficult to imagine she would have been anything but optimistic about the future changes in American society. 'Justice is often slow, but it will come', Parks maintained.

Just like Nelson Mandela, who you will read about later, Parks had no time for bitterness or blame in the face of adversity. She insisted that, 'hate will destroy the hater' and refused to classify her struggle as against the white community, arguing that there were a lot of friendly white people on the side of the civil rights movement, who sacrificed as much as she did in the quest for justice.

Chapter Eleven

Rabbi Menachem Mendel Schneerson

Imagine you could open your eyes to see only the good in every person, the positive in every circumstance, and the opportunity in every challenge

Rabbi Menachem Mendel Schneerson, known simply as 'The Rebbe', was the most remarkable Jewish personality of modern times.

As the seventh and final leader of the Chabad-Lubavitch movement, he took an insular Hasidic group that was devastated by the Holocaust and transformed it into the most influential movement in the Jewish world. The Rebbe dedicated his life to helping hundreds of thousands of people, Jewish and non-Jewish, in their daily struggles.

Born in 1902 in Ukraine, the persecutions that the Rebbe experienced in his own childhood did not crush his sense of self but made him more determined to forge a better future. In 1928, the Rebbe married the sixth Rebbe's daughter, Rebbetzin Chaya Mushka, in Warsaw.

The young couple moved to Berlin, where the young Rabbi broadened his secular education at the University of Berlin. That was until Hitler rose to power in 1933. Moving to Paris, the Rebbe continued his studies at the Sorbonne University. The Rebbe was widely considered a genius, both in Talmud, Jewish law and in a range of secular topics such as maths, science and engineering.

On the eleventh of June 1940, three days before Paris fell to the Nazis, the Rebbe fled to Vichy and later to Nice, until he managed to escape Europe in 1941. Arriving in New York, the Rebbe quickly set about bolstering and disseminating Judaism.

After the death of his beloved father-in-law, Rabbi Yosef Yitzchak Schneerson, in 1950, the Rebbe reluctantly ascended to the leadership of the Lubavitch movement a year later. Chabad Lubavitch had long been involved in outreach work and managed to have an impact on Jewish communities across the world. As well as continuing those clandestine operations, the Rebbe sought to revive world Jewry after the trauma of the Holocaust.

A global network of emissaries, known as 'Shluchim', left New York and spread out to the four corners of the world to assist communities worldwide: building schools, community centres, youth camps and even drug rehabilitation centres.

The Rebbe's actions attracted hundreds of thousands of followers and admirers across the globe. The Rebbe's dynamic personality captured the attention of political leaders such as Robert F. Kennedy, New York Mayor Rudy Giuliani and former Israeli Prime Ministers Begin, Sharon and Rabin. Figures as diverse as the musician, Bob Dylan and actor, Jon Voight were also drawn to the Rebbe's teachings.

The Rebbe died in the early hours of the twelfth of June 1994 but his legacy lives on. To this day, his resting place in Queens, New York receives thousands of visitors each day for prayer.

Upon his death, President Clinton paid tribute to, 'a monumental man who as much as any other individual, was responsible over the last half a century for advancing the instruction of ethics and morality to our young people'.

In 1978, the US Congress issued a resolution to President Carter to designate the Rebbe's birthday as the National Education and Sharing Day. It is notable that every single US president, from Ronald Reagan through to Donald Trump, issued a proclamation recognising and paying tribute to the Rebbe's efforts for a better education for all American citizens.

The Rebbe was no stranger to adversity and suffering. He had to contend with the brutal murder of his brother by the Nazis and his father's death in exile from the Soviet Union in 1944.

The question can rightly be asked: How did a Rabbi dressed in traditional rabbinical clothing and speaking mainly in Yiddish, manage to turn a small movement, decimated by the Holocaust, into a worldwide phenomenon?

Take Responsibility

Encouraging his emissaries to take responsibility for their actions and become leaders created an environment where they would be able to maximise their potential. As the Rebbe said, 'I will help as much as I am able. But unless you work independently, what will be gained if I distribute new teachings?'

The death of the previous Lubavitcher Rebbe, a fearless leader, was a demoralizing blow for the movement. The small Hasidic sect had been founded in Russia and suffered tremendously by the time the Rebbe reluctantly assumed control. The group had sprung up in modern day Belarus and vicious persecution under the Soviet regime saw thousands of prominent activists sent to their deaths in exile.

In the 1950s, there were only a handful of Lubavitcher Hasidim in the United States, as well as a collection of Russian refugees and Holocaust survivors that had recently joined him.

The Rebbe never saw himself in such a prominent leadership role, preferring to work behind the scenes. Nevertheless, he finally acceded to the requests of the followers and set about on a purpose; not only the rebuilding of his own community, but also to revive Judaism out of the ashes of the Holocaust.

The Rebbe achieved all this by operating with a unique leadership style. A devolved system was established, with responsibility for the building of local communities placed into the hands of his emissaries. To the Rebbe, leadership meant enabling individuals to be leaders themselves, giving them the responsibility to carry out his work. Whilst the Rebbe himself appointed, or at least approved, each emissary, over time, they were encouraged to formulate their own local plan with little support from headquarters. In response, the loyalty of his followers was unwavering, with no shortage of volunteers for each role.

Lubavitch became an organization where action came from the bottom up. There were new initiatives from the Rebbe, but Shluchim, the emissaries themselves, were expected to take the ball and run with it.

The late Rabbi Adin Steinsaltz, a biographer of the Rebbe, described the Rebbe's strategy in militaristic terms. 'Under the Rebbe, Chabad did not function like a smooth military machine; it worked instead like a group of partisans, mounting uncoordinated forays', he said.

In his book, *The Leadership Experience,* Richard L. Draft, a Professor of Management at Vanderbilt University, provides an insight into differing styles of leadership. According to Hershey and Blanchard's Situational Leadership® model, the Rebbe's 'entrusting style of leadership' was possible because his followers had a high level of ability and readiness to accept responsibility for their own tasks.

As of 2019, Shluchim were based in most major cities across the United States and in more than one-hundred other countries.

Responsibility, taken either alone or shared with others, is a crucial aspect in overcoming problems. It is present in almost every aspect of our life, from getting up on time in the morning to paying our bills on time. By taking responsibility, we own our actions and choices. Successful people take responsibility for their actions and inspire others to buy in and join them in facing down their challenges.

One cannot deny the brilliance of the Rebbe's approach. He made every one of his emissaries, followers and even petitioners feel that they were an invaluable part of his programme to create a better world. Rabbi Lord Jonathan Sacks, the late Chief Rabbi of the United Hebrew Congregations of the Commonwealth, stated 'some become great leaders because they create followers ... The Rebbe was a great leader because he created leaders'.

Focus on being positive
Insisting on looking at things from a positive perspective was a fundamental aspect of the Rebbe's approach. He confirmed, 'I worked on myself to always look at things in a positive light; otherwise, I could not have survived'.

The Rebbe focused solely on positivity. He often invoked the saying of his predecessor, the third rebbe, the revered Tzemach Tzedek, whose secret for emotional well-being was encapsulated in the phrase, 'think good and it will be good'.

The Rebbe believed that this principle had the power to transform feelings of sadness or worry, freeing oneself to focus on positive deeds and activities. In other words: If you change the way you look at things, the things you look at change.

Elie Wiesel, the Nobel prizewinning author, came to see the Rebbe after the Holocaust. The victim of unspeakable suffering during those dark years, he expressed his reluctance to bring children into the world. The Rebbe changed his mind by telling him that to do so would be the best revenge against those who had tried to obliterate the Jewish people.

The Rebbe believed in the goodness of man and in the positive potential of every human being. 'Look within yourself and you will find that you are far better than you have ever imagined', he was often known to say. Such a positive message could not fail to turn the tide in the battle to rekindle Judaism after the horrors of the war.

The Rebbe took positivity incredibly seriously, even refusing to use certain words which expressed negativity. Even more strikingly, he would actively rephrase common words and colloquial phrases that many of us say or write without a second thought. For example, he disliked using the word deadline, with its connection to death and would not call a spiritual getaway a retreat, because that word implies going backwards, when in fact, the opposite should be true.

Shortly after the Yom Kippur War of 1973, a group of disabled veterans of the Israel Defence Forces visited the Rebbe. The Rebbe rejected the notion that these individuals were disabled but challenged them to see themselves as 'exceptional'. The Rebbe never saw disabilities in people. Rather, he chose to focus on their abilities.

As a result, the Rebbe's every word and teaching were designed to stimulate and provoke positive change in the lives of the people with whom he interacted. As an example, the Rebbe told a man who had been released from prison, 'focus on the benefits of being free rather than dwelling on memories of your prison time. This may be difficult at first, but you can do it'.

In his book *Positivity Bias*, Rabbi Mendel Kalmenson, himself an emissary of the Rebbe, provides several important steps that empower a person to live a life of positivity. 'Our perspectives are so powerful; they can lead us to find fault with paradise or to express gratitude even while in a state of extreme suffering', he states.

There are many times in our lives when our natural response is to prepare for the worst. Yet, how often did things turn out differently? The disaster we anticipated did not materialise. Ultimately, that negativity served no purpose. Follow the example of the Rebbe; look positively upon your experiences and you will come to understand that it is not the events of our lives that shape us, but the meanings we assign to those events.

Take bold action
The Rebbe believed that taking audacious action, against the prevailing customs would be a powerful way of rebuilding the community. 'Here in America, people like to hear things expressed in the form of a statement, preferably a provocative and shocking statement. I don't know if this is the best approach, but as our sages have said, ''When you come to a city, do as its custom''', he observed.

For centuries, Jews were in the habit, particularly in the public sphere, of hiding their Judaism. Keeping a low profile and seeking to avoid anti-Semitism sentiment was the prevailing custom.

Other Hasidic communities followed an inward-looking approach. Chabad, under the direction of the Rebbe, took the opposite view, reaching out to the masses of assimilated Jews formed the core of its agenda. The United States was home to the world largest Jewish community, albeit largely secular and assimilated in nature. A decline in religious practice had occurred in the first part of the twentieth century and there was nothing to suggest this would reverse. That did not deter the Rebbe.

The Rebbe, was encouraged by his father-in-law's proclamation on arrival in New York in 1940 that, 'America is no different', meaning the movement's success in old Europe would be replicated in the New World. The Rebbe had the foresight to see that Jewish values were entirely consistent with the American ideals of freedom and service of God.

The Rebbe observed that big, audacious statements were successful in provoking the greatest reaction in contemporary American society. He was prepared to risk ridicule from other Jewish groups, keen to keep a low profile, in the pursuit of his goals. Bold tactics, at first mocked, began to work; Jewish practice became front and centre in mainstream American society.

Public rallies were held in the 1950s and Grand Chanukah Menorah lightings took place in major cities. Jimmy Carter was the first president to light a menorah outside the White House in 1979. Every president since has acknowledged Chanukah with a special menorah-lighting ceremony.

In 1969, the first Chabad Houses was set up in Los Angeles by Rabbi Shlomo Cunin. Since that time, these Jewish Community centres, providing educational programmes for the entire Jewish community, regardless of affiliation or level of observance, have sprung up across college campuses, from Stamford to Harvard.

In 1974, the Rebbe introduced the 'Mitzvah Tanks', mobile Jewish centres that visited strategic locations in towns and cities. Large posters on the sides of the vans spoke of 'Mitzvot (Commandments) On The Spot For People On The Go'. If most of American Jewry had ceased to go to synagogue, then the Rebbe reasoned that he would take the synagogue to them. Rabbinical students approached Jewish adults in the street asking if they would like Shabbat candles or wanted to attend a Jewish class.

Whilst other Orthodox Jewish groups frowned upon technology, the Rebbe saw the opportunities that technology presented. Radio, satellite television and the internet were all valid ways of reaching out to the masses.

According to the late Rabbi Lord Jonathan Sacks, 'the Rebbe did something absolutely extraordinary; he said to himself: If the Nazis searched out every Jew in hate, we will search out every Jew in love'.

Our challenges or setbacks may require bold action. In our own lives, it might be time to ask if we should maintain the status quo or instead to take bold steps in the face of our own challenges.

Over the course of his leadership from 1951 to his death in 1994, the Rebbe, using bold methods, succeeded, in both reviving Jewish practise amongst the masses and expanding the religious community whose very presence was nearly obliterated in the Holocaust.

Develop a sense of urgency

Getting on with things was a key part of the Rebbe's approach. He did not believe in waiting. 'I have been asked, "Now that you have attained the age of seventy, what are your plans? It would seem that this is an appropriate time to rest a bit ..." My response to that is that we must begin to accomplish even more'. The Rebbe said this in what many might call old age.

The Rebbe displayed an intense sense of urgency, demanding much from his followers and even more from himself. The Rebbe believed that if something was worth doing, it should be done immediately. There was no time to delay.

During his decades of leadership, he worked over eighteen hours a day and never took a single day of holiday. He was often seen leaving his office at three in the morning with a stack of papers, only to return early the next morning having completed his workload. He rarely left Crown Heights, Brooklyn except for visits to his father-in-law's gravesite in Queens, New York. Additionally, the Rebbe set aside two or three evenings each week to meet with anyone who wanted to visit him. These visits began at eight o'clock and often extended until dawn. Over the years, the Rebbe advised thousands of people, Jews and non-Jews alike, in business and delicate personal matters brought to him.

The Rebbe was focused on the idea that one should never be satisfied. He always challenged people to do more, often exclaiming, 'every living thing must grow!'

In 1972, on his seventieth birthday, instead of announcing his retirement, the Rebbe proposed the establishment of seventy-one new institutions to mark the beginning of the seventy-first year of his life. He was vehemently opposed to the idea of retirement, seeing it as a waste of precious years. People may wish to explore other vocations and put talents and experience into different avenues. But he believed that, 'there should be no retirement from life or from man's divine purpose to continue to make a difference in our world'.

In 1977, the Rebbe had a major heart attack and at seventy-five years of age, it would have been the ideal time to bow out into semi-retirement. Remarkably, the Rebbe returned to public life just thirty-eight days later. More determined than ever, it appeared that the heart attack marked the beginning of an increase in his activities which continued for the next fifteen years.

The late Rabbi Adin Steinsaltz was involved in three full time jobs; writing, outreach work in Russia and a network of schools in Israel. Under strain from his varied assignments, he asked the Rebbe if he should reduce his workload. The Rebbe's response was definitive - he should 'continue to do all these things and do more things'.

Despite transforming Chabad-Lubavitch and world Jewry significantly, the Rebbe was never satisfied with his achievements. One must not confuse this dissatisfaction with unhappiness or discontent. A Shaliach, updating the Rebbe about his work, asked if he was happy with what he had reported. The Rebbe smiled and gave his reply. 'Happy, I most certainly am, but by nature, I am never satisfied with what has already been done in an area where even more can be achieved,' he said.

Reframe your challenges

'Tell your father that he should finish the mission he was sent to the hospital for: to inspire the others there to intensify their spiritual commitments.' This was the reply received by a petitioner, concerned about her father's mental state whilst in hospital, in a letter from the Rebbe.

Instead of focusing on the negative impact a hospital environment may have on her father's well-being, the Rebbe suggested an entirely different approach. If her father could see that his presence there had meaning, that he could still do good, despite being ill, he would have something to live for. It sounds remarkably simple, but how many people would have thought to put such a positive spin on such a difficult situation?

As the Rebbe's reputation grew, many politicians of international stature and influence began to visit his headquarters in Brooklyn on a regular basis. When Shirley Chisholm was elected in 1968 to represent New York's twelfth District, which included her neighbourhood of Crown Heights in Brooklyn, she made headlines as the first African American woman elected to Congress.

However, she soon found her career path blocked by racism. Bowing to political pressures from Southern politicians, the House's leadership assigned Chisholm to the Agriculture Committee, a place where she would be out of the way. Chisholm lived a block away from the Rebbe and told him how upset she had been at this action.

'What a blessing God has given you!' the Rebbe told Chisholm. 'This country has so much surplus food, and there are so many hungry people. You can use this gift that God gave you to feed hungry people. Find a creative way to do it'.

Chisholm happened to meet Senator Bob Dole on her first day in Washington. Dole, the one-time presidential candidate, was looking for help in assisting the economic plight of Midwestern farmers who were losing money on their crops. Chisholm remembered her meeting with the Rebbe and over the next few years, worked to expand the national Food Stamp Programme, which allowed poor Americans to buy subsidized food.

At her retirement party, Chisolm stated, 'a Rabbi who is an optimist taught me that what you may think is a challenge is a gift from God. If poor babies have milk, and poor children have food, it's because this Rabbi in Crown Heights had vision'.

The Rebbe saw every adversity as an opportunity, whether the challenges brought with it the potential for spiritual or material improvement. Facing up to adversity in business would enable a person to, 'become a stronger and more effective businessman than before, with an added dimension of experience and a keener acumen, to put to good use when things begin to turn upwards'.

He also expounded the Jewish view that difficult tests were given from God precisely because a person can overcome the challenge. Viewed in this context, embracing one's challenges becomes a whole lot easier.

We have already spoken of the Rebbe's militaristic approach to challenges. It is, therefore, no surprise that the Rebbe urged people to go on the attack when faced with mental health challenges such as anxiety. 'Half of winning any battle is understanding the enemy and once you understand the root of your fears, you are well on your way to conquering them. When you become aware of fear or anxiety, do not give way to depression; instead, attack and improve the situation', he advised.

Reframing is a technique used in therapy to help create a different way of looking at a situation, person, or relationship by changing its meaning. The Rebbe's approach bears a striking resemblance to that currently found in Cognitive Behaviour Therapy, an approach pioneered in the 1960s by Dr Aaron T. Beck.

If we can learn to view our current challenges in a different way, then what may first seem like an obstacle, can become the start of a new opportunity. Sometimes the more difficult an obstacle, the greater the opportunity that lies within.

Chapter Twelve

Eleanor Roosevelt

You can often change your circumstances by changing your attitude

Eleanor Roosevelt is best known as the First Lady of the United States. It was a role she held from 1933 to 1945, during the four terms in office of her husband, President Franklin D. Roosevelt (FDR). However, this period marks but one chapter in an eventful life story.

Adversity was a regular visitor in her life, but the tenacious New Yorker refused to let hardship stand in her way. She is famous for advocating for those less fortunate in society; doing so at a time when campaigning for such causes was frowned upon.

Roosevelt experienced an unhappy childhood, having suffered the deaths of both parents and a brother at a young age. After marrying her distant cousin, FDR, in 1905, she could easily have settled for a life of privilege. Nevertheless, she resolved to overcome her difficulties to establish a legacy of her own.

The Roosevelts' marriage was a difficult one. The couple had six children although one, Franklyn Jr, died as a child, which devastated the young mother. FDR's domineering mother, Sara, lived with the family and acted a constant critic to her daughter-in-law. Revelling in the role of the stereotypical mother-in-law, Sara was on hand to criticise Eleanor at every opportunity.

In 1918, Roosevelt was devastated to discover her husband's affair with her good friend and social secretary, Lucy Mercer. Divorce was not considered an option as FDR had ambitions to become president and divorce at that time would almost certainly have put paid to any presidential run.

According to their son James, the state of the marriage after the incident was, 'an armed truce that endured until the day FDR died'.

The incident marked a turning point, though. Eleanor decided to seek comfort in giving to others, through her activities in public life. Throughout the 1920s, she became influential as a leader in the New York State Democratic Party. During her husband's term as Governor of New York, Roosevelt travelled across the state to make speeches and report back to her husband at the end of each trip.

In March 1933, she assumed the role as First Lady of the United States and is regarded as arguably, the most controversial occupant of the role in the country's history. Determined to stay in the public eye, she hosted a weekly radio show and wrote a monthly magazine column, called *My Day*.

In the first year of her husband's administration, she single-mindedly set out to match her husband's presidential salary and reportedly, earned seventy-five thousand dollars from lectures and writing, most of which she gave to charity. She also focused on helping the country's poor, rallying against racial discrimination, and travelling abroad to visit US troops during the Second World War.

Following her husband's death in 1945, Roosevelt remained involved in politics for the last seventeen years of her life. She lobbied the United States to join and support the United Nations and became its first delegate, serving from 1945 to 1952. She also served as the first chair of the UN Commission on Human Rights and oversaw the drafting of the Universal Declaration of Human Rights. Upon her death, President Harry S. Truman called her the 'First Lady of the World' in honour of her human rights achievements.

How was someone described as introverted and withdrawn in nature, able to grow into the formidable personality who worked so tirelessly on behalf of the disadvantaged?

Confront your fears

Eleanor Roosevelt had a simple mantra when it came to facing tasks she instinctively recoiled from: 'Do one thing every day that scares you', she said. Eleanor was described as a shy and reserved infant, who came out of her shell to become a colossal public figure.

Roosevelt spoke of a home life, in which her mother, a famous socialite, humiliated her frequently by referring to her as 'Granny' due to her plain appearance. 'She often called me that for I was a solemn child, without beauty and painfully shy'. This made Eleanor, 'sink into the floor with shame'.

Matters were not helped by the fact that her father was a troubled man, suffering from depression and alcohol and drug dependence. Her mother died from diphtheria when Eleanor was only six years old. Her father, unable to overcome his demons, died two years later after jumping from a window.

After her parents' deaths, Eleanor was sent to live with her grandmother, whose lack of compassion further risked alienating the vulnerable child. Her saving grace arrived in the form of her schooling at Allenswood Academy in London, where she spent three years. The move forced her out of her comfort zone, enabling her to become more confident. There, she met an inspirational role model, Headmistress Marie Souvestre, who opened her eyes to a range of social and political issues.

Roosevelt returned to America a more self-assured and mature young woman and married her distant cousin, Franklin Delano Roosevelt in 1905. Pursuing the route that was expected of a prominent politician's wife would have been the predictable path for her to take, but events appeared to change her mindset. Firstly, the discovery of the affair of her husband's infidelity appears to have prompted Eleanor to become increasingly outward looking. She began to live a more autonomous life and often escaped to a cottage in upstate New York, which she shared with two friends. Together, they started a furniture factory which provided jobs for unemployed workers.

Roosevelt decided that she would reinvent herself as a public campaigner, in her own right, regardless of her introverted nature. She noted in her autobiography that she was, 'always afraid of something: of the dark, of displeasing people, of failure. Anything I accomplished had to be done across a barrier of fear'.

Once she started speaking out about social issues, she threw herself wholeheartedly into public life. She campaigned diligently for her husband's gubernatorial race in New York and for his presidential campaigns. When her husband was stricken with paralysis in 1921, it was Eleanor who travelled and gave speeches in his place.

In 1933, at the point of FDR's election as president, she also had to occupy the role expected of a First Lady. Nevertheless, she resolved to change the role forever, with her regular columns and radio shows.

Psychologists have long heralded the strategy of exposure and response prevention in the treatment of anxiety. The method involves asking patients to deliberately and repeatedly come into contact with circumstances that are anxiety provoking (spending time in crowded locations, touching certain objects or animals) in the belief that repetition of such tasks will lessen or decondition the anxiety reaction. Tremendous results have been seen, with few strategies as potent in producing direct and effective relief from anxiety and fear.

As Eleanor Roosevelt showed, the approach clearly has a major role to play in a non-clinical setting. Her life story serves as a case study for those seeking ways to step out of their comfort zone and embrace their fears. 'You gain strength, courage and confidence by every experience in which you really stop to look fear in the face. You are able to say to yourself, "I have lived through this horror. I can take the next thing that comes along." You must do the thing you think you cannot do', she once said about confronting one's fears.

Focus on others

A selfless approach was at the heart of Roosevelt's mindset. She summed up this view by saying, 'since you get more joy out of giving joy to others, you should put a good deal of thought into the happiness you are able to give'. Eleanor's determination to cast aside the insecurity and fear caused by childhood events and her husband's subsequent infidelity were manifested in her dedication to the needs of others.

She believed that there was no better way to assert her own personality and overcome her difficulties than by focusing on the needs of the wider, less privileged community. In doing so, she was able to gain a confidence that was previously lacking.

From an early age, the young Eleanor was often found helping her mother by rubbing her temples during her frequent migraines. She felt needed and wanted when she was of service to anyone who could not help themselves.

In August 1921, whilst on vacation, FDR was diagnosed with a paralytic illness. FDR's physician, Dr William Keen, praised Eleanor's dedication to her husband's rehabilitation. 'You have been a rare wife', he said, proclaiming her, 'one of my heroines'.

Prior to her husband becoming President, she threw herself into public life and service to others. She participated in the League of Women Voters, joined the Women's Trade Union League and worked for the Women's Division of the New York State Democratic Committee. She became an advocate of the rights and needs of the poor, of minorities and of the disadvantaged. As First Lady, Eleanor travelled across the United States, reporting back to the President after she visited government institutions and programmes and numerous other facilities.

She was a controversial advocate of civil rights for black Americans, which was highly divisive at the time, as well as a champion of women and workers' rights. She was disliked by many who saw her as a dangerous liberal and by those who were uncomfortable with such a formidable woman.

There is little doubt that her self-confidence was boosted every time she successfully backed a worthy cause.

Roosevelt's political involvement did not end with her husband's death in 1945. Appointed in 1946, she served for more than a decade as a delegate to the United Nations, the institution established by her husband. There, she embraced the cause of world peace. In 1960, President John F. Kennedy requested that she chair his Commission on the Status of Women, which released a trailblazing study about gender discrimination.

How does helping others ultimately help a person with their own travails? Focusing on the needs of others allows a person to forget their own troubles. There is an idea in Jewish philosophy, believed to derive from the book of Job, that speaks of the optimal way to get your own prayers answered - it is to first focus on the needs of others and pray for their requirements.

Roosevelt experienced tremendous heartache in her personal life. She chose to move on from that pain by focusing on the needs of others. It is why, by the time of her death in 1962, *The New York Times* called her, 'the object of almost universal respect'.

Show foresight

Creating a vision was important to Roosevelt. 'It is today that we must create the world of the future', she claimed. Indeed, Roosevelt spent most of her time thinking of the future and in doing so, ended up on the right side of history on many subjects. Whether it was in warning of the impending war in Europe, women's rights or racial inequalities within America, she foresaw the topics, problems and issues that were looming and acted to make a difference.

Eleanor, like her husband, FDR, was quick to see the imminent catastrophe in Europe. In a twist of fate, she had moved into the White House five weeks after Adolf Hitler became chancellor of Germany. She kept herself well informed on the anti-Jewish policies of the Nazi regime. As First Lady, Eleanor used influence to intervene on behalf of refugees. In February 1939, she joined the list of prominent Americans who supported passage of a bill to permit the entry of twenty-thousand German refugee children of fourteen years of age and under, into the United States over the course of two years. Eleanor told reporters the bill was, 'a wise way to do a humanitarian act'.

As the Nazi horrors became clear, she worked behind the scenes to try to influence her husband and in public, through her newspaper column, *My Day*. Whilst Congress favoured America neutrality in the war, Eleanor Roosevelt used a broadcast prior to Pearl Harbour in November 1941, to attack her husband's isolationist opponents.

Back home, she viewed racial discrimination as a blatant form of injustice that had been tolerated for too long. She cultivated relationships with civil rights leaders and stressed her distaste for segregation. In 1939, the influential Daughters of the American Revolution refused to allow Marion Anderson, an black singer, to perform in their auditorium. Roosevelt resigned as a member of the group and in doing so, took a bold stance against the prevailing attitudes of the time.

Following the controversy, Anderson was invited to sing at a public recital before seventy-five thousand people on the steps of the Lincoln Memorial in April 1939. Roosevelt had the foresight to see that her high-profile resignation would bring the issue into the national spotlight.

Not only did Eleanor serve as a role model for women, she also hosted the first press conferences ever held by a First Lady, which were covered by female reporters only, encouraging women to become more politically active. Working alongside Molly Dewson, head of the Women's Division of the DNC, she lobbied her husband to appoint more women. This culminated in the appointment of Frances Perkins as the first woman to head the Department of Labor.

Foresight, in the most basic of terms, can be considered an act of looking to and thinking about the future. The ability to anticipate change can be a key component in overturning difficult situations.

It is little wonder that several of this generation's women politicians identify closely with Roosevelt. 'I think she was one of the greatest Americans in our history', Hillary Clinton told *Sunday Morning* host, Jane Pauley. Where Eleanor led, many female politicians and activists subsequently followed. Like Eleanor Roosevelt, we must have the foresight to take risks and challenge the status quo where necessary.

Stick to your beliefs

Roosevelt was committed to what she believed. 'Have convictions. Be friendly. Stick to your beliefs as they stick to theirs', she would say. Her moral fortitude was one reason she was so respected. A fascinating television interview between Frank Sinatra and Eleanor Roosevelt in 1959 can be found on YouTube. In that clip, host Sinatra extolled the virtues of his good friend, who he described as the most admired woman of our time. The two chatted for some time in a frank and warm exchange. Just like the famous singer, Roosevelt firmly insisted on doing things her way.

When FDR took office as president in 1933, Eleanor significantly changed the role of the First Lady. Eleanor held her first press conference on the sixth of March 1933, just two days after Franklin's inauguration. It was the first of over three-hundred and forty-eight that shaped her role in the administration's New Deal programme to combat the Great Depression. The public was drawn in by the First Lady's exploits and adventures which she recounted in her daily column, *My Day*. She began writing the column in 1935 and continued until her death in 1962. She wrote numerous articles and advice columns for women's magazines, such as the *Ladies' Home Journal*, which serialized the first part of her autobiography in 1937 and enabled her to reach readers across the United States.

On several occasions, she lambasted her husband for his stance on a given issue, vehemently disagreeing with government policy. She was distressed by her husband's stance on refugees during the Second World War and lobbied behind the scenes against official US policy. She relentlessly petitioned FDR on policy matters. At one stage, Franklin asked her to write no more than three memos a night. As a result, in 1939, *Time* magazine showcased her on its cover and called her the 'world's foremost female political force'.

Had she not acted with independence and taken a stand against injustice, it is unlikely that the period would have seen so much change in American society. Eleanor always insisted that she had to do what she believed was right. Her continued support of the civil rights movement and an anti-lynching bill earned her death threats from white supremacists, who put a twenty-five-thousand-dollar bounty on her head in the 1960s.

It is remarkable to think that such independent action was possible in the first part of the twentieth century. After the death of her husband, she continued to call out injustice wherever she saw it. She put pressure on the US government with her criticism of their lukewarm commitment to the United Nations, forcing them to make a greater contribution to the fledgling organisation.

As the chair of the United Nations commission drafting the Universal Declaration of Human Rights, Eleanor played a crucial role in its passage, uniting countries and brokering compromise.

Staying true to one's beliefs can be difficult at the best of times, let alone in difficult times. Standing up for your own values when they often conflict with the majority can be daunting. If you feel strongly enough about an issue, nobody has the right to tell you to change your beliefs. The subject of Chapter Sixteen, Winston Churchill, issued the famous saying, that could well have been applied to the life of Eleanor Roosevelt, 'you have enemies? Good. That means you've stood up for something, sometime in your life'.

As *The New York Times* stated in its obituary of her, 'in the White House and for some time thereafter, no First Lady could touch Mrs Roosevelt for causes espoused, opinions expressed, distances spanned, people spoken to, words printed, precedents shattered, honours conferred, degrees garnered'. Without strong beliefs, none of that would have been possible.

Choose carefully which advice to use or discard

'What about criticism? I am always being asked if it troubles me, or makes me angry, or hurts me. Should we be affected by criticism regardless of its source?' Eleanor Roosevelt may have been famous for her writing, but it was her capacity to both listen and ignore, that rank amongst her most remarkable traits. Eleanor knew, that to understand the issues of the day, she needed to learn about ordinary people and discover what mattered to them. She also knew that over the years, she had built up quite a collection of enemies, who were not shy in sharing their opinions.

In her first year as First Lady, she travelled over forty-thousand miles. On these tours around the country, she went into the homes of workers, women, and children, pulling up a chair and sitting at their kitchen tables. 'Listening to such a woman talk, taking in the surroundings, one finds oneself, little by little, coming to understand the feelings of that other human being'.

She would use her voice and body language to demonstrate her care about the subject being spoken about. On a campaign trip in New York, Eleanor took a ride with a family to catch her train after a speech. The daughter, who was ten years old at the time, remembered vividly that, 'she was warm and personable, she had the voice of someone who was really listening to you, someone who really cared about what you said'. Her empathy for the ordinary and disadvantaged was said to be untypical of someone growing up in such a privileged manner.

Eleanor Roosevelt's most vocal critic was 1941 Pulitzer Prize winning journalist, Westbrook Pegler. He was a fervent opponent of the New Deal and a forceful opponent of both Franklin and Eleanor Roosevelt, although he often reserved his most vicious reprimands for Eleanor. 'I have been accused of rudeness to Mrs Roosevelt when I only said she was impudent, presumptuous and conspiratorial, and that her withdrawal from public life at this time would be a fine public service', he said. Did Eleanor let such stinging criticism affect her? It is intriguing to read Eleanor's own thoughts on how one should differentiate between constructive and destructive criticism.

Whilst acknowledging that no human being enjoys being disliked, Eleanor believed that there was an intrinsic value in listening to constructive criticism, if, 'it came to us from people whom we know and whose judgement we trust and who we feel really care, not only for us as individuals, but for the things which may be affected by the actions or attitudes which we take'.

However, when criticism was really a cover for political attack, such criticism serves no purpose. 'Destructive criticism is always valueless and anyone with common sense soon becomes completely indifferent to it. It may of course, be cruel at times', she explained.

Quoting her Aunt, Mrs William Sheffield Cowles, she ends by stating that one should not, 'be bothered by what people say as long as you are sure that you are doing what seems right to you but be sure that you face yourself honestly'.

While the ability to take in feedback is vital to our growth, we need to be careful about what information we take on board and what should be dismissed as harmful.

Eleanor Roosevelt experienced her fair share of praise and vitriol. It was her ability to empathise and listen to people of all races, religions, and nationalities, whilst blocking out the jeers of critics, that resulted in the outpouring of grief upon her death in 1962.

Chapter Thirteen

Helen Keller

We could never learn to be brave and patient, if there were only joy in the world

Helen Keller, the American educator and advocate for the deaf and blind, was born in Alabama in June 1880. She was not born with her terrible afflictions. Before her illness, she was said to be highly advanced for her age, speaking at just six months old and walking by the time she was one.

Life changed forever when, at just nineteen months old, Keller contracted an unknown illness, thought to have been either scarlet fever or meningitis. The illness resulted in the devastating loss of both sight and hearing.

As Keller grew up, she developed a basic form of sign language with her childhood friend, Martha Washington, the young daughter of the family cook. By the time she was aged seven, the two friends had invented more than sixty signs to communicate with each other. However, Keller was prone to wild outbursts and family members recommended that the unruly child be institutionalised. In the late nineteenth century, the expectation was that such children would quietly disappear from public view, living out their days in a remote institution.

Keller's mother refused to contemplate such a move, instead researching ways to improve the life of her child. Eventually, the Kellers took their daughter to see Alexander Graham Bell, the inventor of the telephone, who at the time, was working with deaf children. Bell suggested the family travel to the Perkins Institute for the Blind in Boston, Massachusetts. It was there that the family was introduced to one of the school's recent graduates, Anne Sullivan.

The meeting was a success, with the Keller and Sullivan going on to work together for nearly fifty years. Keller spoke of the day of Sullivan's arrival 'as my soul's birthday'. With the help of her teacher and mentor, she made remarkable progress and learned to communicate effectively. Keller became the first deaf and blind person to earn a degree at twenty-four years of age.

Keller wrote her first book, *The Story of My Life,* around the time of her graduation, which covered her extraordinary progress from disabled child to college graduate. As a leading disability activist, she forced society to talk about taboo topics such as blindness and she successfully lobbied for services for the deaf and blind as well as for wounded veterans.

She became a well know international celebrity and lecturer and she even testified before the Congress. In 1920, she helped found the American Civil Liberties Union, reinforcing her reputation as an activist whose focus extended beyond her own challenges. She campaigned to improve the rights and conditions of those in all manners of difficulties.

During her lifetime, she received many honours for her campaigning, including the Theodore Roosevelt Distinguished Service Medal in 1936. On the fourteenth of September 1964, President Lyndon B. Johnson awarded her one of the United States' two highest civilian honours, the Presidential Medal of Freedom. Keller's life story was a triumph over crushing adversity and devastating affliction.

It is difficult to contemplate the loss of even a single sense. To lose both sight and hearing would be a knockout blow to many. As someone who spent her life devoted to helping others, it is appropriate to look at the life and legacy of Helen Keller and ask; how was a woman with so many obstacles before her, able to achieve so much?

Find a mentor

'The most important day I remember in all my life is the one on which my teacher came to me', Keller said in her autobiography. She worked with that teacher, Anne Sullivan, from the age of seven until her mentor's death, in 1936.

Arriving on the recommendation of the Perkins Institute for the Blind, Sullivan was meant to follow the teaching methods used by Perkins' founder, Samuel Howe. However, she soon realised that this rigid routine would not suit her new pupil. She refused to be restricted by the inflexible curriculum that had been prescribed for young Helen. Sullivan came to the realisation that to bring out the best in Keller, she must adopt a firm but fair approach to her pupil. She made the decision to enter Helen's world, observing her interests and adding language and words to those activities. Formal lessons were subsequently abandoned. Teaching through nature, she provided Keller with a carefully designed curriculum, that gave her opportunities to learn through hobbies such as horse riding and sailing.

From that point on, it was clear that Keller would flourish under Sullivan's guidance. Within one month, her vocabulary had grown by more than a dozen words a day. Sullivan achieved this by teaching her pupil finger spelling and a series of unconventional exercises. This allowed Helen to make a physical connection between an object and its identity. Within six months, Keller had a vocabulary of five-hundred and seventy-five words and had mastered multiplications as high as five and had learned the Braille system.

Sullivan was not only Helen Keller's teacher but also a trusted friend and role model. Her nurturing and caring attitude allowed Helen to grow into an altruistic and considerate adult, who became dedicated to emulating her mentor in working for the well-being of the blind and deaf.

Like Keller, Anne Sullivan was born a healthy child only to develop an illness which left her visually impaired. The two forged an instant connection with teacher able to relate to her student and understand the pain behind her childhood tantrums.

When Keller enrolled at the Cambridge School for Young Ladies and later, Radcliffe College of Harvard University, the dedicated Sullivan was by her side to support her learning. In

Helen Keller's own eyes, she believed that her success was due to the constant support and encouragement from her teacher.

The importance of a mentor cannot be understated. Mentors offer encouragement and lift us up when we are falling. A mentor is, in the words of entrepreneur and television host Oprah Winfrey, 'someone who allows you to see the hope inside yourself', providing you with the much-needed wisdom and guidance you need.

We will never know what would have been achieved had Sullivan not entered Keller's life. Sullivan herself rejected the portrayal that she was Keller's saviour. She argued that the job tutoring Helen Keller was the only one she had been offered, therefore, she had no choice but to make it work. We can perhaps only put Sullivan's words down to modesty, for she was central to the progress made by Helen Keller. A mother figure one minute, a disciplinarian the next, Sullivan was much more than just a teacher. She was able to unlock the potential locked inside a little girl who could not see, speak, or hear.

Stick to your task

'We can do anything we want if we stick to it long enough'. Keller stood fast to this principle even though not much, if anything, was expected of her after her illness rendered her blind and deaf. Whilst she initially developed a basic method of communication, her early years were full of ferocious outbursts and tantrums. She looked destined to spend her childhood unschooled and unable to fully communicate with her family. Her ultimate end was expected to be the well-trodden path of institutionalisation. Her uncle told her mother, 'you really ought to put that child away ... she is mentally defective and it is not pleasant to see her about'.

By nightfall on her first day with Sullivan, Keller had learned thirty words. The young student was frustrated, at first, because she did not understand that every object had a word identifying it. When Sullivan attempted to teach Keller the word for 'mug', her young student became so upset she broke the mug. Teacher and student had to toil daily to achieve their shared aims. In order to write, Keller placed paper over a board that had the alphabet grooved into it by Sullivan. With patience and practice, Helen was able to remember how to move her pencil so that she could form the letters herself and then write words sentences and eventually, whole books.

By the end of the first year, Keller was able to spell nearly a thousand words and even write letters to her family and friends. Sullivan even challenged Helen to start a journal before her eighth birthday. She was also able to experience music by feeling the beat and developed a connection with animals through touch.

When the time came, Keller made up her mind to attend the most prestigious of colleges, Harvard. However, Harvard did not yet accept women, so Keller was forced to accept her second choice, Radcliffe College. Keller met with resistance from friends who tried to persuade her that a college environment was no place for a deaf-blind person. Ignoring the doubters, she easily passed the entrance exams to Radcliffe.

While at Radcliffe, she wrote a graphic account of her own miraculous education as a child. She was commissioned to write six personal narratives under the title, *The Story of My Life*, by an editor of the *Ladies' Home Journal*. Despite struggling with her college education, Keller finished the series in 1902 and released a full-length book of the same title in 1903.

What sets Keller apart is that no similarly afflicted person before had done more than acquire the simplest of language skills. Most of her fellow students at Radcliffe had never even met a deaf and blind person. Yet Helen Keller had no time for outdated beliefs. She resolved to work harder than any other student to achieve her goal of a degree. In 1904, the twenty-four-year-old Helen Keller achieved the previously unthinkable end result, graduating with honours.

The New York Times lauded Keller's achievement of gaining entry to college, stating, 'the obstacles appear insurmountable. But that is the principal reason why Helen Keller is inclined to surmount them'.

Be happy with what you have

Enjoying what she had at any given time was an important part of Helen Keller's approach to dealing with her challenging situation. 'Be happy with what you have while working for what you want', she stated. Keller had every reason to be resentful of the hand she had been dealt. It is striking to note that many of her writing and speaking engagements were about happiness. 'I take happiness very seriously. It is a creed, a philosophy and an objective'.

Having experienced the dramatic breakthrough in communication under Sullivan's tutelage, Keller's ability to communicate and experience nature appears to have left her in a state of perpetual appreciation.

Keller and Sullivan travelled together to a small town in Wisconsin to deliver a lecture in January 1916. A local newspaper lauded her words, speaking of a 'message of optimism, of hope, of good cheer and of loving service ... a message that will linger long with those fortunate enough to have received it. The wonderful girl who has so brilliantly triumphed over the triple afflictions of blindness, dumbness and deafness, gave a talk with her own lips on happiness and it will be remembered always as a piece of inspired teaching by those who heard it'.

The title of Helen's 1903 book, *Optimism*, allowed her to share her underlying positivity with readers, despite having experienced her fair share of misfortune. To Keller, happiness does not come through the attainment of material possession, 'for if happiness is so to be measured, I who cannot hear or see have every reason to sit in a corner with folded hands and weep'.

Rather, Keller states that if she can be happy whilst lacking so much, then so too, can others be. 'If I am happy in spite of my deprivations, if my happiness is so deep that is a faith, if in short, I am an optimist, my testimony to the creed of optimism is worth hearing', she confirmed.

Like the theories of Viktor Frankl, discussed at length in Chapter One, Keller was adamant that one's attitude is what counts in life, not one's circumstances. 'I demand that the world be good and it obeys'.

The months during the pandemic have certainly been trying. People have been threatened with the loss of health, livelihood and loved ones. Yet, many have come to see the beauty of a simpler life, one which can still be meaningful, without the need to visit exclusive restaurants, exotic locations, or go on days out. Many people have spoken of rediscovering a love of nature, walking and other outdoor pursuits.

No-one would wish to endure the type of disabilities experienced by Helen Keller. Yet she consistently exuded contentment. 'My life has been happy because I have had wonderful friends and plenty of interesting work to do', she claimed.

Being content does not mean being enthralled with every situation we find ourselves in. Rather, it means finding fulfilment in what we have and appreciating the good in our lives. There is a teaching in the Jewish oral tradition, the Mishnah, which tells us how to define a rich person: 'Who is rich? He who is happy with his lot'.

Helen Keller lived a rich life because she focused on being happy with what she had, not what she could not change.

Challenge the status quo
Keller had an interesting but profound take on her sight disability, stating philosophically that, 'the only thing worse than being blind is having sight but no vision'. In an age of prejudice and stigma, Helen Keller not only changed perceptions about blindness but also became the driving force behind efforts to improve treatment of the deaf and the blind. Before Helen Keller became established in the public's consciousness, the deaf and blind were often treated in a

dismissive way. It was felt that such people could never become productive members of society. Keller lived a life in defiance of these views; riding horses and bicycles and playing chess and backgammon.

One story sums up Helen's determination to invoke change. Two days before her college entrance, she learned that the tests had been copied for her into American braille, one of five such systems at the time. Unfortunately, she had only ever used English braille for her mathematical studies. Keller spent the next two days studying American braille and somehow managed to pass. Exasperated by this situation, she spent years lobbying for a single standardised braille system, resulting in the adoption in 1932 of the standard English braille system across the world.

Her lecture tours took her around the world, advocating on behalf of the disabled. She could rightly point to her own achievements and by doing so, was able to remove the stigma surrounding sight and hearing disorders. If she could graduate from college and become a multiple author of books, why could others in difficult positions not achieve similar results?

Helen Keller was not scared to express her outspoken voice in other formats. She began to write of blindness, a taboo subject in women's magazines because of its relationship to venereal disease. Her articles for the *Ladies' Home Journal* did much to dispel outdated notions regarding disability.

Amongst her peers, Helen Keller led by example. She worked on behalf of the American Foundation for the Blind (AFB) for nearly half a decade. She met with President Roosevelt in 1935 and it was her persuasiveness that led to Roosevelt personally endorsing talking book machines. Her influence extended beyond the realms of her own interest groups. She campaigned for wounded veterans, women's suffrage, workers' rights and the rights of women to use birth control.

Keller's willingness to challenge the accepted practices of the day caused a shockwave through society, resulting in profound changes that are still felt to this day. By 1937, thirty states had established commissions for the blind and she continued to appear before state legislatures to give a personal example of what similar people could accomplish. Not only did Helen Keller personally break down barriers that had once seemed impenetrable, but in advocating on behalf of her peers, she ensured they remained down permanently.

Believe your goals can be achieved

Staying up-beat about the chances for your success was important to Keller. 'Nothing can be done without hope and confidence', she confirmed. Keller became a well-known celebrity and lecturer by sharing her experiences with audiences. Her disabilities did not stop her from becoming a strong and confident woman. Much of the credit, as has been shown, was given to her teacher and mentor, Anne Sullivan, who taught Helen that she could achieve whatever she desired despite being blind and deaf. Writing about her first days of learning under Sullivan's guidance, Keller declared that, 'the more I handled things and learned their names and uses, the more joyous and confident grew my sense of kinship with the rest of the world'.

As a student at Perkins School for the Blind, she assertively fronted a fundraising campaign to establish a kindergarten for the blind and to pay for the education of Tommy Stringer, a poor boy from Pennsylvania who was deaf-blind, like her.

Of course, Helen had times when her self-confidence was affected. Aged eleven, Keller was accused of plagiarism having written a story called, *The Frost King*, which bore resemblance to a story written by another author. Helen was deeply scarred by the incident and for a short time, had no confidence in herself. It was only when Sullivan arranged for Helen to write a biography of her life to date for the children's magazine, *Youth Companion,* that Keller was able to throw herself into the work with, 'renewed confidence'.

Keller won her friends effortlessly and exuded energy and assertiveness. Such was her confidence in her ability to make her own way in life, that when Andrew Carnegie, the successful industrialist and philanthropist, offered her a regular pension income in 1910, she turned him down, proclaiming that she needed to make it on her own and hoped the self-made industrialist would understand.

In March 1930, she testified before Congress, astonishing the committee with her eloquence. advocating to improve the welfare of blind people. She confidently asked the lawmakers to close their eyes and for a few moments, imagine the world of the blind.

Anne Sullivan had taught Helen Keller to be confident and as a result, she was not intimidated by meeting great statesmen or lecturing before huge crowds. During her lifetime, Keller met twelve US presidents, beginning with Grover Cleveland and ending with John F. Kennedy. She met and had an impact on many leading figures, like Winston Churchill.

Perhaps it was because Keller had climbed so many mountains and exceeded so many expectations that she felt nothing was beyond her reach.

Difficult times bring challenges to almost everyone's self-confidence. Even Helen Keller had times when she doubted herself. Nevertheless, remaining confident helps one overcome the worst of challenges. Confidence provides the belief that targets can be obtained, no matter how difficult they may be to achieve.

The Politicians

Chapter Fourteen

Margaret Thatcher

You may have to fight a battle more than once to win it

It has been said that the great military and political leaders are often referred to by their surname, for example, Napoleon, Churchill, Mandela ... and Thatcher. There is little doubt that Mrs Thatcher, was loved and loathed in equal measure and that included within her own political party and cabinet.

She spent her whole premiership under threat from the IRA, losing two friends, Airey Neave and Ian Gow, in terrorist attacks. Despite being only inches away from death when the IRA bombed the Grand Hotel in Brighton in 1984, Thatcher literally shook off the dust and gave a rousing speech the next morning to the Conservative Party Conference.

Things could have been vastly different had she not been turned down for a job at ICI in 1948. Her application was declined on account of her performance at interview, in which she appeared, 'headstrong, obstinate and dangerously opinionated'.

Born Margaret Roberts on the thirteenth of October 1925, she was raised in a cold-water flat above the grocery store owned by her father, Alfred. She won a scholarship to Kesteven and Grantham Girls School and then, when she was seventeen years old, won a further bursary to attend Somerville College, Oxford, where she studied chemistry.

As a woman, she was prevented from joining the Oxford Union debating society but soon became a member of the Oxford University Conservative Association and its president in 1946. Thatcher graduated in 1947, earning a master's degree in chemistry. Her plan was to study law, but she lacked the funds to pay for her further education. She, therefore, became one of the first women to be hired as a chemist by British

Xylonite Plastics. Thatcher practiced briefly as a barrister, specialising in tax and patent law, having passed her bar finals just four months after giving birth to twins.

In case anyone thinks that Thatcher's political rise was without setback, in 1950, she campaigned to be the Member of Parliament for Dartford and as expected, she was defeated. She ran again the next year and lost again. Undeterred, she was finally elected to the House of Commons in 1959.

A steady but unspectacular rise saw her occupy Shadow Cabinet roles as well as a series of junior governmental posts. Her highest profile role came as Secretary of State for Education and Science from 1970 to 1974.

In December 1975, the Conservative Party chose Mrs Thatcher at its leader. In her role as Leader of the Opposition, she attempted to build the Party in her own image and took advantage of the 'winter of discontent' in 1978-79 to promote herself as the leader to rescue the country from its economic problems.

Saying it would take years to cure Britain of the havoc wrought by socialism, Mrs Thatcher warned, 'Things will get worse before they get better'. Whilst winning a comfortable majority in 1979, a long road lay ahead.

Unafraid of ruffling feathers, Thatcher was involved in numerous confrontations. In a ten-week war, British forces retook the Falklands Islands from the occupying Argentinian force in 1982. She famously took on and defeated the Miners Union, led by Arthur Scargill, in 1984. Thatcher is also credited with helping bring an end to the West's decades-long Cold War with the Soviet Union.

However, by 1989, she had become an unpopular and a divisive figure. The introduction of the unpopular Poll Tax confirmed to many that she was out of step with society. In 1990, she reluctantly stood aside as both party leader and Prime Minister. On her death in 2013, David Cameron stated that people failed to appreciate the 'thickness of the glass ceiling she broke through'.

How then, was Margaret Thatcher, a grocer's daughter from Grantham, able to defy the odds to succeed as the country's first female Prime Minister?

Never give up

'You turn if you want to. The lady's not for turning', said Thatcher, a quote she is often remembered for. It was political opponent Shirley Williams, who stated, 'Margaret Thatcher was neither the cleverest nor the most eloquent politician of her generation. But she was without question, the most determined'.

This determination was shown at an early age. Nothing was ever going to be handed to her on a platter. Like Tory party notables a quarter of a century later, many at Oxford University underestimated her. They had not recognised her single-mindedness and determination to get to the top. Once in office, she was driven by an unquestionable belief that it was she and she alone, who knew what was best for Britain.

In December 1975, Mrs Thatcher, in what many regarded as an act of political audacity, decided to stand for the Conservative Party leadership. One bookmaker, Ladbrokes, put the odds against her at fifty to one. In other words, she had no chance. Yet somehow, Thatcher finished ahead of Edward Heath on the first ballot and defeated the other male candidates in a second ballot. It was a lonely and difficult experience to be a female politician during that period. 'There will not be a woman Prime Minister in my lifetime – the male population is too prejudiced', Thatcher stated herself in 1970.

When she took office as Prime Minister in 1979, Britain was on its knees, economically. Unions had helped bring the country to a standstill during the 'winter of discontent' with power cuts and three-day weeks. Thatcher was determined to crush what she saw as, 'the enemy from within.'

It did not start well. At one point, polls showed that she had become the most unpopular British Prime Minister since the war. A deep recession had a stranglehold on the country with over two million unemployed. Despite hostility from within the party, Thatcher would not back down, adamant that only tough policies would suffice to turn around the economy. By 1983, her refusal to back down had been vindicated. Encouraged by victory in the Falklands War, as well as an improving economic situation, Mrs Thatcher decided to go to the polls and won an impressive three-hundred and ninety-seven seats.

The victory was a vindication for Thatcher. With her positions endorsed by the electorate, she proceeded to increase her grip on power and implement further changes to the British economy. She revelled in the nickname given to her by Soviet propagandists. 'Yes, I am an iron lady', she boasted.

Even Thatcher's many enemies recognised and respected her determination. There was no more implacable opponent than Labour politician, Tony Benn. Yet he came to recognise that, 'she said what she meant and meant what she said ... she just had a clear idea and followed it through'.

Difficulties struck regularly during the Thatcher era. In such times, it is possible to react in two ways. You can, like many of her successors, dither and avoid taking difficult decisions, or you can take a firm approach, tackling problems head on. The latter was the policy boldly adopted by Thatcher and one that allowed her to navigate around her many challenges.

Stand your ground

Thatcher believed in taking a firm leadership stance confirming, 'You cannot lead from the crowd.' British settlers had lived on the remote islands in the South Atlantic, since the 1820s. Claimed by Argentina, negotiations over the future of the Falkland Islands had been deadlocked for years. Then, the Argentine military rulers launched an invasion in April 1982 and reasoned that with barely any military presence on the Falklands, no British Government would be willing to risk so much for a small parcel of land that many had not even heard of.

Over the course of the next seventy-four days, the British armed forces retook the islands in a victory that ensured Thatcher's legacy as a brave and fearless politician. Despite fears within her cabinet and group of advisers and against the wishes of her close ally, President Ronald Reagan, she boldly acted where many others would not have.

'We must recover the Falkland Islands for Britain and for the people who live there who are of British stock', she stated.

Why were her actions so brave? According to historian, Chris Collins, of the Margaret Thatcher Foundation, her political future rested on a decisive victory. If the war had been lost, it would have destroyed her. The Argentinian military dictatorship had clearly not understood who they were dealing with.

There was a saying in British politics that one never picked a quarrel with the Pope or the National Union of Mineworkers. Mrs Thatcher disagreed. In 1984, the government announced plans to shut down several unprofitable mines. In response, Arthur Scargill, the president of the union, called a strike that became violent. Thatcher had seen how the miners' strike had taken down Ted Heath's government and was determined to stand her ground. Her courage to stand by the principles of her economic plan overrode her fear of the consequences. On the third of March 1985, almost a year after it had started, the strike came to an end. To her many admirers, the victory boosted her image as a strong and brave leader.

Her insistence on, 'business as usual', brought tremendous admiration from the country and her courage may well have been a reason behind an unprecedented third election victory in 1987.

Kenneth Clark, Health Secretary in her Government from 1988-1990, stated that Thatcher's bravery rubbed off on cabinet colleagues. 'She gave us all the courage to do what we all believed ought to be done', he confirmed.

Mrs Thatcher displayed tremendous bravery at the time of the Brighton hotel bombing in October 1984, when she survived an attempt on her life. Two people were killed and several injured, including two senior cabinet ministers.

The morning after the bombing, despite only narrowly avoiding injury, she insisted on carrying on with her speech to the Conservative Party Conference. She tore up her original speech and delivered a memorable address. 'This attack has failed … all attempts to destroy democracy by terrorism will fail', she emphasised to a tumultuous response from her audience.

That was bravery.

Keep working hard

Fundamental to her approach was hard work. She observed, 'I do not know anyone who has got to the top without hard work. That is the recipe. It will not always get you to the top but should get you pretty near'. Some will dispute the argument that Margaret Thatcher was the greatest peacetime Prime Minister of the last century. Others may have disliked her abrasive style. But few can dispute her work ethic. The working day began at six o'clock in the morning and rarely ended until the last of the ministerial red boxes was completed in the early hours of the following morning. Part of her formidable reputation was built on the narrative of how little she slept, which she wore proudly as a badge of honour. 'I have always had an onerous timetable, but I like it', she proudly stated in an interview on the first anniversary of taking office.

There are countless stories of how Margaret Thatcher's long hours and vast appetite for work astonished her colleagues. According to Harvey Thomas, Head of Press at Conservative HQ for thirteen years, 'she had the ability to dismiss fatigue, apparently at will'.'

Her father, Alfred, taught her the virtues of hard work, through his own efforts as a grocer and local politician. Sheer hard work also took her to Oxford whilst she also managed to juggle having twins in 1952 with her Bar exams.

Hard work was in fact, the core of her political philosophy, which came to be known as Thatcherism. Coming from a modest background, she believed that everybody should succeed on merit alone. The economic 'medicine' she prescribed needed to be downed with a considerable serving of hard work. In Thatcher's worldview, socialism created an elite who had not earned their status by hard work and talent, as in a free market economy.

One Christmas, Thatcher's close friend and former Conservative Party treasurer, Lord McAlpine, stayed with her at Chequers, the Prime Minister's retreat, during the holidays. 'She worked right through Christmas. When everyone else went off to bed, she went off to work', he reported later. Thatcher viewed weekends as an annoying interruption to her daily routine, a problem she attempted to solve by turning Chequers, into a second office. Her biographer, John Campbell, author of *The Iron Lady*, says her routine helped make her 'the best informed person in the room'.

The Falklands War showed her in her real colours. She had practically no sleep for three months. She just catnapped. On the night of victory on the fourteenth of June 1982, when the Argentinians surrendered at Port Stanley, she was drained, having been up at night writing personal letters to bereaved families.

Thatcher's work ethic had an infectious effect on those around her and perhaps even more significantly, to those watching on.

Start building relationships

'I like Mr Gorbachev. We can do business together' said Margaret after her first meeting with the leader of the USSR. Many have argued that Mrs Thatcher pursued a lonely political path, rejecting advice and refusing to work in consensus. Whilst this certainly held true in domestic matters, it was far from the case on the international stage.

Mrs Thatcher played a major role in helping end the Cold War. It was on her say so that she introduced Mikhail Gorbachev to US President Ronald Reagan, helping the two come together to end the Cold War.

Through her friendship with Ronald Reagan, she helped create the illusion that the UK and the United States were in some way equal world powers. From their first meeting in 1975, Mrs Thatcher and President Reagan, then Governor of California, quickly became, in the words of Nancy Reagan, political soulmates, dedicated to freedom and committed to stopping communism.

'As soon as I met Governor Reagan, I knew that we were of like mind, and manifestly, so did he', Thatcher said. Reagan was equally effusive, writing a thank you note after their first meeting in London, stating, 'please know, you have an enthusiastic supporter out here in the 'colonies'.

To understand why the alliance was so important to the global problems of the day, one needs to examine the international tension at the start of her tenure as Prime Minister in 1979.

The prevailing attitude of many, if not all, commentators in the West had come to view the Cold War as unwinnable. The Soviet Union invaded Afghanistan in 1979. In response, US President Jimmy Carter announced a boycott of the Moscow 1980 Summer Olympics. In 1984, the Soviet Union countered with its own boycott of the 1984 Summer Olympics in Los Angeles. Tensions increased between the two countries when the US announced they would deploy missiles in West Germany and were further worsened in 1983 when Reagan branded the Soviet Union an, 'evil empire'.

Even when the two disagreed on significant issues, such as the recapture of the Falkland Islands in 1982, the warm relationship between the two helped prevent disagreements get out of hand. Margaret Thatcher once sent a tough note to President Reagan, one strong enough to have broken diplomatic relations with any other two countries. Reagan's reaction was, 'well, that's Maggie'.

Moreover, she was quick to recognise the reforming qualities of new Soviet leader, Mikhail Gorbachev. She convinced Reagan that he could be trusted and acted as, 'an agent of influence in both directions', as Sir Percy Cradock, her foreign policy adviser, put it. Likewise, Gorbachev respected her, believing that Thatcher was a politician with a strong voice. Two months before the general election of 1987, she went on a walkabout in Moscow and was mobbed by a cheering crowd.

One of the biggest challenges in building a relationship is understanding that everyone is different. Accepting and celebrating these differences are key starting points for any relationship. It was Theodore Roosevelt, the former American President, who said that the most important single ingredient in the formula of success is knowing how to get along with people. Relationship building is key in almost all aspects of life, be it in personal relationships, at work with colleagues or in trying to build a successful business.

By the time she left office, the Berlin Wall had fallen and Eastern Europe was released from the stifling rule of communism. A year later, the Soviet Union itself was consigned into the dustbin of history. Through shrewd alliance building and a human touch that remained largely hidden on the domestic front, Thatcher helped the world become a safer place.

Communicate a clear message
To Thatcher, her mission was clear, summed up by her statement, 'I am in politics because of the conflict between good and evil and I believe that, in the end, good will triumph'. As part of a group of visiting American businessmen in 1984, Steve Jobs was invited to attend a dinner with Margaret Thatcher at

the American Embassy. Whilst there are no reports of what the two discussed, it is possible that the two bonded over a shared love of communicating a simple message.

By the mid-1970s, Britain was the sick man of Europe, a staggering combined total of twenty-nine million working days had been lost to strikes in 1979 alone. The first step for the Conservative leader was to defeat the Labour incumbent, James Callaghan. To do so, Thatcher turned to the advertising agency, MC Saatchi, to craft a clear but effective slogan. Saatchi devised a striking advertising campaign in anticipation of a forthcoming election. The message was straightforward and could not have been clearer. The poster's design was a picture of a winding queue outside an unemployment office. Above the office was the slogan, 'Labour isn't working', with the phrase, 'Britain's better off with the Conservatives', in a smaller text below.

The poster featured on every newspaper front page, every television station and the more Labour kept complaining about it, the more coverage it received. By the end of the first week, the poster was known across Britain.

In 1979, Mrs Thatcher entered Downing Street as Prime Minister, quoting St Francis of Assisi as she stopped to speak to the gathering press outside. Thatcher delivered her now famous address with poise and clarity, pledging that, 'where there is discord, may we bring harmony. Where there is error, may we bring truth. Where there is doubt, may we bring faith. And where there is despair, may we bring hope'.

Thatcher was also comfortable in front of the camera and showed her skill in dramatic moments. In the aftermath of the Brighton bomb, in 1984, she was asked by John Cole, the BBC's political editor, whether she would deliver her planned speech to the Conservative Party conference. 'The conference will go on,' she said resolutely. As the camera lights brightened, indicating that she was on air, she looked directly into the lens, defiantly adding, 'The conference will go on, as usual'. The clip, shown on the BBC news, helped convey to the country her clear refusal to be intimidated by terrorism.

Too often, modern day voters complain that they do not really understand the message being given by political parties or leaders. Mrs Thatcher left voters with little doubt about what she stood for and what she would deliver when in office.

Chapter Fifteen

Nelson Mandela

Difficulties break some men but make others

There can be few human beings who have endured adversity with less bitterness and self-interest than Nelson Mandela. Leaving Victor Verster Prison in February 1990, where he had spent two of his twenty-seven years incarcerated, Mandela, aged seventy-two years old, found a country racially divided and on the brink of bloody civil war.

With an astonishing lack of resentment about his incarceration, Mandela was able to soothe the concerns of the country's white minority to ensure that there would be no reprisals. He insisted that there was a place for everyone in the new South Africa.

Born in 1918, Nelson Mandela joined the African National Congress (ANC) in 1943, opposing the policies of South Africa's white minority government. Mandela, or Madiba as he was also known, studied law at university before becoming a lawyer in Johannesburg. Together with Oliver Tambo, he opened South Africa's first black law firm in 1952. Having joined the African National Congress in 1943, he led the 1952 Campaign for the Defiance of Unjust Laws, traveling across the country to organize protests.

After many years of non-violent protest, Mandela helped set up the armed wing of the ANC in 1961. After years of engaging in a cat and mouse struggle with the apartheid authorities, Mandela was sentenced to life imprisonment in June 1964.

He spent the next twenty-seven years of his life in prison, often performing hard labour. The conditions were harsh, and Mandela was allowed only one visitor and one letter every six months. Apart from dealing with the difficulty of prison life, Mandela endured many further setbacks, such as tuberculosis, periods of solitary confinement and regularly having his study privileges revoked.

On the eleventh of February 1990, Mandela finally walked free from prison. After his release, he preached racial tolerance and worked to transform the ANC from an armed liberation group into a mainstream political party prepared to take the reins of government.

Mandela and President De Klerk worked together to change the constitution. In 1991, the system of apartheid came to an end. As a result, both Mandela and de Klerk shared the 1993 Nobel Peace Prize. The Nobel committee in Oslo stated that, 'by looking ahead to South African reconciliation instead of back at the deep wounds of the past, they have shown personal integrity and great political courage'.

Mandela went on to become South Africa's first ever black President in 1994. When he put together his first cabinet as president of a democratic nation, Mandela went out of his way to include members of the defeated National Party, the party of apartheid and of the ANC's main rival, the Zulu nationalist Inkatha Freedom Party.

All political careers, it is said, end in tears, but not Nelson Mandela's. Unlike Robert Mugabe in Zimbabwe, there were no attempts to cling onto power. In 1999, he did what he said, in serving one term as President and then stepped aside with grace, to focus on other projects.

After his tenure ended, he continued to campaign for noble causes. In 2007, he founded a group called 'The Elders', an independent group of world leaders working together for peace and human rights.

On the fifth of December 2013, Nelson Mandela died at the age of ninety-five. Few people have experienced as much adversity yet responded in such a constructive manner.

How did Mandela manage to achieve so much against the backdrop of so many difficulties?

Define your vision

Mandela had a clear vision. 'The struggle is my life. I will continue fighting for freedom until the end of my days', he stated. Even as a young man in his twenties, Mandela had a vision to end the apartheid system in South Africa. Mandela joined the African National Congress in 1942 and never wavered from his aims. When he was released from prison in 1990 and then elected President in 1994, he set about turning that vision into a reality. He accomplished so much because he had a clear vision of what steps were necessary to unify both black and white people in South Africa. Many leaders believe that victory for their own cause should result in the weakening of their enemies. This is not how Mandela saw things. At his trial in 1964, he made clear that he was as opposed to black domination as he was of white domination. 'I cherish the ideal of a democratic and free society in which all people will live together in harmony with equal opportunities', he proclaimed.

In his inauguration as the first post-apartheid President of the South African Republic, he set out his vision for a 'Rainbow Nation … the society in which all South Africans, both black and white, will be able to walk tall, without any fear in their hearts'.

In 1995, Mandela had the foresight to realise that the Rugby World Cup, being hosted in South Africa, could be used as a tool to support his vision. He urged the black community to back the team, despite rugby being seen mostly as the sport of the whites. Rugby was seen by many blacks as a symbol of segregation and the last stronghold of whites. Mandela resisted pressure to scrap the springbok, the team's reviled emblem, and urged national unity around the team.

What better image of unity could there have been than Mandela, himself wearing the team's cap and shirt, presenting the trophy to captain, Francois Pienaar, a white Afrikaner. Perhaps only a Hollywood script writer could have dreamt up such a moment.

Pienaar was glowing in praise for Mandela's role, stating that Mandela was a leader, 'with a fantastic vision, who realised that sport is important for the Afrikaner white community'.

Ten days before the final, the former prisoner had delivered a speech in Soweto. Arriving in a springbok cap and repeatedly pointing to it, he urged his audience, 'to stand by them, because they are our kind'.

Having a vision allows us to have a larger picture of how we wish our life or business to be. According to adventurer, John Graham, a vision is a mental picture of the result you want to achieve - a picture so clear and strong it will help make that result real. A vision is not a vague wish or dream or hope. It is a picture of the real results of real efforts. It comes from the future and informs and energizes the present.

If we can learn anything from Mandela, it is to live our lives around an important cause and never lose sight of what it is that we are striving to achieve. Mandela showed that adversity can drive a person towards that vision. The future is no longer invisible for those who create a vision for their life.

Play the long game

Acting when the time was right to do so was a key part of Mandela's philosophy. 'We should not let an illusion of urgency force us to make decisions before we are ready', he said. As a young man, Mandela was known to be hot headed and impatient. He wanted instant results. However, prison taught him the importance of playing the long game. He came to see that making quick decisions often led to mistakes. Whilst in prison, he calculated that the apartheid regime could not last forever. He was, therefore, prepared to wait for events to unfold. When they did, it was the apartheid government of F.W. De Klerk that itself realised, it could not go on ruling over the majority indefinitely.

As a student of history, he realised that a system that had developed after hundreds of years of colonial rule, would not disappear overnight. Mandela was known to regularly start sentences with the words, 'in the long run'. He was convinced that freedom was an unstoppable force. The date and time that this would happen were simply trivial matters.

At his famous Treason Trial in 1956, in which he and one-hundred and fifty-five other defendants were acquitted after four years in court, he told the court that he wished to talk with the government. He said that he would accept an agreement whereby for five years, the black population had only partial representation in parliament, after which the situation would be reviewed again. He was always prepared to take a slower route to ease the concerns of the white population.

On the thirty-first of January 1985, the President of South Africa, P. W. Botha, made a surprising announcement in parliament: he offered Nelson Mandela his freedom, provided he, 'unconditionally rejected violence as a political weapon'. Ten days later, came Mandela's reply, read by his daughter Zindzi at a mass meeting of seventy-thousand people in Jabulani Stadium, Soweto.

After over twenty years in prison, most people would have renounced violence as a condition of release. But not Mandela. He refused to compromise. 'I cannot sell my birthright, nor am I prepared to sell the birth right of the people to be free', Mandela declared.

What was the point of accepting the government offer, he said, when apartheid still effectively reduces freedom to almost nothing? Mandela was prepared to remain in prison, patiently waiting for the changes he expected to arrive.

Despite being in his seventies upon his release from prison, he was prepared to wait patiently for a long period of transition before the country's first free elections took place. Mandela displayed further patience and flexibility in dealing with Inkatha's Chief Buthelezi, the Zulu tribal leader, who had not committed to the path of reconciliation. Mandela worked to convince Buthelezi to have Inkatha participate in the 1994 elections, a step which Buthelezi took only days before the election.

The need for patience is more relevant in our times than ever before. People want the vaccine for Covid-19 to reap instant results, not in twelve months' time. It is hard to accept the changes to our freedoms and lifestyle.

Impatience has its roots in frustration. It is a feeling of stress that starts when you feel that your needs and wishes are being ignored. There are many times we might have made a better deal or done a better job on a task, if only we had acted less quickly.

The Hebrew word for patience – savlanut – refers to the capacity to endure difficulty or inconvenience without complaint. For some, the greatest challenge of all is patience with self. We all have the potential for excellence but when it does not happen immediately, we get upset.

On becoming President in 1994, Nelson Mandela had to temper expectations to an eager public and urge patience. The required changes would not happen overnight. Change takes time. In the meantime, by displaying patience, in the manner of Mandela, we can give ourselves time to reflect on the bigger picture.

Forgive wherever possible

Mandela confirmed a powerful belief when he said, 'as I walked out the door toward the gate that would lead to my freedom, I knew if I didn't leave my bitterness and hatred behind, I'd still be in prison'. Was Mandela angry about his treatment at the hands of the apartheid regime? Absolutely. However, he had the foresight to see that forgiveness was essential to moving forward: both for himself and the country.

South Africa under Mandela could, like in many other countries, have descended into chaos and score settling. Show trials, mass rounding up and assassinations have long been the hallmarks of similar regime changes. Nevertheless, Mandela stated, 'you will achieve more in this world through acts of mercy than you will through acts of retribution'.

Mandela's greatest legacy was his total belief in reconciliation, as the only way in which South Africa could prosper. When the apartheid government began to negotiate secretly in the years before his release, it demanded to know how an ANC government would protect the interests of a white minority. Mandela told them that the whites were Africans as well and that ... the majority would need the minority.

Not only was he willing to forgive but work with those who had harmed him. Ever the strategist, Mandela stated that, 'if you want to make peace with your enemy, you have to work with your enemy. Then he becomes your partner'.

Mandela approached people with trust and attitude of hopefulness. His message of forgiveness was extended to all South African whites, regardless of their level of support for the previous apartheid regime. The gestures were not superficial, political stunts. He invited Percy Yutar to lunch, the man who headed the prosecution against Mandela and his co-accused and who had asked for the death sentence. After their meeting, Yutar spoke of him as a saintly man whilst Mandela commented, 'I wanted South Africa to see that I loved even my enemies whilst I hated the system that had turned us against one another'.

In 1995, he visited Betsie Verwoed, the ninety-four-year-old widow of Hendrik Verwoerd, one of the architects of apartheid. She expressed pleasure for his visit and he for the, 'typical Afrikaner hospitality', she had shown him.

Mandela's release from prison in February 1990 had been awaited and feared in equal measure. Many members of the white South African minority were terrified of the vengeance that often-followed revolutions. When Mandela chose instead to speak of a 'Rainbow Nation', he calmed many of his opponents fears in one fell swoop. It was this spirit of forgiveness that his government set up the Truth and Reconciliation Commission in South Africa. Rather than vengeance, the commission heard testimony that intended to heal the painful wounds that apartheid had inflicted. The model has been admired the world over for its success.

Forgiving yourself is often even harder. We are often haunted by previous mistakes and failings. A voice in our head repeats our mistakes over and over. The focus, like Mandela's, should be on the present and the future, not the past. Forgiveness can take time and much work but in forgiving ourselves, we often provide closure. In the words of Canadian author, Robin S. Sharma, 'forgiveness is not just a blessing you deliver to another human being. Forgiveness is also a gift you give yourself'.

Letting go is not easy. People naturally look for someone or something to blame for difficulties. Whether the feeling is justified or not, is irrelevant. If we remain in this state of mind, we will never be free. Mandela knew that to carry on holding the baggage of resentment and bitterness, would mean that he would still be in prison long after his release.

'Suffering can embitter and it can ennoble', explained Archbishop Desmond Tutu, who presided over the commission at Mr Mandela's request, 'and we were very fortunate that, in Madiba, it did the latter.'

Live life with integrity

Observing that, 'those who conduct themselves with morality, integrity and consistency need not fear the forces of inhumanity and cruelty', Mandela emphasised the importance of people in the political process. He tried hard to discourage a cult of personality around him and insisted that he was far from a saint. In old age, Mandela readily admitted that in his youth, he was a bit of a troublemaker and show-off. However, Mandela's success was largely due to his integrity. People knew what he stood for. On his release from prison, efforts to improve his own personal wealth and standing were simply not part of his agenda. Improving the livelihood of his people, ensuring their dignity as human beings and the betterment of his country would be his focus.

His belief in the greater good over his own comfort has already been discussed in his refusal to meet the criteria for his own release in 1985 by the government of P.W. Botha. As a result, many leading supporters of the old apartheid regime, who once denounced him as a terrorist, came to admire and even to venerate him.

Many of Africa's post-war governments failed because of the moral corruption of the leaders and parties in power. With Mandela, there were none of the scandals concerning the improper use of state resources, no lucrative contracts given out to cronies. He lived much of his time as president in a modest house in Johannesburg, where he made his own bed.

Mandela acknowledged his shortcomings. His achievements are all the greater because he admitted to errors. Mandela conceded that during his presidency, he did not act quickly enough, in respect of the HIV-AIDS epidemic that struck the country. Out of office, Mandela sought to right this wrong, campaigning for effective education and treatment for South Africans, after announcing that his son had died of AIDS in 2005.

South African photographer, Steve Bloom, whose father, Harry Bloom, was a political activist, tells the following story which summed up Mandela's integrity, 'during the 1950s, my parents, who were anti-apartheid activists, knew Nelson Mandela. I remember the story he told them about the occasion he saw a white woman standing next to her broken car in Johannesburg. He approached her and offered to help. After fiddling with the engine, he fixed the car. Thankful for his help, she offered to pay him sixpence'.

"Oh no, that's not necessary," he said, "I am only too happy to help."

"But why else would you, a black man, have done that if you did not want money?" she asked quizzically.

"Because you were stranded at the side of the road," he replied.

Mandela was the world's most admired public figure because of sincere gestures, like this. This was the man who, after all, invited his former jailer to attend his presidential inauguration as a VIP guest.

Integrity is unwavering honesty that shows a consistent and uncompromising adherence to moral and ethical principles. When people can be trusted to display integrity during difficult times, they become known as people who can be trusted and relied on to keep their word. Betraying principles and violating their supposed ethical code has been the hallmark of many politicians - not Mandela.

Staying loyal to your values, even in tough times, is crucial. Our character is often tested during hard times. Leaders are often under the microscope. If you are an employer, employees are often watching to see whether you are a person who sticks to their guns and does what they say.

Use humour

Seeing the funny side of things was important to Mandela. He emphasised, 'I like to make jokes even when examining serious situations. Because when people are relaxed, they can think properly'. Two months after Mandela had arrived at Robben Island, his lawyer George Bizos visited his client in prison. Mandela apologised to his lawyer for not introducing his guard of honour, identifying each of the eight guards surrounding him. Bizos would recall many years later, 'that they were so stunned that they actually behaved like a guard of honour, each respectfully shaking my hand'.

Mandela's humour was certainly a central part of his character. In many ways, Mandela adopted an approach to adversity that was right out of the book of Viktor Frankl. He was determined not to treat Robben Island as a place of constraint and suffering, but rather, as a place for intellectual debate and education.

The long period of detention had taught him altruism and the importance of a sense of humour. It was not the light-hearted, jocular banter that can be attributed to many politicians on the campaign trail. Rather, Mandela was able to use his humour to inject some observation or statement that transformed that humour into a serious point that caused you to think. He seized the opportunity, while people were still laughing, to challenge the perspective being promoted.

As a result, Mandela was able to defuse critics, win over doubters and charm the media using his sharp words. The humour and jovial manner were not just a ploy to woo crowds or disarm guests.

Robyn Curnow, a journalist for CNN, states that Mandela used humour to put people at ease. 'More often than not, he would poke fun at himself with classic comic timing. He would often start off a speech by thanking everyone for coming to listen to, "Such an old man"'.

A well-known story in South Africa is how, during multiparty talks before the 1994 democratic election, he would often tease the leader of a right-wing Afrikaner party, General Constant Viljoen, by saying, 'we have to let the white man talk; after all, he is from the supreme race'. A cheeky grin would subsequently appear, by which time, the chilly atmosphere would have been warmed up by nervous laughter.

His humour was the skilled and disciplined response of a person who had learned that the only way to speak the truth in the face of oppression was to cloak it in wit. He used humour as a tool to diffuse confrontations before they turned ugly or violent.

Ahmed Kathrasa, the veteran anti-apartheid activist, was jailed for life alongside Mandela in 1964. He spoke about the sense of community of life on Robben Island, with great warmth, fellowship, friendship, humour and laughter.

In 2004, at the age of eighty-five, Mr Mandela retired from public life to spend more time with his family and friends and engage in quiet reflection. 'Don't call me, I'll call you', he jokingly warned anyone thinking of inviting him to future engagements.

It is hard to imagine anyone surviving so many years in prison without maintaining a sense of humour. Mandela himself joked of his time in prison as a long holiday for twenty-seven years. A sense of humour is often our most useful tool when facing setbacks. Philosophical people, like Mandela, can 'laugh at adversity and make jokes about their misfortune'.

Chapter Sixteen

Winston Churchill

Success is never final. Failure is never fatal. It is the courage to continue that counts

Winston Churchill was the victorious wartime leader who saved Europe and indeed, the world from the spread of Nazism. Despite many triumphs in a long and colourful life, Churchill encountered many setbacks, in an existence not short of adversity.

Churchill was born into a wealthy and aristocratic family, in 1874. His school life was chequered, having experienced poor health, displaying bad behaviour and only narrowly passing his entrance exam into Harrow School.

Churchill's first attempt at winning a parliamentary seat ended in failure in 1899. He went onto pursue a career as a war correspondent, before being captured as a Prisoner of War during the Boer War in South Africa. He was taken to a prison camp in Pretoria but a month later, he made his escape and travelled three-hundred miles to safety. After becoming a national hero, he joined the army and began fighting in the war itself.

Churchill persisted in his attempts to enter parliament and successfully stood for the Conservatives in 1900. A long and colourful political career followed, but it was his experiences as First Lord of the Admiralty during the First World War that marked a low point in his life.

A quarter of a century before leading Britain in the Second World War, Churchill directed a military debacle at Gallipoli. Initially, blamed for the failure of the campaign, he was forced to accept a humiliating demotion to the position of Chancellor of the Duchy of Lancaster. This did not mark the lowest point in Churchill's life; that came in 1921, with the death of both his mother, followed by that of his beloved daughter, Marigold.

Churchill later returned to front line politics but encountered a huge political setback in 1925, as Chancellor of the Exchequer, when he returned Britain to the Gold standard in his first budget. By fixing the price at the pre-war rate, it was argued by economists at the time, that the decision led to economic depression, unemployment and the 1926 General Strike.

The period between 1929 to 1939 is often called his wilderness years as events conspired against him. Most notably, his views against German aggression in Europe were largely ignored. In December 1936, during the abdication crisis, Churchill also suffered one of the most humiliating days of his political career. He backed King Edward VIII, advising him to ignore the government's ultimatum to abdicate or abandon plans to marry Wallis Simpson. This led to a humiliating encounter in the House of Commons, where he was shouted down by all sides whilst attempting to come to the defence of the monarch.

Churchill had, however, correctly identified the growing strength of Germany's armed forces. He had predicted that the situation in Europe would lead to war and it did. In 1940, whilst remaining unpopular with many in the establishment, he became Prime Minister.

Despite proclaiming victory in the Second World War in May 1945, the man who had led Britain in war was not voted back into power in peacetime. Churchill remained in politics and after the general election of October 1951, again became Prime Minister until his resignation in April 1955.

Had he died before 1940, it is likely his obituary would have been less than flattering. By 1945, he was regarded as the saviour of the nation. Having seen so many dark days; made so many fundamental errors and experienced so many black moods, how did Winston Churchill turn into the national legend that he will forever be remembered as?

Never give in

'If you're going through hell, keep going' were the powerful words used by Churchill to encourage others in difficulty. Churchill's career undoubtedly had its up and downs. It is hard to think of a greater setback than that which occurred during his tenure as First Lord of the Admiralty during the First World War. The failed attempt to seize control of the Dardanelles and Gallipoli Peninsula resulted in over two-hundred fifty thousand allied casualties. It has been argued that the disaster prolonged the war and destabilised the Middle East.

The episode would haunt Churchill's political career for years to come. Churchill's wife thought her husband would never recover from his grief. Churchill lamented, 'I am the victim of a political intrigue. I am finished!'

Following the catastrophe, Churchill resigned from the government. He became an officer in the army and served on the Western Front until early 1916. To his credit, few would have been able to recover from such a damaging experience. The findings of the Dardanelles Commission later exonerated him of responsibility and he was recalled to the cabinet as Minister of Munitions.

Churchill had shown his refusal to give up early on in life. His well-known speech impediment saw him visit several doctors in the hope of correcting the problem. Despite this, Churchill came to be known as a great orator. He persevered and worked on his pronunciation, famously rehearsing such phrases as, 'the Spanish ships I cannot see for they are not in sight'. He taught himself to practice his speeches well in advance and developed the art of effective, loaded pauses.

The ability to fight back would serve Churchill and the nation well, in later years. He replaced Neville Chamberlain as Prime Minister in May 1940. On that very same day, Hitler invaded France and the Low Countries.

Those first few weeks as leader were marred by catastrophes, as France surrendered and then, on the fourth of June, three-hundred and thirty-eight thousand allied troops were evacuated from Dunkirk. Churchill's famous speeches and broadcasts were carefully constructed to raise British morale while sending a message of defiance to Germany. Churchill addressed the nation and vowed that, 'we shall defend our island, whatever the cost may be, we shall fight on the beaches, we shall fight on the landing grounds, we shall fight in the fields and in the streets, we shall fight in the hills; we shall never surrender'. Churchill's words prompted the Labour MP, Josiah Wedgwood, to say, 'That was worth one-thousand guns and the speeches of one-thousand years'.

Churchill's spirit began to rub off on the war itself. Severely outnumbered in the Battle of Britain, the RAF valiantly defeated the Luftwaffe and forced Hitler to abandon his invasion plans. In 1941, Winston Churchill returned to his old school, Harrow. His twenty-minute speech may not be as well-known as some of the more memorable addresses, but perfectly encapsulated the philosophy by which he lived his life and serve as a timeless lesson that can be applied to any of our own battles.

'Never give in, never give in, never, never, never, never- in nothing, great or small, large or petty - never give in except to convictions of honour and good sense. Never yield to force; never yield to the apparently overwhelming might of the enemy,' were his inspiring words.

Think ahead

Churchill developed the ability to foresee likely outcomes. 'Dear Germany, do destroy us last!' he remarked in 1935. Churchill's foresight was largely ignored during the 1930s. Robert Rhodes James, one of his biographers, wrote, 'By the end of 1933, Churchill was widely regarded as a failed politician, in whom no real trust could be reasonably placed; by June 1935, these opinions had been fortified further'.

Having retreated to his home at Chartwell in Kent to write books and newspaper articles, it was largely thought that his political career was over. The war-weary political establishment was loath to listen to his opposition to the rise of the Nazi Party in Germany. Churchill's preoccupation with Hitler was even viewed as scaremongering.

Churchill's concern at the speed of German re-armament was justified in March 1935, when Hitler announced German parity with British air power. He wrote an article for *The Strand Magazine* in November 1935, so scathing of Hitler, that the Germany government protested and banned its publication in Germany. He insisted that Hitler's promises were worthless and that giving in to the German dictator would lead to the subjugation of the British people. Only after the invasion of Poland, did it become clear to many that Churchill was right.

This ability to think ahead and embrace modernity had long been a characteristic associated with Churchill. In 1911, after becoming First Lord of the Admiralty, he saw that one-day, coal would be replaced by oil and made the decision to use oil as the primary source of power for naval vessels.

In 1914, a month before the First World War began, Churchill secured for the British Crown a fifty-one per cent controlling interest in the Anglo-Persian Oil Company for £2.2 million. That decision was enough to ensure British naval supremacy during the war. He had already ensured the Royal Navy was well prepared for battle having studied German naval progress and manoeuvres since his appointment, in 1911.

Without Churchill, the country may never have moved to modern warfare which helped win both World Wars, including the use of tanks and radar. Interestingly, he also saw the significance of keeping British soldiers and civilians healthy during the war and set up several projects to determine the best diets and exercise regimes for peak physical performance.

Long before his famous 'Iron Curtain' speech against Communist Russia, Churchill had seen the threat of communism against the West. In 1931, he demonstrated remarkable foresight before an audience in New York, by saying that the 'struggle of the future would be between English speaking nations and communism'.

Foresight is not so much about predicting what will happen (this is impossible) but about anticipating what may happen. Churchill's success as a statesman and leader can clearly be attributed, amongst other things, to his remarkable ability to see the challenges that lay ahead.

Believe in your destiny

Churchill did not shirk his responsibility when his moment arrived. 'All my past life had been a preparation for this hour and for this trial', he stated. Churchill's foresight would have been for nothing had he not become Prime Minister in May 1940. For Churchill this was a matter of fate. Though not a religious believer, even at an early age, Churchill felt that his life had purpose; all his prior struggles were but a preparation for the final trial as Prime Minister.

Churchill had an extraordinary sense of destiny, openly expressed at the age of sixteen when he told a school friend that at some time in the future, London would be in danger of invasion and 'It will fall to me to save the capital and save the Empire'.

In his six-volume history, *The Second World War*, Winston Churchill reflected on the moment he became Prime Minister in May 1940. 'I felt as if I were walking with destiny, and that all my past life had been but a preparation for this hour and for this trial', he said.

Perceived as a failure for much of his life, in the 1930s, Churchill was the last person anyone would have expected to lead Britain into war. But Churchill had a sense of mission - the defence of his country against foreign aggression.

Instead of feeling overwhelmed by the task ahead, he felt relieved. He believed he had cheated death so many times in the past because of the greater destiny that had to be fulfilled. A romantic believer of his country's greatness, it was as if he had come to see his long political exile in the 1930s as some kind of sabbatical before he assumed his role as the nation's saviour.

Whilst most certainly a flawed and complicated character, his sense of purpose helped guide him through difficult decisions when the fate of the free world was at stake.

When it came to decisions like the sinking of the French fleet, he made many difficult choices which historians continue to debate. 'This was the most hateful decision, the most unnatural and painful in which I have ever been concerned', he wrote. Whether a tough choice proved to be morally right or wrong, he made such decisions based on his underlying aim of protecting the nation.

How important is purpose in one's life? As discussed in Chapter One, the theory proposed by Viktor Frankl considers meaning and purpose to be the primary driver in a person's life.

As Churchill himself said, 'it is not enough to have lived. We should be determined to live for something'.

Focus on a hobby

Churchill always held a broad range of interests. 'The cultivation of a hobby and new forms of interest is, therefore, a policy of first importance', he once said. Churchill is known as the heroic wartime leader who led the Allies to victory in 1945. Such a role required courage, strategic expertise and sound judgement. What may be less known is the emphasis Churchill placed on activities that helped him unwind. In 1943, Churchill arrived in Casablanca for a summit with US President, Franklin D. Roosevelt. The Prime Minister insisted that the two leaders take a break to spend a few days in Marrakesh.

'You cannot come all the way to North Africa without seeing Marrakesh', Churchill told an unconvinced Roosevelt, who wanted to return to the United States. Churchill then opted to remain for an additional day to capture the sunset on canvas. That piece was his only wartime painting, but it allowed him to return to London revitalised.

Churchill first took up painting during the First World War. 'Just to paint is great fun', he wrote in his 1948 book,

Painting as a Pastime. Painting helped Churchill's unsettled mind, especially in dealing with tragedies such as the death of his youngest daughter, Marigold, in 1921. For him, it provided solace from personal grief and served as a welcome distraction from the bigger matters in his career.

Painting came to Churchill's rescue again in 1955, when he finally retired from office. At the age of eighty, he said, 'if it weren't for painting, I couldn't live; I couldn't bear the strain of things'.

The 1930s were possibly the quietest times in Churchill's professional life. In such times, he needed to keep himself busy, quite possibly to keep the 'Black Dog' of depression at bay. A master of the English language, his writing proliferated at an astonishing rate. In total, he wrote forty-three books, even winning the Nobel Prize for Literature in 1953.

Not one to sit around doing nothing, another hobby Churchill indulged in strangely enough, was bricklaying. He set about renovating his beloved home at Chartwell in Kent. A qualified member of the Union of Bricklayers, he laid a red brick wall around the vegetable garden with a trowel in one hand and a cigar in the other.

Despite his many responsibilities, Churchill appeared eminently capable of switching off, commenting that, 'to be really happy and really safe, one ought to have at least two or three hobbies, and they must all be real'.

Churchill showed the importance of reserving time for activities that helped improve mental health and wellbeing. It is also important to note the emphasis Churchill placed on exercise, such as swimming. A guest visiting Chartwell on Christmas Day, discovered the entire Churchill family in bathing suits in the drawing room.

Whether it was his enjoyment of fine brandy, his interest in butterfly breeding, farming or horse racing, Churchill taught that to be active in other pursuits is sometimes as important as the time spent on bigger challenges.

Develop a routine to suit you

'Don't think you will be doing less work because you sleep during the day. That's a foolish notion held by people who have no imagination. You will be able to accomplish more', Churchill confirmed. Most people would do well to achieve a fraction of Churchill's achievements in a lifetime. Between the two wars, he wrote a five-volume memoir of the First World War, an autobiography of his early years, a biography of the first Duke of Marlborough, several books of essays and speeches and over four hundred articles. That was in addition to the range of hobbies already noted, and his various roles in government and as a serving MP.

What is most striking is the nature of Churchill's daily routine. Unusual? Most certainly. Unproductive? Most certainly not. In fact, Churchill went so far as to claim his productivity was boosted by the routine he set for himself.

He regarded his midday naps as sacrosanct, vital for maintaining his mental balance and renewing his energy. Even during the Blitz, Churchill would disappear to his private room in the War Rooms after lunch and sleep. He would then return to Downing Street for a bath, change into new clothes and return to his work.

One should not confuse Churchill's curious habits with laziness; it was a schedule that simply worked for him. Having spent years in the military, Churchill was adept at keeping to a disciplined schedule. F. W Deakin, the chief researcher for Churchill's biography of his ancestor, John Churchill, recalled that, 'he was totally organized, almost like a clock. His routine was dictatorial. He set himself a ruthless timetable every day and would get very agitated, even cross, if it was broken'.

Churchill started the day at Chartwell at eight o'clock in the morning, with a full English breakfast and the occasional glass of wine. His bed served as his office, where he reviewed the newspapers, dictated letters, read and worked on his speeches until late morning.

After taking a bath, he dressed and began his day. A hearty lunch was taken, before a leisurely walk around the gardens and pond. This was followed by his nap of exactly one hour. The nap, he claimed, allowed him to get thirty or more hours out of every twenty-four. The evening hours were spent playing cards with his family, taking another bath, and having dinner. Churchill's second work shift of the day began at eleven o'clock in the evening and usually ended at around two o'clock in the morning.

The historian, Paul Johnson was a boy in 1946, when he approached Churchill in the street and asked to what he attributed his success in life. 'Conservation of energy. Never stand up when you can sit down. And never sit down when you can lie down', came Churchill's prompt answer. Indeed, one must remember that Churchill did not become Prime Minister until he was sixty-six, a post he held for a second time into his eighties. Therefore, it made sense to preserve his energy for when it most mattered.

Boris Johnson, another Churchill biographer, described Churchill as a '100-horsepower mental engine', when one-hundred horsepower was a lot. 'His makeup meant that he had to work; he was simply incapable of idleness'.

The Entertainers

Chapter Seventeen

Walt Disney

All the adversity I've had in my life, all my troubles and obstacles, have strengthened me … You may not realize it when it happens, but a kick in the teeth may be the best thing in the world for you

Walt Disney is best known as an animator, movie producer and creator of Mickey Mouse. Disney stands alone as the record holder for the most Academy Awards earned by an individual, winning a total of twenty-two Oscars from fifty-nine nominations. Not bad for a once penniless animator, who transformed a small studio into the world's largest media empire.

Disney's childhood was not a happy one. His father was a tough disciplinarian who dispensed regular beatings. As a young boy, he found his escape in drawing and animation, hawking his pictures to neighbours and family friends. When Disney was sixteen years old, he dropped out of school to fight in the First World War but was rejected for being underage. He joined the Red Cross and drove an ambulance for a year in France. On his return home in 1919, he started working life as a newspaper artist. Eventually, Walt decided to start his own animation business, but things began badly. His first enterprise resulted in bankruptcy. He relocated to Los Angeles where he teamed up with brother Roy, to set up Walt Disney Studios in 1923.

Disney's first successful film came in 1928, when *Steamboat Willie* starring Mickey Mouse, was released. Disney himself played the voice of Mickey and the cartoon was an overnight sensation.

His first full-length animated film was *Snow White and the Seven Dwarfs*, which premiered in 1937 and won eight Oscars.

Disney went on to produce over one-hundred feature films, the last of which was the cult classic *Mary Poppins*. Disney was also one of those first to see the potential of television as an outlet for entertainment, creating classics such as *Zorro* and *Davy Crockett*, as well as the much-loved *Mickey Mouse Club*.

Despite the massive success, there were plenty of low points. *Pinocchio* and *Fantasia* were both released during the Second World War and neither did particularly well. Losses were made on both productions and the studio was heavily in debt by 1941. *Bambi* was another flop that lost over two-hundred thousand dollars.

With almost childlike zeal, Disney refused to let disappointments stand in his way of his vision. He was an early pioneer of the theme park industry, opening his seventeen-million-dollar Disneyland Theme Park in July 1955 in Anaheim, California.

Few individuals have had a greater impact on both the entertainment industry and popular culture of the twentieth century. One of the studio's most popular cartoons, *Flowers and Trees*, was the first to be produced in colour and the title song to the 1933 classic, *The Three Little Pigs*, *Who's afraid of the Big Bad Wolf* became an unofficial theme tune for the country during the Great Depression.

Disney experienced his fair share of misfortunes along the way. Bankruptcy, a mental breakdown, and a crippling studio strike were all devastating events. Yet, his story provides an example of someone who grew up in hardship, faced adversity and still managed to accomplish unparalleled success. What was the secret behind his success?

Learn from your failures
Looking back, Walt saw failure as having a beneficial impact, saying, 'I think it's important to have a good hard failure when you're young ... I learned a lot out of that'. In early 1921, Disney started his first company, Laugh-O-Gram Studio, and obtained a contract for six animations. However, Disney had made a bad

deal in signing a distribution contract, with the company receiving only one-hundred dollars up front with the balance of eleven-thousand dollars to be paid after all films had been delivered. This gave the company no working capital to make the films or pay salaries. Disney attempted to revive his company through the production of *Alice's Wonderland*, a short film displaying live human action with animation. Unfortunately, things went from bad to worse. The film was completed too late to save the studio. In 1923, faced with mounting debts and no money to pay creditors, Disney was forced to file for bankruptcy.

The failure could have resulted in humiliation and ended his career there and then. However, from a creative point of view, *Alice's Wonderland* proved a tremendous encouragement for Disney. He took the film with him when he moved to Los Angeles and in 1924, received backing for a series of short films, which proved to be a major step on the way to making the Mickey Mouse animation series.

Laugh-O-Gram taught Disney that he was no financial expert. He took the decision to team up with his financially savvy older brother, Roy, who from then on, took most business decisions for him.

By 1928, Disney had created Oswald the Lucky Rabbit. Unfortunately, Disney had not realised that the character was copyrighted under the distributor, Universal, rather than in his own name. In February 1928, Disney travelled to New York, in the hope of negotiating a larger fee for producing the series but found his distributor, Charles Mintz, threatening to start his own studio if Disney refused to accept payment reductions. Disney refused Mintz's demand and lost most of his animation staff.

Instead of plotting his revenge, Disney shrugged his shoulders and moved on. On the long train ride home, he came up with an idea to create another character, Mickey Mouse, who would soon become the most successful cartoon character in film history. Walt learned from his naïve mistake and registered the Mickey Mouse trademark in May 1928.

Even after Disney gained acclaim, his projects were not immune from failure. The opening of Disneyland in 1955 is remembered as 'Black Sunday' by critics, with malfunctioning rides and broken water fountains amongst the initial teething problems. But Disney learnt from the experience and Disneyland grew into what it is today.

Walt Disney was able to forgive himself for his fundamental business mistakes and used failure as a valuable learning tool. He made the frank admission, 'I've made some bad ones, (mistakes) but fortunately, the successes have come along fast enough to cover up the mistakes'.

Stick at it

'If you can dream it, you can do it', said Walt. Being fired from his first job with the *Kansas City Star* newspaper for not being creative enough, spurred Disney on to start his own business. At the time, the only thing he had to show for his previous decade's work was an incomplete short reel he had created called *Alice's Wonderland*. After that failure, he swore to make amends, and travelled to Hollywood to become an animator and live-action film director.

Disney sent letters soliciting distributors for the reel although he received nothing but rejection letters in return. He was fortunate to eventually catch the attention of Margaret Winkler, a New York film distributor, who offered one-thousand five-hundred dollars for six Alice comedies. The animations were well received and Winkler ordered more. Shortly after, Disney and his brother, Roy, created the Disney Brothers Studio which later became the Walt Disney Company.

In his attempts to put Mickey Mouse onto the big screen, Disney tried tirelessly to get bankers to fund his efforts. When he approached MGM studios in 1927, he was told that the idea would never work. After all, a giant mouse would terrify women. Yet Disney would not hear of it and Mickey Mouse ended up as one of the most celebrated animated figures of the twentieth century.

Snow White is another case in point. Industry experts scoffed at attempts to produce the first animated feature length movie. Nothing like it had been attempted before. Although initially sceptical, Disney's animators were won over at an impassioned meeting in 1934. The project went considerably over budget, pushing the overall cost to a remarkable $1.5 million. Disney was determined to complete the project, personally showing raw footage of the film to bank manager, Joseph Rosenberg, to obtain the funds needed to finish. Through Disney's sheer persistence, *Snow White and the Seven Dwarfs* met its deadline and held its premiere in December 1937.

If Walt Disney had listened to those around him, his theme parks would never have been built. The plans were described as absurd, but Disney refused to listen to the negativity. The opening day of Disneyland was also a disaster, but Disney assured the press that, 'we'll settle down and get this place operating', before adding, 'it may take a month before everything's going smoothly'. Such was his resolve to get things right, that he was a constant presence at the park, even staying in a hidden apartment in Main Street on site, where he would sometimes be spotted at the window as he looked out over his staff.

According to nephew Roy Disney, 'if Walt had one great gift, it was that he kept his head down and kept trying ... Over the years, he was told that his ideas were impractical, impossible and would never work ... Walt proved the only way to get things done is by sticking to your ideas and your beliefs'.

Too often in life, people give up after a rejection or two, feeling that instant acceptance is what is needed to validate the viability of an idea or project. Disney, on the other hand, was prepared to tolerate rejection because he was so determined to see his projects succeed.

Take Risks

Walt once said, 'I dare to take risks'. Like many successful entrepreneurs, Disney was somewhat of a 'calculated risk-taker', literally betting the house on his projects succeeding. Occasionally, the risks failed but at other times, the gambles paid off.

When Walt Disney was at his lowest ebb, his creation of Mickey Mouse was a huge risk, given the initial feedback he received. Yet, without taking that chance, Disney would never have succeeded.

During the 1930s, shortly after the Great Depression, when most of America was struggling, Disney was willing to push the boat out for the *Snow White* production. 'We had a little money rolling in', he said, 'but not enough to finance such a big deal. Our assets were pretty impressive though we had our studio and a backlog of marketable pictures, so we could get credit backing'.

No expense was spared, with Disney procuring the best animators to ensure the film succeeded. The risk paid off; *Snow White* went on to earn eight-million dollars as well as an academy award.

Away from the film studio, Disney had always dreamt of an amusement park, a real-life version of the fantasy world Disney escaped to in his youth. Getting the money to finance the project was the major problem. So, Walt mortgaged his life insurance and assets to purchase an orange grove near Anaheim, California, in 1955. The project was mockingly called, 'Walt's folly'. Even brother Roy thought that a 'fanciful, expensive amusement park would lead to financial ruin'.

With his reputation and finances at stake, Disney pressed on with the project, keeping his promise to open the park only a year after construction begun. Again, the gamble paid off. An estimated seventy million people, in a country of one-hundred and sixty-five million, tuned in to watch the unveiling co-hosted by actor and future President, Ronald Reagan. The opening may have been shambolic, but visitors arrived in droves and within weeks, Disneyland was a success.

Disney got to the top because he was bold and willing to push boundaries. A risk taker certainly, but one who knew when to back himself. Never was this more evident than in his last major success, the adaptation of *Mary Poppins* into a cinematic masterpiece. Producing the motion picture himself, the film was unique for featuring both live action and animation. He was told no one would sit through an animated feature film and in the case of *Mary Poppins*, animation could not be mixed with real life actors. Children the world over continue to enjoy the film to this day, making it a risk that paid off.

Taking risks brings confidence and helps people move beyond their fears. Playing it safe may be virtuous and bring steady results, but as T.S. Eliot, the British poet said, 'only those who will risk going too far can possibly find out how far it is possible to go'.

Disney demonstrated the difference between blind risk, which is foolish and rarely works out and intelligent risk taking, which is based on a forensic examination of the situation and calculated action. Without risk-taking, successful people like Disney would not have achieved a fraction of their eventual achievements.

Wear your heart on your sleeve

Walt claimed, 'I have never been interested in personal gain or profit. This business and this studio have been my entire life'. His career suffered numerous setbacks but his legacy as an inspirational cartoonist and animator lives on. The driving force behind his success was not his desire for financial reward; rather it was his enthusiasm for his projects.

Disney's passion for drawing began at a young age. He started by drawing cartoons for his school newspaper and by the time he was eighteen years old, decided to become a newspaper cartoonist. He was inspired at the time by Lewis

Carroll's *Alice in Wonderland* and by cartoon-strips in newspapers.

At the height of his career, he became so immersed in the production of the films that he even spoke of the characters as if they were real people. *Snow White and The Seven Dwarfs* was an example of his passion rubbing off on others. Although initially, taken aback by the thought of drawing an eighty-minute animated film, the animators were captivated by Disney's presentation. 'He was doing something no other studio had ever attempted', art director Ken Anderson said, 'but his excitement over *Snow White and The Seven Dwarfs* inspired us all'. Disney film editor, Norman Palmer, captured the feeling amongst Disney employees. He stressed, 'Walt's enthusiasm made overachievers of us all. He transmitted his excitement to all of us'.

It was this enthusiasm that saw him willingly give up his apartment and living out of the office in an attempt to get his first business venture, Laugh-O-Gam, to succeed.

One day, Walt made a presentation to a company he wished to sponsor an attraction at the new theme park. He managed to convince the board that it was a great deal for the company and they agreed there and then to the sponsorship. After Disney had left, one board member, who had been so taken to Walt's passion, turned to his fellow board members and said, 'I have a question. What did we just buy?'

Towards the end of Disney's life, the flame continued to burn deep inside him. He kept pushing for bigger, more adventurous projects. Even whilst suffering with terminal cancer, Disney's final months were spent preparing to build his most ambitious project to date, the Experimental Prototype Community of Tomorrow (EPCOT), in Central Florida.

In a 1953 profile of Walt, AP reporter Bob Thomas wrote, 'one element characterizes all movies bearing the Walt Disney label. That is enthusiasm. It is not hard to account for. It comes from the head man himself'.

To those currently experiencing difficult times, the message from Disney and indeed, others within this book, is to retain enthusiasm for whatever it is you are passionate about. For as Winston Churchill maintained, 'success consists of going from failure to failure without loss of enthusiasm'.

In difficult times, many people find themselves disillusioned by failure or defeat. Disney's enthusiasm to carry on, despite hardship and the Great Depression of the 1930s, serves as a lesson to aspiring entrepreneurs and those who have been harshly affected by the current economic realities. Peter Ellenshaw, the British born special effects creator, worked on many Disney features. He called Disney's enthusiasm, 'contagious ... we all felt it. Walt's enthusiasm powered everything we did'.

Know your limitations

Walt was clear about what he could and couldn't do, stating, 'I have always had men working for me whose skills were greater than my own. I am an idea man'. Disney was someone who was aware of his limitations. But rather than seeing this in a negative light, this realisation allowed him to focus on his own strengths.

Many Disney critics argue that his behaviour was characteristic of a control freak, unwilling to surrender control over business matters to others. There is no shortage of literature available which voices this view. However, there is also ample evidence to counter this argument. After his first bankruptcy, Disney resolved to leave financial matters to the experts whilst he focused on directing and producing.

Disney's success was in large part, due to his unassuming brother, Roy, the sensible, financial operator behind Walt's successes. The two men clashed regularly over the years, but the conflicts were always creative in nature. Alone, it was doubtful either would reach their potential but together, they were an unstoppable force. Roy's financial and managerial proficiency freed up Walt to dream and create. Additionally, Roy acted as devil's advocate to coax the best out his brother.

Roy helped Walt understand how to execute on his grand ideas and pulled him back when his ambitions exceeded what was financially possible. It was not until Walt moved to Los Angeles in 1923 and teamed up with his older brother that he began to see any kind of success.

Roy's most famous contribution was in helping to acquire the land that would become the home of Walt Disney World. In the early 1960s, Walt and Roy embarked on a secret plan, known simply as Project X to scour the country for a location for a second theme park. Had people known that Disney was interested in buying up swamp land in Florida, the price of the land would have increased ten-fold and jeopardised the project. Instead, Roy partnered with a Florida law firm to form a series of companies designed to disguise the ultimate buyer of land.

In the animation department too, Disney was prepared to accept help from talented colleagues. Ub Iwerks was an illustrator who Disney had worked with since 1919. Iwerks assisted Disney on the design of Mickey Mouse, revising the initial sketches to make the character easier to animate. By this point, Disney was starting to move away from animating and entrusted the design of the character to Iwerks. As a Disney employee put it, 'Ub designed Mickey's physical appearance, but Walt gave him his soul'.

He originally planned to called Mickey Mouse 'Mortimer'. However, his wife, Lillian, thought it sounded, 'too sissy' and suggested the name Mickey instead. As was often the case, taking his wife's advice turned out to be sound judgement.

Disney also listened to his doctors when he was on the verge of a breakdown in 1932. He understood that a long rest was required. On his return, he realised that to preserve his creative energy, he needed to take a slight step back. Walt got the advice to relax, exercise and develop a few hobbies.

Disney demonstrated that asking for help, is not a sign of weakness, but rather a strength.

Chapter Eighteen

Audrey Hepburn

Nothing is impossible. The word itself says I'm possible

Audrey Hepburn is best known as the star of the classic movie *Breakfast at Tiffany's*. Her iconic image is so well known that she has been described as a recognisable brand in her own right.

Behind the beauty, style and elegance, lies a deeply painful story, filled with obstacles, all of which served to shape the character of a remarkable woman.

Born in Belgium, Hepburn was the daughter of an English banker and a Dutch baroness. When she was six years old, her parents separated. Audrey's father was a known Nazi sympathiser, something which caused her tremendous anguish. Her mother also appeared to harbour fascist sentiments, although her views changed during the war.

An introverted child, Hepburn was sent to boarding school in England at age five. Before the onset of the Second World War, Audrey's mother took the family to the Netherlands to benefit from Holland's neutrality. The move was futile as Holland was subsequently occupied by the Germans in May 1940. It was there that Audrey witnessed the heart-breaking sight of deportations of neighbouring Jewish families to the death camps. In 1942, Audrey's uncle was arrested and murdered in retaliation for acts performed by the Dutch resistance.

Hepburn did her bit to resist the invading forces. She volunteered to help the sick and wounded and danced in secret to raise funds for the Dutch resistance. It is also alleged that she helped deliver messages on behalf of the movement. Nazi reprisals included rounding up Dutch women and girls to work in German kitchens; Hepburn was rounded up, but somehow managed to escape.

In 1945, the joy of liberation brought with it the harsh reality that her dreams of becoming a professional ballerina had been crushed by ill health. When she was sixteen years old, she weighed just eighty-eight pounds and suffered from asthma, jaundice and anaemia.

Hepburn switched attention to the stage, starring as a chorus girl in London West End musicals before appearing in minor roles in several films. Her breakthrough moment came in 1951, when she starred in the Broadway play, *Gigi*.

It was the romantic comedy, *Roman Holiday* that turned Audrey Hepburn into an overnight sensation. She became the first actress to win an Academy Award, BAFTA and Golden Globe for performance in the same role. A hugely successful film career followed. She won another Oscar for her role in the box office hit, *My Fair Lady*.

Considerable personal heartbreak followed; she suffered four miscarriages and two broken marriages before finding happiness with Dutch actor, Robert Wolders.

Her humanitarian work, on behalf of suffering children, was no less impressive. She worked in Africa, South America, and Asia between 1988 and 1992. In 1989, Hepburn was appointed a Goodwill Ambassador of UNICEF. She never forgot the international aid that she benefited from towards the end of the German occupation and wanted to show her gratitude to the organisation.

In December 1992, Hepburn received the United States' highest civilian award, the Presidential Medal of Freedom. Despite being so slight and vulnerable, what qualities allowed Hepburn to leave such an impressive legacy?

Never give up
'Your soul is nourished by all your experiences ... it gives you baggage for the future — and ammunition, if you like', Hepburn once said. The terrible suffering, encountered as a girl, lived with Hepburn throughout her life. 'Don't discount anything

awful you hear or read about the Nazis. It's worse than you could ever imagine', she once said.

Those harsh experiences served to mould her outlook on life and prepared her for difficult experiences in her professional life in Hollywood. The Hepburn family, like many other Dutch households, suffered terribly during the 'Hunger Winter' of 1944, relying on boiled grass and tulip bulbs, grinding them into flour to make cake and biscuits.

Audrey's experiences could have been written by a Hollywood scriptwriter. Still a teenager, she danced before silent crowds, raising money for the Dutch resistance. The events came to be known as black evenings. The windows were blacked out, so the Germans did not know what was going on. None of the spectators dared to applaud, in case it alerted passing German troops.

Hepburn ignored the potential consequences and risked her life for the Dutch Resistance, ferrying messages to British and American fliers who had been shot down over Holland and delivering the resistance newspaper to Dutch loyalists.

Adversity can break some people, but not Audrey Hepburn. Her response was to show her resilience. Her wartime efforts provided her with a platform in which she developed her mental toughness. She was able to put a positive spin on those early life difficulties, speaking of her time in Holland as one that offered a tremendous learning opportunity. 'Being without food, fearful for one's life, the bombings ... all made me appreciative of safety, of liberty'.

Anyone can learn to become resilient in the face of adversity. Just like Audrey Hepburn, the way in which a person engages with their circumstances, determines their fate. It was the belief of the writer, William Arthur Ward, that, 'adversity causes some men to break; others to break records'.

War often forces a person to mature quickly and those trying circumstances provided Audrey Hepburn with the inner strength to pursue her career with vigour. 'It made me resilient and terribly appreciative for everything good that came afterwards', she said. Once she had been through such testing experiences, the stress of an audition simply could not compare to the battles she had already triumphed over during the war.

Show humility

Audrey Hepburn's view of herself was always a humble one, a self-perception confirmed when she said, 'I never think of myself as an icon. What is in other people's minds is not in my mind. I just do my thing'. Hepburn brushed off compliments about her style and acting ability. She would regularly joke that she did not deserve to be cast in the roles alongside Hollywood's greats. Yet, she remains a Hollywood icon who is regularly voted as one of the best actresses of all time. Fashion writers regularly enthuse about her style in *Breakfast at Tiffany's*, with Hepburn holding a cup of coffee, staring into a shop window.

A large part of Hepburn's success and popularity, which remains to this day, came about because of her modesty and down-to-earth nature. She enthralled audiences with star performances in *Sabrina, Funny Face* and the classic 1961 movie, *Breakfast at Tiffany's*. Nevertheless, she never really seemed to belong in the superficial world of Hollywood.

Despite the success of the film, *Roman Holiday*, she insisted she was still learning her trade and was humble enough to admit it rather than let fame go to her head. She rejected praise, in all aspects of her life, not because it helped her image, but because it was genuinely part of her personality.

Fred Zinnemann, the film director, cast Audrey in the role of Sister Luke, in *The Nun's Story* in 1959. He spoke of how delightful it had been to work with the young actress. 'There was no ego, no asking for extra favours; there was the greatest consideration for her co-workers', he confirmed.

On her trips to Somalia as part of her humanitarian work towards the end of her life, she was known to roll her sleeves up and take an active part in activities on the ground. UNICEF director, James Grant, told an interviewer, 'what you see in

Audrey Hepburn is exactly what you get. There is no public or private persona. She is what she seems to be. It may sound boring, but Audrey is one of the most special human beings I've ever met in my entire life'.

C.S. Lewis, the British writer confirmed the value of humility. He may even have had Hepburn in mind when he famously stated, 'humility is not thinking less of yourself, it's thinking about yourself less'.

Sean Hepburn Ferrer, Audrey's son, also testified to his mother's modesty, 'when people complimented her, she would always shy away and ultimately explain how those who surrounded her were the reason for her success'.

Hepburn's humility endeared her to admirers worldwide and showed a human side that contrasted sharply to the attitudes of other Hollywood stars at the time.

Get your priorities right

Despite her glamorous life in Hollywood, Audrey Hepburn never forgot the most important people in her life: her family. She was married twice. Her first marriage to actor, Mel Ferrer, produced a son, Sean; whilst her second marriage to Andrea Dotti, resulted in a second son, Luca. She once said, 'I may not always be offered work. But I will always have my family'.

According to Luca, she was never happier than when she was home with her family. In 1966, Audrey Hepburn did what many working mothers would love to be able to do: she put her career on hold. This was no great sacrifice for Audrey, for being at home for her children when they arrived home each day is what she truly yearned for. She noted that this was preferable to being miserable on a movie set wondering how her kids were getting on.

After a difficult childhood, in which she was estranged from her father at a young age, all Audrey really dreamed of was a warm home and children.

The small village of Tolochenaz-sur-morges in Switzerland became her refuge. Spending time at a place she referred to as La Paisible, 'a place of peace', with her children and dogs, brought her contentment and respite from the health problems she is believed to have suffered from.

In a frank interview with Maggie Gogler in March 2020, Sean Hepburn spoke of the normality of his upbringing. 'The greatest gift she gave us and me, is that she gave it (fame) all up, to be a full-time mum. We had a normal house with a regular mum, that whenever you woke up in the morning, she made you breakfast, always picked you up from school, bought all the necessary school supplies etc.'.

After her second marriage, in 1969, to Dr Andrea Dotti, an Italian psychiatrist, she announced that in future, she would only undertake work in Rome or Switzerland. 'My family always comes first', Hepburn insisted - 'Being separated from my children is too high a price to pay'.

Many actors have left everything behind to seek fame and fortune in Hollywood but according to Barry Parris, author of the book *Audrey Hepburn*, all she really wanted was to be married to a decent guy and have children.

After two failed marriages, Audrey finally met actor and businessman, Robert Wolders in 1980. He accompanied her on all the trips she made to Africa and Central America on behalf of UNICEF and the two lived out an almost idyllic life over her final thirteen years. Audrey called this period the happiest time of her life. 'It took a while, but I got here', she once joked, a few years prior to her death when she was sixty years old.

Audrey Hepburn loved acting, but she was also aware of the pitfalls of life in Hollywood. According to her publicist and close friend, Henry Rodgers, 'she never had a burning desire to become and remain a move star, as do most actresses, but instead, cared only for personal happiness, peace, love, her children and a husband whom she loved and who loved her'.

Family is one of the most active sources anyone can have to provide positive support and wisdom for the journey of life. Audrey Hepburn understood this and after so many difficult experiences, it was around her family that she lived out her final years in quiet serenity.

Turn negatives into positives

Hepburn's approach was a combination of being selfish and selfless. She said, 'As you grow older, you will discover that you have two hands, one for helping yourself, the other for helping others'. Audrey suffered greatly when her parents divorced early on in her life. Her wartime experiences have also been discussed, as has her two divorces. She also suffered four miscarriages, one of them after being thrown from a horse on the set of *The Unforgiven*. The actress later admitted, 'after yet another miscarriage, I was almost on the verge of insanity'.

She spoke of the need to turn all these experiences into a positive: 'I couldn't conquer those feelings by acting indecisive. I found the only way to get the better of them was by adopting a forceful, concentrated drive'.

Her experiences created a stronger character, something some actors never get around to developing. She took her negative feelings and experiences and used them as a springboard towards success. Her light-hearted nature was demonstrated in her ability to shine in comedy productions, a trait revealed in her early films *Roman Holiday, Funny Face* and *Sabrina*.

In the 1956 film, *War and Peace*, she was cast in the role of Natasha. Her own experiences during the Second World War enhanced her appreciation for the experiences of her character and allowed her to identify with the role.

There are many examples of people who turn their adversity into success by contributing to the lives of others. Audrey Hepburn was one of these people. By recalling her own personal suffering during the war, Audrey Hepburn showed that the most constructive response to suffering is kindness. In 1988, Audrey Hepburn became a Special Ambassador for UNICEF. In 1990, on behalf of the orgnisation, she travelled to a remote, mountainous area of Vietnam to raise funds for poor children.

The trip served as a precursor to her most heart-wrenching tour to Somalia in 1992. As a spokesperson for children in crises, she threw herself into her humanitarian work. On her arrival in a country ravaged by civil war, Hepburn watched as one-hundred dead children were loaded onto a truck. 'I walked right into a nightmare, Hepburn recalled. 'No stories in the press could prepare me for what I saw. The unspeakable agony of it!', she continued.

The mission brought the world's attention to the plight of Somalia. CNN joined forces with other media outlets to provide coverage of the horrors of war and famine. Soon, food arrived under the protection of the United Nations peacekeepers and the US Navy. President Bush sent thousands of American troops to Somalia to curb the violence. Mass starvation was quelled and all because a dignified, compassionate and selfless woman remembered her own upbringing and choose to live her life by the philosophy of serving others.

Difficult experiences in life may be inevitable. Audrey Hepburn showed that turning negatives into positives, whilst not easy, is entirely possible.

Take Your chances

Hepburn was clear about the need to both see and take opportunities when they presented themselves. She stated, 'I've been lucky. Opportunities do not often come along. So, when they do, you have to grab them'. In 1951, the film *Monte Carlo Baby*, was being shot in the South of France. The French novelist, Colette, saw Audrey on a crowded filmset and proclaimed that she had discovered the perfect actress for a Broadway play, based on one of her novels. 'My dear', Colette told her, 'I have just cabled New York to tell them to stop looking for a Gigi. I have found her'.

Whilst it was certainly a case of being in the right place, at the right time, Audrey still had to prove herself on the biggest stage. She had to undertake a crash course in acting and producer, Gilbert Miller, was filled with doubt before the premiere in Philadelphia. However, he stuck with Hepburn and she was soon being hailed as the new star of the stage. The theatre critic, Walter Kerr, described her performance as, 'fresh and frisky as a puppy out of a tub'.

In auditions for the 1953 film, *Roman Holiday*, Hepburn so impressed the director, William Wyler that he opted to choose her, a relatively unknown actress, ahead of the favourite, Elizabeth Taylor. When Hepburn acted out a scene from the film, the cameraman kept the film rolling after the director's cut. The unscripted filming showed Hepburn at her natural, sparkling best. 'She was absolutely delightful ... acting, looks, and personality ... she was absolutely enchanting, and we said, 'That's the girl!' Wyler remembered.

Many successful people fully admit they were never the most talented amongst their peers. They often speak of that one person who was blessed with far more talent, but who never made it. Talent does not necessarily equal success.

What matters is the ability to take that chance when it presents itself. There is no shortage of competition in life. It is imperative, therefore, to invest the time and effort in preparation for that big moment, the big game, job interview, examination, audition, or presentation.

Gregory Peck, Hepburn's co-star, already had eighteen films and four Oscar nominations under his belt whilst *Roman Holiday* was Audrey's first major role. Peck later admitted that the real star of the film was Audrey Hepburn. 'We all knew that this was going to be an important star and we began to talk off-camera about the chance that she might win an Academy Award in her first film,' he remembered. Hepburn did indeed take her chances when they arrived.

Chapter Nineteen

Bruce Lee

Do not pray for an easy life, pray for the strength to endure a difficult one

Bruce Lee died over forty-five years ago, but his legacy lives on. It endures not only in the films he made and the martial arts he taught, but also in the philosophy he left behind. The iconic image of this martial arts star has long been associated with triumph over suffering. Along the way, he shared with the world, a rich collection of teachings, which can provide inspiration to anyone experiencing hardship.

The son of a Chinese opera star, Lee was born in San Francisco in 1940. His family returned to Hong Kong, where he appeared in several films as a child.

Despite this, Lee's childhood was not an easy one. He struggled in school, as racial tensions simmered between Chinese students and British schoolchildren. Having been bullied after school, he came home one day and told his parents he wanted to learn how to defend himself properly. When he was sixteen years old, Lee was introduced to Yip Man, a local teacher of the martial art, Wing Chun. Lee attended sessions every day after school, excelling in the discipline, having chosen organised competition over street fighting.

Lee did, however, have one further altercation on the streets. A police detective visited the Lee household and warned Robert Lee, that if his son got into another fight, he might have to put him in jail. This forced his parents into sending their son back to his country of his birth. Leaving his family and friends for the United States was a worrying prospect. He barely knew anyone and arrived with only one-hundred dollars in his pocket. He made his way to Seattle where he worked in the restaurant of a family friend. After enrolling in the University of Washington, Lee began to teach martial arts, opening his first school in 1959. After meeting his wife Linda, the couple moved to Oakland, California, where he opened another school.

At a martial exhibition in 1964, Lee was spotted by television producer, William Dozier, which led to him playing the role of Kato in the series *The Green Hornet*. During this time, Lee also worked on developing his own martial art, named Jeet Kune Do. The format is often acknowledged as the forerunner for modern mixed martial arts (MMA). Lee appeared in tournaments around the country and taught martial arts to private clients including the actor, Steve McQueen.

Like other ethnic minority actors, Lee suffered from the racial prejudice that was endemic in Hollywood. When *The Green Hornet* was cancelled, he pitched an idea called *The Warrior* to Warner Bros. Though Lee had worked tirelessly on the project, the studio ignored his credentials, instead selecting a white actor, David Carradine, with no knowledge of Kung Fu, for the main role.

In 1969, Lee suffered a back injury during a training session. He was told that he would never be able to practice Kung Fu again and might even struggle to walk. Initially depressed by the news, Lee turned his attention to reading and writing to stay active. His philosophy was eventually collated posthumously into his book, *Tao of Jeet Kune Do*.

Once recovered, Lee returned to Hong Kong, where freed of the constraints of Hollywood, he became a major movie star in Asia. Hollywood finally took note, and Warner Bros. offered Lee the chance to star in *Enter the Dragon*. Tragically, just six days before its 1973 release, Lee died. *Enter the Dragon* went on to become one of most profitable films of all time and cemented Lee's place as a phenomenal martial artist and cultural icon.

How was Bruce Lee able to overcome racism, injury and regular career setbacks to become the person who is so widely admired to this day?

Know Yourself

'Always be yourself, express yourself, have faith in yourself', Lee once said. From a young age, Bruce Lee was a non-conformist and questioned the established order. This may well have been forged from his own feelings of being different and born out of a failure to fit in with his peers. His mother, Grace, was half-German and at the time, the Chinese community in Hong Kong was not particularly accepting to those of mixed heritage. Twelve months into his training with Yip Man, the other students found out about his mother's ancestry and refused to train with him. Yip was in agreement with the view of his students but had too much respect for his young protégé to stop teaching him. A standoff ensued with the students, leaving Lee feeling that he had no choice but to leave of his own accord.

Lee was appalled by the attitude of his fellow students. After years of studying classic martial arts, Bruce Lee founded his own style, called Jeet Kune Do. He came to describe other forms of martial arts as 'organised despair' which held people back from fully expressing themselves. However, when it came to teaching his own students, Lee was adamant that his students should not agree or disagree with his methods but rather, grow from them. He wanted every student to see what worked best for them and develop their own styles. His technique required students to spend a lot of time studying their own thoughts, body and energy. It was about allowing the individual room to grow rather than making him fit into a box.

In later life, Lee lamented the fact that he had lacked the gumption to bring his own skills to the role of Kato in *The Green Hornet*. It was his first big break in Hollywood and he later stated that he simply turned up and did what he was told to do by the director. Before accepting future roles, he sought assurances that he would be able to express himself fully within the role.

It is interesting to note that whilst Lee needed his independence, this did not come at the expense of finding a mentor. Lee's wife Linda stated that his early years were frustrating because he struggled to find a mentor who could help him find direction. He told Linda, 'a good instructor functions as a point of the truth, exposing the student's vulnerability; forcing him to explore himself both internally and externally, and finally integrating himself with his being'.

Steve McQueen, the legendary film star, was a good friend of Lee's. He stated that Lee was, 'very much into finding out who he was'. Lee's advice to people was, 'know yourself. No matter what you do in life, if you don't know yourself, you're never going to be able to appreciate anything in life'.

Make things happen

Lee was another who focused on identifying opportunities, saying, 'to hell with circumstances, I create opportunities'. Bruce arrived back in the United States and spent his early days as a newspaper 'stuffer' (inserting loose adverts into the printed pages) for *The Seattle Times*. Even in those difficult early days, Bruce had made plans. He began teaching martial arts in backyards and city parks. He forced himself back to school, gaining a high school diploma and enrolled in the University of Washington.

By the age of thirty, he possessed thousands of books in his library, mainly titles on martial arts, philosophy and self-help. But Lee was not simply a man of theory; rather, he was a man of action.

Being an Asian actor in the Hollywood of the time was challenging. It was hard for anyone from a minority to get a fair crack of the whip. Conflicts such as the Vietnam and Korean Wars influenced many Americans' views of Asian people, according to Bao Nguyen, the director of the documentary on Lee called, *Be Water*. 'The face of the Asian American or Asian male was very much the face of the enemy to a lot of Americans', he says, 'and so, those type of foreign policy decisions and conflicts created these stereotypes and portrayals of Asians on screen as villains, as enemies'.

The final straw for him came in December 1971 when he received a telegram from the film company, Warner Bros. saying that 'due to pressures from the network regarding casting', he had been dropped from *The Warrior* television series. Despite the story being about a character with a Chinese background, with a Chinese man as the leading character, one of the reasons Bruce was given for being dropped was that he looked too Chinese!

Unable to secure anything other than a supporting role, Lee could have stayed in America and continued to win bit-part roles. Instead, he returned to Hong Kong and attempted to take advantage of his growing reputation in Asia. In 1971, Lee played his first leading role in *The Big Boss*, which proved to be a huge box office success across Asia. He followed this up with an even bigger hit in the form of the 1972 film, *Fists of Fury*. For the third film, he formed a film partnership with Raymond Chow, called Concord Productions. Bruce wrote, directed, and produced the iconic film, *Return of the Dragon*.

No one can control circumstances or outcomes but that does not mean that events need to stand in the way of dreams and aspirations. Successful people are always the most proactive; they look ahead at future goals and make things happen.

Many people passively wait for things to happen, but not Bruce Lee. In November 1972, because of his concerted efforts in Hong Kong, Warner Bros. offered Lee the chance to star in *Enter the Dragon*, a film that became one of the greatest martial arts films of all time.

Stay calm in life
Lee sought calm, once saying, 'all in all, the goal of my planning and doing is to find the true meaning in life – peace of mind'. In August 1973, just three weeks after Bruce Lee's death, *Enter the Dragon* was released in cinemas. One of the most iconic scenes in the film features Lee on a boat headed to an island where a major martial arts tournament is set to take place. A

fighter called Parsons, played by Peter Archer, attempts to intimidate fellow competitors on the boat by attacking some helpless boys who are also on the boat. After the attacks, Parsons approaches Lee and asks him what his fighting style is. Lee calmly replies, 'my style is the art of fighting without fighting'. Lee's character was focused on the forthcoming tournament and nothing was going to direct his calm focus away from that.

Martial Arts was simply a vehicle to achieve his ultimate ideal; peace of mind. In his book, *The Tao of Jeet Kune Do*, Lee stated, 'there will be calm and tranquillity when you are free from outside influences and are not disturbed. Being calm means having no illusions or disillusionment with reality'.

One should not think that serenity was a natural state for Lee. A complicated character, his biggest fight was always against himself. The way that Bruce Lee sought to achieve peace of mind was in practice, where he conditioned not only his body, but his mind as well. In 1964, Lee married Linda, a woman who was also, very much a calming influence on him.

Lee spoke a lot about water. He spoke about formlessness. 'Be Water' was a response he gave in an interview with Canadian journalist, Pierre Berton and this reply made the concept famous. 'Empty your mind. Be formless, shapeless, like water. You put water into a cup, it becomes the cup. You put water into a bottle, it becomes the bottle. You put it into a teapot, it becomes the teapot. Now water can flow, or it can crash. Be water, my friend', he said.

Calm and silence allow for psychological security and self-control. The first item on Bruce Lee's daily 'to-do list' was not weightlifting or strengthening exercises - it was always meditation and mental training. He simply sat and focused his attention on his body, allowing his mind to settle and his senses to register what was present, everywhere. It was, he believed, the most important part of his day.

Embrace Change

A very real understanding of the importance of change was central to Lee's view of personal awareness. 'To understand your fear in change is the beginning of really seeing', he once said. When Bruce Lee began teaching Kung Fu in America, many in the Chinese community believed that he was betraying his culture by sharing the secrets with the wider community. Bruce Lee considered such thinking outdated. Lee was challenged to a fight by Jack Man Wong, a leading Kung Fu practitioner in Oakland's Chinatown. Jack presented him with an ultimatum on an ornate scroll in Chinese, which stated that if he lost a fight, he would have to close his institute or stop teaching non-Chinese students. If Lee won, then he would be able to continue to teach Kung Fu to anyone that wished to learn.

The fight only lasted one minute with Bruce the victor, but despite the emphatic victory, the experience made Lee wonder why it took him 'so long' to beat Jack.

He decided to re-examine his style of Kung Fu and began to integrate other martial arts into his routine including Karate, Muay Thai and Judo. Jeet Kune Do emerged as a hybrid philosophy of martial arts. It was not about change for change's sake but rather, a recognition that life is constantly changing and one needs to adjust accordingly.

The Kung Fu that Lee had been taught in Hong Kong could not serve him with the same degree of success now that he was in America. He, therefore, borrowed concepts and techniques from other schools of martial arts to ensure his success. 'Absorb what is useful. Discard what is not and add what is uniquely your own' is the iconic quote from Lee which best summed up the lessons he had learned.

It has been said that one of the most important qualities of successful people is their willingness to adapt. Change is something that can be embraced with the excitement that new possibilities lay in waiting.

Bruce Lee stressed the importance of knowing that nothing stays the same. Everything is in constant motion and transformation. He believed that individuals, societies, and cultures need to move with the times. The world, Lee stated, was constantly evolving and there was much healing to be done. Refusing to accept this truth only causes suffering. Change often brings fear, and many times people resist.

As Lee said, to resist change is to resist life. If a person is adaptable, Lee believed, they are better able to deal with all that life throws at them. It ensures the person themselves remain in a changeless state. When people do not accept change, it simply inhibits their capacity to learn and grow.

Walk On

Lee believed that you couldn't let obstacles get in your way. 'Walk on and leave behind all the things that would dam up the inlet or clog the outlet of experience' was his mantra. In 1969, Lee skipped out his usual warm up routine and severely injured a nerve in his back during a routine weightlifting session. The injury threatened his livelihood and his ability to practice martial arts again. Lee had in fact been told that he may never walk normally again.

His childhood nickname had been Mo Si Ting (never sit still) which shows just how hard Lee found it to be out of action. Lee was distraught and determined to do whatever was necessary to come back from the setback. He became a researcher of his injury, his body, physiology, and biomechanics to create his own route to healing. Many others never recovered from similar injuries. Lee believed that obstacles should never get in your way and used the down time to read books on mental and physical recovery and to write his commentary on martial arts. This all helped him to make a remarkable recovery.

One day, he took one of his business cards and wrote, 'walk on' on the back. He put this card on a wooden stand, in clear sight, to act as a reminder to press on with his recovery.

No matter what anyone else said, he would always 'walk on'. Lee had already come up with the motivational phrase in a 1966 interview, stating that it was something he wanted to teach his son, Brandon, in his own life.

Although Lee grew frustrated and had several moments of doubt, these were simply isolated experiences. He refused to stay in a negative moment. He had already gleaned tremendous knowledge from his previous setbacks and was determined to use this challenge to become stronger.

In a letter to a friend, Mito Uyehara in August 1972, he wrote that, 'whether I like it or not, circumstances are thrust upon me and being a fighter at heart, I sort of fight it in the beginning but soon realise what I need is not inner resistance and needless conflict; rather by joining forces to readjust and make the best of it'.

Letting go offers freedom. Like in sports, when people 'walk on' and let go of their mistakes and refocus attention to the here and now, it gets rid of the inner resistance and needless conflict which serves no positive purpose at all.

To Bruce Lee, it was futile to add the tension of emotional despair to his injury situation. Worrying about the possibility of a return would just make his recovery even harder. In such situations, one needs to let the negativity go and simply, 'Walk on'. It was a philosophy which helped him to make a remarkable recovery.

Chapter Twenty

Ella Fitzgerald

Just don't give up trying to do what you really want to do. Where there is love and inspiration, I don't think you can go wrong

Ella Fitzgerald, known as the 'First Lady of Song', was a brilliant jazz singer. Referred to by no less than Bing Crosby as, 'the greatest', she sold over forty million albums in a glittering career. Her composed demeanour gave no hint of the heartbreak and anguish she encountered at various stages of her life.

Born in 1917, she grew up never having known her father as her parents separated shortly after her birth. Her childhood, whilst coinciding with the turbulence of segregation and the Great Depression, was for the most part, happy.

In 1932, Ella's world fell apart. The death of her mother, Temperance, triggered a deeply unsettling phase in her teenage life. Her stepfather became abusive, forcing her to move in with an aunt in Harlem. Her school performance declined as she began mixing with the wrong crowd. Her behaviour led authorities to place her in an orphan asylum in the Bronx. She was later sent to the New York Training School for Girls, a segregated reform school in upstate New York, where staff were alleged to have abused the students.

Eventually, Ella fled the institution in 1934. Still not yet eighteen years old, she escaped back onto the streets of New York City, where she danced for tips until she could find a band leader who would hire her as a dancer.

An amateur night contest at Harlem's Apollo Theatre in November 1934, changed her life. When she entered that contest, Ella went on stage with the intention of dancing, but soon froze. Facing derision from a boisterous crowd, a terrified

Ella decided to sing. The jeers of the crowd soon turned into rapturous cheers. The unknown singer won first prize on the night, but more significantly, convinced her that she could perform on the big stage. The transformation was enough to impress arranger, Benny Carter, who had been the band leader that night. Carter undertook to assist Ella at the start of her career, introducing her to other band leaders before collaborating on several occasions later in her career. Only months after being homeless, the eighteen-year-old singer was now intent on making her way in the industry.

She won further talent competitions and caught the eye of Charles Linton at the Harlem Opera House. Linton was a vocalist in the famous Chick Webb Band and is credited with bringing her to the attention of Webb himself.

The renowned band leader was hesitant to sign her up. 'The belief was that she was something of a rough diamond', recalled Mario Bauzá, who played lead trumpet for Webb. It was only the audience's response to her singing that persuaded Webb to offer her a job. It was alongside Webb at the Savoy Ballroom in Harlem, that Fitzgerald really made a name for herself.

She made her first recording in 1935, Love and Kisses with Webb and had her first hit with *A- Tisket, A- Tasket*. By the time Webb died in 1939, she had made such an impression, that she led the band for the next two years. The awards kept coming. By 1958, she had become the first black American woman to win a Grammy Award, the first of thirteen that she would win in her career.

Demonstrating her adaptability, she moved into acting, singing in four films. Most notably, she played the role of singer, Maggie Jackson, in Jack Webb's 1955 jazz film, *Pete Kelly's Blues*. Despite finding stardom, her early difficulties followed her into adulthood. In 1941, searching for stability, she married Benny Kornegay, a local dockworker. Upon learning that Kornegay was a convicted drug dealer, the marriage was annulled in 1942. Her second marriage to famous bass player, Ray Brown, also ended in divorce.

As was often the case for other black American performers, racial discrimination was part of everyday life. In 1954, on her way to one of her concerts in Australia, she was prevented from boarding the flight. Such disgraceful treatment spurred her on to campaign tirelessly against racial prejudice.

In her later years, Fitzgerald endured serious health problems. She suffered from diabetes, which led to her having both of her legs amputated below the knee in 1993; her ailments also affected her eyesight.

Having undergone a quintuple coronary bypass surgery in 1986, many journalists wrote her off, believing she would never sing again, but Fitzgerald proved them all wrong. On the twenty-seventh of June 1991, Ella, who had, at that point, recorded more than two-hundred albums, performed at Carnegie Hall for her twenty-sixth and final performance.

Upon her passing in 1996, her loss was felt by many, including those stars who believed that her trailblazing career had paved the way for their own. Dionne Warwick was one such performer, praising her as someone who, 'made the mark for all female singers, especially black female singers, in our industry'.

How did someone with such a difficult start in life manage to become one of the most loved singers of all time?

Allow inspiration to guide you

Ella believed in inspiration. 'Just don't give up trying to do what you really want to do. Where there is love and inspiration, I don't think you can go wrong', she said. The name Ella Fitzgerald may not mean as much to younger readers as it will to older ones. This should not stop anyone appreciating the legacy that she left on modern music. Many of today's favourite stars have spoken openly of the indirect influence she had on their own music. Adele, the English singer-songwriter grew up with little music around her. She spoke of only finding her passion for music after discovering an Ella Fitzgerald vinyl record in a junk shop. 'I didn't listen to it for a year and half, but I loved it when I put it on. It's the technique, Ella Fitzgerald is like an acrobat with her voice, you really believe what she's singing'.

Lady Gaga surprised many when she joined forces with Tony Bennett to release a jazz album in 2014. It is no surprise that she describes Ella as her, 'absolute favourite jazz singer' and someone she likes to wake up listening to every morning.

Doris Day, the actress and jazz singer, also spoke about the influence of Ella on her career. 'The one radio voice that I listened to above others belonged to Ella Fitzgerald. There was a quality to her voice that fascinated me and I'd sing along with her, trying to catch the subtle ways she shaded her voice, the casual yet clean way she sang the words', said Doris.

Where did Ella Fitzgerald gain her own inspiration to sing? Ella was a jazz enthusiast from her earliest days. She was an admirer of Louis Armstrong and Bing Crosby. Speaking in 1988, she stated how much she adored Connee Boswell of the Boswell Sisters. 'She was tops at the time. I was attracted to her immediately. My mother brought home one of her records and I fell in love with it. I tried so hard to sound just like her'. Ella listened carefully to the radio and imitated her hero, studying her solos and style. With their regular radio shows and record releases, Ella had plenty of time to listen and catch onto their unique manner.

In the words of her biographer, Stuart Nicholson, Ella Fitzgerald, 'lived to sing. It was the focus of her whole life, providing her with a career that lasted over seven decades'. Without the influence of Boswell on her own singing style, it is unlikely she would have risen to the levels she did.

On that momentous night in 1934, when she entered an amateur contest at the Apollo, after being unable to dance, the first thing that came to mind was Connee Boswell. Fitzgerald recalled that, 'I knew her records of *The Object of My Affection* and *Judy*, so I sang those songs and won the contest by imitating her'.

Fitzgerald's career, in turn, has acted as an inspiration to so many of today's stars, leading to the view that without the inspiration of Ella Fitzgerald, the world of jazz would have been a poorer place.

Get out of your comfort zone

Off stage and away from her friends, Ella was quite timid and introverted. Before going on stage, it was said that she would pull back the stage curtain slightly, look out at the audience and say to her band, 'I hope they like me'. Eventually, she was able to channel her nerves and use the energy to perfect her music.

But stretching herself was part of Ella's performance process. As this quote confirms, she knew where she needed to be. 'Once up there, I felt the acceptance and love from my audience. I knew I wanted to sing before people the rest of my life'. In 1983, the vocal group, The Manhattan Transfer, sang with Fitzgerald. Janis Siegel, the group's singer, remembers their rehearsal. 'We were all around the piano', Siegel said. 'We did our little four-part harmony party and then she scatted a couple of choruses. And she turns to us and said, 'Was that all right?' And I was so flabbergasted. It's like God asking angels after he just created the world and turned and said, 'Well, whaddya think? The Grand Canyon? Could it use a little tweaking?'

She was also self-conscious about her appearance and for a while, even doubted her abilities. Once on stage, however, this reticent young lady was surprised to find that her fear diminished, rather than increased. Like so many performers, she transformed into a different person whilst on stage, becoming emboldened and feeling at home in the spotlight.

Once a show came to an end, she often reverted to her usual introverted self. In *Ella Fitzgerald: A Biography of the First Lady of Jazz*, Mario Bauzá - who played alongside Fitzgerald in Chick Webb's orchestra - explained, 'she didn't hang out much.

When she got into the band, she was dedicated to her music … She was a lonely girl around New York, just kept herself to herself, for the gig'.

Despite her talent, when Chick Webb first saw her, he whispered to Charles Linton, 'you are not putting "that" on my bandstand'. With her unkempt hair, eyeglasses and modest clothing, this was a girl who had essentially come from the streets and had very little parenting in her upbringing. Therefore, she had to be guided by members of Chick Webb's band about basic matters, such as personal grooming and hygiene.

In 1908, psychologists Robert M. Yerkes and John D. Dodson explained that a state of relative comfort created a steady level of performance. To maximize performance, however, they believe that a person needs to feel a state of relative anxiety, a space where stress levels are slightly higher than normal. This space is called 'Optimal Anxiety' and it exists just outside of our comfort zone. Gravitating towards our comfort zone is part of our natural state. Departing from it increases risk and anxiety. But for real growth and accomplishment, it is necessary to get out of one's comfort zone. Granted, it is a hard thing to do, but someone as shy and timid as Ella Fitzgerald showed that it is perfectly possible.

Accept help when it is offered
Accepting assistance from others was an important factor in Ella's success. Norman Granz was a music impresario. When he first heard Ella Fitzgerald in his hometown of Los Angeles in the early 1940s, he did not think much of the young star. The singer was equally cautious after Granz eventually warmed to her and later asked to become her personal manager. He was a hard man to please. She explained, 'Norman … felt that I should do other things, so he produced *The Cole Porter Songbook* with me. It was a turning point in my life'.

The relationship was not always an easy one, but it worked well for them, both professionally and financially. In the words of his biographer, Tad Hershorn, the combination of Granz's business shrewdness and Fitzgerald's talent elevated her from one of jazz's most beloved singers to the international 'First Lady of Song'.

Upon joining forces, the two worked together to refine her talent and build up her reputation. Granz wanted his star performer to appear at better venues, for more pay and leave behind what he called, '52nd Street money'. He moved Ella onto the hotel circuit, playing such prestigious venues as the Starlight Room of New York City's Waldorf Astoria Hotel.

On setting up Verge Records in 1956, Granz placed Ella with the fledgling label. That year, Granz pulled off the masterstroke of getting Ella to record with Louis Armstrong in what are regarded as iconic jazz masterpieces, *Ella And Louis* (1956) and *Ella And Louis Again* (1957) along with *Porgy And Bess* (1957).

In 1944, Granz had already launched his Jazz at the Philharmonic (JATP) concert series, which had brought Ella together with other leading jazz artists. The rules he stipulated for the concerts included non-discrimination clauses in musicians' contracts, equal pay, integrated audiences, travel and accommodations. Hershorn's biography of Granz showed what a giant of a man he was, doing what so few did at the time, putting principles before profit. Granz was unique in the business world for the emphasis he placed on fairness and equality as well as having a true passion for jazz. He believed music had a role in breaking down segregation. Born in Los Angeles to Russian Jewish immigrants, Granz faced his own battles with anti-Semitism and understood the difficulties faced by black American performers. On one occasion, a white man complained about sitting next to a black man. Granz was happy to give the spectator his money back but refused to let him change his seat.

Phoebe Jacobs, president of the Louis Armstrong Educational Foundation, spoke warmly of the collaboration, which did not initially appear to be a natural fit. Whilst the two never spent much time together socially, in the areas where it mattered, the two simply clicked and formed a great team. 'Music was the common denominator. He treated her like she was a queen. He was dedicated to presenting her in the atmosphere she should enjoy befitting her talent. He was a very savvy guy and Ella respected and trusted him implicitly'.

Being part of a team means working with those who have strengths you lack but who share the same vision. The Granz-Fitzgerald team brought together two people from diverse backgrounds. People from different walks of life can often bring their own standpoint, fuse the different elements together and ensure that the whole becomes greater than the sum of its parts.

'Ella was easy', Granz said, late in life. 'All she needed was a good manager'. She did not just find a good manager in Norman Granz; she found a great one.

Value your friendships

'I owe Marilyn Monroe a real debt', Ella remarked about her dear friend. Not only was Monroe a big Ella Fitzgerald fan, but she was also a great friend who used her influence to boost Fitzgerald's career. When once asked to name her favourite singer, Marilyn Monroe did not hesitate before answering, 'Well, my very favourite person, and I love her as a person as well as a singer, I think she's the greatest and that's Ella Fitzgerald'.

Monroe had been a frequent visitor to New York night clubs and was a huge fan of jazz. It was an enduring friendship that lasted until Monroe's premature death in August 1962.

Like many people, Monroe was troubled by the absurdity of black jazz performers being prevented from drinking at the bar or speaking to their fans, whilst performing in white-only clubs. The pair bonded quickly over common struggles including tough childhoods, failed marriages and difficulties coming to terms with their stardom. Film star Monroe was intent on improving her own singing and spent hours listening to Fitzgerald's records. In November 1954, she finally got to see Fitzgerald perform in Los Angeles.

By 1955, Fitzgerald expressed a desire to play the Mocambo in Los Angeles, a prestigious, white-only club on Sunset Boulevard in Los Angeles. Marilyn Monroe had learned that the club owners were reluctant to book Fitzgerald; it was not so much that race was a factor, but rather the feeling that she was not glamorous enough.

Monroe took it upon herself to personally broker Fitzgerald's first appearance at the Mocambo. She approached the owner with a deal. If he agreed to let Ella play, she guaranteed to attend every night and bring along other celebrities. The irresistible offer was accepted by the club owner, who hired Fitzgerald for a couple of weeks in March 1955. Having the likes of Frank Sinatra and Judy Garland show up on the opening night was a huge boost. Fitzgerald returned to the Mocambo twice more in the next year and a half, generating the club's largest business after the release of *Ella Fitzgerald Sings the Cole Porter Songbook* in 1956.

The story of this unlikely friendship continues to inspire. In 2008, *Marilyn and Ella*, a play by the American writer, Bonnie Greer, about the friendship between Fitzgerald and Monroe, opened at the Theatre Royal, Stratford East, London.

It is no exaggeration to state that Marilyn Monroe's love and friendship helped change the course of Ella's career, something Fitzgerald herself acknowledged, 'It was because of her that I played the Mocambo. She told him (the owner) and it was true, due to Marilyn's superstar status, that the press would go wild. The owner said yes, and Marilyn was there, front table, every night. The press went overboard ... After that, I never had to play a small jazz club again'.

Accept what's done is done

A positive outlook on the future was important to Ella. 'It isn't where you came from; it's where you're going that counts', she felt. Fitzgerald had a tough upbringing. She did not adjust well to the death of her mother and ended up moving to Harlem to be with her Aunt. There, she dropped out of school and ended up 'running numbers'- selling tickets for a Mafia-run illegal lottery.

According to the journalist, Frank Rich, 'as a girl in Harlem, she knew scoundrels as low as any in Threepenny Opera; she worked for a numbers runner and as a lookout at a bordello'.

Her truancy from school eventually led to a place in a segregated reform school in upstate New York, where staff mistreated its residents. State investigators testified that of the school's four-hundred and sixty residents, its eighty-eight black residents were segregated into the two most crowded and dilapidated of the school's seventeen cottages.

A BBC documentary: *Ella Fitzgerald: Just One of Those Things*, was released in May 2020. It revealed the trauma Ella experienced at the reformatory. 'It was Dickensian and much, much worse if you were black', said producer Reggie Nadelson. 'The black girls were held in solitary confinement and beaten by male staff'.

Ella herself never spoke often about her upbringing. Instead, all that she tried to do was use her experiences as a springboard for success. She reflected on those difficult days with an awareness of how they helped her mature. Rather than being weighed down by those traumatic memories, she used her difficulties as a way of summoning up emotions prior to her musical performances.

According to Harlem historian, John T. Reddick, this came over in her music. She performed with a lightness which gave no indication of a difficult past. 'Despite whatever difficulties she had in her life, you could hear the joy'.

Chapter Twenty-One

Amelia Earhart

The most difficult thing is the decision to act, the rest is merely tenacity. The fears are paper tigers. You can do anything you decide to do

Amelia Earhart was a best-selling author and aviator, who achieved fame in 1928 as the first woman to fly across the Atlantic. Earhart became a role model for women, making a successful career out of writing, flying and several lecturing tours. Her, all too short life, was immortalised in the 2009 film, *Amelia,* starring Hilary Swank.

Born in Kansas in 1897, she was an unconventional child, earning a reputation as a tomboy who favoured pony-riding, tree climbing and hunting over more traditional pursuits for girls at that time. Signs of her later activism were evident in her formative years during which she kept a scrapbook of newspaper clippings about successful women in male dominated careers.

Earhart's childhood was complicated. Her upbringing was unconventional, given she was brought up in the house of her grandparents, before re-joining her mother and father at the age of ten. Her father, Edwin, was a lawyer of some promise, but found it easier to obtain a job than keep one. By the time she had returned to live with her parents, her father was in the grip of alcoholism. Amelia and her sisters spent long stretches of time back at their grandparents as the married couple sought to work through their marital difficulties.

Socially awkward, Earhart had trouble making friends, with her yearbook caption reading, 'A.E. - the girl in brown who walks alone'.

On seeing her first plane at the Iowa State Fair in Des Moines in 1908, she was initially unimpressed, describing the plane as, 'a thing of rusty wire and wood and not at all interesting'. By 1920, her views had altered. After taking her first flight, she said, 'as soon as we left the ground, I knew, I myself, had to fly'. At the time, there were less than one-hundred female pilots in the United States but this acted as no deterrent. Within a few days, she has taken her first flying lesson and six months later, bought her own airplane.

Earhart went on to set several aviation records in her short career. Her first record came in 1922 when she became the first woman to fly solo above fourteen-thousand feet. Unfortunately, this coincided with a spate of personal issues. A chronic sinus problem that developed during the Spanish flu pandemic of 1918 regularly reappeared, significantly affecting Earhart's flying activities.

The Earhart family had previously lived off an inheritance from Amelia's grandmother. By 1924, funds had dried up and Earhart was forced to sell her plane. Around that time, her parents also divorced. In 1925, she enrolled in Columbia University but was forced to abandon her studies due to limited finances. Further plans to study at Massachusetts Institute of Technology were also shelved due to insufficient finances.

Earhart was forced to find work as a teacher and then social worker. Gradually, she got back into flying in 1927, becoming a member of the American Aeronautical Society's Boston chapter.

In April 1928, Earhart received a phone call asking her if she would you like to fly across the Atlantic. In an instant, she agreed. There was one caveat: Owing to the prevailing customs at the time, a woman could not possibly be expected to undertake such a trip alone. To her frustration, she was merely a passenger. Arriving in the UK, twenty hours after taking off from Newfoundland, she became a record holder, albeit a frustrated one. She had no desire to play second fiddle to anyone.

On the twentieth of May 1932, Amelia finally achieved her aim. Despite difficult weather conditions and mechanical problems, Earhart became the first woman to fly solo across the Atlantic, turning into an international star in the process.

By 1935, Amelia was planning one final venture: a flight around the world. Sadly, her attempt to be the first person to circumnavigate the earth around the equator resulted in her disappearance on the second of July 1937. The plane wreckage has never been found and she was declared lost at sea in 1939.

Earhart's life and career are celebrated annually on the twenty-fourth of July. Remembered as more than just a pilot amassing distance and altitude records, it is fascinating to examine how Amelia Earhart managed to leave a legacy which showed that women, just like men, could shine in their chosen profession?

Push your boundaries

Amelia's way was always to try and get the most out of life. 'The most effective way to do it, is to do it', she once said. In 1920, at an air show in Long Beach, California, a crack First World War pilot, Frank Hawks, was offering ten-minute flights for ten dollars. Earhart, always one to embrace adventure, borrowed a ten-dollar bill off her father and took Hawks up on his offer.

Those growing up with Earhart attested to her restless nature. When she was just six, the family paid a visit to the St Louis World Fair. Amelia asked her mother if she could ride the roller coaster. Her mother refused, saying that it was, 'too dangerous for little girls', but being turned down never deterred her. Instead, she went home and built her own roller coast ride, with the help of her sister, 'Pidge'. A wooden box was tied across wood planks, greased with lard. The box and Amelia crashed on its first attempt, resulting in a bruised lip and torn dress. Instead of tears, Amelia exclaimed, 'oh Pidge, it's just like flying'.

National Geographic's book, *In Praise of Difficult Women* features women throughout the world who have pushed societal norms and boundaries. It comes as no surprise to see the appearance of Amelia Earhart; a young woman who was always pushing the boundaries, determined to extract the maximum out of life.

After her first trip across the Atlantic, she returned to New York City with a ticker-tape parade in an open top vehicle through Manhattan. She expressed her frustration at feeling, 'just baggage, like a sack of potatoes. Maybe someday I'll try it alone'.

Earhart helped found the Ninety-Nines, a group of female pilots and acted as the first president. Today, the Ninety-Nines are an international organization with thousands of licensed members. By breaking records, Earhart and other women in aviation were pushing boundaries and showing they should be regarded as equal to men in every sense of the word.

Earhart pledged to use the money she made from celebrity appearances, lectures and a best-selling memoir to fund her own solo trip across the Atlantic. On the twenty-second of May 1932, she achieved her aim, taking off from Newfoundland, landing fifteen hours later in Northern Ireland. The records kept tumbling, with Earhart becoming the first woman to fly solo across the United States, East to West, and the first woman to fly solo from California to Hawaii.

Earhart pushed hard against the rigid boundaries that existed at the time. 'Even as a child, as a little girl, she said she should be allowed to do anything a boy would be allowed to do', says Louise Foudray, the caretaker and historian for the Amelia Earhart museum in Atchison, Kansas.

Trust yourself
Self-reliance was a strong belief of Earhart. She followed an independent minded approach, stating that 'the woman who can create her own job is the woman who will win fame and fortune'. As a precocious child, Amelia never liked accepting

help from anyone else. Moreover, her difficult upbringing had a profound influence on her and shaped her views on self-reliance.

Her parents' tempestuous marriage is said to have contributed to her progressive viewpoint. Her mother was raised in a wealthy family, whilst her father struggled to keep his wife in the ways she had grown accustomed. This may have been an aggravating factor in his own battle with inadequacy and alcoholism and the couple's eventual divorce in 1924.

Seeing her father move from job to job and the turbulence that caused, persuaded a young Amelia to adopt an independent mentality. She worked her way to financial independence as a nurse's aide at a military hospital in Canada during the First World War and later, as a social worker in Boston. This helped her pay for her flying lessons and her first plane, nicknamed Canary.

Book publisher, George P. Putnam had romantically pursued Earhart for some time, having originally co-ordinated her flight across the Atlantic and helped build her brand on her return to America. Earhart's ideas on marriage were progressive. She believed in equal responsibilities for both parties and defied convention by keeping her own name rather than adopting the title Mrs Putnam. In fact, Putnam got used to being called 'Mr Earhart'.

In 2013, the National Portrait Gallery in Washington D.C. featured a special exhibit on Earhart's career with a special focus on her contribution as a feminist. According to Frank Goodyear, the associate curator of photographs, her intention behind the founding of the Ninety-Nines, the group of female pilots, was not just to promote women in aviation, but to also encourage them to lead independent lives, professional lives, outside the home.

When Amelia Earhart returned home after becoming the first women to fly across the transatlantic, she became what today may be termed, an influencer. Celebrity endorsements followed, from Lucky Strike cigarettes to women's clothing and sportswear. Recognizing the power of her celebrity, she only had two aims; to fund further adventures and to ensure self-sufficiency.

Accept Your Limitations

'Our strength grows out of our weaknesses' is an oft quoted phrase by Ralph Waldo Emerson and it could justifiably be applied to Amelia Earhart, who may well be the most famous female pilot in aviation history, due in part, to both her aviation career and her mysterious disappearance.

Earhart was a skilled pilot but far from being naturally gifted. Her initial flying lessons provided evidence of some rudimentary shortcomings. A crash occurred during her initial flying lessons, which were given by Neta Snook. The crash is believed to have come about owing to Earhart's inability to check fuel levels before take-off. Earhart acknowledged that the process of learning to fly was, 'rather a long-drawn-out' one and she admitted that her first solo-flight landing was exceptionally poor.

Far from being a naturally gifted pilot, Earhart persisted to become a competent pilot, building up her flying time, and ironing out her technical deficiencies. In a 2012 article in *The Washington Post* by Donna Trussell, it was suggested that Amelia's bravery and intelligence made up for any aviation flaws. Her contemporaries thought she was not a natural flier and crashed a lot, but her team always explained the mishaps away as mechanical failure, not pilot error. However, Earhart absorbed herself in flying. She read everything she could on the subject and spent much of her time at the airfield.

Earhart's first around-the-world attempt ended in near disaster on the twenty-first of March 1937, when she damaged her Lockheed Electra 10E after losing control during take-off from Hawaii's Luke Field. While the plane was being repaired, a Navy Lieutenant Commander, named Phillip Van Horn Weems, wrote to Earhart encouraging her to undergo navigation training and Morse code, which was essential for gaining long range bearings from the Coast Guard cutter specially stationed at Howland Island for this purpose.

Earhart, also, directly participated in the promotion of commercial aviation. In 1929, she took a job with Transcontinental Air Transport (TAT) as assistant to the general traffic manager. In her book, *The Fun of It*, Earhart wrote that, 'my job was to sell flying to women, both by talking about it and by watching details of handling passengers, which were calculated to appeal to feminine travellers'. Her job was to make sure women passengers were comfortable and satisfied with the service so that they would continue to travel by air.

Knowing one's limitations is not a weakness. No one can work on their weaknesses if they do not acknowledge they exist. Entrepreneurs come in all shapes and sizes; some are communicators, others are suited to developing products away from the limelight. Nobody is good at everything. Accepting limitations is not a weakness.

A fearless spirit made up for any shortcomings, which were many and included her struggling to get to grips with sophisticated radio and navigation equipment. She recognized her limitations and continuously worked to improve her skills. She was able to become an intelligent and competent pilot who was never unnerved, a crucial requirement for anyone on the flight deck.

Never give up

'You can do anything you decide to do. Adventure is worthwhile in itself', proclaimed Earhart, in a view which was reflected in her own experiences. Almost immediately upon taking her first flight in 1920, Earhart decided to become a pilot. No experience? No problem, she taught herself aviation mechanics, absorbed all she could about airplanes and flying and hung out at the airfield. No money? Just take any work that comes your way to find that passion. Earhart juggled several unusual jobs, including working at a phone company, a photographer and driving a gravel truck.

Whilst Earhart's father admired her dedication and was willing to help pay for her flights, he was concerned about the amount of time she might spend with a male instructor. What did Earhart do? She found a female pilot to teach her. Such was her determination that there were no problems, only solutions.

Anita 'Neta' Snook started teaching Amelia on the third of January 1921. Despite having little money and no career to fund her newfound hobby, Earhart was smitten and determined to do whatever it took to be a successful pilot. Fast forward to an air derby in October 1922, when Earhart, having only twenty months experience behind her, flew her plane to fourteen-thousand feet and set a world altitude record for a female pilot.

Worried what the other, more experienced pilots, would think of her, she even slept in her new leather jacket for three nights to give it a more worn look. So eager was she to fit in that she even cropped her hair short in the manner of other female pilots.

One of Amelia's greatest goals was to become the first person to complete a circumnavigation of the equator in a plane. The only way to fund such a project was to undertake other ventures. The ventures themselves were never about fame for fame's sake. She set to work as a writer and lecturer, even designing her own female clothing line. In 1935, she got paid ten-thousand dollars to become the first person to fly from Hawaii to the mainland United States, 'Easily the world's No. 1 airwoman', *TIME* magazine described her that same year.

Without such dogged determination, there was no way Amelia Earhart could have accomplished a fraction of her immense achievements.

Move ahead despite the uncertainties
'Flying may not be all plain sailing, but the fun of it is worth the price', said Amelia once, confirming that risk taking was almost built into her psyche. Certainly, flying in the 1920s did

not come without its risks. In those early days, anything could happen. Formal runways were the exception rather than the rule and often, propellers stopped working for no apparent reason. There were certainly safer ways to spend a Sunday afternoon.

In 1920, forty pilots had been hired by the government to deliver 'aerial' mail, and by 1921, thirty-one of them had died. Amelia was undaunted; after all, the risks were part of the fun.

In a letter to her husband, written in case a dangerous flight turned out to be her last, she wrote, 'please know I am quite aware of the hazards'. She said, 'I want to do it because I want to do it. Women must try to do things as men have tried. When they fail, their failure must be but a challenge to others'.

Elinor Smith, a fellow pioneering aviator, became the youngest licensed pilot in the world, aged sixteen. At an air show in August 1929, she observed Amelia in action. She spoke glowingly of her admiration for Amelia, stating that her performance was, 'gut courage that transcended the sanity of reasoning'.

The Sports Stars

Chapter Twenty-Two

Muhammad Ali

Impossible is temporary. Impossible is nothing

Muhammad Ali was one of the greatest sporting icons of the twentieth century. Crowned 'Sportsman of the Century' by *Sports Illustrated* and 'Sports Personality of the Century' by the BBC, Ali was a legend who transcended the sport of boxing. His willingness to speak out on controversial topics such as religion, race and politics, moved him from the back pages to the front. Inside the ring, Ali defeated every top heavyweight in his era, in what has become known as the 'golden age of heavyweight boxing'.

Born Cassius Clay in Louisville, Kentucky in 1942, he grew up in the segregated South, experiencing the same racial prejudice and discrimination as his peers. Young Cassius did not perform well at school and by the end of his schooling, was barely in attendance. He could hardly read or write when he graduated from high school in 1960, ranked three-hundred and seventy-sixth in a graduating class of three-hundred and ninety-one.

At twelve years of age, Ali discovered a gift for boxing. His rise to fame went relatively unnoticed until his gold medal at the 1960 Olympic Games in Rome. Having turned professional that same year, Clay went on to win his first nineteen fights before his first title bout with Sonny Liston in February 1964.

In the build up to the fight, Clay's persistent taunting of the reigning champion belied the fact that he was a rank outsider to win the fight. At the end of the sixth round, Liston couldn't continue and Clay ran around the ring shouting, 'I am the greatest!' and 'I shook up the world!' The next day, having converted to Islam, Clay changed his name to Cassius X, and then, in March 1964, to Muhammad Ali. Ali held the title in the rematch before defending his title a further eight times.

Then came the event, which became known as the biggest fight of his lifetime. Ali decided to resist the draft into the US Army on moral grounds. On the twentieth of June 1967, Ali, was convicted and sentenced to five years in prison and fined ten-thousand dollars. The biggest tragedy to many boxing commentators was that his forty-three months suspension from the ring deprived fans of seeing Ali in his prime years.

Ali finally returned to the ring on 1970 and got a chance to regain his title in March 1971 against Joe Frazier, in a bout billed as, 'The Fight of the Century'. Frazier won on points to hand Ali his first ever defeat. Ali gained revenge in a rematch before taking a title fight against George Foreman in Africa, in what became known as, 'The Rumble in the Jungle'.

The fight has been referred to as, 'the greatest sporting event of the twentieth century' and was watched by a record estimated television audience of one billion viewers worldwide. By the time of the fight, in 1974, Ali was thirty-two years old and Foreman was at the time, a strong favourite to win. But Ali revelled in his underdog status, causing a major upset in beating Foreman.

In 1975, Ali took on Joe Frazier for a third time, this time in what became known as the 'Thrilla in Manilla'. Ali absorbed sustained punishment from a relentless Frazier, but somehow kept going to win on a technical knockout.

By now, Ali's star was fading. On the fifteenth of February 1978, an aging Ali lost his title to Leon Spinks. After avenging the defeat, Ali was meant to retire but undertook two more fights, which both ended up in defeat. Worryingly, Ali had begun to demonstrate signs of ill health, struggling with vocal stutters and trembling hands in the months leading up to the fight with Larry Holmes. Amazingly, boxing authorities cleared him to compete. Those around him begged him to retire but Ali fought on one more time, losing a ten-round decision against Trevor Berbick in 1981.

The fact that Ali was diagnosed with Parkinson's disease in 1984 came as no surprise. It was estimated that he had been subjected to over two-hundred thousand blows during his career.

The illness may have slowed down his reactions, but he continued to fight for causes he believed in. Ali had the honour of lighting the flame during the opening ceremony of the 1996 Summer Olympics in Atlanta. The gesture is said to have done more to raise awareness of the disease than any other moment in history. In 2005, he received his country's highest civilian honour, the Presidential Medal of Freedom, from President George W. Bush.

Ali could have faded into a quiet, well deserved retirement. He remained in the public spotlight, travelling the world for charitable and humanitarian causes, before dying when he was seventy-four years old, in 2016.

How did this remarkable man achieve so much, in the face of so much opposition and prejudice?

Believe in yourself

Ali was never short of self-confidence. 'It's hard to be humble when you're as great as I am', he said once, emphasising this point. Indeed, for Muhammad Ali, the notion of being an unpretentious, modest boxer, who let his fists do the talking, was never on the cards. He made no apology for the arrogance he displayed, both in and out of the ring.

Ali had no desire to play the role he believed society expected of him. In February 1964, the day after beating Sonny Listen, he made the spectacular announcement that he was a member of the Nation of Islam — ridding himself of his 'slave name', renouncing Christianity and insisting that he be called Muhammad Ali. He was brazen and outspoken about the civil rights struggles of the time. He bragged, 'I am America. I am the part you won't recognize. But get used to me — black, confident, cocky. My name, not yours. My religion, not yours. My goals, my own'.

Although as Cassius Clay, he made headlines as an Olympic Gold medallist in 1960, he had yet to achieve the widespread fame that would soon follow. However, the self-belief was evident from an early age. Even at twelve years old, when he was a slight beginner, he had an impudence about him that made him stand out to the older amateurs in the gym in Louisville.

George King first met Clay during a tournament at the Columbia Gym. 'We were down there, grown men, and he didn't give a damn', says King. 'That's just the way he was. He'd pick at you, mess with your head, tease you to death'.

If Ali was an underdog for his first fight with Sonny Liston, then nobody had told him. Liston was thought to be amongst the greatest and most ferocious heavyweights of his time. Clay was the young twenty-two-year-old upstart. *LA Times* reporter, Jim Murray, had stated that the only thing at which Clay could beat Liston was reading the dictionary.

Liston, with his criminal past and connections to the underworld, was not someone most people were prone to upsetting. In February 1964, after Clay, had gone around taunting Liston as an, 'ugly bear', he pulled up to Liston's home in Denver after midnight in a bus and blasted the horn to taunt him. When Liston did not respond, Clay walked up to his windows with a flashlight to peer inside.

After a powerful display from Clay on fight night, Liston was unable to continue past the sixth round. 'I told ye', Ali said to reporters after the Liston fight. 'I told ye. I just played with him. I whipped him so bad and wasn't that good? And look at me — I'm still pretty'.

The self-belief and illusion of infallibility were instrumental in enabling Ali to get through several difficult contests later in his career. At the 'Thrilla in Manila', Joe Frazier inflicted such damage on Ali that, despite winning, he later described it as a near-death experience.

A story is told how shortly after the Olympics, an eighteen-year-old Cassius Clay was driving his Cadillac convertible through the black part of Louisville ahead of his first professional fight. He was accompanied by Wilma Rudolph, featured in Chapter Twenty-Three. Almost standing as he drove the car, the youngster yelled over and over, to everyone he passed, 'I'm Cassius Clay! I am the greatest!'

Stick to what you believe

Ali refused to back down on matters of belief and principle. 'There are only two kinds of men, those who compromise and those who take a stand', he stated defiantly. In 1967, the United States was deeply entrenched in the Vietnam War and like many other men, Ali was drafted into the army. He was convinced that supporting the war would violate his principles.

Despite his conviction and sentence for draft-dodging, Ali remained outside of prison pending an appeal but faced up to an indefinite suspension from boxing. He was stripped of his titles and had his passport taken away, along with the ability to make a living. To make ends meet, he began lecturing at universities and gatherings across the country.

By 1968, 19,560 Americans had died in the Vietnam War and another 16,502 would die that year alone. As the anti-war movement grew, Ali became a hero. 'It has been said that I have two alternatives', Ali told a crowd of college anti-war protesters. 'Either go to jail or go to the army. But I would like to say that there is another alternative. And that alternative, that alternative is justice. And if justice prevails, I will neither go to the army, nor will I go to jail'.

Banned from boxing, Ali would spend the next four years appealing that verdict. It was not an easy period for him. He was denounced by fellow black athletes such as Jackie Robinson and Joe Louis. On television, talk show host David Susskind berated Ali as, 'a disgrace to his country, his race and what he laughingly describes as his profession'.

On the twenty-eighth of June 1971, Ali won possibly his biggest victory: The Supreme Court unanimously overturned his conviction, saying his draft board failed to specify why his conscientious objector application was denied. Fittingly, it was declared that the sincerity of Ali's beliefs and their foundation in religious training were beyond doubt.

Ali's life turned full circle in 2005. His hands shaking because of his Parkinson's, he accepted the Medal of Freedom, at the White House. 'The American people', said President George W. Bush, 'are proud to call Muhammad Ali one of our own.'

Great people are those who stand by their principles, despite the uncertainty and unpopularity which may result because of their actions. Ali was ultimately successful in overcoming his challenges, largely due to his unyielding refusal to give up on his ideals.

'His biggest win came not in the ring but in our courts in his fight for his beliefs', Eric Holder, the former US attorney general said, after his death.

Back up your beliefs with actions

Ali believed he had to find expression for his beliefs in his actions. He summed up his attitude: 'At home, I am a nice guy: but I don't want the world to know. Humble people, I've found, don't get very far'.

Ali's early years in the boxing game were not easy. Aged eighteen, the young Cassius Clay, as he was then, got his taste of how little his newfound celebrity status mattered in segregated America.

Having returned from Rome in 1960, where he had beaten Poland's Zbigniew Pietrzykowski to become the Olympic light-heavyweight champion, the young Clay was refused a table in a 'white people's' burger restaurant in his hometown of Louisville, Kentucky. Despite his fame, he was still called 'boy' on the street. He was so angry, he claimed to have thrown his Olympic medal into the Ohio river.

On the thirteenth of March, 1963, before a sold-out Madison Square Garden crowd, Doug Jones gave Ali his toughest fight. In round one, Jones hit Clay with a left hook that sent Clay spinning into the ropes. Somehow Clay stayed on his feet and won by a unanimous decision, but the crowd did not like it. Clay was unpopular with fans and they hurled beer, programmes and peanuts at him. Clay picked up a peanut and ate it. Ali learned that he did not mind being disliked. In fact, he realised that it even motivated him and was good for business.

Four years later, he became the heavyweight champion of the world, defeating Sonny Liston. His brashness did not endear him to white Americans and made Liston appear a more sympathetic character. Ali soon became the fighter most fans wanted to see lying flat on his back. The boxing crowds often booed Ali and rooted loudly for his opponents. 'The Louisville Lip' was the name the sportswriters gave him and scolded him for his bad manners.

Shortly after Ali beat Sonny Liston in 1964 to win the heavyweight championship of the world, he annoyed many Americans and sports writers, by changing his name from Cassius Clay to Muhammad Ali. But he did not care.

The Vietnam War was popular at the time in the United States and the sight of Ali, refusing to serve incensed the sporting, media and political establishments. The boxer had converted to the Nation of Islam a few years earlier and he explained his resistance to the war by saying, 'I ain't got no quarrel with them Viet Cong'. Ali instantly became a pariah — perhaps the most hated man in the country.

The irony is that by standing by his principles and not caring about popularity, Ali started to gain the respect of the wider public. As his biographer, Jonathan Eig remembers, it was as if people now turned around by 1971 and said, 'Wow, Ali was right. That war has been a disaster. No wonder he didn't want to fight over there'.

Many people want to be liked, so they make the mistake of making decisions, based on what might be popular rather than what is right for them.

Some of the greatest people of our time have not always been liked. But what ultimately makes them great, or truly respected, is that they act in a way they believe to be right. Ironically, Muhammad Ali now wins most popularity contests hands down, precisely because of the respect he garnered for caring little about popularity when acting on his original decisions.

Find your own way

A famous quote from Ali exemplifies his unique style. 'Float like a butterfly, sting like a bee, your hands can't hit, what your eyes can't see', he would say. Ali believed in doing things his way not the way others might expect things to be done.

Muhammad Ali had a unique fighting style. He moved seamlessly in the ring. Ali's signature style of dancing, dodging and movement in the ring confused opponents and wore them down. He avoided punches by leaning back, a technique which most coaches frowned upon. To Ali, the technique felt natural, so he ignored the advice to stop doing it. According to some writers, his style broke every rule in the book, but it was effective. In the twenty-nine fights he won between 1957 and 1960, he was never hurt.

On his return to boxing, Ali was forced to adopt a new style, going toe to toe with opponents. His speed had slowed considerably during his layoff, which was noticeable in his return against Jerry Quarry, in 1970.

'The Fight of the Century' in 1971, against Joe Frazier, confirmed the change. Ali now used his hand-speed to block punches or if opponents caught him, he would hold them against the ropes until the referee separated them.

Despite having eight years on George Forman in their fight, Ali's pragmatic approach saw him adopt a defensive style, named the 'rope-a dope' tactic, in which he rested against the ropes and let his opponent exhaust himself with punches that Ali evaded or absorbed. It required tremendous courage and willpower instead of raw speed, as in earlier days, to defeat his younger rival. To be able to soak up so much punishment from as powerful a hitter as George Forman was no mean feat.

Sometimes it pays to do things differently. You must ask yourself if doing things the conventional way works for you. Fitting inside the box may have its advantages but people like Muhammad Ali showed that on occasion, it pays to adopt your own way.

As Judy Garland said, 'always be a first-rate version of yourself instead of a second-rate version of somebody else'.

Commenting on the two distinct fighting styles that defined his career, one boxing expert later said that the two greatest heavyweights in history were Cassius Clay and Muhammad Ali.

Show others the way

'Service to others is the rent you pay for your room here on earth', Ali once stated, confirming his belief in being a leader of others.

There were many challenges in the career of Muhammad Ali, but none were as great as the challenges he voluntarily undertook on behalf of the black American community. Articulating his views with honesty and arrogance, he emboldened and led others in sport to speak out against racial injustice and inequality.

On a June afternoon in 1967, several of America's best black athletes, including Bill Russell and Lew Alcindor (who later changed his name to Kareem Abdul-Jabbar) met with Muhammad Ali in Cleveland, Ohio. The summit was held to decide whether to issue support to Muhammad Ali over his refusal to serve in Vietnam. In the words of his biographer, Jonathan Eig, 'Ali worked the room like it was his birthday party, cracking jokes and talking to everyone at once'. When difficult questions were raised, he never got defensive. He simply answered assertively.

During the summit, the athletes were told that boxing promoter Bob Arum had negotiated a deal with the government: if Ali travelled around America performing in exhibition fights on military bases, the charges against him would be dropped.

Ali took questions from his fellow professionals but refused to back down. He never did take the government's deal. As a result, he was exiled from his sport for three years. But the other men were impressed by Ali and the leadership he had shown on the issues of racial equality. A joint press conference was held in which all the athletes expressed support for Ali.

It is interesting to note that Ali had several interactions with another leader who had the courage of his convictions, Dr Martin Luther King Jr. Whilst Ali did not support King's methods of non-violent protests and integration, the two had similar views on the Vietnam War.

King officially supported Ali and his actions. 'He's doing what he's doing on the basis of conscience', King said in a news conference. 'He's absolutely sincere. I strongly endorse his actions'. Friends later told Ali's biographer, Michael Ezra, that they thought Ali's public stance had helped prompt King's public opposition to the war.

In 1967, King and Ali appeared together in public, standing together at a rally for fair housing in Louisville, Kentucky. 'In your struggle for justice, freedom, and equality, I am with you,' Ali told King as cameras rolled. King recognized Muhammad Ali's leadership, even as he felt obliged to highlight the two men's differences religiously and politically.

Displays of leadership did not end upon his diagnosis over Parkinson's disease. After his diagnosis, Ali the philanthropist, raised millions of dollars for the Muhammad Ali Parkinson Centre at the Barrow Neurological Institute in Phoenix, Arizona.

Perhaps most interestingly, Ali travelled to Iraq, where fifteen Americans were being held hostage by Saddam Hussein in the run-up to the Gulf War. On the second of December 1990,

Ali and the hostages flew out of Baghdad, heading back to JFK airport in New York. The men remained overwhelmed. 'You know, I thanked him', said former hostage Bobby Anderson. 'And he said, "Go home, (and) be with my family" . . . what a great guy'.

Muhammad Ali did not just change boxing. He led by example to change society.

Chapter Twenty-Three

Wilma Rudolph

My doctors told me I would never walk again. My mother told me I would. I believed my mother

Wilma Rudolph may be an unfamiliar name to many readers, but her story is no less inspiring than any other featured within these pages. Here is a tale of a sickly young girl, unable to walk properly until she was twelve years old, who went on to become the first American woman to win three gold medals in track and field at the Olympics. It is the story of a black athlete, brought up in the racially segregated Deep South, who became a role model for black and female athletes across the world.

Rudolph faced an uphill battle from the start. She was born prematurely in 1940, weighing just four and a half pounds. In the 1940s, babies born at such a weight did not live more than a few days. She was the twentieth of twenty-two children born to her father across two marriages.

Stricken with double pneumonia, scarlet fever and polio at the age of five, her first major challenge was finding a hospital willing to treat a black child with such ailments. Doctors fitted her left leg with a steel brace and with hard work and determination, she was able to defy the odds and walk unaided before her teenage years.

Growing up in segregated Tennessee came with additional challenges. Rudolph attended the all-black Burt High School, where she played on the basketball team. A naturally gifted runner, she was soon spotted and asked to join a summer track camp at Tennessee State University. There, she met her future coach and mentor, Ed Temple.

Her progress was so remarkable that by sixteen years-of-age, she had been selected to compete for the United States team in the 1956 Melbourne Olympic Games, only four years after she had cast away her leg brace. She proceeded to win a bronze medal as part of the 400-metre relay team.

After finishing high school, Rudolph attended Tennessee State University, where she studied education. Four years later, she starred at the 1960 Olympics in Rome, winning the 100-metres, 200-metres and securing another team gold in the 4 x 100-metre relay team. In doing so, she became the fastest woman in the world and the first American woman to win three gold medals on the track in one Olympic Games.

Not many people managed to outshine the brash and effervescent Cassius Clay, but Wilma managed to do just that. Clay won a boxing Gold in Rome, but Rudolph's achievements outshone even his.

Nicknamed 'The Tornado', she became a household name as the Olympics were broadcast live on television for the first time. Rudolph played an important role in furthering the rights of the black community by insisting that the homecoming parade and gala banquet held in her honour should be one of the first non-segregated events held in her hometown of Clarksville.

At the time, athletes competed on an amateur basis. As a result, Rudolph did not earn significant money from her career. She successfully moved into a teaching and coaching position after her retirement. In 1977, she shared her life story in her autobiography, *Wilma*, which was turned into a film for television later that year. Tragically, she died prematurely in November 1994 after a brave battle with brain cancer, aged just fifty-four years old. Her extraordinary determination and kindness are what people remember most about her. Bill Mulliken, a 1960 Olympics teammate of Rudolph said, 'she was beautiful, she was nice and she was the best'.

Rudolph's legacy lay in in her ability to demonstrate that it was entirely possible to succeed despite poverty and disability. The Wilma Rudolph Foundation she founded continues to help and inspire children overcome their challenges.

'Believe me, the reward is not so great without the struggle', was her constant mantra to children seeking her advice. One week after her death, *Sports Illustrated* magazine proclaimed, 'the Wilma Rudolph story is the stuff of fairy tales, only in her case, the fairy tale came true'.

Has any Olympic champion ever had to work so hard just to be able to run, let alone end up as a multiple champion?

Appreciate your family

Wilma believed that the energy and support from her family was important to her. 'When you come from a large, wonderful family, there's always a way to achieve your goals', she once stated.

Wilma Rudolph was born during the Second World War in Tennessee, the heartland of the segregated South. Her mother, Blanche, worked as a maid for six days a week in the homes of wealthy white families whilst her father worked as a porter and handyman. The family got by, but it was by no means a privileged upbringing.

When Rudolph was four, she became seriously ill with double pneumonia and scarlet fever. When she finally recovered from those afflictions, it was discovered that she has contracted polio. Doctors predicted that the child would never walk again. For years, she struggled to place one foot in front of the other.

With little medical care available to the local black American residents, Rudolph's parents were forced to take her to faraway Fisk University Medical School in Nashville. The facility was over fifty miles away and Rudolph and her mother made the trip twice weekly for two years. It was there that she received water and heat therapy, until she was able to walk with a metal brace, by the age of six. The bus trips themselves were traumatic for young Wilma. She later recalled the humiliation of being told where to sit on the bus; where she and her mother could and could not eat whilst in the neighbourhood.

Rudolph had parents who had no hesitation in doing whatever it took to get the right treatment for their daughter. She also benefited from the support provided by her many siblings. At least four times a day, without fail, Blanche or one of the children worked on Wilma's leg, massaging it and wrapping it in steaming hot towels. Those first few years were difficult. The leg showed little improvement and the pain continued. Her family continued to believe that she would be able to walk again and persisted with the massages.

By the time she was eight, Rudolph became so mobile that she was able to walk with only the brace for support. At that age she was also able to start school.

The youngster hated those leg braces, which she referred to as, convicts' leg irons and spent most of her time trying to figure out how to get them off. With the help of her family, that is exactly what she set out to do. She began to take off her brace and strategically positioned her brothers and sisters around the house to enable her to practice walking. Defying the opinion of respected medical professionals, it was clear she was on the verge of being able to walk unaided. By the time she was twelve years old, she was challenging every boy in the neighbourhood to races and easily beat most of them.

There was no doubt in Rudolph's mind of the important role played by her strong, supportive family in her recovery. She later wrote that, 'with all the love and care my family gave me, I couldn't help but get better'.

Find a mentor
Wilma firmly believed that you couldn't achieve success on your own, stating that, 'no matter what accomplishments you make, somebody helps you'. From early in her life, Rudolph was already able to count on the support of a loving and devoted family in her battle to walk. In the next stage of her life, several other mentors played a role in allowing the latecomer to make up for lost time.

It was not until high school, that Rudolph was to meet the mentor who would profoundly change her destiny. While playing for her high school basketball team, Rudolph caught the eye of Ed Temple. Temple was women's track coach at Tennessee State University for forty-four years and went on to be the unpaid coach of the US Women's Olympic track team in 1960 and 1964. Temple's credentials were second to none. He operated a strict schedule of three training sessions a day, in all weathers, the first starting before six o'clock in the morning. He produced forty Olympians who between them, won thirteen gold medals.

With Wilma aged only fourteen, Temple knew a natural athlete when he saw one and was impressed with the youngster's speed. He persuaded her to train with him during her summer break from school. A gentle man, he was a feared and respected disciplinarian and acted as a father figure to his young athletes. He drove the team to meets in his own car and had the school track, an unmarked and unsurfaced dirt oval, lined at his own expense. But Temple was no pushover. He made the girls run an extra lap for every minute they were late to practice. Rudolph once overslept and was thirty minutes late for practice. Temple made her run thirty extra laps. The next day she was at the track thirty minutes early.

Coach Temple taught Rudolph to learn to relax her body whilst running by breathing properly and keeping her hands loose. He also taught other technical basics, such as running with open hands and not running whilst leaning backwards.

Rudolph went on to win all nine events she entered at an Amateur Athletic Union track meet in Philadelphia, Pennsylvania. Fast forward one year and she was competing in her first Olympics; aged just sixteen. There, she became the youngest member of the 1956 US track and field team, in Melbourne. During the games, she was awarded her first medal, a bronze in the women's 400-metre relay.

In his role as mentor, Ed Temple offered Rudolph not just technical advice but provided the encouragement and objective voice which enabled his young protégé to succeed. Temple had been around the block, so to speak and had the life experiences not yet experienced by his sixteen-year-old disciple. His advice ensured she steered clear of common mistakes. Temple provided the tough love in a way that may have been resented in the short term, but in the long term, was a process that Rudolph came to appreciate.

Develop a growth mindset

A quote from Wilma after winning her bronze medal in Melbourne, demonstrates her belief in always trying to improve. She had given the medal to her schoolfriends but 'when I got it back, there were handprints all over it. I took it and I started shining it up. I discovered that bronze doesn't shine. So, I decided I'm going to try this one more time. I'm going to go for the gold'.

As the youngest member of the United States team at the 1956 Melbourne Olympics, Rudolph had a decision to make. Was she content with the modest glory she had experienced in Melbourne? Or did she have the hunger, commitment, and self-sacrifice needed to become an Olympic champion in four years' time? Rudolph decided that she was capable of the latter. In 1958, Rudolph followed Ed Temple to Tennessee State, where he continued to coach her whilst she majored in elementary education. She had already given birth to a baby girl, Yolanda, who was cared for by her family whilst she was at college.

Temple insisted that his athletes maintain high standards in their academic studies. Wilma found the course work and training requirements difficult but managed to meet all the requirements set by Temple. She managed to juggle her responsibilities as a member of the track team, the Tigerbelles, her studies and her family.

The training intensity took its toll when she found herself ruled out of most of the 1958 season through injury. She rebounded in 1959, only to pull a muscle at a crucial race in Philadelphia. Ed Temple supervised her recovery and by 1960

Rudolph was ready to go to Rome. Early in 1960, she began training seriously for Rome and won both the 100- and 200-metre dashes at the US Olympic trials and qualified for the team.

In Rome, the day before her first race, she went jogging. While crossing a field, she stepped into a small hole and twisted her ankle. After having her ankle taped tightly and packed in ice, she managed to beat her own world record time in the 100-metres and set an Olympic record in winning the 200-metres. On the seventh of September 1960, Rudolph joined up with her Olympic teammates from Tennessee State to win the 4 x 100-metre relay and obtain her third gold medal.

Rudolph believed in the growth mindset, working hard from childhood to achieve her aims. She refused to be held back by her leg problems and kept working on her exercises until she no longer needed a brace. It was her growth mindset that gave her the perseverance and dedication to walk, and then move onto winning three gold medals in Rome. When asked about her legacy as a world-class athlete, she commented, 'I just want to be remembered as a hard-working lady with certain beliefs'.

Give to others
Wilma possessed an altruistic approach to life and strongly believed that her talents could be directed towards helping others. 'My thoughts about my life, my great moment, if I left the Earth today, would be knowing that I have tried to give something to young people', she declared.

As well as being a top athlete, Rudolph was also regarded as a civil rights and women's rights pioneer. Following her victories in Rome, she resolved to play an even bigger role in changing society.

When she returned from Rome, Tennessee Governor Buford Ellington, who was known as, 'an old-fashioned segregationist', planned to head the celebrations. Rudolph let it be known that she would not attend any type of segregated event. She insisted that her homecoming parade and subsequent banquet be open to all residents. As a result, her victory parade was the first racially integrated event in Clarksville. Over one-thousand people attended the banquet, marking the first time that both blacks and whites had gathered for the same event in the town's history. This 'first' brought Wilma as much joy as any of her Olympic gold medals.

Following her retirement in 1963, she graduated from university and dedicated her life to helping others. In May 1963, Rudolph participated in a civil rights protest in her hometown of Clarksville to desegregate one of the city's restaurants. Within a short time, the mayor announced that segregation would end in all municipal facilities.

From 1967, she worked for Job Corps, a free education and training organisation for young people. She became involved with a programme called, 'Operation Champion', where well-known athletes went into poor inner-city areas for youth sports training. She also worked as a track coach at Indiana's DePauw University and served as a US goodwill ambassador to French West Africa.

According to Rudolph, her greatest achievements were not her exploits in Rome. They came from the work done by her foundation, which focused on community-based sports programmes for young athletes. Rudolph wanted to ensure that young athletes had the life skills available to deal with life's difficulties. 'I tell them that the most important aspect is to be yourself and have confidence in yourself. I remind them that triumph can't be had without struggle'.

Before her death, Rudolph said, 'I would be very sad if I was only remembered as Wilma Rudolph, the great sprinter. To me, my legacy is to the youth of America to let them know they can be anything they want to be'.

Never give up
A determined approach was fundamental to Wilma's approach. This view is summed up well when she said, "I

can't', are two words that have never been in my vocabulary. I believe in me more than anything in this world'.

Despite her childhood problems, Wilma Rudolph never doubted that she would walk. One of the proudest moments of her life came was when she walked into church completely unaided at the age of nine and a half. She finally felt accepted having walked amongst her peers who had cruelly taunted her because of her deformity. However, she was determined that this would just be the beginning. She never settled for mediocrity, she was determined to go beyond her taunters, to do something none of them would ever do.

The 1956 Olympics in Melbourne were a mixed experience for the sixteen-year-old athlete. She was disappointed with her own performance but inspired by Betty Cuthbert, who won gold medals in her favoured races. Watching Cuthbert win those medals from the side of the track made her determined that four years on, wherever the Olympics would be held, she was going to be there and she was going to win Gold for the United States.

In the 1960 Rome Olympics, the pressure was on, having smashed records in the Olympic trials. Unphased, Wilma spoke of looking at the other runners in the tunnel and feeling deep inside, that she could beat any of them.

For some people, adversity takes the form of economic hardship. For others, it may be prejudice or a physical or emotional challenge. Wilma Rudolph made the decision not to become a victim and was determined to take control of her life.

Wilma Rudolph was the keynote speaker at the fourth Annual Conference on Women in 1986, where the theme of her message was determination. Rudolph stressed that the same discipline and self-belief that took her to Olympic gold, could be used, 'to become the best lawyer, doctor and secretary'. She told a packed audience of four-thousand women that 'anything that anybody in this room wants to accomplish, you can. But you have to believe it'.

Never underestimate the power of determination.

Chapter Twenty-Four

Jesse Owens

Life doesn't give you all the practice races you need

Jesse Owens seemed to spend his life in a perpetual state of struggle - fighting against himself, battling racism and just simply trying to make ends meet.

Winning four gold medals at the 1936 Olympics in Berlin, did not grant much respite from his difficulties. The Games, held in Hitler's Germany, seemed to encapsulate his life; at once, the finest, yet most humiliating of experiences.

Born James Cleveland Owens in Oakland, Alabama, in 1913, he was the youngest of ten siblings. Growing up, his teacher confused 'J.C.' with Jesse and so, the name Jesse stuck. Like other black youngsters growing up in the segregated South, life was an unending cycle of poverty and hardship, yet young Jesse stated he was happy, with no comprehension of just how poor the family was. Owens was a sickly child and had a brush with death at a young age. For sharecroppers like Jesse's father, life was a daily battle. Too much or too little rain could result in crop failure, making all the difference between food or hungry stomachs.

When he was nine years old, his parents moved the family to Cleveland, Ohio, in the hope of a better life. The move did little to alleviate the family's financial situation, but it was in his new hometown that Owens discovered his love for running. At his junior high school, Owens met coach, Charles Riley, who he credited with setting him on the road to success.

Deprived of an athletic scholarship and prevented from living on campus on account of his colour, it was his time at Ohio State University that proved critical to his development. Owens came to prominence, in forty-five sensational minutes at the Big Ten Championships in Ann Arbor,

Michigan, on the twenty-fifth of May 1935. He equalled the world record for the 100-yard dash and the long jump, as well as setting a record for the 220-yard dash and the 220-yard-low hurdles.

The achievements were simply a prelude for what was the follow. To the consternation of Hitler, Owens went on to win gold medals in the 100-metres dash, in the long jump, the 200-metre dash and the 4 x 100-metre relay. These results were more than had been achieved by any other American track and field athlete in a single Olympic Games.

The irony was that despite incurring the wrath of the Nazi press and rumours of a snub by Hitler, the Games were, in many ways, a more liberating experience for the athlete. For once, Owens was able to train and stay in the same accommodation as his white teammates.

'When I came back, after all those stories about Hitler and his snub, I came back to my native country and I couldn't ride in the front of the bus. I had to go to the back door. I couldn't live where I wanted. Now what's the difference?' he said after his return.

Owens' treatment worsened on his return home. He had to take a service elevator up to the reception honouring him at the Waldorf Astoria Hotel in New York. No invitation to the White House or phone call from President Roosevelt was forthcoming.

Owens' attempts to capitalize on his fame were met with hostility from amateur sporting officials, who withdrew his amateur status, thus ending his career. Within months, the commercial offers ran dry and Owens was forced into a series of menial jobs, becoming a janitor, gas station attendant and manager of a dry-cleaning firm in the years after Berlin. Worst still, he was forced to accept money to race against cars and horses. 'Those races made me sick', Owens said. 'I felt like a freak'.

Having endured financial problems and several failed businesses, Owens was finally able to churn out a respectable living on the speaking circuit. In 1976, the recognition he had long sought finally arrived, as President Ford presented him with the Presidential Medal of Freedom.

At the age of sixty-six, Owens died of lung cancer in Tucson, Arizona. A life of remarkable highs and devastating lows, but one which, in the words of President Carter, 'symbolised the human struggle against tyranny, poverty and racial bigotry'.

How was Owens able to overcome a life that saw more than its fair share of poverty, racism, injustice and hard times?

Develop your character

Jesse believed his success was down to several factors combined. 'We all have dreams. But in order to make dreams come into reality, it takes an awful lot of determination, dedication, self-discipline, and effort', he stated.

The event that changed Jesse Owens life almost took place without him. On the morning of the twenty-fifth of May 1936, as Owens was supposed to be warming up for the 100-yard final of that Big Ten Championship in Ann Arbor, Michigan, he was writhing in pain. Larry Synder, the Ohio State track and field coach told his young charge that it wasn't worth risking further damage to his fragile back.

"If you can't go, you can't go," Synder told his star athlete.

"Coach, I'm okay. Let me try," Jesse replied.

But Owens was not okay. Five days before, Owens had fallen down the stairs at a fraternity party in Columbus. A badly bruised lower back made him an immediate doubt for the upcoming meet. Owens had to be helped in and out of the car in which he had travelled to Ann Arbor. Once there, he could barely bend enough to touch his knees. He even took a thirty-minute hot bath as a final attempt to loosen his aching limbs.

David Albritton, Ohio's gifted high jumper had to pull Owens' shirt over his head. He too, urged his close friend to pull out of the event. But Owens was adamant he would be competing. Finally, Coach Snyder, relented, agreeing to let his young protégé compete on an event-by-event basis. Almost by magic, as he settled into position, the pain left him and despite a slow start, he crossed the line in 9.4 seconds, equalling the world record.

Within the next forty-five minutes, the twenty-one-year-old set the world record in the long jump, the 220-yard dash and the 220-yard low hurdles. *Sports Illustrated* magazine believed that Owens' one day achievements in Ann Arbor had no equal, not just in athletics but in any sport. It is, they claim, the greatest single day performance in athletic history.

In somewhat poetic language, the magazine states, that 'to find a similar scale of achievement, one has to journey to the realm of art and think of Mozart needing only six weeks to compose his final three symphonies in the summer of 1788 or of Shakespeare writing *Henry V, Julius Caesar* and *As You Like It* all in the same year'.

What made the difference that day in Ann Arbor, was not simply talent. In ignoring the relentless pain, in defying the pleas of his coach, in focusing solely on his desired goal, Owens had showed the importance of character.

In a sport which can last less than ten seconds, Owens himself, recognised the most important attribute in coming out on top. 'It all goes so fast, and character makes the difference when it's close', he confirmed.

Know yourself
Being aware of yourself and your strengths and weaknesses was acknowledged by Owens. He stated, 'I wasn't in Berlin to compete against any one athlete. The purpose of the Olympics, anyway, was to do your best. As I'd learned long ago from Charles Riley, the only victory that counts is the one over yourself'.

In 1927, Jesse Owens met the man who he credited with teaching Owens his athletic skills. A short, middle aged man with a thick Irish accent, Riley was the school's physical education teacher and track coach. Riley noticed how Jesse outran his peers in gym class and asked Jesse to train with him for ninety minutes each morning before school.

Riley was relentless, working on Jesse's technique, ensuring he ran with a straight head and high knees. When Jesse was fifteen years old, Riley had a 100-metre race set up on the sidewalk of a street in Cleveland. To his astonishment, Jesse finished in eleven seconds. The next day, Riley returned with a new stopwatch in case there had been a mistake. Jesse simply repeated the feat. At this stage, Jesse was already amongst the fastest people on earth.

Like any good coach, technique was only one part of Riley's genius. It was the mental side in which Riley excelled. After a difficult race, he took the frustrated youngster to a racecourse and made him watch the horses all day. He wanted to show Jesse the effortless strides of the horses and the calmness of their faces.

The skill of detaching oneself from a hostile environment, to take the pressure off oneself and focus solely on one's best performance, could well be Charles Riley's greatest legacy. It is a powerful message that transcends sport and is as relevant to each of our lives as it was to Jesse Owens' in the cauldron of the Olympic stadium in Berlin. Owens, as we have seen, encountered considerable adversity after Berlin. In his motivational speeches to business executives and public offices, Owens stressed that, 'the struggles within yourself – the invisible, inevitable battles inside all of us – that is where it's at'. In other words, life is essentially about competing against yourself, not others. It is a point not restricted to the sporting arena.

When we realise, we are competing against ourselves, not against others, it changes out perspective in life. It can be liberating. Like Jesse Owens, the best approach is to keep your eyes forward, focused on the track in front of you, running your own race and ignoring those in the other lanes.

Identify your hidden talents

'Owens does not so much take (a room) over as envelop it, He is friendly to all, outgoing and gracious'. This quote by Tony Gentry, Owens' biographer, summed up Jesse's presence when in the company of others.

The American Athletic Union (AAU) sought to reap the financial rewards after the Olympic games and arranged several race meetings across Europe for Jesse and his teammates. It did not remunerate its athletes to perform, paying out only nominal expenses.

Owens purposely missed a flight to Sweden, before returning home to Cleveland. He argued that the athletes were being treated like trained seals. When Jesse left the tour without permission, AAU official were furious and decided to ban him for life. 'It was a strange time', Jesse's wife, Ruth recalled. 'People kept telling him they were gonna do this or that for him. It was just fancy talk'.

The challenge lay in finding regular income. For the next few decades, Owens toiled, trying to find an income worthy of his status as an Olympic champion. He was forced onto the exhibition circuit, forming a softball and a basketball team whilst taking a summer job as a playground director.

In May 1939, less than three years after Berlin, a new low was reached. The Jesse Owens Dry Cleaning Company, which bragged of a, 'Speedy Seven Hour Service By The World's Fastest Runner', collapsed. To complete his misery, the US Tax authorities forced him into personal bankruptcy. The following year, he accepted a position as a salesman with the Lyons Tailoring Company. His position was terminated after less than two months.

The exhibition performances resumed until age caught up with him by 1952. At rock bottom, Owens was able to look inward and discover hidden talents. In 1955, the government appointed him as a goodwill ambassador, in which he flew to foreign countries and met the people and leaders of those countries. When he returned to Chicago, he was appointed head of the Illinois Youth Commission, organising athletic meetings and training camps for troubled youngsters.

It was then that Owens found his calling, amongst the youth of the nation. His main project over the last period of his life was a competition called the Jesse Owens' Games, made up of track and field meets for boys and girls beginning on a regional basis and ending in a national championship.

'When you see thousands of young people together, then competing against each other, you know it just has to eventually bring a new kind of understanding of other people and other nations' folkways. This is a wonderful thing because these young people are the greatest commodity the world has', he stated.

He also built his own PR firm. An in-demand speaker, Owens' oratory skills served to inspire generations of future athletes as well as the top business. His speeches hailed the values of patriotism, clean living, and fair play. His style was captivating, a 'kind of all-round super combination of nineteenth century spellbinder and twentieth century plastic PR man, fulltime banquet guest, eternal glad-hander and evangelistic small-talker', according to journalist William Oscar Johnson in *Sports Illustrated.*

For Jesse Owens, it took a failed business, bankruptcy, and years of demeaning exhibition events before realising that his talents really lay in inspiring others.

Use the underdog mentality

'In one week, in the summer of 1936, on the sacred soil of the Fatherland, the master athlete humiliated the master race'. *Race*, a 2016 biographical sports drama film about Jesse Owens, shows an awestruck Owens emerging from the changing rooms, to the sight of a packed stadium awash with Nazi regalia. Swastika flags flew high above the stadium in Berlin, itself a testament to German engineering prowess. The Germans wanted to use the Games for propaganda purposes, demonstrating that their nation was the rightful heir to the Greek Empire.

As Owens looked up on the starting line for the biggest moment of his career, the 100-metre final, he stood as a lone underdog, the antithesis of everything that Nazi Germany stood for. Hitler was said to be furious about Owens wins. He famously refused to shake hands with any of the winners, as he would certainly not contemplate shaking the hand of Owens.

As Larry Schwartz said in his ESPN article, 'score it: Owens 4, Hitler 0'. The story is one of triumph over evil, as a single black athlete defeated the powerful Third Reich. It was in this context that the writer Scott Smith called Jesse, 'the ultimate sports underdog'.

Fighting against the odds brings out the best in many people, including Jesse Owens, who later wrote, 'my whole life was wrapped up, summed up – and stopped up – by a single incident: my confrontation with the German dictator, Adolf Hitler, in the 1936 Olympics'.

Change your approach to fit the situation

Despite the adversity that kept presenting itself to Owens, he was always pragmatic about dealing with it, trying to move his life on. 'In what other country in the world could a poor black kid like me go all the places I've been, see all the things I've seen and make so many friends?', he asked.

A short time before leaving for Berlin, Owens, together with his close friend, the high-jumper, Dave Albritton, had travelled across America with Ohio State University's athletic squad. On their return from an event, they stopped for a meal in Richmond, Indiana. While their white friends were seated around the empty tables, Owens, Albritton and another black athlete were stopped from entering. The restaurant manager mumbled, 'White folk only …' Albritton, without hesitation, stepped towards him with clenched fists. 'Now then, Papa', Owens said to Albritton, 'take it easy'.

'Jesse', his wife insisted, 'was not a bitter man. He liked moving ahead with life. He was gearing up for the Olympics - and nothing was going to stop him'.

The incident was certainly not a one off. Another story is told how a few months later, on another team trip, Owens was prevented from driving into a roadside café. When his white team-mates brought out Albritton and Owens chicken sandwiches, the owner rushed out, trying to prevent the handover. Owens had to again calm his friend down.

What a sad sight it must have been, in later years, to see someone of Owens' stature reduced to racing horses, Remarkably, Owens did not see it that way. He knew that at the time, American society was designed for the black man to fail, not prosper. He had a young wife and daughter to support and resolved to do everything he could to make a living. Even if that required racing against a horse. 'People said it was degrading for an Olympic champion to run against a horse', Owens said. 'But what was I supposed to do? I had four gold medals, but you can't eat four gold medals'.

Owens was realistic after returning from Berlin, realising that despite his success, he would struggle to receive special treatment. 'I came back to my native country and I couldn't ride in the front of the bus. I had to go to the back door. I couldn't live where I wanted'.

Owens was never going to let society's injustices prevent him from succeeding, even if victory came despite, rather than because of, the system. Pragmatists like Owens have goals but are focused on the practical, the methods they can take to achieve them. Idealists, on the other hand, tend to focus on big ideas, focusing more on the end than the way of getting there.

Sometimes, people regard pragmatism as negative and cynical, but it is one which acknowledges the whole picture, warts and all. It is no less aspirational; it just acknowledges that along the way, there may be many obstacles in the road that need to be navigated.

Owens knew that American society was racist and unfair, but tellingly, his attitude was always one of realism and gratitude. 'We never had any problems', he said. 'We always ate. The fact that we didn't have steak. Who had steak?'

Chapter Twenty-Five

Althea Gibson

Shaking hands with the Queen of England was a long way from being forced to sit in the colored section of the bus going into downtown Wilmington

Before the 2019 US Open, a statue of Althea Gibson, the first black tennis player to win a Grand Slam, was unveiled outside the Arthur Ashe Stadium at Flushing Meadows in New York. This was a long overdue honour for a champion who, after her career was over, felt she had received scant recognition for her pioneering efforts while playing the sport.

Gibson was born in South Carolina in 1927. She was the daughter of sharecroppers. But with agriculture suffering significantly during the Great Depression, the family moved north to New York City.

Following the example of her father, she took up boxing to earn kudos in the local area. 'A street-brawling chronic, truant and eighth grade dropout' was how she was described. Gibson's future seemed gloomy. After leaving school aged thirteen, she spent time living in a shelter for abused children, fearful of her violent father.

Finding a path to success was a challenging one, but one thing in Althea's favour was her sporting prowess. She had been fortunate to grow up in a block closed to traffic, designated as a play street. Volunteers from the Police Athletic League set up recreational equipment, with a paddle tennis court close to her home.

Goodhearted community members spotted her potential as a tennis player and in 1940, directed her to the local Cosmopolitan Club. There, she excelled and started a journey which led to her playing at national level. Barred from participating in white-only tournaments, in 1941, she entered and won her first tournament, the New York State Championship, organised by the American Tennis Association (ATA), a competition formed exclusively for black competitors.

Gibson's success attracted the attention of Dr Walter Johnson, and Dr Hubert Eaton, physicians active in the black tennis community. The good doctors took Gibson under their wing, providing her with not just sporting opportunities, but the familial warmth and the education she never received at school.

Initially, Gibson struggled to become a fixture on the tennis circuit. Her determination and hard work paid off, beginning in 1950 when she became the first black woman to play in the US National Championship. But she had to wait for success in a Grand Slam as her breakthrough victory at the French Championships in 1956 showed.

Suddenly, everything seemed to click. Writing in her autobiography, she called the 1957 season, 'Althea Gibson's year'. In July, Gibson won Wimbledon, following this up with a victory at the US National Championship. A ticker tape parade and welcome at City Hall in New York followed. The Associated Press named her 'Female Athlete of the Year' in 1957 and 1958, a year in which she retained her Grand Slam titles in London and New York City.

By this time, her tennis career was coming to an end, however. The amateur era brought its share of glory but offered little in the way of financial reward, even for a player of Gibson's prowess who had won eleven Grand Slam titles in singles, doubles and mixed doubles. Gibson lamented the fact that, 'being the Queen of Tennis is all well and good, but you can't eat a crown … The landlord and grocer and tax collector are funny that way: they like cold cash'.

In 1959 she made an album, *Althea Gibson Sings*, and starred in the film, *The Horse Soldiers*, co-starring John Wayne and William Holden. She signed a one-hundred-thousand-dollar deal to play in exhibition tennis matches before Harlem

Globetrotter games in 1959 and took up golf in 1960, becoming the first black woman on the LPGA tour in 1962.

Racial discrimination remained a problem. Many hotels banned black people and some club officials refused to allow her to play. When she did compete, she was often forced to dress for tournaments in her car, as black golfers were banned from the clubhouse. Despite this, she was one of the LPGA's top fifty money winners for five years.

Tough times followed and she suffered ill health, marital problems and poor finances.

Summing up her career, Alan Schwartz, president of the United States Tennis Association (USTA) said, 'she simply changed the landscape of tennis. Arthur Ashe's job was not easy, but if he had to climb a hill, Althea Gibson had to climb a mountain. She was the original breakthrough person'.

Althea Gibson's contribution to the success of both Venus and Serena Williams has not been lost on either of the sisters. In 1997, Venus said, 'Althea Gibson paved the way for us'.

So, what traits enabled Gibson to overcome such hardship?

Play to win
Althea was always clear about how much victory meant to her. 'The loser is always a part of the problem; the winner is always a part of the answer. The loser always has an excuse; the winner always has a programme. The loser says it may be possible, but it's difficult; the winner says it may be difficult, but it's possible', she stated.

In August 2019, the city of East Orange, New Jersey, unveiled a monument at a local park in memory of a 'trailblazing sports icon and civil rights pioneer', who had lived in the city for over twenty years. Gibson's long-time friend, Frances Gray, spoke at the event, and highlighted her close friend's competitive nature, a trait synonymous with all sporting champions.

A talented singer and saxophonist, she didn't enter competitions just to perform but always to win. She was, as the title of her authorised biography suggests, *Born to Win*. A runner up in the Apollo Theatre's amateur talent contest in 1943, she made her professional singing debut at the Waldorf Astoria Hotel in 1957. 'If you sat down with her to play chess, you sat down to lose', Gray wryly noted, 'If you went bowling and you bowled, 200, she bowled 201'. As well as writing Gibson's biography, Francis Grey kept Gibson's memory alive through the Althea Gibson Foundation, a non-profit organization dedicated to giving city kids a chance to play tennis and golf.

Gibson was given two second-hand tennis rackets when she was thirteen years old. She learned to play at the Cosmopolitan Tennis Club in Harlem and won her first ATA title in 1941, in New York. Winning Wimbledon in 1957 did not come without its challenges. Victory had eluded her the previous year and such was her will to win on the grass courts of London, SW19 that she took a difficult decision to sacrifice her defence of her title at the French Championships to concentrate on sharpening her skills on the unique court conditions in England. On the day of the final, Gibson was undaunted by the blistering heat on Wimbledon's Centre Court. The burden of being top seed and possibly becoming the famous tournament's first black winner, may have gotten to some, but not Althea. She strolled to a straight sets win over Darlene Hard.

Many people are content to win a title once, only to fade into obscurity once they have achieved their ambition. Continuing to win is a much more difficult challenge, as Gibson herself acknowledged in one of her often-remembered remarks, 'in sports, you simply aren't considered a real champion until you have defended your title successfully. Winning it once can be a fluke. Winning it twice proves you are the best'. Indeed, Althea did return to win the Wimbledon title in 1958, backing up her initial success the previous year.

'Even as a girl, Althea was in a league of her own', said Bill Davis, a player on the ATA circuit, who was Gibson's training partner. 'She had unbelievable determination'.

Keep trying

Althea believed in sticking at her task and she was ecstatic when that resulted in triumph. 'At last! At last', she proclaimed, after winning Wimbledon.

On Saturday night, the sixth of July 1957, Gibson was on top of the world. It was the night of the Wimbledon Ball. In time-honoured fashion, the men's single winner, Australian Lew Hoad, took to the dancefloor alongside the new ladies' champion, Althea Gibson. The day was unique in many ways. For one, Gibson had become the first black player to win the title in London. Moreover, although a coincidence, it was the first of only four times that Queen Elizabeth II attended the final.

During the Ball, Gibson, the talented singer, grabbed a band leader's microphone and began to sing, *'I Can't Give You Anything but Love'*. The meaning behind the lyrics to the song were not lost on the audience; they came to represent her persistence, against all the odds, in reaching her present heights.

That breakthrough win at Wimbledon had been a long way coming. Seven long years earlier, after winning the 1950 Eastern Indoor Championship, Gibson remained frustrated in her quest to enter the full range of tournaments. Initially, the tennis authorities closed rank to keep her from performing at the US National Championship at Forest Hills, the forerunner of the US Open. To qualify for an invitation to the 1950 nationals, the USLTA insisted that Gibson would need to win one of the major preliminary grass-court events, all of which were invitational tournaments. No such invitations were forthcoming.

Finally, Gibson received a grudging invite to the Orange Lawn Tennis Club in New Jersey, where the Eastern Grass

Court Championships were taking place. The disappointment of a second-round exit was tempered by the fact that although she had not won the event, she still received an invitation to play at Forest Hills. And so, in August 1950, Gibson became the first black player to compete in the US National Championship. This was followed a year later by her appearance at Wimbledon, again, the first by a black player.

Through her twenties, Gibson dug deep and worked hard to improve her game. She was not exactly a journeyman, but she had not set the game alight either. Gibson, who spent two years as a physical education instructor at university, became unhappy with her inability to break through to the top ranks. She even considered leaving the tour and joining the army.

In 1956, together with her close friend, Angela Buxton, she won the Wimbledon doubles. However, to be considered a great, Gibson knew she needed to achieve sustained success in the singles format. Granted, she had won the French Championships in 1956, but victory was tantalisingly close in all the other Grand Slam tournaments. Gibson reached the quarter finals at Wimbledon, together with the finals of the Australian Open and US National Championship. Would Gibson ever reach the heights she knew she was capable of?

The answer came a year later, in which she dominated the sport. She won Wimbledon without the loss of a set. It had been a long journey. Her first battle had been to be allowed to compete against white opponents. Once that struggle was won, it was only the beginning. Many more years of improvement and dedication on the court were needed before Gibson could claim the titles she craved. Neither of these victories could have succeeded without patience.

It is worthwhile to note that nothing comes overnight, things take time. Like the words sung by Gibson at her victorious Wimbledon ball, the world becomes a more tolerable place when we acknowledge that, 'Rome was not built in a day, you have to pay, kid, for what you get'.

Find a mentor

Gibson understood that you couldn't do things on your own. 'No matter what accomplishments you make, somebody helped you', she confirmed.

In 1941, Althea had pretty much given up on high school. She was being threatened, with the prospect of attending a reform school, should her delinquency continue.

At the time, Buddy Walker, an accomplished but poorly paid saxophonist, was moonlighting as a Police Athletic League (PAL) instructor. Walker noticed Gibson playing paddleball and immediately saw the raw talent of the youngster. According to filmmaker, Rex Miller, who made a documentary on Althea's life in 2014, Walker invited Gibson to play tennis on local courts and took her to the Cosmopolitan Club, one of two clubs in Harlem with black ownership and a predominantly black membership in Harlem that counted doctors, lawyers and professionals amongst its numbers.

'As they like to tell the story, she was a little rough around the edges', Miller said. 'But a lot of folks at the Cosmopolitan Club mentored her, not only in tennis, but also just how to conduct herself in this new group of people that she was being exposed to'.

By mid-summer, Althea was taking lessons from Fred Johnson, a one-armed teaching professional at the club. Her game, which had previously been all about power, also began to have an elegance to it. With financial help from famous boxer, Sugar Ray Robinson, Gibson captured junior national championships and in 1947, her potential caught the eye of two ATA officials, Dr Robert Johnson, and Dr Hubert Eaton. Dr Johnson, who also helped Arthur Ashe, took Althea to one side and asked her if she would like to play at Forest Hills someday. Her previous unwillingness to co-operate and accept help, changed after she met the men who have been described as the two godfathers of black tennis in America.

While enthusiastic about her talent, the two men felt her lack of education and discipline would impede her development. It was, therefore, arranged that Dr Eaton would take Althea to live with his family for the winter and put her through high school; in the summer, she would travel the ATA tennis circuit with the Johnsons.

Her manners were so bad that the Eatons initially made her eat in the kitchen. Over time, she began to blossom under his tutelage and even thrived in the more refined environment. She put the hours in at school, finishing among the top ten in the graduating class. She went on to enrol as a scholarship student at Florida A&M, where she went on to earn her degree.

Althea Gibson, whose favourite word as a teenager was 'no', came to accept the help of the community and according to tennis legend, Billie Jean King, made a huge difference in her life. 'It's not necessarily unique to the African-American community, but everybody stands on somebody's shoulders', said former New York Mayor, David Dinkins, a long-standing friend of Gibson.

Express gratitude

Gibson appreciated the importance of thanking those who had helped her. 'Believe me when I say I am sincerely grateful to you for what you have done for me. I do hope to make you proud of my sacrifices', she said.

Although they were two good mentors, Doctors Eaton and Johnston, could only take Althea so far. Whilst Gibson thrived on the black-only ATA tour, she was not allowed to play in white tournaments.

The USLTA rules officially outlawed racial or ethnic discrimination but players qualified for the US National Championship by their performances at USLTA tournaments, most of which were held at white-only clubs. That changed in 1950, when former national champion, Alice Marble, wrote a scathing magazine article challenging the USLTA's stance. Marble was a white tennis player who won the US singles titles four times and Wimbledon in 1939.

'If tennis is a game for ladies and gentlemen', she wrote in a letter to *American Lawn Tennis* magazine, 'It's time we acted a little more like gentlepeople and less like sanctimonious hypocrites. If Althea Gibson represents a challenge to the present crop of women players, it's only fair that they should meet that challenge on the courts'.

Unmoved, New Jersey's Maplewood Country Club refused to let Althea on its courts during the New Jersey State Championship. However, the Orange Lawn Tennis Club in South Orange, New Jersey, allowed Althea to compete. She advanced to the second round. She then received an invite from the USLTA to play in the US National Championship.

Althea Gibson expressed profound gratitude for the help she received in obtaining this invitation. She wrote a six-page letter to Marble, which was published in the *Baltimore Afro-American* newspaper of the thirtieth of January 1951:

'Dear Miss Marble. Your open letter was read with a mixed feeling of sorry and elation. I am elated over the opportunity I had to play at Forest Hills, but I am sorry for the slurs you received and friends you have lost. I do believe that you have gained more true respectful friends than you have lost by writing the very fine article you wrote on my behalf in the Tennis Magazine'.

'Alice Marble's letter was a turning point', said Bob Davis, Gibson's former warm-up partner and a black tennis historian. 'It said things we couldn't say. It was something that Althea Gibson was truly grateful for'.

Don't back down

Gibson was willing to sacrifice herself in pursuit of her goal. 'I always wanted to be somebody. If I have made it, its half because I was game to take a wicked amount of punishment along the way', she commented.

In the summer of 1950, the US National Championship at the West Side Tennis Club in Forest Hills, Queens, reached a pivotal moment after Gibson had won her first-round match. Now, on one side of the court was the favourite, Louise Brough, a Californian and the reigning Wimbledon champion. On the other side was the tall, Harlem-raised young woman, Althea Gibson, the first black player to play in the iconic tournament, the forerunner of the United States Open.

According to Bertram Baker, executive secretary of the ATA, as well as a New York Assemblyman, the darkening weather, which descended into lightening and torrential rain ultimately causing the match to be extended into the following day, was only matched by the vulgarity of some of the chants against Gibson.

'It was American apartheid, like South Africa', David Dinkins said. 'But that's the way we were. Most tennis was played at country clubs and places that didn't admit people of color, so it was tough for her'.

Gibson went onto lose the match the next day but had shown she would not be cowed by the prejudice of the crowd. Naturally sporty and muscular, Althea's streetwise attitude is said to have been born out of her father forcing her to fight him on the roof of their apartment block, telling her to always get in the first punch. It was a trait that never left her and once refined, helped her win many battles in the future.

She described Harlem as a mean place to grown up in, where a kid had to prove herself by fighting to prevent her from being considered an 'easy mark'. As she grew up, and moved away from the streets, she may have stopped fighting battles with her firsts, but her willingness to battle continued.

Whilst she was never intent on making political statements and could not be said to be an activist in the traditional sense, she never backed down either. By entering hostile environments and winning tournaments, rather than arguments, she was creating opportunities for black athletes for generations to come.

It did not get any easier when Althea left the tennis environment for the world of golf and became the first black player on the LPGA tour. She joined in the same month as George Wallace, Governor of Alabama promised, 'segregation now, segregation tomorrow and segregation forever'. At one event, Althea was even forced to change her shoes in the parking lot.

Mentally strong people, like Althea Gibson, have healthy habits. They do not waste time feeling sorry for themselves, lament their circumstances or how others have treated them. Instead, they take responsibility for their role in life and understand life is not always fair. They are prepared to enter hostile environments and stand by their principles or beliefs, confident that they are doing the right thing.

Althea Gibson's road to success may have been a challenging one but as Billie Jean King observed, 'I never saw her back down'.

Chapter Twenty-Six

Ben Hogan

I always outworked everybody. Work never bothered me like it bothers some people

Ben Hogan, known as 'The Hawk', ranks as one of the most successful golfers of all time. Few sporting champions have faced the physical and mental challenges which Hogan had to overcome on his way to glory. Hogan battled difficult life events off the course, with the same fortitude that saw him win nine career Majors on it.

Alongside Gary Player, he is the fourth most successful golfer of all time, behind only Jack Nicklaus, Tiger Woods and Walter Hagen. Despite losing his best playing years to the Second World War, Hogan is one of only five men to have won all four of the Major championships. He also lays claim to the Triple crown, having won the US Masters, the US Open and the Open Championship in the same year.

Born in Texas in August 1912, Hogan's father suffered from ill health before committing suicide. According to some reports, nine-year-old Ben was in the room with him when he shot himself. Whether or not the young boy witnessed the event, the trauma is likely to have stayed with him throughout his life and could well be the reason he was described as such an introvert.

The family experienced significant poverty after the death and the Hogan children were put to work to help make ends meet. Ben ended up selling newspapers and by the age of eleven, was walking the seven miles to a local country club to make money carrying golfers' bags.

Hogan dropped out of high school during his senior year and turned professional in the golf industry six months short of his eighteenth birthday at the Texas Open in San Antonio, in late January 1930.

Not as naturally gifted as many of his contemporaries, Hogan struggled to make the grade in his early years, failing to win a tournament until he was twenty-seven years old. The financial challenges of life on the tour were considerable. On more than one occasion Hogan found himself playing for his dinner.

After the war, in which he served in the US Air Force, Hogan worked relentlessly on his game and took his first PGA title in 1946. Two years later, he won another PGA and his first US Open. Between 1945 and 1949 Hogan won an astonishing thirty-seven tournaments and was twice the leading money winner of the year.

Whilst 1949 started as well as the previous four years, things were soon to change. Travelling with his wife on a country road through Texas, Hogan's vehicle was involved in a head-on collision with a Greyhound bus. The accident saw Hogan suffer significant injuries, yet remarkably, within sixteen weeks, he had resumed his golfing duties in time for the 1950 season. Even more astonishingly, just a year after doctors questioned whether he would walk again, Hogan won the US Open.

Hogan's career went from strength to strength. 1953 marked the high point in his career. He won the Masters, by five strokes and the US Open, by six. Making his only appearance across the 'pond', at the Open Championship, at Carnoustie, he won by four strokes. All of this achieved despite the constant pain that served as an ongoing reminder of that near-death car accident.

A ticker-tape parade on Broadway welcomed him home with the achievement still known as one of the single greatest seasons in the history of professional golf. To provide some context, only Tiger Woods near perfect season in 2000 came close to matching Hogan's achievement.

However, the accident had left both physical and mental scars and Hogan curtailed his appearances in future years, before ultimately retiring and entering the golf club manufacturing business.

A career that saw sixty-three victories and nine Majors would be regarded as impressive even before one considers the difficult childhood, the earlier technical deficiencies and the near fatal crash that almost cost him his life.

The life of Ben Hogan and his successful battle with adversity serves as an inspiration to those in the golfing world and beyond. What traits did the 'Hawk' display that enabled him to triumph over his many adversities?

Keep practicing

Hogan understood the benefits of practice. 'If you can't outplay them, outwork them', he once commented. In his book, *Five Lessons: The Modern Fundamentals of Golf,* Hogan spoke about the final hole at the 1950 US Open when his two-hundred-yard two-iron shot stopped forty feet from the cup, helping him into the playoff, which he subsequently won. The crowd erupted into cheers, amazed at the shot. To the unsurprised Hogan, it was just an example of the power of practice. 'I didn't hit that shot then', he wrote. 'I'd been practicing that shot since I was twelve years old'.

Golf fanatics know the work that top professionals undertake on the practice ground, but it is important to remember that in Hogan's days, such dedication was rare and even frowned upon. Hogan saw practice as the only way of correcting his major technical deficiency, a hook, that he had described as being, 'like a rattlesnake in his pocket'. The solution to getting rid of the problem was hard work and practice, becoming known in golfing circles as, 'the secret', which allowed him to make his swing almost automatic.

Gary Player, the legendary South African golfer, saw a direct correlation between Hogan's triumphs and the hard work and consistent practice. Dedication to his craft was the key to building the persistence needed to be successful. Byron Nelson, the champion who grew up with Hogan, agreed with Player, noting that, 'nobody had to work as hard to play golf as Ben. Nobody'.

Practise was not just a result of a bad performance. There were times when Hogan returned to the practice ground immediately after winning a tournament. A story is told of Hogan undertaking a mammoth three-hour practice session just minutes after a brilliant day, in which he had shot a score of sixty-six to lead a tournament. With no hint of humour, Hogan commented, 'when I'm not playing, I like to be practicing. I enjoy every minute of it. To tell you the truth, I'd just as soon do this'.

It seems prudent to ask if other golfers could have come back from the near fatal crash that Hogan was involved in on the twenty-ninth of March 1949. On his way home to Fort Worth from a tournament in Arizona, the near fatal crash caused significant damage. The medical procedures that followed caused him chronic pain, swelling and fatigue, which he endured for the rest of his life. But he was as determined to work as hard on his rehabilitation as he had done on his golf swing.

If you want to succeed at something and have technical flaws in your chosen area, then you can take heart from the career of Ben Hogan. Hogan believed that there was no such thing as a born golfer, 'or a born anything'. To Hogan, it was all dependant on hard work and practice.

Prove them wrong

Hogan was motivated by the negative views of others in relation to his perceived abilities. 'People have always been telling me what I can't do. I guess I have wanted to show them. That's been one of my driving forces all my life', he once said.

In 2018, ahead of that week's Masters, Tiger Woods was asked if a victory for him would mark sports greatest comebacks. (As an aside, Woods did not win, but he did return the year after to achieve a remarkable victory and one of golf's most remarkable recent comebacks.) Woods was adamant that 'one of the greatest comebacks in all of sport is the gentleman who won here, Mr Ben Hogan. I mean, he got hit by a bus and came back and won Major championships … the pain he had to endure, the things he had to do just to play and just how hard it was for him to walk, and he ended up walking thirty-six holes (in one day) and winning a US Open'.

In that accident, on the second of February, the car driven by Hogan, accompanied by his wife, was hit head-on by a Greyhound bus. To protect his wife, Hogan threw his body over to the right, avoiding the steering column that could have easily crushed him. Instead, he suffered such severe injuries that doctors predicted he would never walk again. Hogan had another near brush with death before surgeons operated to stop blood clots from entering his heart.

In December of that year, fellow golfer, Jimmy Demaret, told the press at the Miami Open that he felt Hogan would not make a comeback. Hogan not only taught himself to walk again, but he also taught himself to play golf again. He was chipping and putting by May 1949. In rehabilitation treatment for ten months, it was said that Hogan practiced his swing until his hands bled.

His damaged legs had to be wrapped in elastic to keep the swelling down and he limped as he walked, but, incredibly, in January 1950, he was back playing at the Los Angeles Open, in which he finished in a tie for first, before losing an eighteen-hole play-off.

Before each round at the 1950 US Open at Merion, Hogan soaked for an hour in a hot bath filled with Epsom salts. He kept the pain to himself in order not to show any weakness. Less than eighteen months after the near fatal collision, Hogan defied excruciating leg cramps to win the US Open at Merion. That was just so typical of Hogan, always more comfortable when defying the odds.

Beating the odds, when things are stacked against you, can bring out the best in a person. It means they must persevere and keep going, despite what people say about their chances of succeeding. If you are the type of person like Ben Hogan, who enjoys proving people wrong, you can learn to remain positive in the face of adversity. Whatever anyone has said about your chances of success, history is full of stories of those who succeeded having at first, been written off.

Set high standards

Hogan was never happy with his performances, believing he could always improve his performance. Nonetheless, he did acknowledge when he played well. 'I think I played the best nine holes of my life on those holes. I don't think I came close to missing a shot', he once commented.

Ben Hogan was not a natural at golf, in the same way that legends such as Sam Snead or Jack Nicklaus were. A late developer, it took him fifteen years as a professional to get his game together, cure that troublesome hook and reach great heights.

Like many top sportsmen, Hogan was not satisfied with anything other than the best of standards. He was known to have once asked his caddy for the distance to the pin, only to receive an imprecise reply of '117 or 118 (yards)'. In complete seriousness, Hogan turned around and asked, 'Well, what is it?'

The perfectionism followed him off the golf course and into the factory, when in 1953, he started the Ben Hogan Company, a golf club manufacturing business. Hogan promised to do things differently and to manufacture clubs 'as near perfect as modern-day tools can perform'.

Having launched the company with a partner from Dallas, Texas, he was pleased with the new clubs that had been produced at a cost of one-hundred and fifty-thousand dollars, until he tried them out. 'It was obvious that they weren't up to my standards', he said. 'I had approved the model, but we were training new people and they were badly made. 'These can't go out', I said. Orders were coming in like crazy, but we never shipped any of those clubs. We took them out back and broke every one'.

After his retirement from playing, Hogan went to the office every day and regularly had clubs destroyed if he felt they did not meet his own high standards. As late as 1987, he told Nick Seitz in *Golf Digest*, 'this sounds stupid, but I thought I was always in a slump'. Sam Snead wrote of Hogan, 'You got the feeling that Ben hated -- I mean, hated -- the mistakes he made'.

Ben Hogan would undoubtedly agree with Tony Robbins, when he says that, 'goals don't lead to success. High standards do'.

Commit to the right mindset

Hogan knew the power of the mind in achieving his goals. 'Golf is twenty per cent talent and eighty per cent management', he once stated.

In 1953, Ben Hogan was victorious in the 1953 Open at Carnoustie. Scottish golf fans fell in love with the man they dubbed the 'Wee Ice Mon', after his cool and calculated performance in lifting the Claret Jug in his first and only attempt. Part of the current course is named for him, 'Hogan's Alley', whilst across the street is the Hogan House Hotel.

It is unknown whether the 'ice mon' nickname was originally designed to mock Hogan's clinical, emotionless approach to the game or whether it paid tribute to his calm temperament. Writer, Will Grimsley, called Hogan a cold, detached artisan on the course whilst Gene Sarazen, a seven-time Major winner stated that Hogan played with the, 'frigidity of dry ice'.

A story is told that, during a tournament, Ben Hogan stood over the ball, gripping his putter and contemplating a putt. Suddenly, a train came hurtling past and belted out a loud whistle! Unmoved, Hogan simply rolled the ball into the hole at the same time. In the press conference after the tournament, Hogan was asked by a member of the press if he had not been bothered by the train's whistle. Hogan gave a puzzled look and replied, 'What whistle?'

The 'Wee Ice Mon' moniker has come to represent Hogan's calm temperament and that, symbolizes something extremely positive about Hogan's approach to his profession.

In his 1957 book, *Five Lessons: The Modern Fundamentals of Golf*, Ben Hogan presented his ideas about the essential elements of a proper golf swing. Many golf teachers still recommend the book, over sixty years after its release. One of the main reasons, apart from the technical aspects, that the book is so widely regarded is that it is written by a player with the calm mindset desired by all players.

Hogan's recovery from his catastrophic injuries, could well have been down to his mindset. If any sport is given to maintaining a balanced mindset, it is golf. Anyone who has ever picked up a club knows that the game is, essentially, a mental game that requires emotional balance as much as, if not more than, technical ability.

When tackling challenges, it often come down to our mindset. As we have already discussed, people with a fixed mindset are often discouraged by setbacks, such as a poor shot on the golf course; the setback is too great for their fragile confidence and does not bode well for future performance. Those with a balanced outlook, like Hogan, view setbacks as learning opportunities. Mistakes are too good an opportunity to waste on a tantrum. The good news is that research has shown that neuroplasticity, our brains ability to change, continues even into old age.

Hogan himself summed up the importance of a balanced mindset when talking about Tommy Bolt, a player known for his temper tantrums. 'If we could have screwed another head on his shoulders, he could have been the greatest who ever played'. Had Bolt understood the power of neuroplasticity, the ability to change, then it could have been him and not Hogan, who came to be considered as one of the greats of the game.

Always look to improve

As one of the game's greats, knowledge, as the source of improvement and success, was a key factor for Hogan. 'I learn something new about the game almost every time I step on the course', he observed.

Continuing professional development is the term used to describe the learning activities that professionals such as lawyers, accountants and teachers engage in to develop and enhance their abilities. It enables learning to become conscious and proactive, rather than passive and reactive.

In much the same way, Hogan used every experience on the course towards his own continuing professional development. In 1937, Hogan and his wife Valerie were all but down to their last five dollars. He was virtually broke and on the verge of quitting the tour. By finishing sixth in the PGA tournament in Oakland, California, in early 1938, he won prize money of three-hundred and eighty dollars and was persuaded to carry on.

Hogan explained to Jerry Potter, a writer for *USA Today*, how much emphasis he placed on his golfing education. 'I was trying to make a living. I had failed twice to make the tour. I had to learn to beat the people I was playing'. Education took the form of watching how some of his competitors shaped up, 'how they swung a club, the way they hit a ball'.

In 1946, Hogan suffered two of the most devastating back-to-back losses in Major championship history. At the Masters, he had an 18-foot putt to win his first Major tournament. Hogan ran his first putt three feet past the hole, then missed the next shot. Two months later at the US Open in Cleveland, he was faced with an identical situation on the final green. Hogan three-putted again, to miss out on the title.

Many golfers struggle to overcome one devastating loss, let alone two in quick succession. Instead, Hogan returned to the practise ground and studied ways in which he could learn from his bitter disappointments. Hogan recovered to win the 1946 PGA Championship at Portland Golf Club, his first Major championship.

In his book, Hogan showed his commitment to lifelong learning, by stating, 'the more you know about a goal, the more you can keep on learning, almost indefinitely'. In other words, learning is for life, not just for difficult times.

The Ben Hogan story shows that continuous development allows a person to meet his or her challenges head on. As food nourishes our bodies, so to, continued learning feeds our minds.

Chapter Twenty-Seven

Fanny Blankers-Koen

I'll show you

Francina 'Fanny' Blankers-Koen was a Dutch athlete, famous for winning four gold medals at the 1948 Olympics in London. Such was her impact on sport, that the date that would have marked her one-hundredth birthday was commemorated by Google with a special Doodle that pictured her racing down the track. Nicknamed 'The Flying Housewife', she smashed through the barriers in place against married women at the time, setting in motion changes that positively affected the careers of female athletes forever.

A natural athlete, she had a talent for several sports, initially focusing on swimming, before switching to the track when she was seventeen years old. A year later, in 1936, she met her coach and future husband Jan Blankers, who persuaded her to enter the Dutch Olympic trials. Aged eighteen, she made the team for Berlin, competing in the high jump and the 4 x 100-metre relay. The games were an important learning experience, rather than a roaring success, as she finished sixth in the high jump whilst placing fifth in the relay.

Her first world record came in the 100-yard dash at the European Championships in Vienna in 1938. At the time, she was being spoken about as a future Olympic champion. Unfortunately, the Second World War put paid to her ambitions. The rescheduled 1940 Olympics set for Helsinki were cancelled just a week before the Nazis invaded the Netherlands.

During the war, she married her coach and had two children. In line with the conservative views of the time, it was presumed that this would spell the end of her career. Fanny had clearly not read the script, as instead, she used the wartime to build up her power, speed and technique. Competing in national events, she managed to become world record holder at the 80-metre hurdles, high jump and long jump.

Nearing the end of the Second World War, the Nazi occupation caused famine and food scarcity in the Netherlands, making it difficult for Blankers-Koen to eat enough food during her training. She became ill and had to stay in bed for six weeks. Like other housewives in the country, she was forced to cycle around and find whatever she could to eat or burn in her woodstove.

By the time of the 1948 Olympics, the thirty-year-old was thought to be too old to succeed, whilst other less progressive critics suggested she should have been back at home with her children. Defying the cruel taunts of her detractors, Blankers-Koen won four gold medals in the London Games and could have won even more had she not been restricted to entering three individual races as well as the sprint relay.

Such was her fame that according to *Smithsonian* magazine, during the Games, 'she was as well-known to Olympic patrons as King George of England'.

She returned home; not to millions in sponsorship endorsements, as would happen today, but to the more modest gift of a bicycle from the people of Amsterdam. As an amateur, she could not even benefit from the modest financial rewards that were on offer, instead travelling around the world to promote female participation in sport.

Her last Olympic Games, in Helsinki in 1952, were an anti-climax; aged thirty-four, she suffered from blood poisoning and a skin complaint that hindered her preparations and forced her to withdraw from the sprints and the relay.

To put Fanny's achievements into context, in the seventy-two years since her medal haul, only Carl Lewis has equalled her record and the Netherlands have only produced a further two Olympic Gold medallists in the sport.

In a country that has produced sporting stars as great as Johan Cruyff, Ruud Gullit and Marianne Vos, Dutch athletics coach, Charles Van Commenee, labelled his compatriot as simply the 'greatest sports person we have ever produced as a nation'.

How did a mother and housewife, aged over thirty, manage to confound the critics and become known as one of the greatest female athletes of all time?

Develop the will to win

Fanny was very competitive in everything she was involved in. An article published by the Associated Press observed, 'with her bike at a stoplight, she insisted on being the first off. Cards, any game, she always wanted to win'. Indeed, despite her modesty, Blankers-Koen's biographer, Kees Kooman, portrays her as a deeply competitive athlete. 'Fanny wasn't only the shy, nice Dutch housewife. Sport was everything to her and she wanted to win in everything. If she was out on her bike and someone was ahead of her, she had to beat them. When she was sixty-five years old and she was told about someone knitting a sweater in a week, she was so jealous she had to do it herself'.

Kooman felt that such a single-minded approach was a necessity for any champion like Fanny. Whilst she had a natural talent, her competitive nature ensured that she was able to perform in so many different events.

As a teenager, she enjoyed most competitive sports including swimming and tennis. The only reason she is said to have chosen athletics over swimming is because the Netherlands had many other star swimmers at the time and her chances of winning were much higher in track and field.

The Second World War did not discourage Fanny from engaging in sporting competition. Having won all the championships available to win in the Netherlands, she was excluded from further competition. In sheer desperation, she entered a men's race and came in fourth in the 100-metre dash, with a time of 11.5 seconds.

In February 1946, she gave birth to a daughter, little Fanneke. A dedicated performer, Fanny returned to training only two months after the birth. That August, she also participated in the Dutch Championships and won five titles. Fanny followed this up by winning the 80-metre hurdles and obtaining a gold medal in the 4 x 100-metre relay at the European Championships in Oslo.

Competition pushes some people to do better than others. Pursuing goals with great intensity paid off for competitors like Fanny Blankers-Koen. It is interesting to note that most of her twelve world records were accomplished in her thirties, after she had given birth. Her relentless will to win made up for any advantages that her younger rivals would have had over her. In winning with such regularity, she broke down ageist and sexist barriers that existed against mothers in sports.

Successful people triumph over adversity because their will to win is so great. Fanny Blankers-Koen showed that the attribute can literally lift you to unimaginable heights.

Prove your point
Proving her point to people was important to Fanny, especially after she received criticism for decisions she had made. Famously, she once vowed, 'I'll show you'.

Fanny Blankers-Koen arrived in London for the 1948 Olympic Games with a point to prove. Qualification meant leaving her two children behind in Amsterdam for the duration of the games, something for which she received a great deal of criticism.

Whilst she arrived in London as the holder of six world records and two European championship golds in Oslo, won two years earlier, she remained relatively unknown to the British public. One of her greatest challenges came not on the track, but in dealing with the prevailing customs of the time. Fanny recollected that she received, 'very many bad letters. People writing that I must stay home with my children'. She was also told that it was unbecoming of a woman to run on a track with short trousers.

It was not just sexism that the Dutch athlete faced. The British team manager, Jack Crump, took one look at Blankers-

Koen and said she was, 'too old to make the grade'. It is interesting to think what might have been said had it been revealed that she was already three months pregnant and training only twice a week.

Blankers-Koen won golds in the 100-metres, 200-metres, 80-metre hurdles and 4 x 100-metre relay in the rain, but possibly her greater achievement was proving a point to her critics. She was not too old to completely dominate the field and win every event she entered. As a mother, she had shown that she deserved to be taken seriously as an athlete.

Praised by *The Guardian* as, 'easily the outstanding all-round woman athlete of the day', there was still a hint of sexism in its praise of Fanny. 'Off the track she is as feminine as man's capricious heart could wish. On it, not only is she an expert technically as most men champions but her actual foot and leg movements are straight like a man's rather than a woman's and temperamentally, she is a lesson to all'. Another reporter wrote that she ran, 'like she was chasing the kids out of the pantry'.

Blankers-Koen changed public perceptions of what a married mother of children was capable of. Since that time, there have been so many stories of women athletes who have returned from pregnancy to succeed in their sports. Channelling the doubts of others into motivation, rather than unproductive anger, like Fanny Blankers-Koen did, can be hugely effective.

Use a guiding hand
Listening to those close to her became a benefit for Fanny. 'You can go home if you wish', Jan said to Fanny. 'But in time, you will be sorry. Just go out there and try to make the final, that will be enough'.

Sobbing in the Wembley dressing rooms moments before the start of her 200-metre heat, Fanny Blankers-Koen told her husband and coach, that she wanted to go home. She had already won two gold medals and was mentally and physically exhausted. Jan's brief but powerful pep talk did the trick. She went back out onto the Wembley track and stormed into the final. On the sixth of August, she left the rest of field trailing in her wake as she achieved the biggest margin of victory in a 200-metre Olympic final, a record that still stands to this day.

It was not the first time during the games that Jan had been on hand to soothe his wife's nerves. Having won the 100-metres, she had told her husband, 'I am an Olympic Champion and I don't want to run anymore'. She believed that she had already achieved her goal and claimed that she was missing her children. Jan simply told her to go to bed and rest for the following day's 80-metre hurdles heats, an event she went onto win with ease.

Perhaps, it was homesickness, the pressure, or a reaction to the pre-games taunts of her critics that had taken it out of her. Maybe, it was even a mixture of all three. As Fanny leaned through the tape to claim victory, Jan was on hand at the finishing line to joke, 'see, you aren't too old after all'.

Jan Blankers, a former Olympic triple jumper, had met his future wife at an athletics competition a year before the 1936 Olympic Games. He was immediately taken by her natural ability but felt that he could improve her faults with his coaching ability. He became her coach and the couple were married in August 1940.

Dutch athletics coach, Charles Van Commenee, is keen to highlight the role that Jan, fourteen years his wife's senior, played in her rise to the top. 'He was a very progressive coach, ahead of the game. He played a very important role in pursuing excellence and trying to get her to do more and get better. He encouraged her to get the best out of herself and win more medals; in that era, that was a big deal. Women were often not encouraged to be competitive in that era'.

Blankers was the coach of the Dutch team for the Berlin Olympics and was at the forefront of promoting his future wife's career. She was only eighteen years of age and her medal hopes were slim, but Jan Blankers insisted that she be invited to join the Dutch Olympic team. Jan very quickly learnt

Swedish, for example, in order to study trendsetting Scandinavian books on physiology. After the war, he regularly assembled his team of women in a log cabin far from the bustle of the city. There, he organised meticulously prepared group training sessions which were unheard of at the time.

Would Fanny have achieved as much without her husband? By the time of her triumph in 1948, she had spent twelve years under the tutelage of him. What is certain is the fact that had Jan Blankers not been trackside in 1948, we may be talking about the double gold medallist Fanny Blankers-Koen, rather than as the holder of four Olympic gold medals.

Say no to complacency

At a glittery ceremony held in Monaco at the end of 1999, the International Amateur Athletic Federation awarded Fanny Blankers-Koen, by then, an elderly, eighty-one-year-old, the title of Female Athlete of the Twentieth Century. 'You mean it is me who has won? I must say I am surprised', was Fanny's response and so typical of the modest, down-to-earth athlete, who tended to downplay her achievements. Unpretentious to the end, she rejected excessive praise of her achievements, stating, 'all I've done is run fast. I do not see why people should make much fuss about that'.

A story is told of how Blankers-Koen attended the Munich Olympic Games in 1972 and met Jesse Owens (See Chapter Twenty-four). The story serves to illustrate the modesty with which she conducted herself. The two had met briefly at the 1936 Olympics when the Dutch teenager managed to obtain Owens' autograph.

"I still have your autograph" she told her hero, "I'm Fanny Blankers-Koen."

Owens replied, "You don't have to tell me who you are, I know everything about you!"

Blankers-Koen was, in many ways, the sporting equal of Owens, but in her own eyes, she was still the young girl from Utrecht.

Keeping her feet on the ground and refusing to become complacent about her achievements was the hallmark of this Olympic Champion. It has been said that one of the dangers of success is the fact that it can breed complacency. Such arrogance can cause a person to underestimate their future challenges. Sport is littered with occasions when teams thought that they only had to turn up to win, only to be surprised by the challenge that lay waiting for them.

How do we guard against complacency? Blankers-Koen showed that you need to keep your feet on the ground and not believe in past glories. Successful people continue to learn and adapt, and never think of themselves as the finished article.

Ada Kok, the Dutch swimming star, spent time with Blankers-Koen when she was a coach of the Dutch Olympic Squad at the 1964 Olympics in Tokyo. She explained that Fanny's approach was one which was ingrained in Dutch sporting culture. 'It may be a very bad Dutch habit, but our well-known sportspeople were more recognised and honoured abroad than in the Netherlands', said Kok. 'The Dutch are more like, "Act normal and keep both feet on the ground," no matter how famous you become in your sport'.

Keep going even at the end
The Second World War looked like it was going to deprive Fanny of her opportunity to become an Olympic champion. 'People were being taken away, and friends of mine in the underground were shot and people were hungry and were in the streets begging for food,' she remembered.

In 1939, Fanny Blankers-Koen was getting ready to prepare for the 1940 Olympic Games in Helsinki. In consultation with her coach Jan, it had been decided that she would focus on the 100-metre sprint and the high jump events.

Only one month after her engagement to Jan, the Netherlands was invaded by Nazi Germany on the tenth of May 1940. The Second World War cut short many promising sporting careers and it seemed as if the Dutch athlete's career may have been another to add to the list.

The Olympic Games had been scheduled to take place only two months later in Helsinki, Finland. Due to the cancellation of the Helsinki and 1944 Games, due to be held in London, it seemed that Blankers-Koen was destined never to win an Olympic gold.

Some of her best performances may have taken place during the war, but the war years were not particularly kind on a personal level. Whilst Fanny resumed outdoor training only six months after the birth of Jan Blankers Junior, in August 1941, the young child suffered a severe illness in the summer of 1942 that further interrupted her career.

The long and severe winter of 1944-1945 was catastrophic for many Dutch families as what became known as the 'Hunger Winter' took hold. Fanny and other athletes were forced to take a break from competing. Even at her most optimistic, during those dark years, she could not have envisaged that just three years later, she would be standing on the winner's podium at Wembley Stadium on four separate occasions.

From a competitive standpoint, everything was against Fanny Blankers-Koen as the war ended. She was over thirty years of age by the time of the 1948 Olympics, competing eleven times in eight days, outperforming her younger opponents and never losing.

Her extraordinary, four gold medal-winning performance at Wembley showed it is never too late to achieve one's goals. Kees Kooman, her biographer, suggested that, 'if it hadn't been for the Second World War, she would have won seven, eight, nine Olympic gold medals'.

To those despondent at the thought of not yet overcoming their setbacks, remember the life and late development of Fanny Blankers-Koen. After all, as novelist George Eliot pointed out, 'it is never too late to be what you might have been'.

The War Heroes

.

Chapter Twenty-Eight

Virginia Hall

The most dangerous of all Allied Spies: We must find and destroy her

Virginia Hall's extraordinary story is unfamiliar to many. Often referred to as, 'the most important spy you have never heard of', she left behind no revealing memoir, never gave an interview and rarely spoke about her exploits. Like most spies, Hall operated in the shadows and intended to keep it that way. Her main concern was not fame and fortune but keeping her cover out of the public domain. That is why you will not see many quotes attributed to her in these pages; intelligence agents are not predisposed to sharing their thoughts in public.

In recent years, historians have begun to reveal the remarkable stories during in the Second World War, which bore her hallmark. Had she spoken, her modesty would have prevented her from boasting about being top of the Gestapo's most wanted list in Nazi-occupied France.

Hall became the United States' most decorated female civilian during the Second World War and is recognized as the architect of several spy tactics that are still used by the Central Intelligence Agency (CIA) today. In recent years, the agency has publicly called her a war heroine and named a training building after her.

Virginia Hall was born in Baltimore, Maryland in 1906 to a wealthy family and was brought up on a farm. A bright and talented student, she studied multiple languages including German, Italian and French. She was something of an all-rounder, elected class president, editor-in-chief of the school newspaper and captain of the field hockey team.

After studying at Radcliffe and Barnard College, she breezed through graduate school at the American University in

Washington, DC. Hall then continued her education in European cities such as Paris and Vienna. Whilst abroad, she earned a diploma in economics and international law and became fluent in several languages.

After finishing her studies, in 1931, Hall accepted a role as a consular clerk at the US embassy in Warsaw, Poland before being transferred to Izmir, Turkey.

In 1933, disaster struck when she fell and accidentally shot herself in the leg whilst hunting. Her leg had to be amputated below the knee. The blow would have finished off the careers of lesser people, but not Hall. In September 1934, having learned to walk again, she returned to the US Consulate in Venice, complete with a prosthetic leg (which she had nicknamed Cuthbert), in tow.

In 1939, on the eve of the Second World War, she resigned from her position, having failed in her final appeal to gain a waiver to take the US Foreign Service exam.

After France declared war on Germany, Hall enlisted in the French ambulance corps during the 'Phony War' from September 1939 to May 1940. When Paris fell to Germany in May 1940, she decided that she would continue the fight against the Nazis. She was appalled by the Nazi regime and their policies against European Jews, so made her way to London via neutral Spain in August 1940.

Hall was hired by the US Embassy, but the adventurous young lady had no interest in spending the war behind a desk. In February 1941, she resigned her position as a code clerk stating that she was looking for other employment. Hall had, in fact, been recruited by the British Special Operations Executive (SOE).

Upon joining the SOE, Hall was sent to France to collect intelligence on German operations there and to assist and arm the French resistance. In 1942, she was forced to escape through the Pyrenees Mountains on foot, not an easy ask for an amputee. Whilst there she spent time in an infamous Spanish prison for failing to have the proper papers.

On her return to London, she joined the Office of Strategic Services (OSS), the predecessor to the CIA. In May 1944, she was sent back to France with the cover identity of Marcelle Montagne, a farmhand in a rural village. Disguised as the older peasant woman, she secretly coordinated supply drops for the resistance, reported on German troop movements and took part in several attacks on infrastructure and German soldiers.

At the end of the war, the French government awarded her the Croix de Guerre avec Palme, whilst she also received an OBE from the British and the Distinguished Service Cross from US General, William Donovan. Hall finally retired from public service in 1966.

Her story is on display at the CIA Museum inside the spy agency headquarters in Langley, but in keeping with the common theme of her life, it is off limits to the public.

Despite her disability, she made an immeasurable contribution to the Allied war effort. What skills and talents did she possess that ensured she was able to overcome every obstacle in her path?

Be creative

'She could be four different women in the space of an afternoon, with four different code names.' This quote was once said about Virginia Hall. She was known for her creativity and ability to safely escape. She used makeup and duplicity to evade capture by the Gestapo, who had spent months hunting her for assisting the French Resistance.

In September 1941, Hall arrived in Germany on behalf of the SOE. However, her superiors were not overly optimistic about her chances of success. The region was crawling with Gestapo agents and at that time, Hall had no experience whatsoever in the dark arts of espionage.

Yet Hall showed herself to be a natural. She was able to keep one step ahead of the enemy. Entering France as a *New York Post* reporter in August of 1941, she soon established a secret network of loyal French citizens, codenamed 'Heckler'.

Her work enabled many British pilots, whose aircraft had been downed, to escape safely.

Hall was based out of the French city of Lyon. She took up residence in a convent and persuaded the nuns to work with her. She also made the acquaintance of a brothel owner and ensured that the French prostitutes collected information from their German clients.

Klaus Barbie, the notorious 'Butcher of Lyon' and Gestapo chief, made it his personal mission to find Hall. She was forced to flee the country, on foot, via a fifty-mile hike over the Pyrenees. The weather was freezing and her prosthetic leg was in bad shape.

In 1944, months before the D-Day invasion at Normandy, Hall entered France again, this time masquerading as a sixty-year-old peasant woman. Prior to her return, she sat with a makeup artist in London to learn how to draw wrinkles on her face. She also visited a dentist to grind her teeth down so that they would resemble those of an elderly French milkmaid.

Owing to her disability, she was unable to parachute onto the continent like other agents. Instead, she was dropped off in France by a British boat, on the night of the twenty-first of March 1944. Her hair was dyed grey and her limp adapted to resemble that of an older woman forty years her senior. Hall's second tour in France was even more successful than the first. She blew up bridges, called in airdrops and sabotaged German positions. In perhaps her most daring exploit, she managed to free twelve male captives from Mauzac prison.

Virginia Hall was able to use sexism in her favour, owing to the prejudice of the Gestapo at the time. The Germans had no inclination that a woman could act as a spy. However, they soon came to realise that their principal adversary was a limping lady whose creativity helped to thwart their attempts to dominate the European continent.

Work under the radar

A humble approach was important to Hall. 'Many of my friends were killed for talking too much', she once stated.

In 2018, Gina Haspel became the first female Director of the CIA. She spoke of, 'standing on the shoulders of heroines who never sought public acclaim'. She was, 'deeply indebted to women who had served the agency and its wartime predecessor the Office of Strategic Services (OSS) for making her appointment possible by challenging stereotypes and breaking down barriers'.

When Hall received the Distinguished Service Cross in September 1945, in recognition of her work in France, President Truman intended to hold a public ceremony to award the medal. Hall refused, stating that she was, 'still operational and most anxious to get busy'. As a result, only her mother was there to see the proudest day of her daughter's life.

The consummate professional, she had no interest in telling her own story, receiving medals or partaking in ceremonies. She acted out of a duty to her country and because of her passionate determination to defeat Nazism. Virginia would only say about her achievement, that it was, 'not bad for a girl from Baltimore'.

Hall's niece, Lorna Catling, recalled meeting her aunt after the war. 'She came home when I was sixteen years-of-age and she was pale and had white hair and crappy clothes'. Did Hall regale her niece with tales of the war? 'She never talked about it', Catling noted.

Even after Hall returned from Europe and began working for the CIA, she was often kept on the side-lines. Yet many CIA officers stated that the techniques she developed in France were still used by the agency to this day, including during Operation Jawbreaker in Afghanistan before and after the attacks on the eleventh of September.

As a result of her desire to operate below the radar, both during and after the war, she never truly received the formal recognition she was due during her lifetime. None of this serves to diminish the tremendous assistance she gave the Allied war effort.

Very often, the low-key approach is the sensible one. The phrase, 'loose lips sink ships', originated on posters used by the United States Office of War Information. Sometimes, self-promotion is necessary, for example in a job interview. But other times, it serves no purpose at all.

There is a Japanese proverb that translates as, 'the nail that sticks out gets hammered down'. In other words, if you talk too much and gain too much attention, you become a target. Virginia Hall knew that in her line of work, keeping a low profile and acting under the radar, was the only way that she could succeed.

Harry Truman, the president who wanted to present Hall with her medal after the war, undoubtedly understood Hall's rejection. After all, it was he who said, 'it is amazing what you can accomplish if you don't care who gets the credit'.

Go beyond your limits

Hall believed in constantly challenging herself. 'We can all achieve great things, if we put our mind to it. By embracing the spirit of adventure, we can test ourselves, push our boundaries, and laugh a lot along the way', she once said.

Virginia Hall was born into a wealthy family and was expected to marry and raise a family amongst the elite circles of Maryland. But there was one thing standing in the way of this expectation; she just loved adventure. She was a lover of the outdoors and enjoyed hiking, horse riding and hunting. The love of exploration is what took her to Europe before the war, studying across the continent before yearning to become an ambassador.

Upon resigning from the State Department in 1939, her aim was adventure. She found it on the eve of the war in 1939, in her role driving for the French Ambulance corps (known as the Services Sanitaires de l'Armee). The job was not one for the faint-hearted. Evacuating soldiers from the front line whilst driving an ambulance with a prosthetic leg was not an easy one. From the tenth of May 1940, the day the Germans invaded France, until the fall of Paris on the fourteenth of June 1941, Hall risked life and her remaining limbs to evacuate the wounded to safely. As Hall tended to the injured, fighter planes stooped down to spray the roads with machine gun fire.

Spying is a tough business. It is estimated that of the four hundred SOE agents sent to France, up to a quarter never returned, either executed or sent to a concentration camp. On her second expedition to France in 1944, Hall acted as an effective guerrilla leader, arming and training battalions of French resistance fighters for sabotage missions ahead of the Allied invasion. In a radio report, she stated that her group had derailed freight trains and blown up four bridges. In her role in France, Hall's love of adventure drove her to take part in those daring missions that did irreparable damage to the Nazi war machine before Europe's eventual liberation.

Find a way
Virginia once said, 'if you really want to do something, you'll find a way. If you don't, you'll find an excuse', words which epitomised her approach to overcoming problems.

Hall had hoped to use her position as a consular official, first in Warsaw and then Izmir, as a steppingstone to become a diplomat within the US Foreign service. She was determined to become the first female ambassador in United States history.

Unfortunately, she had two things standing in her way. The first was her gender. It was rare for a woman at that time to be considered for such a role. Secondly, her disability resulted in more discrimination. The US State Department would not allow individuals with disabilities to work as US diplomats.

Hall refused to give up on her dream, trying on multiple occasions to join the Foreign Service. In 1934, she was back at a consular desk, this time in Venice, Italy. Once again, she tried to force her way into the US Foreign Service. At that time, only six out of the one-thousand five-hundred US Foreign Service officers were women.

In 1937, Virginia asked to complete the US Foreign Service exam a third time. To her dismay, she was again rejected by the State Department, who explained that Hall's disability, 'is a cause for rejection and it would not be possible for you to qualify for entry into the Service under these regulations'.

Hall appealed to both the wheelchair-bound President Roosevelt and Secretary of State, Cordell Hall. The Secretary of State demonstrated the lack of empathy shown to both women and the disabled in his reply, noting that, 'she could (still) become a fine career girl in the Consular Service'.

In Estonia, Virginia launched a final appeal to Assistant Secretary of State, G. Howland Shaw, requesting a waiver to take the Foreign Service exam. When her appeal was turned down, she refused to feel sorry for herself. Instead, she sought to fulfil her ambitions outside the State Department.

Churchill had set up the fledgling SOE, 'to set Europe ablaze'. Despite her false limb, she impressed an undercover agent and completed a demanding agent training programme. SOE agents normally remained in the field for just six months. Hall was so successful that she spent over fifteen months in Lyon organising the French resistance.

Demonstrating the same resolve, Virginia Hall let nothing stand in her way.

Believe in your talent
Hall believed in emphasising what you are good at, a belief confirmed with her quote, 'to find out what one is fitted to do, and to secure an opportunity to do it, is the key to happiness'.

Hall played a crucial role in organising large networks of resistance fighters and directing their assistance to the Allied invasion. To stay one step ahead of Klaus Barbie and the Gestapo, required preparation of the highest degree. What was most remarkable about Hall was the number of roles she could play, all of which required different talents.

Hall learned bomber signalling, Morse code, hand-to-hand combat, canoeing, map reading, weaponry and operational planning. She was the only female graduate of her class and became the first British female agent inserted into France, codenamed 'Germaine'.

Working alone in France for the SOE, she pretended to be a journalist, giving her the opportunity to interview people and file stories to send back to military planners in London. She was able to make new contacts, calculate who she should bribe, act as team leader for other agents and distribute wireless sets for transmission back to London.

In 1942, she became engaged in resistance operations in Marseille. She offered her apartment as a safehouse for downed RAF pilots, resistance operatives and SOE agents and she also provided routine intelligence reports to London.

In 1944, working for the CIA predecessor, the OSS, she formed the Cosne resistance, overcoming the men's lack of enthusiasm to work for a woman. She organised the resistance into four groups of twenty-five men and gave each group specific instructions to sabotage local German units. Overseeing the coordination of airdrops that provided explosives, weapons, and other forms of support equipment, the resistance set about destroying railroad lines, bridges and disrupting communications.

By D-Day, Hall had over one-thousand five-hundred men under her command. She reported daily to London on the state of operations and German troop movements, and pinpointed locations for attacks.

When the defeated Germans retreated, Hall transferred to the Central Section of OSS and was deployed to Italy in December 1944. Her ability to speak both Italian and German proved invaluable, as was her previous involvement in creating resistance networks. Replicating her success in France, she managed to establish contact with the Austrian underground in the Innsbruck region and performed the role of a radio operator, in order to transfer intelligence to the Americans.

After the war, because she spoke Italian fluently, she was dispatched to Venice, where for several years she collected and transmitted economic, financial, and political intelligence with special emphasis on the communist movement and its leaders.

People who rebound from adversity begin by believing that they have the talent to overcome their challenges. Before defeating any challenges, a person needs to know what it is they are good at. Virginia Hall made the most of her talents, which included quick thinking, the ability to speak several languages, risk taking, bravery, flexibility, thinking ahead of the enemy and being organised.

Virginia Hall's operational preparedness and effective use of the resources available marked her out as an agent of tremendous ability. Hall used her talents to benefit a cause she believed in, the defeat of Nazism and victory of the allied cause. In doing so, she adhered to the viewpoint of Roman Philosopher, Cicero, who believed, 'not for ourselves alone are we born'. Indeed, the world became a better place because people like Virginia Hall used their talents for the benefit of others.

Chapter Twenty-Nine

John McCain

*It is your character and your character alone, that will
make your life happy or unhappy*

John McCain, the Vietnam War veteran and Senator for the
State of Arizona, was the Republican nominee for the 2008 US
presidential election. McCain lost the election to Barack Obama
but continued to play a prominent role in US politics until his
death from brain cancer in 2018. His public clashes with
President Trump were well documented. In the years before his
death, McCain became one of the most outspoken Republican
critics of the Trump administration.

McCain was born into a military family and entered the
United States Naval Academy after finishing school. Following
in the footsteps of his father and grandfather before him, he
became a naval aviator and flew ground-attack aircraft from
aircraft carriers.

His combat duty began in 1967, when he was thirty years
old, flying missions during the Vietnam War. His first brush
with danger came soon after, when he cheated death during a
fire onboard *USS Forrestal* which killed one-hundred and
thirty-four military personnel. McCain told *The New York Times*
how he managed to escape from his burning jet and was
attempting to help another pilot escape when a bomb
exploded.

McCain earned a Bronze Star for missions flown over
North Vietnam and was praised for his aggressive and skilful
airmanship. While on a bombing mission during Operation
Rolling Thunder over Hanoi in October 1967, his plane was
shot down, seriously injuring him in the process. He was
captured by North Vietnamese troops and subject to

interrogation and torture before being moved to a prison, nicknamed 'The Hanoi Hilton', in December 1969.

McCain was viewed as a valuable bargaining chip to the North Vietnamese since his father was a well-known US Naval Commander. McCain stood strong and refused to be used for propaganda purposes. He also declined an offer of release, ahead of those captured before him, in line with military code. As a result, he suffered several severe beatings at the hands of his captors.

It was not until March 1973 that McCain was released, a full five and a half years after his imprisonment. McCain was awarded the Silver Star, Purple Heart and Distinguished Flying Cross for his bravery.

After nearly a year of rehabilitation, McCain returned to flying duties, although it was clear that his injuries had severely curtailed his ability to progress within the Navy.

Upon retiring from military service in 1981, McCain promptly entered politics. He was first elected to office in November 1982, winning a seat in the US House of Representatives. He was re-elected in 1984. In 1986, after the retirement of Arizona senator and prominent Republican, Barry Goldwater, McCain won election to the US Senate. McCain came to be known as a conservative politician who held those in the upper echelons of his own Republican Party to account.

McCain put himself forward for the Republican nomination for president in 2000 but lost out to George W. Bush. McCain eventually secured the Republican nomination in 2008 but was unable to reverse the momentum that had turned in favour of his Democratic opponent, Barack Obama.

By 2016, as a respected elder of the party, he regularly clashed with Republican presidential nominee, Donald Trump. He famously withdrew his support for Trump after *The Washington Post* released recordings of Trump making demeaning remarks about women. Elected for a sixth term in the Senate on the same day as Trump's surprise win over

Hillary Clinton, McCain continued to clash with Trump, despite suffering from further bouts of ill health.

Showing his independent streak, McCain refused to vote for the repeal of Obamacare and defied Trump by continuing to investigate potential Russian interference in the presidential election. After being diagnosed with brain cancer in 2017, McCain was forced to reduce his role in the Senate to focus on treatment.

In August 2018, McCain finally succumbed to cancer. His funeral was televised from the Washington National Cathedral, with former US Presidents George W. Bush and Barack Obama giving eulogies. He pointedly asked that Trump not attend any of the services held in his honour.

John McCain, the great survivor, in both the military theatre and political arena, had finally yielded to an even more malevolent enemy, cancer. His death was felt most keenly, in his adopted home state of Arizona, where one member of the public praised him as, 'always taking the right side, the side of the good people, regardless of his politics. It's going to be very difficult to fill his shoes'.

A life that saw so many dramatic moments; torture, narrow escapes from death, solitary confinement, and political intrigue, is unquestionably worthy of investigation. How did such a remarkable man manage to overcome so many struggles?

Be loyal to your cause
McCain explained, 'I knew my release would add to the suffering of men who were already straining to keep faith with their country. I was injured, but I believed I could survive. I couldn't persuade myself to leave'. His conduct during his time in a North Vietnamese prison became the story of legend. It is known the world over as an example of placing loyalty and love for his jailed comrades over his own self-interest.

To his contemporaries in Naval School, such behaviour did not come as much of a surprise. McCain may never have been a high achiever, but his fellow graduates knew that he always had their back. 'He was everyone's friend', said roommate Bill Hemingway, 'if you had a problem with a class, he was there to help you. People admired and respected that because he was so selfless'.

When McCain was captured, he spent weeks in hospital, having suffered a broken left arm, a shattered right arm, and significant damage to his right knee. McCain's interrogators pressed him for information and threatened to end his medical treatment if he did not cooperate. Writing in his 2000 memoir, *Faith of My Fathers*, McCain simply gave his capturers the names of the Green Bay Packers' offensive line and said they were members of his squadron. When asked to identify future targets, he recited the names of several North Vietnamese cities that had already been bombed.

In 1968, when McCain's jailers discovered that his father, John S. McCain Jr. had been named Commander of US Forces in the region, he was offered early release. It was an offer he flatly refused, unless the North Vietnamese released every one of his comrades who were captured before him. Accepting release would have meant violating the military code of conduct, which stated in Article III that: I will accept neither parole nor special favours from the enemy.

McCain refused to be used as a tool for propaganda and declined to meet anti-war groups in Hanoi seeking to use his well-known surname for propaganda reasons. 'Now, McCain, it will be very bad for you', his guard told him. Indeed, such loyalty had a price: it resulted in his prolonged imprisonment, beatings and near starvation.

Lesser men would have been excused for giving in but not McCain. Out of loyalty, he put his comrades and country before his own needs. John McCain used this principle to help find the mental strength to survive his ordeal. McCain's allegiance to his country inspired other prisoners with his leadership, giving them the courage to survive further years in captivity. Modest as ever, McCain simply told the *Arizona Republican* in 2007 that in rejecting early release, 'I just didn't think it was the honourable thing to do'.

Go your own way

'Glory belongs to the act of being constant to something greater than yourself, to a cause, to your principles, to the people on whom you rely and who rely on you', McCain commented.

McCain was a conservative, but he was not bound by dogma or petty partisan politics. He considered each policy on its merits, without worrying what the polls or party spin doctors thought. He had no problem taking liberal positions on issues like campaign finance and was one of the leading Republican advocates for government action to address climate change, working alongside Joe Lieberman, the Democratic Senator from Connecticut, to cut and cap greenhouse gas pollution.

His passion for bipartisanship often caused dismay within his own party but McCain saw the value of working across the floor when he passionately believed in an issue. Controversially, he worked for more than a decade to create a bipartisan deal on immigration reform that would include stricter border security combined with a path to citizenship for millions of undocumented immigrants.

McCain also had that rare quality in a politician; the ability to openly admit when he had made a mistake. He spoke about how he regretted voting against the creation of a federal holiday to honour Dr Martin Luther King Jr and was apologetic about choosing Sarah Palin as his running mate for the 2008 presidential campaign.

Whilst he had no love for the Affordable Care Act, known as Obamacare, he also saved it. When McCain returned to Washington for the first time after his diagnosis of brain cancer, he gave a speech that called for bipartisan health-reform legislation. Disgusted with his party's rushed, partisan legislative move, McCain's notorious thumbs-down gesture on the Senate floor in July 2017 - the deciding 'no' vote that blocked the repeal of portions of the Affordable Care Act - was a pivotal moment for the US and summed up his refusal to toe the line in favour of his belief in the democratic process.

Likewise, in his battles with Trump, he was prepared to call out wrongdoing wherever he saw it. He took Trump to task after the then-presidential candidate clashed with Khizr Khan, the father of a soldier killed in Iraq. McCain criticized 'spurious nationalism' in an apparent jibe on Trump's 'America First' policy.

John McCain is known for many things but perhaps his most enduring trait could be encapsulated in one word: maverick.

Reject bitterness

By some people's rationale, John McCain might have been justified in being bitter about what had happened to him. But he was everything but bitter. 'My job has been reconciliation and healing', he confirmed.

McCain was repeatedly asked if he harboured continuing ill feeling to his captors. 'I have no bitterness, it's not a luxury I can afford', he replied in a 2006 interview.

McCain described his five-and-a-half-year imprisonment as a hellish experience, in which he twice tried to hang himself. Displaying a remarkable lack of bitterness, he played an important role in the 1990s in American efforts to restore diplomatic relations with Vietnam.

Twenty-two years after returning home from Vietnam, he sat in the Oval Office urging President Clinton to establish diplomatic and economic relations with the former enemy. 'It doesn't matter to me anymore who was for the war and who was against it', McCain told Clinton. 'I'm tired of looking back in anger and I'm tired of America looking back in anger. It's time to put the past behind us, Mr President, and do what's right for both countries.' In July 1995, President Clinton established diplomatic relations with the former enemy, before visiting Hanoi in 2000, on the first presidential visit to Vietnam since 1969.

In his 2005 book, *Character is Destiny*, which focused on 'thirty-five character traits that every young person should know, and every adult should remember', McCain included a chapter about forgiveness which discussed Nelson Mandela. He remarked how Mandela had displayed a similar lack of bitterness in helping his countrymen reconcile. 'People must learn to hate and if they can learn to hate, they can be taught to love, for love comes more naturally to the human heart than its opposite'.

Despite his role in normalizing diplomatic ties with Vietnam, McCain remained critical of the communist rulers of Vietnam. He could never find it within himself to exonerate those who had personally tortured him and killed his fellow prisoners.

Even in political defeat, John McCain never tolerated bitterness. After losing a particularly nasty and at times, personal primary race with George W. Bush for the 2000 Republican nomination, he spoke how even being considered for the top job was, 'an honour for a guy who stood fifth from bottom of his class at Annapolis (Naval College)'.

Look yourself in the mirror

'All my heroes, fictional and real, would have been ashamed of me', McCain once said, emphasising his belief in the importance of self-awareness.

One of McCain's biggest regrets came in 1999 when he was competing with Bush for the Republican nomination. Heading to South Carolina for a key primary, the presence of the Confederate flag on top of the State Capitol became a key issue in the election.

Asked by CBS reporter, Bob Schieffer, what the flag meant to him, McCain answered that the flag offended many Americans as a symbol of racism and slavery but that, as a descendant of Southerners, he understood its historical significance. The response clearly angered conservative voters in South Carolina, whose support he needed to beat Bush in the primary. Instead of reiterating his previously stated belief that the flag was a symbol of racism and slavery, McCain bowed to political pressure and pulled out a written statement from his pocket, reluctantly issuing a bland statement that said he could 'understand both sides' of the argument.

He would come to regret not saying what he really believed: that the flag should be permanently removed. McCain pulled no punches when reflecting on his own contradictory behaviour, 'I had not just been dishonest. I had been a coward, and I had severed my own interests from my country's. That was what made the lie unforgivable'.

McCain lost the South Carolina primary race by fifty-three percent to forty-two per cent and Bush went on to win the Republican nomination. Having reflected on his actions, McCain returned to South Carolina a few months later to publicly apologise for his words.

McCain had already shown himself to be someone capable of making amends for his conduct. In 1989, the Keating Five scandal saw McCain and four other Senators investigated over allegations that they intervened on businessman Charlie Keating's behalf with the director of the agency that oversaw the operation of the country's savings and loans. Keating was so sure that he would benefit from his influence with the senators that he boasted to reporters about his 'bribes'.

Whilst McCain had not broken any laws, he was reprimanded for his poor judgement in a scandal that nearly ruined his political career. McCain called the Keating scandal, 'my asterisk' and a permanent 'bad mark on my record'.

McCain reflected on his behaviour and became a passionate advocate of campaign finance reform. His years-long battle led to the Bipartisan Campaign Reform Act of 2002, supported alongside his Democratic colleague, Senator Russ Feingold of Wisconsin.

When making a mistake, it is always best to take responsibility for it. Honesty shows integrity and people come to respect those who reflect on their own mistakes with frankness. It takes a lot more courage to admit one's wrongdoings than simply gloss over them.

John McCain had a remarkable capacity for self-criticism and self-evaluation. In decades of covering politics, the journalist, Todd S. Purdum, stated that he had never encountered anyone with McCain's 'unflinching combination of bracing candour, impossibly high standards and rueful self-recrimination'.

Be Civil

Certain core values were essential for John McCain as he lived his life. As he was once described by President Joe Biden, 'John lived his life bound by a timeless code — decency, respect, and civility above all else'.

Senator McCain was known for grand acts of civility. Perhaps one of the most notable stories that demonstrates this human decency came on the presidential campaign trial in 2008.

On the day Obama accepted the Democratic Party nomination for president, in Denver Colorado, McCain put out a video congratulating Obama on winning the nomination. 'Too often, the achievements of our opponents go unnoticed. So, I wanted to stop and say congratulations, how perfect that your nomination would come on this historic day. Tomorrow, we'll be back at it. But tonight, Senator, job well done'.

On the tenth of October, 2008, just a month before the election, McCain attended a traditional town hall meeting at Lakeville South High School in Minnesota. McCain was hosting a Question-and-Answer session when a woman was given the microphone to ask McCain a question.

Stating that she could not trust Obama, 'As an Arab', McCain politely took back the microphone and began shaking his head. 'No, ma'am. He's a decent family man, a citizen that I just happen to have disagreements with on fundamental issues and that's what this campaign's all about', McCain said.

In the concession speech of his second bid for the White House, McCain acknowledged the historic nature of President-elect Barack Obama's win and what it symbolised for race relations in the country. He implored his supporters to work with Obama in a bipartisan fashion.

'I didn't like the outcome of the 2008 election. But I had a duty to concede, and I did so without reluctance', McCain said in a statement. 'A concession isn't just an exercise in graciousness. It is an act of respect for the will of the American people, a respect that is every American leader's first responsibility'.

Being civil and gracious, just like the late John McCain can get a person further than contemporary wisdom suggests. McCain's graciousness did not go unnoticed. In 2017, upon hearing that McCain had been diagnosed with cancer, President Obama issued a supportive statement that, 'cancer does not know what it's up against'.

Chapter Thirty

Irena Sendler

I kept silent. I preferred to die than to reveal our activity

The story of Irena Sendler is a powerful one, but one that deserves to be told. Irena Sendler was a Polish social worker, who risked her life to rescue two-thousand five-hundred Jewish children from the Warsaw Ghetto during the Second World War. A Nobel Peace Prize nominee, her story remained relatively unknown until 1999, when a group of high school students in Kansas City discovered her story during a school research project.

Born in 1910, Irena was brought up in a town near to Warsaw. She went on to study Polish literature at Warsaw University, although she was appalled at the ghetto bench system, which saw Jews forced to sit together in designated areas of the lecture halls. Student cards featured the word 'Jew' or 'Polish'. In protest, a defiant Irena defaced her card in public, resulting in a three-year suspension from the university.

In 1931, Irena married Mieczysław Sendler and the couple moved to Warsaw shortly before the German invasion of Poland. Her husband was captured and held in a Prisoner of War camp until 1945. On Yom Kippur in October 1940, the city's Jewish population of four-hundred thousand were herded into an area of 1.3 square miles. By mid-November, the area was sealed, forming the largest ghetto in Nazi-occupied Europe. Ghetto life was intolerable, with thousands a month dying because of the conditions. The German administration deliberately limited food supplies to the absolute minimum.

Sendler became a social worker and was placed in charge of the city's canteens, which aided those in need. At the outset of the war, Sendler used the canteens to provide clothing and medicine to the city's Jewish population. The Germans were terrified that typhus would spread outside the ghetto, so they were more than happy to let medical workers like Sendler deal with the sick and the dead.

However, her work was undertaken at huge risk, as providing any kind of help to Jews was punishable by death, not only for those assisting but also for their entire family.

In 1942, Sendler, known as 'Jolanta', was appointed as head of the Children's Division of Zegota. Together with a team of twenty-five colleagues, she helped smuggle out as many children as possible from the ghetto. Sendler and other social workers undertook risky missions, using various means available.

In the hopes of one day reuniting the children with their families - most of whom died in the Nazis' death camps - Sendler wrote the children's real names on slips of paper that she kept at home. When German police arrested her in 1943, a colleague hid the slips, which Sendler later buried in a jar under an apple tree in a friend's garden. Some two-thousand five-hundred names were recorded.

Sendler was sent to the notorious Pawiak Prison, where she was tortured. She refused to reveal the identity of her accomplices and was sentenced to death. She was only spared the hangman's noose when colleagues managed to bribe the prison guards. For years, she needed crutches and a wheelchair because of her injuries. Sendler was eventually released in February 1944, going into hiding and continuing her work.

When the war ended and she came out of hiding, Sendler hurried to her neighbour's yard where the jars had been buried. She dug them up and began searching for the children she had saved to reunite them with their real families. Sadly, most of them had died in the Ghetto or the camps and very few of the children saw their parents again.

On the nineteenth of October, 1965, Yad Vashem, Israel's Holocaust Memorial Organisation, recognized Irena Sendler as Righteous Among the Nations and made her an honorary citizen of Israel in 1991. Due to the post-war communist regime's anti-Semitism, few Poles were aware of Zegota's work, despite the unveiling of a plaque honouring the organization, in 1995, near the former Warsaw Ghetto.

Standing at only 4'11" tall, her appearance resembled a porcelain doll rather than a fearless resistance leader. How did she find the courage to smuggle so many Jewish children to safety?

Jump in and help

Irena believed that if someone needed help, you had to provide it, saying, 'I was taught by my father that when someone is drowning you don't ask if they can swim, you just jump in and help'.

As a leading activist in Żegota, the Polish underground organisation which provided help for Jews, Irena arranged a network to help those trapped inside the Warsaw Ghetto. When the deportations to Treblinka started in 1942, she literally rescued thousands of children from almost certain death.

Compassion was part of her education at an early age, a trait which she had observed first-hand as a child. It was only natural that she refused to stay inactive.

Her father was a doctor, known for his empathy towards his patients. He treated many of the poor villagers free of charge. The physician had taught his only child to respect all people regardless of their social status or ethnicity. Sadly, he died from typhus when Irena was only seven. After his death, the Jewish community offered to support his widow and only daughter, although this was politely declined.

In the 1930s, Warsaw University was an unwelcoming place for Jewish students, although Irena mixed freely with her Jewish friends. Jews were forced to sit separately from other students on the Ghetto benches. One day, Irena went to sit on the Jewish side of the room. When the teacher told her to move, she answered, 'I'm Jewish today'.

Even before her heroic actions in the ghetto, Irena had shown that standing idly by, was simply not part of her makeup. It was entirely predictable that when the Nazi forces occupying Poland predictably began rounding up Jews in 1940, Sendler jumped in.

Shirley Chisholm, the Congresswoman, mentioned in Chapter Eleven, was another person who could not contemplate inaction. She stated that, 'You don't make progress by standing on the side lines, whimpering and complaining. You make progress by implementing ideas'.

It is actions, rather than words, that should always be the first course of action. 'Irena represents the often-forgotten truth, that no one should be indifferent', said Elzbieta Ficowska, one of the children she rescued.

Use the art of persuasion

'The one question every parent asked me was, "Can you guarantee they will live?" We had to admit honestly that we could not, as we did not even know if we would succeed in leaving the ghetto that day. The only guarantee', she said, 'was that the children would most likely die if they stayed'.

On the twenty-second of July 1942, the Jewish Council of Warsaw published a Nazi notice in the ghetto, stating that almost all its inhabitants would be deported to camps in the east. By the twelfth of September 1942, approximately three-hundred thousand of the ghetto's inhabitants had been deported to the Treblinka extermination camp or murdered. Roughly fifty-thousand people remained in the ghetto.

Realising how desperate the situation was, Sendler concluded that her only hope of saving lives was to convince parents to part with their children. Even the many secular Jewish parents were horrified at the thought of giving up their children to Catholic homes or convents, where they might be baptized. Sendler, herself a young mother, found it distressing to have to convince parents to part with their children, entrusting them to a non-Jewish stranger. Sendler was haunted for the rest of her life by the parents' pleas, particularly from those who could not bear to be apart from their children.

Most of the children who left with Sendler's group were taken into Roman Catholic convents, orphanages and homes and given non-Jewish aliases. All the children were first placed in one of the emergency care centres. There, they would receive new identity documents, mostly from Polish children who had died. They were then placed with carefully selected foster families, or most often with nunneries, such as the Franciscan Sisters. The children were given Christian names and taught Christian prayers in case they were tested. Each family was made to promise to return the children to any surviving family members at the end of the war. Sadly, not everyone kept their promise, although Irena spent years after the war, with the help of her lists, trying to track down missing children and reunite family members.

Persuasion is a trait that is sometimes cynically viewed as being synonymous with marketing and sales. However, the capacity to convince others, to change opinions and views, could well be one of life's most important skills.

It was only through Sendler's skills of persuasion, in the most difficult circumstances, that two thousand five-hundred young Jewish children were rescued from adversity and the unimaginable horrors of the Holocaust.

Remain humble

A humble approach was fundamental to Sendler. She was happy to accept that, 'every child saved with my help is the justification of my existence on this Earth, and not a title to glory'.

In the autumn of 1999, a schoolteacher from rural Kansas encouraged three students to work together on a National History Day Project on unsung heroes. The aim of the project was to teach respect and tolerance and to find a historical example for the school motto, 'He who changes one person, changes the world entire'.

A group of four girls joined forces to enter their project in the programme. Their teacher, Norman Conard, showed them a short clipping from a March 1994 issue of *News and World Report*, which said, 'Irena Sendler saved many children and adults from the Warsaw Ghetto in 1942'. From this tiny reference in a news magazine, the girls researched Irena's remarkable story.

Though recognized by Yad Vashem in 1965, Sendler was largely unknown before Conard became involved. As the students delved further into the topic, they grew more and more inspired. The project was turned into a fifteen-minute play they called, *Life in a Jar*, playing to over three-hundred and seventy-five audiences across North American and Europe. As the story gathered momentum, students and teacher travelled to Poland to meet Irena. In 2009, the Hallmark Channel produced *The Courageous Heart of Irena Sendler,* a film for CBS and an award-winning book followed in 2011.

Although the children she saved had known her only as Jolanta, as her story made the news, she began to receive communication from people who recognized her face from the photos, 'I remember your face! You took me out of the Ghetto!'

At that first meeting in Warsaw in 2001, one of the four schoolgirls told Sendler she was a hero and her inspiration. 'I am not a hero', Sendler said. 'A hero is someone doing extraordinary things. What I did was not extraordinary. It was a normal thing to do'.

One of the students, Sabrina Coons, could barely believe that 'after all she has done, she is so modest. She always talks about other people, gives them credit, never herself'.

Modesty leads to composure, a trait that was necessary for Irena in leading her team during its dangerous missions in the Ghetto. Modest people like Sendler do not feel they are superior. Rather than seeking approval, or glory, they are more interested in working with others to achieve their overall goal. This, in turn, results in a collective unit, working together to overturn adversity.

It comes as no surprise that Sendler deflected away the praise she received and quickly played down her role, whilst emphasising that played by others.

'I could not have achieved anything were it not for that group of women I trusted who were with me in the ghetto every day and who transformed their homes into care centres for the children', she declared. 'These were exceptionally brave and noble people'.

Think outside the box

Sendler knew that her organisational strength could be put to good use. As she confirmed, 'I'm sure I have many faults but there's one thing I can boast about. I'm a good organizer'.

Zegota made an excellent choice in selecting Sendler to head the organization's Children's Bureau. She had considerable experience in outwitting the Germans as a social worker, having frequently entered the Warsaw Ghetto using passes from the Department of Sanitation. Wearing the Star of David as a sign of solidarity with the Jews, Sendler and her close colleague, Irena Schultz, had distributed food, money, and medicine to the ghetto inhabitants.

Irena and her friends used a variety of methods to spirit children out of the Ghetto. She used boxes, suitcases and even coffins, whilst sedating babies to silence their cries. Other children escaped through a network of basements and secret passages.

Elzbieta Ficowska was only five months old when she was placed in a carpenter's box and smuggled out of the Warsaw Ghetto. She was placed with a Polish family on the 'Aryan' side of the wall, and the young woman who carried her out of the Ghetto added tiny little Elzbieta's name, parents' names and new address to a piece of tissue paper, on which were written the details of other children she had smuggled out. This was one of the many names which were placed in the jar that Irena later buried under an apple tree in the back yard of a friend's home.

Another child spoke about waiting by a gate in darkness as a German soldier patrolled nearby. When the soldier passed, the boy counted to thirty, then made a mad dash to the middle of the street, where a manhole cover opened and he was taken down into the sewers before being spirited to safety.

Being imaginative is not always about creating something new but also with a little ingenuity, making old things work better. It is about allowing your mind to wander and encouraging the creative process.

By the time that the Nazis began to liquidate the Ghetto, Sendler knew that she had to act, something she did with resourcefulness. 'I became convinced of the necessity to organize efforts to escort children out of the ghetto to the Aryan side of the city', she said. 'Hitler created hell for all of us in Poland. But the kind of hell he made for the Jews was even greater'.

Be courageous
Irena was clear about her path, once saying, 'I lost no time in reflecting (on the danger) … knowing that I and my heart had to be there, had to be a part of the rescue'.

For two years, Sendler's secret missions were successful. Then, in October 1943, the Gestapo finally caught up with her. As the Nazi soldiers ransacked her house, Sendler flung the lists of children to her friend Janina Grabowska, who hid the records in her loose clothing.

She was arrested and held in the city's notorious prison, where she was beaten and tortured. Despite the cruelty inflicted upon her, she refused to divulge the names of any of her accomplices or to divulge the location of any of the children.

Irena was sentenced to death, a verdict that she acknowledged with dignity. Unbeknown to her, Zegota had induced one of the German guards to accept a bribe and Irena was helped to escape just before the sentence could be carried out. The guard added her name on the list of those who had been executed. The next day, the Germans boasted of her death.

As she left the prison, she could not help but notice posters all over the city proclaiming her death. She was forced to spend the rest of the war in hiding, in much the same way of the two thousand five-hundred children she had helped to rescue. Despite her injuries and the need to keep a low profile, she still bravely did all she could to help rescue more children. The necessities of her secret life even meant that she was prevented from attending her mother's funeral.

Following the film Schindler's list, Oskar Schindler's inspiring efforts to save 1,200 Jewish workers became more widely known. What most people might not realise is that Irena Sendler saved more than twice that number of Jewish children, whilst being detained and tortured in the process.

It is obvious that Sendler was a brave woman, described by Elzbieta Ficowska, as having, 'a Margaret Thatcher personality'.

On one occasion, Irena was taking seriously ill children out of the Ghetto in an ambulance. She had the help of an ambulance driver and a dog. When the children would start to cry, she became extremely fearful about detection. Yet, she had a plan in place. She would hit her dog on his paw and he would begin to bark. This set off a chain reaction among the Nazis' dogs, and chaos would erupt. Over time, her preparation helped override her fear and she was able to act courageously.

Without courage, strengthened over time, it is unlikely Irena Sendler would have been able to save so many children from near certain death.

Conclusion

The Formula Defined

The objective of this book has been to examine the adversity faced by thirty inspiring personalities, with the aim of discovering a strategy that can be implemented in the face of our own challenges.

Whilst each story has been unique, I believe that we have identified several key commonalities that led to our subjects' successful responses to adversity.

The thirty illustrious individuals in this book experienced their fair share of poverty, bereavement, jail, prejudice, segregation, economic crisis, wars, divorce, sickness, injury and defeat.

Whilst we have been presented with over one hundred techniques that were successfully employed to combat hardship, a shorter, more pragmatic approach allows us to gain the most from our learning journey. That's why I have devised my seven-point formula for overcoming adversity.

Before revealing the formula in its entirety, let us first outline the seven key components that comprise it.

1. Purpose

This book started with an analysis of the life of Victor Frankl, who placed purpose at the core of his philosophy, logotherapy.

What exactly do we mean by purpose? Quite simply, we are talking about our driving force or motivation in life. On a basic level, purpose is the reason we get up in the morning. On a deeper level, it may mean adhering to a set of beliefs, principles, or commitment to a cause or way of life that is in line with our own values.

Frankl taught that every human being has within them an inner desire to find purpose in life. I believe this is the crucial first step in tackling our challenges.

Frankl used his time in the concentration camps to provide therapeutic services to despairing inmates. He spoke of counselling two men who believed they had nothing left to live for. 'In both cases', Frankl later recounted, 'it was a question of getting them to realize that life was still expecting something from them; something in the future was expected of them'. For one inmate, it was to think of his child, living in a foreign country, who he could later be reunited with. For the other, a scientist, it was the value that his research and books could provide for the scientific community in the future'.

This gave both men reason for living and allowed them to see beyond their current predicament. For as Frankl wrote, 'a man who becomes conscious of the responsibility he bears toward a human being who affectionately waits for him, or to an unfinished work, will never be able to throw away his life. He knows the 'why' for his existence and will be able to bear almost any 'how'.

Only when we know what we are living for can we deal with the situation in front of us. Nelson Mandela, Muhammad Ali, Rosa Parks, Steve Jobs and many others, lived with a purpose that allowed them to visualise the future, rather than lament the past and present.

Finding purpose is, at the core of 'The Adversity Formula'. Purpose provides the anchor that can be dropped in troubled waters; acting as a stabilising force when all around us is anything but secure.

2. Passion

Passion can be defined as a powerful or compelling emotion or feeling for something. Just like purpose, it is something that is deeply personal to each person. I may be moved by something that simply does not resonate with you.

Examining the life of Stephen Hawking was moving on so many levels. Yet, it was Hawking's passion for science which was the driving force behind his refusal to give up on life. It was a passion that kept Hawking going. That commitment to sharing his passion for science with others, moved him to comment that 'I hope that I can inspire in a new generation of children the wonder that the universe holds for me'.

That curiosity provided the energy for him to move beyond his own physical suffering. Hawking led the way in showing that where passion exists within a person, inner strength to deal with life's challenges naturally follows.

3. Hard work

Hard work cannot simply be defined by the number of hours spent on any given activity. It is far too simplistic to measure work in that way. You will recall that Albert Einstein had a totally different work ethic to Margaret Thatcher. For some, like Churchill, the combination of rest and play, was as an important component in a relentless work ethic.

The story of Madam C. J. Walker showed us that through hard work, we can be lifted to new heights. In Walker's case, without her strong work ethic, it is unlikely she would have persisted with her experiments to find a product to reverse her own hair loss. The transformation from poverty to wealth could never have taken place with purpose and passion alone. It required the inevitable toil that must be employed in all our lives.

In Walker's own words, 'If I have accomplished anything in life, it is because I have been willing to work hard'.

What I feel we have learnt about hard work, is that it involves expending the maximum effort within our own capabilities and needs. Adopting a routine that works best for that individual will provide for the best results.

4. Teamwork

Teamwork is usually defined as a group of people working together to achieve a common goal. It has been no surprise to learn just how central teamwork has been to the success of many.

Perhaps one of the most enlightening moments for me in the writing of this book came when I discovered that whilst the section on sports stars featured only those involved in individual sports, it was the role played by mentors, coaches, and family members that really ensured their success.

This should make us more conscious of the fact that even within individual pursuits, the importance of teamwork can never be discounted.

In 2000, Steve Jobs and his fellow Pixar executives relocated Pixar Amination Studios to the site of a former Del Monte fruit canning factory. The original drawings visualised three buildings with separate offices for animators, computer scientists and Pixar executives. Jobs thew out the original proposals. Instead of the three separate buildings, he insisted on a single vast space, with an atrium at its heart.

Brad Bird, the director of award-winning productions *Ratatouille* and *The Incredibles* gave an insight into Jobs' thinking. 'The atrium initially might seem like a waste of space. But Steve realised that when people run into each other when they make eye contact, things happen', he explained. In other words, great people put teamwork at the core of their strategy.

There was nothing more vital to innovation and problem solving to Steve Jobs than his team's collaboration.

Nothing is ever achieved alone. We must all appreciate the value of having good people around us, be they friends, family, colleagues or mentors.

5. Acceptance

Acceptance involves adopting a mindset that allows us to implement the lessons that life has taught us. More than anything else, it relies on a thorough and honest self-awareness.

Nelson Mandela demonstrated that only through his acceptance of the need for reconciliation, not revenge, would he be able to make South Africa the true beacon of equality that he so desired.

Mandela was not born with this pragmatic viewpoint. It was an 'acquired trait' according to his own words in his autobiography, *The Long Walk to Freedom*. Known for his youthful impudence and bouts of anger towards the treatment of the black community, he came to acknowledge and accept that a multi-racial society was beneficial to the future success of his nation. Violence would be detrimental and futile. As he himself said to younger supporters keen for revenge, 'we can't win a war, but we can win an election'.

In our own lives, we must similarly accept the need for flexible thinking. Nothing is static nor stands still. We must be mentally prepared to accept and adapt to our new realities.

Mandela led the way in accepting that real change takes time.

6. Courage

Courage can mean different things to different people. It can mean confronting one's own pain or fighting bravely against an external force. There can be no doubt just how important courage has been shown to be in these pages.

Courage comes in all shapes and sizes, but only arises when people take calculated risks. *The Courageous Heart of Irena Sendler* is a 2009 television film directed by John Kent Harrison. Those enthralled with Irena's story will be unsurprised at the director's choice of title.

Sendler's bravery can perhaps best be summed up by her view that 'Fear makes you weak; anger makes you strong.' What is clear is that Sendler's actions to save so many children in the Warsaw Ghetto, could not possibly have taken place without bypassing the natural tendency to be fearful.

Was Sendler born with such levels of courage or was it a trait that she developed over time? The answer remains a mystery but is also irrelevant. The story of Katharine Graham showed us that courage can be learnt by even the most apprehensive of personalities.

Fortune favours the brave. In adversity, we often see an opportunity to sink or swim. Whilst playing it safe may be more comfortable, it may not produce the necessary results.

As Robert Schuller said, 'tough times do not last. Tough people do'.

7. Positivity

A positive mindset refers to a state of mind in which one tends to be positive or optimistic in attitude. It does not need to be a natural tendency but can be learnt 'on the job'.

The rewards for positivity, in its many forms, have been shown to be immense. Consistently, we have seen how successful people have been able to reframe rather than bemoan their challenges.

We saw that, in October 1941, when Winston Churchill found the time, despite the rigours of war, to speak to pupils at Harrow, his childhood school. Most people focus on the words we have already spoken about regarding 'never giving in' and it's true, those words were powerful. However, there is much to be taken from his final words that day.

Western Europe had been conquered. The United States had yet to enter the war. But Churchill defiantly asserted that 'these are not dark days; these are great days, the greatest days our country has ever lived; and we must all thank God that we have been allowed, each of us according to our stations, to play a part in making these days memorable'.

Putting a positive spin on whatever life throws at us is essential. However bad things may appear to be, we must remind ourselves that there is always some good within our lives. This will allow you to have perspective and remain calm amidst any setback. Understand that negative emotions like bitterness and self-criticism serve no purpose at all.

We have come to see that it is often not what a person experiences, but how they react, that determines a successful outcome. We have now come to appreciate that those who faced adversity with positivity became bolder, wiser, and better people because of their challenges.

The Formula in three categories

Looking at the seven key elements of the formula as laid out above, I think it is important to understand that they can be grouped into three categories: intrinsic values, extrinsic values, and a healthy mindset.

A look at the categories one by one will help us understand the traits better and how to access them to help us deal with the adversity in our lives:

- Intrinsic Values: Purpose and Passion

The first two components of our formula, purpose and passion, are both intrinsic in nature. That means that they must come from within. No one can force purpose upon you. It is either already in place or be something you wish to discover. Likewise, you cannot be forced into feeling passionate about something. If a subject doesn't resonate with you, you simply won't have a passion for it. If you haven't yet discovered either, don't worry, because it is not too late. Keep looking; no one ever said that there was a time limit on finding purpose or passion. However, it is at the core of the formula because we can only be determined and tenacious to deal with any given situation if it is underpinned by our life purpose and we have the passion to drive us forward enthusiastically to deal with it.

- Extrinsic values: Hard work and Teamwork

The second part of our formula involves behaviours that are extrinsic in nature. That means they arise from outside an individual, as opposed to within. These are the vital practical steps that accompany our intrinsic values. You can have all the purpose and passion in the world but without putting in the hard yards to overcome your challenges, it is unlikely that you will be crossing the finishing line any time soon. Seeking out and surrounding yourself with good people, be they friends, family or colleagues who can support you in times of need is another key component of the formula.

- Healthy mindset: Acceptance, Courage, and Positivity. The final part of our formula may well be the most important. Anyone looking to prevail over their challenges must work relentlessly on three learned elements that heavily influence our mindset: acceptance, courage and positivity. Without a healthy mindset, we are unlikely to be able to develop as individuals. These behaviours act as the lens through which we see our challenges. For example, failure to accept reality or partake in regular self-analysis, makes it harder to face up to our challenges honestly. Only through a patient and calm approach, together with an acceptance of our limitations, can we truly hope to succeed. Courage is necessary if we are to boldly take risks, face our fears and challenge the status quo. Acting with courage may not be natural, to us, but we have seen within these pages that with practice, it can be learnt as easily as any other trait. Finally, positivity is the bedrock of success. Confidence, gratitude, and a sense of humour have all been proven to be vital traits when tackling adversity. A positive and healthy outlook is perhaps the most crucial ingredient in our recipe for success.

For use at all times
We have learnt much from an in-depth study of thirty fascinating individuals that whilst each person utilised their own strategies for dealing with adversity, there were seven key traits common to all, as outlined above.

Further analysis has shown that these seven traits can be combined into three categories enabling us to display the formula as follows:

The Adversity Formula = Intrinsic + Extrinsic + Healthy Mindset

My concluding belief is that the formula can be applied by any person, at any time.

Epilogue

Learning from History

History provides us with an array of stories, events, and lessons from which we can benefit. Indeed, Winston Churchill stated, 'those that fail to learn from history, are doomed to repeat it'.

There are always those who dismiss history as irrelevant and even meaningless. They may have glanced at the book's title and questioned what the lives of Winston Churchill, Rosa Parks, Walt Disney, Wilma Rudolph or Eleanor Roosevelt, amongst others, could possibly teach us about dealing with today's challenges?

This book has been about more than simple facts about inspiring people. Interesting though that may have been, it would have been an opportunity lost, to absorb the many valuable lessons that can be applied for our own times.

When it comes to tackling adversity, we have learned that many things connect those who have been able to overcome it. In every chapter, we saw that every adversity, every disappointment, every bit of distress that is experienced in life, can be turned into a positive.

We have come to see that it is often not what a person experiences, but how they react, that determines a successful outcome. We have now come to appreciate that those who faced adversity with positivity became bolder, wiser, and better people because of their challenges.

I make no claim that this book offers any kind of substitute for professional therapy. Rather, I have tried to reveal how these inspirational individuals overcame their setbacks. By understanding their approach to adversity, you too can find encouragement for the battles that lay ahead for you.

This book was written during the chaos and confusion of the 2020 coronavirus pandemic, but its lessons are enduring.

After all, adversity would not appear to be going out of business any time soon.

Whether you are a student, an aspiring entrepreneur, lawyer, political leader, father, mother, husband, or wife, you will surely have felt an affinity with one or more of those featured above. I hope it will allow you to look at life through a different lens.

Like me, you may have previously thought of adversity as a negative experience, to be confined to a dark corner at the back of your mind. I used to harbour resentment towards the bigger disappointments I experienced in life. After all, isn't that the narrative that modern society gives us? As humans, we tend to paint the world in black and white with no shades of grey. There are winners and losers and failure means losing, doesn't it? Having completed this book, I no longer feel this way. I have come to look at difficult experiences through a different lens.

Whilst writing this book, I was captivated by the documentary *The Last Dance* shown on Netflix. Released to widespread acclaim, I was fascinated by the drive of its main character, basketball star, Michael Jordan. Despite having a net worth of over two billion dollars and leading the Chicago Bulls to six NBA titles, Jordan's most famous quote may be about adversity.

'I've missed more than nine thousand shots in my career. I've lost almost three hundred games. Twenty-six times, I've been trusted to take the game winning shot and missed. I've failed over and over and over again in my life. And that is why I succeed', he summarised, mentioning statistics that are rarely disclosed about his career.

Of the many hundreds of hours of research, I have undertaken during the writing of this book, one of the most inspirational lines I heard came from my wife. When I explained to her how Michael Jordan believes his success has come about as a direct result of failure, she told me that as a primary schoolteacher, she often encourages pupils making errors by proclaiming enthusiastically, 'we love mistakes, it's how we learn'.

I passionately believe that in today's world, we have become too scared to make mistakes. This search for perfectionism, as shown through the countless images of faultlessness we see on social media, leave us devastated when tough times happen or when we make our inevitable mistakes. We only see the finished article; we rarely see the suffering and toil it took to get there. This book has done just that.

It saddens me when I hear some people speak of 2020 as a wasted year. I understand the frustration felt by those unable to progress with long term plans or who have suffered losses.

However, the words of Robert H. Schuller mean more at this time, than ever before: 'Difficult times will pass and at the end of it, with the right tools, we can become better and more resilient people'.

Having probed the lives of thirty remarkable people, I believe that those tools that Schuler refers to, can be found in the approach I have outlined above. If we can focus on applying 'The Adversity Formula', then we too, can triumph at this most unprecedented time in history.

Steven Mason

Bibliography

Prologue

Banks, J., Karjalainen, H. & Propper, C. (2020). *Recessions and Health: The Long-term Health Consequences of Responses to Coronavirus.* IFS Briefing Note BN281. The Institute for Fiscal Studies. Ifs.org.uk

Campbell, J. (2000). *Margaret Thatcher Volume One: The Grocer's Daughter.* London: Jonathan Cape.

Chakravorti, B. (2010). *Finding Competitive Advantage in Adversity.* Brighton, MA: Harvard Business Review, store.hbr.org

Sugarman, M. (2014). *Under the Heel of Bushido: Last Voices of the Jewish POWs of the Japanese in the Second World War.* Chicago, IL: Valentine Mitchell & Company.

Chapter One - Viktor Frankl

Alfermann, D. & Stambulova, N. (2007). *Career Transitions and Career Termination.* In Tenenbaum G. & Eklund R. C. (Eds.), *Handbook of Sport Psychology (p. 712–733).* Hoboken, NJ: John Wiley & Sons, Inc. psycnet.apa.org

Batthyány, A. (Ed.) (2016). *Logotherapy and Existential Analysis. Proceedings of the Viktor Frankl Institute, Vienna, Volume 1.* Basel, Switzerland: Springer International, springer.com

Cooper, B. (2017). *A Short Guide to Setting and Achieving Goals.* Seattle, WA: Rescue Time, Inc, rescuetime.com

Davenport, J. (2007). *Will as Commitment and Resolve: An Existential Account of Creativity, Love, Virtue, and Happiness.* New York, NY: Fordham University Press, research.library.fordham.edu

Frankl, V. (1985). *The Unconscious G-d.* New York, NY: Washington Square Press.

Frankl, V. (2006). *Man's Search for Meaning.* London: Beacon Press, beacon.org

Frankl, V. (2000). *Viktor Frankl Recollections: An Autobiography.* Cambridge, MA: Perseus Publishing.

Frankl, V. (2005). *Frühe Schriften, 1923-1942.* Wien: München Bern Maudrich.

Frankl, V. (2014). *The Will to Meaning Foundations and Applications of Logotherapy.* New York, NY: Plume.

LaCasse, M. (2017). *Rewriting the Narrative with Logotherapy: Review of Man's Search for Meaning.* The American Journal of Psychiatry Residents' Journal. ajp.psychiatryonline.org

Locke, E. & Latham, G. (2006). *New Directions in Goal-Setting Theory.* SAGE Journals, Volume 15, Issue 5. journals.sagepubs.com

Mosby, Inc. (2013). *Mosby's Dictionary of Medicine, Nursing & Health Professions.* Amsterdam, Netherlands: elsevier.com

National Library of Medicine. (2001). *Viktor Frankl and the Genesis of the Third Viennese School of Psychotherapy.* pubmed.ncbi.nlm.nih.gov/11554273/

Pattakos, A. & Dutton, E. (2015). *The OPA! Way: Finding Joy & Meaning in Everyday Life & Work.* Dallas, TX: BenBella Books.

Pattakos, A. (2009). *Living with Meaning: Shift Your Focus of Attention.* Article. 3 July 2009. New York, NY: huffpost.com

Redsand, A. (2006). *Viktor Frankl: A Life Worth Living.* New York, NY: Clarion Books.

Shantall, T. (2020). *The Life-changing Impact of Viktor Frankl's Logotherapy.* Cham: Springer, springer.com

Schatzman, M. (1997). *Viktor Frankl: Obituary.* London: The Independent, independent.co.uk

Southwick, S., Gilmartin, R., McDonough, P. & Morrissey, P. (2006). *Logotherapy as an adjunctive treatment for chronic combat- related PTSD: a meaning-based intervention.* American Journal of Psychotherapy, Vol. 60, No. 2. Lancaster, PA: American Journal of Psychotherapy. pubmed.ncbi.nlm.nih.gov

The Lancet. (2018). Global, regional, and national incidence, prevalence, and years lived with disability for 354 diseases and injuries for 195 countries and territories, 1990–2017: a systematic analysis for the Global Burden of Disease Study 2017. The Lancet Volume 392, Issue 10159, P1789-1858, November 10, 2018. London: thelancet.com

Turner J. *Man's Search for Meaning - Teacher's Guide*. New York, NY: Random House, penguinrandomhouse.com

Washingtonpost.com/archive/politics/1984/04/07/the-pursuit-of-happiness

Chapter Two - Marie Curie

Borzendowski, J. (2009). *Marie Curie: Mother of Modern Physics*. New York, NY: Sterling Publishing, Inc.

Brandt, S. (2009). *The Harvest of a Century*. Oxford: Oxford University Press.

Country Living. (2017). *British Couples in Business Together*. 14 February 2017. countryliving.com/uk/kitchen-table-talent/news/a1302/british-couples-in-business-together/

Des Jardins, J. (2011). *Madame Curie's Passion*. Washington, DC: Smithsonian Magazine, smithsonianmag.com

Froman, N. (1996). *Marie and Pierre Curie and the Discovery of Polonium and Radium*. Royal Swedish Academy of Sciences Lecture: Stockholm, Sweden. nobelprize.org

Goldsmith, B. (2006). *Obsessive Genius: The Inner World of Marie Curie*. New York, NY: W.W. Norton & Company.

History.com Editors. (2010). *Marie and Pierre Curie Isolate Radium*. A&E Television Networks. history.com

Kraft, S. (1995). *France Entombs Madame Curie Amongst the Great Men*. Article. 21 April 1995. Los Angeles, CA: Los Angeles Times, latimes.com

The Lancet. (2020). *Safety and immunogenicity of the ChAdOx1 nCoV-19 vaccine against SARS-CoV-2: A preliminary report of a phase 1/2, single-blind, randomised controlled trial*. 20 July 2020. London: The Lancet, thelancet.com

McHugh, B. (2019). *Marie Curie: 7 Facts about the Ground-breaking Scientist*. Article. 6 November 2019. biography.com

Manson, M. *Screw Finding Your Passion*. Article. markmanson.net

Mansell, S. (2018). *A Potted History of Radium, the Most Radioactive Substance on the Planet.* Article. 19 December 2018. London: The Independent, independent.co.uk

Mme Curie is Dead: Obituary. Martyr to Science. 4 July 1934. New York, NY: The New York Times, nytimes.com

Obama, B. (2018). *Second Annual Obama Foundation Summit.* Chicago, IL: Obama Foundation, obma.org

Ogilvie, M. (2017). *Marie Curie and Her Fellow Scientists.* Article. 6 April 2017. New York, NY: Physics Today, physicstoday.scitation.org

Pasachoff, N. (2008). *Marie Curie: And the Science of Radioactivity.* Oxford: Oxford University Press.

Pycior, H. (1996). *Creative Couples in the Sciences.* New Brunswick, N.J: Rutgers University Press.

Poynter, M. (2015). *Marie Curie: Genius Researcher of Radioactivity (Genius Scientists and Their Genius Ideas).* New Jersey: Enslow Publishing LLC.

Quinn, S. (2011). *A Test of Courage: Marie Curie and the 1911 Nobel Prize.* The Clinical Chemist. watermark.silverchair.com

Quinn, S. (1996). *Marie Curie: A Life.* Cambridge, MA: Perseus.

Sheean, V. (2013). *Madam Curie - A Biography by Eve Curie.* Style Press.

Sullivan L. (2018). *Life as an Ambulance Driver in World War I.* London: Cavendish Square Publishing.

Ward, A. (2002). *The Leadership Lifecycle.* London: Houndmills: Palgrave Macmillan.

Wasternedge, T. (2015). *In Conversation with John McCarthy CBE. The Limits of Resistance.* Article. 22 October 2015. Manchester: robertsoncooper.com

Chapter Three - Albert Einstein

Biography Channel. (2015). biography.com/scientist/albert-einstein

Calaprice, A. & Lipscombe T. (2005). *Albert Einstein: A Biography.* Westpoint, CT: Greenwood Press.

Crockatt, R. (2016). *Einstein and Twentieth Century Politics: 'A Salutary Moral Influence'.* Oxford: Oxford University Press, global.oup.com

DeMeres, J. *Hard Work? It's Not All It's Cracked Up To Be. It May Even Be Irrelevant. Here's Why.* Article. The StartUp. medium.com

Einstein, A. (1920). *Document 31: Ideas and Methods of the Theory of Relativity, Presented in Their Development.* einsteinpapers.press.princeton.edu/vol7-trans/129

Einstein, A. (1931) *The World as I See It, included, in Living Philosophies.* New York, NY: Simon & Schuster. core.ac.uk/download/pdf/31058817.pdf

Einstein A. *"Relativity".* In Janssen, M., Schulmann, R., Illy, J., Lehner, C. & Buchwald, D. K. (eds.). *The Collected Papers of Albert Einstein. Volume 7: The Berlin Years: Writings, 1918 – 1921.* Princeton, NY: Princeton University Press, press.princeton.edu

Einstein, A. (1991). *Autobiographical Notes.* La Salle, Il: Open Court. worldcat.org

Einstein A. (1939). *Letter to The New York Times.* 2 August 1939. New York, NY: The New York Times, nytimes.com

Falk, D. (2018). *Einstein Made His Share of Errors. Here Are Three Of The Biggest.* Article. 14 March 2018. nbcnews.com

Ferreira, P. (2010.) *General Relativity: Einstein's Insight.* Article. 30 June 2010. London: New Scientist, newscientist.com

Gardener, M. (1997). *Relativity Simply Explained.* Mineola, NY: Dover Publications.

Gorvett, Z. (2017). *What You Can Learn From Einstein's Quirky Habits?* Article. 12 June 2017. London: bbc.co.uk

Isaacson, W. (2007). *Einstein.* Prince Frederick, MD: Recorded Books.

Isaacson, W. (2008). *Einstein, His Life and Genius.* New York, NY: Simon and Schuster.

Isaacson, W. (2011). *The Genius of Jobs.* Article. 29 October 2011. New York, NY: The New York Times, nytimes.com

Jobs, S. (2005). *Stanford Commencement Address*. Stanford. news.stanford.edu

Karges, C. (1999). *Ignite Your Intuition: Improve Your Memory, Make Better Decisions, Be More Creative and Achieve Your Full Potential*. Deerfield Beach, FL: Health Communications, Inc.

Kennedy, R. (2014). *A Student's Guide to Einstein's Major Papers*. Oxford: Oxford University Press, global.oup.com

Lovett C. B. (1987). *Men Who Made a New Physics: Physicists and the Quantum Theory*. Chicago, IL: University of Chicago Press, press.uchicago.edu

Levenson, T. (2017). *The Scientist and the Fascist: How Einstein Reacted to Hitler's Rise*. Article. 9 June 2017. Washington, DC: theatlantic.com

Moskowitz, C. (2010). *Einstein's 'Biggest Blunder' Turns Out to Be Right*. Article. 24 November 2010. New York, NY: space.com

Miller, W. (1955). *Death of a Genius*. Article. 2 May 1955. New York, NY: Life Magazine. sundheimgroup.com

Null, G. (2008). *Living in the Moment*. Berkley, CA: North Atlantic Books.

Nussbaumer, H. (2014). *Einstein's Conversion from His Static to an Expanding Universe*. The European Physical Journal H39, 37-62. arxiv.org/abs/1311.2763

Nike News. (2015) *Bill Bowerman: Nike's Original Innovator*. news.nike.com/bill-bowerman-nike-s-original-innovator

Paid, A. (1982) *Subtle is The Lord: The Science and the Life of Albert Einstein*. Oxford: Oxford University Press.

Parker, G. & Bounds, A. (2020). *Brexit: Will Boris Johnson Reverse Thatcherism?* Article. 30 January 2020. London: ft.com

Pipes, T. (2017). *Albert Einstein's Unique Approach To Thinking*. Article. 11 January 2017. evernote.com

Branson, R. (2016). *Simplicity Speeds Up Disruption*. Article. 4 January 2016. The Star Malaysia, thestar.com

Waldrop, M. (2017). *Einstein Relativity Explained in 4 Simple Steps*. Article. Washington, DC: nationalgeographic.com

Weinstein, G. (2015). *Einstein's Pathway to the Special Theory of Relativity.* Cambridge: Cambridge Scholars Publishing, cambridgepublishing.com

Chapter Four - Stephen Hawking

Babu, S. (2018). *Stephen Hawking: Struggle Against Disability And Superstition.* Article. Kerala, India: countercurrents.org

Bailey, L. (2018). *Stephen Hawking's Funny, Surprising and Touching Moments in Popular Culture.* Article. 14 March 2018. London: inews.co.uk

Biography.com Editors. (2014). *Elie Wiesel Biography.* biography.com/writer/elie-wiesel

Blog.iec.ch/2018/03/how-stephen-hawking-overcame-his-disability/

Evans, G. (2018*). Stephen Hawking's Doctors Offered To Cut Life Support.* Article. 8 January 2018. London: indy100.com

BBC News. (2020). *Coronavirus: Hawking's Family Donate Ventilator to Hospital.* Article. 22 April 2020. London: bbc.co.uk

Dreifus, C. (2011). *Stephen Hawking Speaks.* Article. 10 May 2011. New York, NY: The New York Times, nytimes.com

Elgot, J. (2015). *Stephen Hawking: 'I Would Consider Assisted Suicide'.* Article. 3 June 2015. London: The Guardian, theguardian.com

Erickson, J. (2005). *The Art of Persuasion: How to Influence People and Get What You Want.* London: Hodder Mobious.

Ferguson, K. (2011). *Stephen Hawking: His Life and Work.* London: Bantam Press.

Gillespie, T. (2018). *Stephen Hawking: The Genius with a Funny Side.* Article. London: skynews.com

Greenfield, S. (2018). *Stephen Hawking: Obituary.* Article. 14 March 2018. London: The Independent, independent.co.uk

Hartley-Parkinson, R. (2018). *What is ALS The Disease That Stephen Hawking Suffered From A Young Age.* Article. 14 March 2018. London: METRO Newspaper.

Hawking, S. (2013). *My Brief History: A Memoir.* London: Bantam Press.

Hawking, S. (2016). *Reith Lecture.* 26 January 2016. London: Royal Institution of Great Britain.

Hawkins, D. (2018). *What Made Hawking's 'A Brief History of Time' So Immensely Popular?* Article. 14 March 2018. Washington, DC: The Washington Post, washingtonpost.com

Kreitler, P. (2005). *Trends in Black Hole Research.* New York, NY: Nova Science Publishers.

Larsen, K. (2007). *Stephen Hawking: A Biography.* Mumbai, India: Jaico Publishing House.

National Institute of Neurological Disorders and Stroke-Amyotrophic Lateral Sclerosis (ALS) Fact Sheet. ninds.nih.gov

Nytimes.com/2004/12/12/magazine/the-science-of-secondguessing

Oxtra, C. (2019). *Get to Know the Man Behind the Theory.* Capstone Press. capstonepub.com/library/products/stephen-hawking

Penrose, R. (2018). *Mind Over Matter: Stephen Hawking.* Obituary. 14 March 2018. London: The Guardian, theguardian.com

Penzel, F. *Acceptance and OCD.* beyondocd.org

Rees, M. (2018). *Stephen Hawking Obituary: Boy Who Became Master of the Universe.* Article. 14 March 2018. London: The Daily Mail, dailymail.co.uk

Rigby, R. (2019). *Psychology of Wealth: If You Are Worth Millions, Why Bother Working?* Article. 6 December 2019. London: The Financial Times, ft.com

Ryan, F. (2018). *Hawking Won the World's Respect and Gave Disabled People Like Me Hope.* Article. 14 March 2018. London: The Guardian, theguardian.com

Schwartz, B. (2015). *Why We Work.* TED. London: Simon & Schuster UK.

Selby, J. (2014). *Stephen Hawkins Admits He 'Briefly Tried to Commit Suicide' in Discussion on Assisted Dying.* Article. 17 July 2014. London: The Independent, independent.co.uk

Wiesel, E. & Wiesel M. (2008). *Night.* London: Penguin Books.

Williams, R. (2018). *How Technology Gave Stephen Hawking A Voice.* Article. 14 March 2018. London: The Independent, inews.co.uk

Winsor, M. (2018). *The Most Important Pieces of Advice Stephen Hawking Gave To His Children.* Article. 14 March 2018. New York, NY: abcnews.go.com

Withers, L. (2016). *Stephen Hawking Admits His 'Sense of Humour' Inspired Him Through the Tough Times.* Article. 19 January 2016. London; express.co.uk

Chapter Five - Steve Jobs

Balague, G. (2019). *Pep Guardiola.* London: Orion Publishing Group Ltd.

Becraft, M. (2016). *Steve Jobs: A Biography.* Westpoint, CT: Greenwood.

Bickford, J. (2013). *American Comeback.* Las Vegas, NE: American Comeback-Publishing.

Bucero, A. (2018). *Passion, Persistence and Patience: Key Skills for Achieving Project Success.* New York, NY: Business Expert Press.

Business News Publishing. (2016). *Summary: Inside Steve's Brain: Review and Analysis of Kahney's Book.* Troy, MI: Business News Publishing.

De Wolfe, D. (2011). *Lord Sugar's Rules for First Time Entrepreneurs.* Article. 6 June 2011. London: Shortlist Magazine, shortlist.com

Gallo, C. (2015). *As Steve Jobs Once Said, 'People with Passion Can Change the World'.* Article. 8 July 2015. Irvine, CA: entrepreneur.com

Gallo, C. (2011). *The Innovation Secrets of Steve Jobs: Insanely Different Principles for Breakthrough Success.* New York, NY: McGraw-Hill Education eBook.

Gillam, S. (2008). *Steve Jobs: Apple & iPod Wizard.* Edina, MN: ABDO Publishing Company.

Goodell, J. (2011). *The Steve Jobs Nobody Knew.* Article. 27 October 2011. New York, NY: Rolling Stone Magazine.

Gugliemo, C. (1997). *A Steve Jobs Moment That Mattered. Speech at Macworld Boston Conference.* 6 August 1997. Jersey City, NJ: forbes.com

Ichbiah, D. (2020). *The Four Lives of Steve Jobs.* Babelcube Inc.

Isaacson, W. (2011). *Steve Jobs.* New York: Toronto: Simon & Schuster.

Isaacson, W. (2012). *How Steve Job's Love of Simplicity Fueled a Design Revolution.* Article. September 2012. Washington, DC: Smithsonian Magazine.

Isaacson, W. (2012). *The Real Leadership Lessons of Steve Jobs.* Article. April 2012. Brighton, MA: Harvard Business Review.

Investopedia. Article. *Steve Jobs and the Apple Story.* 14 October 2015. investopedia.com

Kramm, J. (1988). *Steve Jobs: The Journey is the Reward.* Glenview, Il: jstor.org

Lavinsky, D. (2012). *Start at the End: How Companies Can Grow Bigger and Faster by Reversing Their Business Plan.* New York, NY: Wiley.

Levy, L. (2016). *To Pixar and Beyond: My Unlikely Journey with Steve Jobs to Make Entertainment History.* London: Oneworld Publications.

Linn, A. (2011). *What Steve Jobs Taught Us: It's Okay to Fail.* Article. 10 May 2011. New York, NY: msnbc.com

Long, A. (2016). *Why Steve Jobs Killed 70% of Apple's Products.* Article. 1 February 2016. Sydney, NSW: hellostepchange.com

McQueen, M. (2016). *Momentum: How to Build It, Keep It or Get it Back.* Chichester: Wiley Blackwell.

Patel, D. (2018*). 10 Ways Successful People Push Through Adversity.* Article. 10 September 2018. Irvine, CA: entrepreneur.com

Safaei, H. (2017). *First-Class Leadership: How Highly Effective Teams Can Achieve Breakthrough Results.* Ontario, Canada: Black Card Books.

Schlender, B. (2015). *Becoming Steve Jobs: The Evolution of a Reckless Upstart into a Visionary Leader.* London: Hodder & Stoughton.

Shenk, J. W. (2014). The Power of Two. Article. July / August 2014. Washington, DC: theatlantic.com

Simpson, M. (2011). *A Sister's Eulogy for Steve Jobs.* Quoted in Article. 30 October 2011. New York, NY: The New York Times, nytimes.com

Weiner, M. (2015). *'Mad Men' Creator Matthew Weiner's Reassuring Life Advice for Struggling Artists.* Quoted in Article. 16 April 2015. fastcompany.com

Weatherhead, A. & Feldman, F. (2008). *Power of Adversity: Tough Times Can Make You Stronger, Wiser and Better.* Charlottesville, VA: Hampton Roads Publishing Company.

60 Minutes. *Steve Jobs Interview.* CBS News. https://sanfrancisco.cbslocal.com/2011/10/06/steve-jobs-offered-rare-insights-during-60-minutes-interview/

Chapter Six - Katharine Graham

ABC News. (2007). *Person of the Week: Katharine Graham.* Article. 26 October 2007. New York, NY: abcnews.go.com

Asirvatham, S. (2001). *Katharine Graham (Women of Achievement).* New York, NY: Chelsea House Publishers.

Berger, M. (2001). *Katharine Graham, Former Publisher of Washington Post, Dies at 84.* Article. 17 July 2001. New York, NY: The New York Times, nytimes.com

Buffett, W. *Kay Graham's Management Career.* Article. ghco.com

CNN. (2001). *Legendary Washington Post Chief Kay Graham Dies.* Article. 18 July 2001. New York, NY: edition.cnn.com

CNN. (2001). Kay Graham: Pillar of the Post and Press. edition.cnn.com/2001/US/07/22/graham.journey/

Davis, D. (2018). *Katharine the Great: Katharine Graham and Her Washington Post Empire.* Los Angeles, CA: Graymalkin Media.

DeBaise, C. (2018). *Start a Successful Business: Expert Advice to Take Your Start-up from Idea to Empire.* New York, NY: Amacom Books, inc.

Diamond, A. (2017). *What the Post Gets Right (and Wrong) About Katharine Graham and the Pentagon Papers.* Article. 29 December 2017. Washington, DC: Smithsonian Magazine, smithsonoianmagazine.com

Fink, C. (1988). *Strategic Newspaper Management.* New York, NY: Random House.

Graham, K. (2017). *The Pentagon Papers Making History at The Washington Post (A Vintage Short).* New York, NY: Vintage.

Hansen, J. (2012). *First Man: The Life of Neil A. Armstrong.* New York, NY: Simon & Schuster.

Hodgson, G. (2001). *Katharine Graham Obituary.* Article. 18 July 2001. London: The Guardian, theguardian.com

Holliday, R. (2016). *Ego Is The Enemy the Fight to Master Our Greatest Opponent.* London: Profile Books.

Los Angeles Times. (1997). *The Life and Times of Citizen Graham.* latimes.com/archives/la-xpm-1997-02-16-bk-29245-story

Meyers, M. (2008). *Happy Accidents: Serendipity in Modern Medical Breakthroughs.* New York, NY: Arcade.

Newyorker.com/magazine/1997/01/20/citizen-kay

Peters, W. (2017). *Leadership Lessons: Warren Buffett, Walt Disney, Thomas Edison, Katharine Graham, Steve Jobs, Ray Kroc.* Boston, Mass: New World City, Inc.

Plush, H. (2016). *'Life's Like Mountaineering – Never Look Down': The Wisdom of Sir Edmund Hillary.* Article. 20 July 2016. London: The Daily Telegraph, telegraph.co.uk

Politico. (2018). *What The Post Missed About Kay Graham.* politico.com/magazine/story/2018/03/04/the-post-graham-academy-awards-217218

Razeghi, A. (2006). *Hope: How Triumphant Leaders Create the Future.* San Francisco, California: Jossey-Bass.

Remnick, D. (2014). *Reporting: Writings from The New Yorker.* London: Picador - On Demand Edition.

Smith, J.Y. & Epstein N. (2001). *Katharine Graham Dies at 84.* Article. 18 July 2001. Washington, DC: The Washington Post, washingtonpost.com

Steinem, G. (2001). *A Great Woman Who Was Everywoman.* Article. 21 July 2001. New York, NY: The New York Times, nytimes.com

Tasler, N. (2009). *The Impulse Factor.* New York, NY: Simon & Schuster.

Telford, D. & Gostick, A. (2012). *Integrity Works: Strategies for Becoming a Trusted, Respected and Admired Leaders.* Layton. UT: Gibbs Smith Publishers.

The New York Times. (1963) *Philip Graham, 48, Publisher, A Suicide.* Article. 4 August 1963. New York, NY: The New York Times. nytimes.com

Walravens, S. (2016). *5 Exercises Sheryl Sandberg: What Silicon Valley Women Do to Build Confidence.* Article. 6 September 2016. Jersey City, NJ: forbes.com.

Chapter Seven - Ole Kirk Christiansen

Baer, D. (2014). *Warren Buffett Tells Manager Their Top Priority is to 'Zealously Guard Berkshire's Reputation'.* businessinsider.in

Basulto, D. (2014). *Why Lego Is The Most Innovative Toy Company In The World.* Article. Washington, DC: The Washington Post, washingtonpost.com

Berman, J. (2014). *The Three Essential Warren Buffett Quotes to Live by.* Article. 20 April 2014. forbes.com

Blakemore, E. (2017). *The Disastrous Backstory Behind the Invention of Lego Bricks.* Article. 21 September 2017. New York, NY: history.com

Brickpedia.fandom.com/wiki/Ole_Kirk_Christiansen.

Christensen, J. *The Quality Story of Lego from Learning by Sufferings to Learning by Play.* PDF. newfutureformula.com

Fenton, R. (2019). *Incredibly Moving Journey for ALS-stricken from Brooklyn.* Article. 8 September 2019. New York, NY: New York Post, nypost.com

Famousinventors.org/ole-kirk-christiansen.

Henriksen I. *An Economic History of Denmark.* Article. eh.net.

Krasnianski, B. *Is Suffering a Blessing in Disguise?* Lecture. New York, NY: chabad.org

Lego. Various articles. Lego.com/en-us/LEGO-History. Bilund, Denmark: lego.com

Mueller, P. S., Plevak, D. J. & Rummans, T. A. *Religious Involvement, Spirituality, And Medicine: Implications For Clinical Practice.* Mayo Clin Proc. pubmed.ncbi.nlm.nih.gov/11761504/

Surowiecki, J. (2009). *Hanging Tough.* Article. 13 April 2009. The New Yorker. questia.com

University of Essex. (2020). *New analysis of the impact of lockdown on UK Jobs.* Article. 18 April 2020. Colchester: iser.essex.ac.uk

Van Looveren, Y. (2017). *LEGO Is World's Largest Toy Manufacturer For The First Time.* Article. 10 March 2017. Antwerp, Belgium: retaildetail.eu.

Chapter Eight - Madam C. J. Walker

Alexandre, S. (2014). *Opportunities Won't Fall in Your Lap: 5 Ways to Go Out and Get What's Yours.* elitedaily.com

American Masters. (2004). *Heroes, Myths and Magic About George Lucas.* Article. 13 January 2004. Arlington, VA: pbs.org

Biography.com Editors (2014). *Madam C. J. Walker.* Article. 2 April 2014. biography.com.

Bundles, A. (2001). *On Her Own Ground: The Life and Times of Madam C. J. Walker.* New York, NY: Scribner.

Bundles, A. (2020). *Self-Made: Inspired by the Life of Madam C. J. Walker.* New York, NY: Lisa Drew Books.

Bundles, A. (2012). *Madam C. J. Walker: Business Savvy to Philanthropy.* photos.state.gov/libraries/amgov/30145/publications-english/Black_Women_Leaders_eJ.pdf

Gugin, L. C. & St. Clair, J. E. (2015). *Indiana's 200: The People Who Shaped the Hoosier State.* Indianapolis, IN: Indiana Historical Society Press.

Haule, A. (2016). *First in Their Field: Madam C. J. Walker.* Article. 18 June 2016. San Diego, CA: Women's Museum of California, womensmuseumca.org

Hess, A. (2017). *4 Lessons You Can Learn From America's First Female Self-made Millionaire.* Article. 15 February 2017. Englewood Cliffs, NJ: cnbc.com

Hine, D. C. (2005). *Black Women in America.* New York, NY: Oxford University Press.

Indiana Historical Society. *Madam C. J. Walker, Empowering Women.* Indianapolis, IN: indianahistory.org.

Kennedy, J.F.K. (1962) *John F. Kennedy Moon* Speech - Rice Stadium. 12 September 1962. Boston, MA: jfklibrary.org

Kettler, S. (2020). *How Madam C. J. Walker Invented Her Hair Care Products.* Article. 10 February 2020. biography.com

Koehn, Nancy F., Anne Dwojeski, William Grundy, Erica Helms, and Katherine Miller. *Madam C. J. Walker: Entrepreneur, Leader, and Philanthropist.* Harvard Business School Case 807-145, March 2007. (Revised April 2011.)

Pattillo, A. (2020). *Military Psychologist Explains Why Grit Matters as Much as Intelligence.* Article. 16 May 2020. New York, NY: inverse.com

Smithsonian. *Malone, A. & Madam C. J. Walker. Pioneers of the African American Beauty Industry.* Washington, DC: Smithsonian National Museum of African America History & Culture.

Stephens, J. (2017). *Why Experimentation Leads to Better Innovation.* Article. 13 January 2017. London: minutehack.com

Washburne, S. (2017). *African American Inventors: Overcoming Challenges to Change America. Lucent Library of Black History.* San Diego, CA: Lucent Books.

Zipkin, N. (2018). *6 Lessons from Madam C. J. Walker, America's First Black Self-Made Female Millionaire.* Article. 21 February 2018. Irvine, CA: entrepreneur.com

Chapter Nine - Colonel Harland Sanders

Anderson, J. C. (2005). *The Human Tradition in the New South.* Lanham, MD: Rowman & Littlefield Publishers.

Bellows, A. (2016). *Colonels of Truth.* Article. 15 March 2016. damninteresting.com

Darden, R. (2002). *Secret Recipe: Why KFC Is Still Cooking After 50 Years.* Irving, Tx: Tapestry Press.

Dawson, V. (2015). *How Colonel Sanders Made Kentucky Fried Chicken an American Success Story.* Article. 6 July 2016. Washington, DC: Smithsonian Magazine.

Emery, D. (2016). *The Life of Colonel Sanders.* Article. 2 December 2016. snopes.com

Handel, S. *The Necessary Pain of Trial-and-Error.* Article. St. Petersburg, FL: theemotionmachine.com

Lodha, H. *The A-Z of Entrepreneurship: 26 Words that Capture What it Takes to be an Entrepreneur.* Hermanlodha.com. Nagpur: Panchsil Prakashan

Keller, G. & Papasan, J. (2015). *The One Thing: The Surprisingly Simple Truth Behind Extraordinary Results: Achieve Your Goals with One of the World's Bestselling Success Books.* London: John Murray Learning.

Nii, J. K. (2004). *Colonel's Landmark KFC is Mashed.* Article. 21, April 2004. Salt Lake City, UT: Deseret Morning News.

Ozersky, J. (2012). *Colonel Sanders And The American Dream.* Austin, TX: University of Texas Press.

Pearce, J. E. (1982). *The Colonel: The Captivating Biography of the Dynamic Founder of a Fast-Food Empire.* New York, NY: Doubleday.

Sanders, H. (2012). *The Autobiography of the Original Celebrity Chef.* PDF. Louisville, KY: KFC.

Smith, J. Y. (1980). *Col. Sanders, the Fried-Chicken Gentleman, Dies.* Obituary. 17 December 1980. Washington, DC: The Washington Post, washingtonpost.com

Whitworth, W. (1970). *Kentucky-Fried.* Article. 14 July 1970. New York, NY: The New Yorker, newyorker.com

Wong, V. (2015). *Everything You Don't Know About the Real Colonel Sanders.* Article. Buzz Feed News, buzzfeednews.com

YouTube. *Interview with Colonel H. Sanders.* youtube.com/watch?v=BUITCIC800c.

Chapter Ten - Rosa Parks

Academy of Achievement. *Rosa Parks.* Article. Washington, DC: achievement.org

Adkins, A. (2015). *Depth of Field Icons: Rosa Parks.* Article. St Thomas-Minneapolis, MN: University of St Thomas, stthomas.edu

Blackside inc. (1985). *With Rosa Parks. Eyes on the Prize: America's Civil Rights Years (1954-1965).* Interview. 14 November 1985. St. Louis, MS: Washington University Libraries, Film and Media Archive, Henry Hampton Collection.

Bill of Rights Institute. (2012). *Rosa Parks, The First Lady of Civil Rights.* Article. Arlington, VA: Bill of Rights Institute, billofrightsinstitute.org

Biography. (2018). *Rosa Parks.* Article. 27 February 2018. biography.com

Briggs, D. (1995). *Faith Guided Rosa Parks' Action.* Article. 20 January 1995. Chicago, IL: Chicago Tribune, chicagotribune.com

Cain, S. (2013). *Quiet: The Power of Introverts in a World That Can't Stop Talking.* London: Viking.

Dholakia, U. (2016). *When Adversity Strikes, Optimism Helps Us Get Through.* Article. 30 October 2016. Psychology Today, psychologytoday.com

Giltay, E. J., Geleijnse, J. M., Zitman F. G., Hoekstra T. & Schouten E. G. *Dispositional Optimism And All-cause And Cardiovascular Mortality*

In A Prospective Cohort Of Elderly Dutch Men And Women. Arch Gen Psychiatry. 2004 Nov;61(11):1126-35. doi: 10.1001/archpsyc.61.11.1126. PMID: 15520360.

Goodin, B. R. & Bulls, H. W. (2013). *Optimism and The Experience of Pain: Benefits of Seeing the Glass as Half Full. Current Pain and Headache Reports, 17(5), 329.* doi.org/10.1007/s11916-013-0329-8.

Goodman, A. (2013). *Rosa Parks at 100: A Great American Rebel for Racial Justice.* Article. 31 January 2013. London: The Guardian, the guardian.com

Harrington, Walt. (1995). *A Person Who Wanted to Be Free.* Article. 8 October 1995. The Washington Post, washingtonpost.com

Jennings, A. B. & Boggs, G. L. (2013). *Rosa Parks, Champion for Human Rights.* Article. 5 February 2013. yesmagazine.org

Kirkman, B., Stoverink A., Mistry, S. & Rosen, B. (2019). *The 4 Things Resilient Teams Do.* Article. 19 July 2019. Brighton, MA: Harvard Business Review, hbr.org

King, N. & Noenickx, C. (2019). *Rosa Parks: In Her Own Words Reveals the Real Person Behind the Icon.* Article. 5 December 2019. Washington, DC: npr.org

Libman, N. (1991). *Rosa Parks Puts Her Faith, Time in Young People.* Article. 8 September 1991. Chicago, IL: Chicago Tribune, chicagotribune.com

Mariscotti, E. (2013). *Corporate Risks and Leadership: What Every Executive Should Know About Risks.* Interview. 10 September 2013. routledge.com

Obama, B. (2013). *Remarks by President Obama at Dedication of Statue Honouring Rosa Parks.* 27 February 2013. Washington, DC: obamawhitehouse.archives.gov

Reed, G. (1995). *Quiet Strength: The Faith, the Hope, and the Heart of a Woman Who Changed a Nation.* Grand Rapids, MI: Zondervan Publishing House.

Remember-them.org/parks.htm

Reyburn, S. (2020). *Rosa Parks in Her Own Words.* Athens, GA: University of Georgia Press, ugapress.com

Rothman, L. (2016). *Listen to a Rare Recording of Rosa Parks Telling Her Story.* Article. 21 January 2016. New York, NY: Time Magazine, time.com

Schatz, K. & Klein S. M. (2015). *Rad American Women A-Z: Rebels, Trailblazers, and Visionaries Who Shaped Our History ... and Our Future.* San Francisco, CA: City Lights Publishers.

The Henry Ford Museum of American Innovation. *What if I don't move to the Back of the Bus?* Article. Dearborn, MI: thehenryford.org

Theoharis, J. (2015). *How History Got the Rosa Parks Story Wrong.* Article. 1 December 2015. Washington, DC: The Washington Post, washingtonpost.com

Theoharis, J. (2014). *The Rebellious Life of Mrs Rosa Parks.* Boston, MA: Beacon Press.

Theoharis, J. (2019). *Rosa Parks' Transformative Two Weeks at the Highlander Research and Education Centre.* Article. 9 April 2019. Beaconside Broadside.

Tynes, T. (2018). *Rosa Parks' Life After the Bus Was No Easy Ride.* Article. 18 April 2018. New York, NY: history.com

Twerski, A. J. (1999). *Visions of the Fathers: Pirkei Avos.* Brooklyn, NY: Shaar Press.

Tousignant, M. (2020). *For Rosa Parks, Standing Up To Injustice Started When She Was A Kid.* Article. 3 February 2020. Washington, DC: The Washington Post, washingtonpost.com

Chapter Eleven - Rabbi Menachem Mendel Schneerson

Allouche, P. (2019). *Six Myths the Rebbe Debunked.* Article. 7 July 2019. New York, NY: The Algemeiner, algemeiner.com

Chabad. *What is Shlichus?* Article. New York, NY: chabad.org

Clark, D. A. (2013). *Cognitive Restructuring in S. G. Hofmann, D. J. A. Dozois, W. Rief, W. & Smits, J. A. J. (Eds.).* The Wiley Handbook of Cognitive Behavioural Therapy. Hoboken, NY: Wiley-Blackwell.

Daft, R. (2015). *The Leadership Experience.* Stamford, CT: Cengage Learning.

Even-Israel Steinsaltz, A. (2014). The Rebbe's Leadership Style. Article. 11 August 2014. London: The Jewish Chronicle, thejc.com

Even-Israel Steinsaltz, A. (2014). My Rebbe. New York, NY: Maggid Books.

Fishkoff, S. (2013). *The Rebbe's Army: Inside the World of Chabad-Lubavitch.* New York, NY: Schocken Books.

Jacobson, S. (2002). *Toward a Meaningful Life the Wisdom of the Sages.* New York, NY: William Morrow.

Lightstone, M. (2017). *Mobilizing the Mitzvah Tanks: The Untold Story of the 'Are You Jewish?' Guys.* Article. New York, NY: chabad.org

Living Torah. (1991). Disc 126: *Programme 503, Breaking Free of the Past 4.* Article. August 1991. New York, NY: chabad.org

Lubavitch.com New York, NY.

Kalmenson, M. (2016). *Seeds of Wisdom.* Brooklyn, NY: Jewish Educational Media.

Kalmenson, M. (2019). *Positivity Bias.* New York, NY: Kehot Publication Society.

Kalmenson, M. (2019). *The Positive Thinking that Drove the Lubavitcher Rebbe's Mission.* Article. 26 July 2019. London: The Jewish Chronicle, thejc.com

Miller, C. (2014). *Turning Judaism Outward: A Biography of the Rebbe, Rabbi Menachem Mendel Schneerson.* New York, NY: Kol Menachem.

Sacks, Rabbi Lord. (2011). *Address to the Gala Banquet of the Conference of Chabad-Lubavitch Emissaries.* 20 November 2011. New York, NY: chabad.org

Schneerson, M. M. (1951). *Sicha 1.* 17 January 1951. chabad.org

Schneerson, M. M. (1972). *Is It Human To Retire? Historic Video Of A Farbrengen (Chasidic gathering) Marking The Rebbe's 70th Birthday.* 26 March 1972. New York, NY: chabad.org

Schneerson, M. M. (1976). *Letter to Mr M.S. Landow.* 27 January 1978.

The World's Real-Time Billionaires. Jersey City, NJ: forbes.com

United States Statutes At Large. Volume 92 Part 1. djvu/254

Zaklikowski, D. *Survival of a Heart Attack a 'Medical Miracle.* Article. New York, NY: chabad.org

Chapter Twelve - Eleanor Roosevelt

Beasley, M. (2010). *Eleanor Roosevelt: Transformative First Lady.* Lawrence, KS: University Press of Kansas.

Cook, B. W. (1999). *Eleanor Roosevelt, Vol. 2: 1933–1938.* New York, NY: Viking.

Freedman, R. (1993). *Eleanor Roosevelt: A Life of Discovery.* New York, NY: Clarion Books.

Gerber, R. (2002). *Leadership the Eleanor Roosevelt Way.* Upper Saddle River, NJ: Prentice Hall.

Grimm Jr, R., Spring, K. & Dietz, N. (2007). *Corporation for National and Community Service, Office of Research and Policy Development. The Health Benefits of Volunteering: A Review of Recent Research.* Washington, DC. nationalservice.gov

Lash, J. P. (1971). *Eleanor and Franklin.* New York, NY: W. W. Norton & Company.

Obituary. (1962). *Mrs Roosevelt, First Lady 12 Years, Often Called 'World's Most Admired Woman'.* Article. 8 November 1962. New York, NY: The New York Times, nytimes.com

Pegler, W. (1942). *Fair Enough: Mrs Roosevelt's Public Life.* Article. 12 February 1942. tc.pbs.org

Persico, J. E. (2008). *Franklin & Lucy: President Roosevelt, Mrs Rutherfurd and The Other Remarkable Women in His Life.* New York, NY: Random House.

Pir, S. (2019). *The Importance of Foresight: Why Intuition and Imagination Will Be Critical in The Future of Work.* Article. flipboard.com.

Roosevelt, E. (1962). *The Autobiography of Eleanor Roosevelt.* London: Hutchinson.

Roosevelt, E. (1941). americanradioworks.org/eleanor-roosevelt-on-isolationists/

Roosevelt, E. (1944). *How to Take Criticism.* Article. November 1944. Ladies Home Journal 61. 2.gwu.edu/~erpapers/documents/articles/howtotakecriticism.cfm

Rosqvist, J. (2005). *Exposure Treatments for Anxiety Disorders: A Practitioner's Guide to Concepts, Methods and Evidence-Based Practice.* New York, NY: Routledge.

The Book of Job 42:10 via Jewish Virtual Library. Chevy Chase, MD: jewishvirtuallibrary.org

Vilhauer, J. (2016). *4 Ways to Overcome Shyness.* Article. 31 December 2016. New York, NY: Psychology Today, psychologytoday.com

Chapter Thirteen - Helen Keller

American Foundation for the Blind. *Helen Keller: National History Day Resources.* Arlington County, VA: afb.org

American Psychological Association. (2012). *Building Your Resilience. Various contributors.* Article. 2012. Washington, DC: apa.org

Berne, E. C. (2009). *Helen Keller: Courage in Darkness.* New York, NY: Sterling.

Bodden, V. (2016). *Helen Keller. Essential Library Series.* Minneapolis, MN: Abdo Publishing.

Breaux, A. (2015). *101 Answers for New Teachers and Their Mentors: Effective Teaching Tips for Daily Classroom Use.* London: Routledge.

Covey, S. & Hatch, D. K. (2006). *Everyday Greatness: Inspiration for a Meaningful Life.* Nashville, TN: Rutledge Hill Press.

Dunn County News. (1916). *Article on Helen Keller.* 22 January 1916. Dunn County, WI: Dunn County News.

Gladstone, J. (2015). *The Common Thread of Overcoming Adversity and Living your Dreams.* New York, NY: Bantam Doubleday Dell Publishing Group Inc.

Gordon, J. (2015). *Helen Keller, Advocate and Traveller.* Article. 18 August 2015. Watertown, MA: perkins.org

Gorman, R. (2008). *Great Lives from History.* Pasadena, CA: Salem Press.

Herman, D. (1998). *Helen Keller: A Life.* New York, NY: nytimes.org

Huang, Al Chung-lian. & Lynch, J. (1994). *Thinking Body, Dancing Mind.* New York, NY: Bantam Books.

Keller H. (2009). *Optimism: An Essay (1903).* New York, NY: T.Y. Crowell and Company.

Keller, H. (1905). *The Story of My Life.* New York, NY: Doubleday and Page.

Keller, H. & Nielsen, K. E. (2005). *Helen Keller: Selected Writings.* New York, NY: New York University Press.

Kennon, C. (2014). *Helen Keller in Her Own Words.* New York, NY: Gareth Stevens Publishing.

Kleege, G. (2013). *Disability Studies Quarterly, Vol 29, No 3. Review of Nielsen, K. (2009) Beyond the Miracle Worker: The Remarkable Story of Anne Sullivan Macy and Her Extraordinary Friendship with Helen Keller.* Boston: Beacon Press.

Kuiper, K. (2010). *The 100 Most Influential Women of All Time.* New York, NY: Britannica Educational Publishing in Association with Rosen Educational Services.

Lash, J. (1980). *Helen and Teacher: The Story of Helen Keller and Anne Sullivan Macy.* New York, NY: Delacorte Press.

Lenson, E. S. (2018). *Overcoming Adversity: Conquering Life's Challenges.* Bowen Hills: Australian Academic Press.

Merrill, D. (2013). *The One-Legged Wrestler Who Conquered His Sport, Then Left It Behind.* Article. 18 March 2003. Chicago, IL: deadspin.com

Mihoces, G. (2011). *"Born with one leg, Arizona St. Wrestler Wins NCAA Title".* Article. 21 March 2011. foxnews.com

New York Times. *Helen Keller at Radcliffe.* Article. 14 August 1899. Conway, MA: disabilitymuseum.org

Nielsen, K. (2009). *Beyond the Miracle Worker: The Remarkable Story of Anne Sullivan Macy and Her Extraordinary Friendship with Helen Keller.* Boston, MS: Beacon Press.

Perkins School for the Blind. *Profiles of Anne Sullivan and Helen Keller.* Watertown, MA: perkins.org

Robles, A. (2013). *Unstoppable.* New York, NY: Gotham Books.

Shattuck, R. (2004). *Helen Keller. July-August 2004.* Cambridge, MS: Harvard Magazine, harvardmgazine.com

The Attic. (2018). *Helen Keller's Moment.* Article. 29 November 2018. theattic.space

Twerski, A. (1999). *Visions of the Fathers: Pirkei Avos.* Brooklyn, NY: Shaar Press.

Wagman-Geller, M. (2017). *Still I Rise: The Persistence of Phenomenal Women.* Miami, FL: Mango Publishing.

Wilkie, K. E. (1969). *Helen Keller: Handicapped Girl.* New York, NY: Atheneum.

Chapter Fourteen - Margaret Thatcher

Armistead, L. (2013). *How Thatcher Brought UK Back from the Wilderness.* Article. 13 April 2013. London: The Daily Telegraph, telegraph.co.uk

Association for Diplomatic Studies & Training. The Extra Special Relationship: Thatcher, Reagan, and the 1980s. Article. Arlington, VA: adst.org

Bannister J. (2014). *Thatcher.* New World City, Inc.

Barber, T. (2020). *The Human Factor: Gorbachev, Reagan and Thatcher, and the End of the Cold War.* Article. 20 March 2020. London: The Financial Times, ft.com

Bracken, S. (2017). *Guts: Find Your Greatness, Beat the Odds, Live from Passion.* Miami, FL: Mango

Cameron, D. (2013). *House of Commons Tribute to Baroness Thatcher.* Statement. 10 April 2013. London: publications.parliament.uk

Campbell, J. (2012). *The Iron Lady: Margaret Thatcher: From Grocer's Daughter to Iron Lady.* London: Vintage.

Cole, J. (1984). *BBC Interview with Mrs Thatcher.* 12 October 1984. London: margaretthatcher.org

Cole, J. (1984). *BBC Interview with Mrs Thatcher.* 17 December 1984. London: margaretthatcher.org

De Castella, T. (2013). *Thatcher: Can People Get By on Four Hours' Sleep?* Article. 10 April 2013. London: BBC News Magazine, bbc.com

ICI. (1948). *Personnel Department Assessment, Rejecting Job Application From The Then Margaret Roberts in 1948.* In Quotes: Margaret Thatcher. London: bbc.co.uk

Fischer, D. (2011). *Science Fiction Film Directors, 1895-1998.* Jefferson, NC: McFarland.

Fisher, M. (2013). *Thatcher: A Divisive Figure, Even in Death.* Article. 8 April 2013. Washington, DC: The Washington Post washingtonpost.com

Flatt, J. M. (2012). *Powerful Political Women: Stirring Biographies of Some of History's Most Powerful Women.* Bloomington, IN: IUniverse.

Friedman, U. (2015). *How an Ad Campaign Invented the Diamond Engagement Ring.* Article. 13 February 2015. Washington, DC: theatlantic.com

Goodlad, G. (2015). *Thatcher.* London: Routledge/Taylor & Francis Group, taylorfrancis.com

Haviland, J. (1984). *Thatcher speech to 1922 Committee, 'The enemy within'.* Article. 20 July 1984. margaretthatcher.org

Howe, G. (2013). *The Margaret Thatcher I knew.* Article. 8 April 2013. London: The Guardian, theguardian.com

Jenkins, S. (2013). *How Margaret Thatcher's Falklands Gamble Paid Off.* Article. 9 April 2013. London: The Guardian, theguardian.com

Leinwand Leger, D. (2013). *Thatcher, Reagan Relationship Altered History.* Article. 8 April 2013. usatoday.com

Lenson, E. S. (2018). *Overcoming Adversity: Conquering Life's Challenges.* Bowen Hills. Australian Academic Press.

Lobel, B. (2013). *Small Business Opinion on the Death of Margaret Thatcher.* Article. 8 April 2013. London: smallbusiness.co.uk

Malnick, E. (2014). *When Margaret Thatcher Met Steve Jobs.* Article. 3 October 2014. London: The Daily Telegraph, telegraph.co.uk

McDonald, W. (2016). *The New York Times Book of the Dead*. New York, NY: Black Dog & Leventhal.

Perkins, A. (2013). *Margaret Thatcher Obituary*. Article. 8 April 2013. London: The Guardian, theguardian.com

Powell, C. (2013). *The Margaret Thatcher I Knew*. Comments. 8 April 2013. London: The Guardian, theguardian.com

Portillo, M. (2013*). Britain Had to Change; Margaret Thatcher Had the Courage to Make it Happen*. Article. 14 April 2013. London: The Guardian, theguardian.com

Reagan, N. (2013). *Statement on the Death of Baroness Thatcher*. Statement. 8 April 2013. Simi Valley, CA: reaganfoundation.org

Shephard, G. (2013). *The Real Iron Lady*. London: Biteback Publishing.

Thatcher, M. (1970). *Interview for Finchley Press*. 26 June 1970. Margaret Thatcher Foundation. margaretthatcher.org

Thatcher, M. (1979). *Remarks on Becoming Prime Minister. Outside No 10 Downing Street*. 4 May 1979. Margaret Thatcher Foundation. margaretthatcher.org

Thatcher, M. (1980*). Speech to the Conservative Party Conference*. 10 October 1980. Brighton. Margaret Thatcher Foundation. margaretthatcher.org

Thatcher, M. (1982). *Interview*. 5 April 1982. ITN. margaretthatcher.org

Thatcher, M. (1984). *Aftermath of The Brighton Bomb. Speech. 12 October 1984. Conservative Party Conference*. Thatcher, M. (1997). Speech to the Heritage Foundation. December 1997. Washington, DC.

Tebbit, N. (2019). *Quoted in Thatcher: A Very British Revolution*. Documentary. London: BBC2. bbc.co.uk

UK Political Information. *General Election Results, 1983 Summary*. ukpolitical.info

Walsh, M. (2018). *My campaign: The Creation of the 'Labour isn't working' Poster of 1978*. Article. 26 October 1978. London: campaignlive.co.uk

Chapter Fifteen - Nelson Mandela

Bartuah, J. (2019). *Nelson Mandela: A Legacy of Integrity.* Article. 18 July 2019. Atlanta, GA: The Perspective, theperspective.org

Bromley, B. (2013). *The Humour of Nelson Mandela.* Article. 12 September 2013. New York, NY: huffpost.com

Bundy, C. (2015). Nelson Mandela. Stroud: The History Press.

Carlin, J. (2009). *Invictus: Nelson Mandela and the Game that Made a Nation.* New York, NY: Penguin Books.

Graham, J. *The Importance of Vision.* Article. Langley, WA: johngraham.org

Gurnede, W. (2013). *Nelson Mandela Sets Standards Which His Successors Have Not Been Able To Live Up To.* Article. independent.co.uk/voices/comment/nelson-mandela-set-standards-which-his-successors-have-not-been-able-live-8987164.html

Keller, B. (2013). *Nelson Mandela, South Africa's Liberator as Prisoner and President, Dies at 95.* Article. 6 December 2013. New York, NY: The New York Times, nytimes.com

Kraft, T. & Pressman, S. (2012). *Grin and Bear It: The Influence of Manipulated Facial Expression on the Stress Response.* Psychological Science. 23. 10.1177/0956797612445312. Newbury Park, CA: Sage Publications, journals@sagepub.com

Kuiper, N. A. (2012). *Humour and Resiliency: Towards a Process Model of Coping and Growth.* Europe's Journal of Psychology, 8(3), 475-491. doi.org/10.5964/ejop.v8i3.464. Geneva: ejop.psychopen.eu

Lodge, T. (2006). *Mandela: A Critical Life.* Oxford: Oxford University Press.

Mandela, N. (1961). *'The Struggle is My Life'.* Press Statement. 26 June 1961. London: ANC, un.org.

Mandela, N. (1964). *Statement During Rivonia Trial.* 20 April 1964. Article. 23 April 2007. London: The Guardian, theguardian.com

Mandela, N. (1985). *Zindi Mandela's Rejection of President P.W. Botha's offer of Conditional Release.* Statement. 10 February 1985. Johannesburg: Nelson Mandela's Foundation, nelsonmandela.org

Mandela, N. (1994). *Speech Upon Inauguration as President of South Africa.* 10 May 1994. Philadelphia, PA: University of Pennsylvania – African Studies Centre, africa.upen.edu

Mandela, N. (1995). *Long Walk to Freedom: The Autobiography of Nelson Mandela.* London: Abacus.

Mandela, N. (2003). *British Red Cross Humanity Lecture.* 10 July 2003. London, museumarchives.redcross.org.uk

Marano, H. E. (2005). *Laughter: The Best Medicine.* Article. 5 April 2005. New York, NY: Psychology Today, psychologytoday.com

Marshall, L. (2013). *Nelson Mandela and the Power of Forgiveness.* Article. 6 December 2013. Washington, DC: National Geographic, blog.nationalgeographic.org

Nicol, M. (2006). *Mandela: The Authorised Portrait.* London: Bloomsbury Publishing.

Paramaguru, K. (2013). *5 Great Stories About Nelson Mandela's Humility, Kindness and Courage.* Article. 6 December 2013. New York, NY: Time Magazine, world.time.com

Parks, M. (1985). *Mandela Rejects South African Terms for Prison Release.* Article. 11 February 1985. Los Angeles, CA: Los Angeles Times, latimes.com

Sharma, R. *Robin Sharma Mastery Sessions.* robinsharma.com

Simmons, S. (2016). *Middot Series #6 Patience, or How to Overcome Road Rage.* Article. 14 August 2016. Jerusalem: aish.com

Smith, D. (2013). *Francois Pienaar: When the Whistle Blew, South Africa Changed for Ever.* Article. 8 December 2013. London: The Guardian, theguardian.com

Stengel, R. (2010). *Mandela's Way.* New York, NY: Crown Publishers.

Van Remortel, S. (2013). *Stop the Vanilla Ice Cream.* Kennett Square, PA: Soundview Executive Book Summaries, hr.com

Chapter Sixteen - Winston Churchill

America's National Churchill Museum. Fulton, MO: nationaalchurchillmusum.org

Anthony, S. (2016). *Kodak's Downfall Wasn't About Technology*. Article. 15 July 2016. Brighton, MA: Harvard Business Review, hbr.org

Attenborough, W. (2019). *Diagnosing Churchill: Bipolar or 'Prey to Nerves'*. McFarland.

Bender, B. (2019). *Handbook of Political Leadership*. Waltham Abbey, Essex: Ed-Tech Press, ed.techpress.com

Churchill, W. (2013). *Painting as a Pastime*. London: Unicorn Press.

Cimino, A. (2018). *Roosevelt and Churchill: A Friendship That Saved the World*. Secaucus, NJ: Chartwell Books.

Edwards, A. (2011). *The Other Lives of Sir Winston Churchill*. Article. 14 March 2011. London: The Daily Express, express.co.uk

Enoch, N. (2012). *A Hero's Return: Never-Before-Seen Photo of Winston Churchill on Horseback after Daring Boer War Prison Camp Escape in 1899*. Article. 2 February 2012. London: The Daily Mail, dailymail.co.uk

Feix, C. (2019). *Churchill's Character: A Rigid Daily Schedule*. Article. 6 February 2019. The Churchill Project: Hillsdale College, winstinchurchill.hillsdale.edu

Gilbert, M. (1971). *Winston S. Churchill: The Challenge of War, 1914–1916*. Boston, MA: Houghton Mifflin Company.

Green, A. (2011). *Beyond Wealth: The Road Map to a Rich Life*. Hoboken, NJ: John Wiley & Sons.

Grosvenor, E. (2018). *The Best of American Heritage: Churchill*. Boston, MA: New Word City.

Haugen, B. (2006). *Winston Churchill: British Soldier, Writer, Statesman*. Minneapolis, MN: Compass Point Books.

Heyman, J. (2019). *The Black Dog Myth*. churchillcentral.com/the-black-dog-myth-how-a-misunderstood-quote-perpetuated-the-myth-of-churchills-mental-state/

International Churchill Society. winstonchurchill.org

Johnson, B. (2015). *The Churchill Factor: How One Man Made History*. London: Hodder Paperbacks.

Crosby Kemper, R. (1995). *Winston Churchill: Resolution, Defiance, Magnanimity, Goodwill.* Columbia, MS: University of Missouri Press.

Kaczor, C. (2019). *Lessons from Churchill's Walk with Destiny.* Article. 16 March 2019. Los Angeles, CA: angelusnews.com

Knapton, S. (2014). *How Churchill Gave Us Tanks, Radar, DNA … and a Velvet Green Air-raid Suit.* Article. 29 November 2014. London: The Daily Telegraph, telegraph.co.uk

Lacouture, J. (1990). *De Gaulle: The Rebel, 1890–1944.* London: Collins Harvill.

Langworth, R. (2012). *Churchill in His Own Words.* London: Ebury Press.

Langworth, R. (2013). *Churchill by Himself: The Definitive Collection of Quotations.* Newburyport, MA: Rosetta Books.

Mack, L. (2017). *Winning Habitudes: 99 Habits and Attitudes of Leaders, Visionaries and Achievers.* Independently Published.

McCain, J. (2008). *Extraordinary Foresight Made Winston Churchill Great.* Article. 20 March 2008. London: The Daily Telegraph, telegraph.co.uk

Perry, J. (2010). *Winston Churchill.* Nashville, TN: Thomas Nelson Publishers.

Rothstein, E. (2005). *Contemplating Churchill.* Article. March 2005. Washington, DC: Smithsonian Magazine, smithsonianmag.com

Severance, J. B. (1996). *Winston Churchill: Solider, Statesman, Artist.* New York, NY: Clarion Books.

Soames, M. (1999). *Winston and Clementine: The Personal Letters of the Churchills.* Boston, MA: Houghton Mifflin.

Schwartz, A. B. (2017). *Medical Mystery: Winston Churchill's Most Secret Battle.* Article. 24 November 2017. Philadelphia, PA: The Philadelphia Inquirer, inquirer.com

Spall, B. & Xander, M. (2018). *My Morning Routine: How Successful People Start Every Day.* London: Penguin.

Stansky, P. (1973). *Churchill.* London: Macmillan.

The Lancet Psychiatry Volume 5, Issue 9, P739-746, 1 September 2018 *Association between physical exercise and mental health in 1·2 million individuals in the USA between 2011 and 2015: A cross-sectional study.*

Van der Book, S. (2009). *Winston Churchill: British Prime Minister & Statesman.* Edina, MN: ABDO Publishing Company.

Van der Vat, D. (2009). *The Dardanelles Disaster.* Woodstock, NY: Overlook Press.

Warren, J. (2014). *Painting: The Hobby that Saved Winston Churchill's Sanity.* Article. 19 December 2014. London: The Daily Express, express.co.uk

Whelan, C.B. (2016). *The Big Picture: A Guide to Finding Your Purpose in Life.* West Conshohocken, PA: Templeton Press.

Chapter Seventeen - Walt Disney

Albert, J. (2015). *They Laughed at Galileo: How the Great Inventors Proved Their Critics Wrong.* New York, NY: Skyhorse.

Austin, D. (2019). *The Hungarian Immigrant Who Funded Walt Disney.* Article. 21 December 2019. New York, NY: Newsweek, newsweek.com

Barrier, J. M. (1999). *Hollywood Cartoons: American Animation in Its Golden Age.* Oxford: Oxford University Press.

Basadur, M. & Goldsby, M. (2016). *Design-Centred Entrepreneurship.* Oxford: Routledge.

BBC. (2011). *Would Walt Have Done That?* bbc.co.uk/news/business-4560192

Biography. (2017). Walt Disney Biography. biography.com

Bodden, V. (2017). *The Story of Disney.* Mumbai: Jaico Publishing House.

Designing Disney. *The Construction of Disneyland.* Article. designingdisney.com

Disney, Roy. E. (1995). *Setting the Record Straight on Roy O. Disney's Role.* Letter. 28 May 1995. Los Angeles, CA: Los Angeles Times, latimes.com

Ellerton, R. (2012). *Win-Win Influence: How to Enhance Your Personal and Business Relationships.* Ottowa, ON: Renewal Technologies, Incorporated.

Entrepreneur. *Walter Elias Disney.* Article. Irvine, CA: entrepreneur.com

Ewen, D. (1977). *All the Years of American Popular Music.* Englewood Cliffs, NJ: Prentice Hall.

Gabler, N. (2006). *Walt Disney: Triumph of American Imagination.* New York, NY: Alfred A. Knoph.

Gabler, N. (2008). *Walt Disney: The Biography.* New York, NY: Aurum: Aldred A. Knopf.

Greffe, X. (2017). *The Artist-Enterprise in the Digital Age.* Tokyo: Springer Japan.

Horwitz, S. & Knych, J. (2011). *The Importance of Failure.* Article. 26 October 2011. Atlanta, GA: Foundation for Economic Education, fee.org

Know, Doctor (2018). *People That Made America A Great Nation.* eBook.

Korkis, J. (2017). *The Laugh-O-Gram Story: Part One.* Article. 22 March 2017. mouseplanet.com

Krasniewicz, L. (2010). *Walt Disney: A Biography.* Westport, CT: Greenwood.

Lambie, R. (2019). *Disney's Snow White: The Risk That Changed Filmmaking Forever.* Article. 8 February 2019. New York, NY: denofgeek.com

Mannheim, S. (2011). *Walt Disney and the Quest for Community.* St. Petersburg, FL: Booklocker Inc.

MacDonald, B. (2015). *Disneyland Got Off to a Nightmare Start in 1955, but 'Walt's Folly' Quickly Won Over Fans.* Article. 10 July 2015. Los Angeles, CA: Los Angeles Times, latimes.com

Mosley, L. (1990). *Disney's World: A Biography.* Chelsea, MI: Scarborough House.

Nesbit, D. (2020). *Clough and Taylor: What Went Wrong?* Article. 11 May 2020. footballpink.net

Pah, J. (2015). *blog.cetrain.isu.edu/blog/5-leadership-qualities-we-learned-from-walt-disney*

Reed, L.W. (2016*). Failure Made Disney Great Real Heroes: Walt Disney.* Article. 15 April 2016. Atlanta, GA: Foundation for Economic Education, fee.org

Robb, B. J. (2015). *A Brief History of Walt Disney.* London: Little Brown Book Group.

Rockefeller's 6 Personal Traits for Success. Bearded Colonel. beardedcolonel.co.uk

Ryan, J. (2018). *A Mouse Divided: How Ub Iwerks Became Forgotten, and Walt Disney Became Uncle Walt.* Brentwood, TN: Post Hill Press.

Shaffer, J. (2010). *Discovering the Magic Kingdom: An Unofficial Disneyland Vacation Guide.* Birmington, IN: Authorhouse.

Thomas, B. (1974). *Walt Disney: An American Original.* Mankato, MN: Creative Education.

Thomas, B. & Vosburgh, L. (1966). *Walt Disney: Magician of the Movies.* New York, NY: Grosset & Dunlap.

Thomas, F. & Johnston, O. (1995). [1981]. *The Illusion of Life: Disney Animation.* New York, NY: Hyperion.

West, M. I. (2018). *Shapers of American Childhood: Essays on Visionaries from L. Frank Baum to Dr Spock to J.K. Rowling.* Jefferson, NC: McFarland.

Williams, P. & Denney, J. (2005). *How to Be Like Walt.* Boca Raton, FL: Health Communications Inc. academia.edu

Williams, P. (2019*). Learning Leadership from Walt Disney, Master of Soft Skills.* Article. 3 September 2019. trainingindustry.com

Chapter Eighteen - Audrey Hepburn

Aten, J. (2019). *Resilience and Humility: An Interview with Dr Joshua Hook on How Humility Helps in Life's Hardships.* Article. 10 January 2019. New York, NY: Psychology Today, pysychologytoday.com

Bright Side. *Remembering the Incredible Woman that was Audrey Hepburn.* Article. brightside.me

Brown, A. (2013). *Overcome Adversity Your Dreams Matter*. London: Breakthrough Publishing.

Cox, A. (2011). *Audrey Hepburn: An Iconic Problem*. Article. 20 January 2011. London: The Guardian, theguardian.com

Fernandez, A. (2019). *Audrey Hepburn's Secret Shame*. Article. 3 April 2019. people.com

Gross, E. (2019). *From World War II to Hollywood and Beyond, Audrey Hepburn's Life and Career Revealed*. Article. 5 May 2019. Closer Weekly, closerweekly.com

Hellstern, M. (2002). *How to Be Lovely: The Audrey Hepburn Way of Life*. Hoddesdon: Portico.

Howe, C. (2015). *How Audrey Hepburn weighed only 88 pounds, suffered from jaundice and anaemia, survived on boiled grass and tulip bulbs and had her dream of becoming a ballerina crushed by the Nazi occupation of the Netherlands*. Article. 22 June 2015. London: thedailymail.com

Fairbanks, B. W. *The Late Show: Writings on Film*.

Gitlin, M. (2009). *Audrey Hepburn: A Biography*. Westport, CT: Greenwood.

Gogler, M. (2020). *Conversation with Sean Hepburn Ferrer*. Article. 29 March 2020. viewofhearts.com

Harris, S. (1993). *Audrey Hepburn Obituary*. Article. 21 January 1993. Los Angeles, CA: Los Angeles Times, latimes.com

Heatley, M. (2017). *Audrey Hepburn: In Words and Pictures*. Secaucus, NJ: Chartwell Books.

Hepburn Ferrer, S. (2003). *Audrey Hepburn: An Elegant Spirit*. London: Sidgwick & Jackson Ltd.

Jackson, D. & Boehm, V. *Audrey Hepburn - Biography*. imdb.com

King, S. (2013). *Audrey Hepburn's 1953 Roman Holiday: An Enchanting Fairy Tale*. Article. 12 December 2013. Los Angeles, CA: Los Angeles Times, latimes.com

Matzen, R. (2019). *Audrey Hepburn and World War II*. London: Mirror Books.

Matzen, R. (2019). *Those Are Things You Don't Forget. How a Young Audrey Hepburn Helped the Dutch Resistance During World War II.* Article. 3 May 2019. New York, NY: Time Magazine, time.com

Madssen, A. (1973). *William Wyler: The Authorized Biography.* London: W.H. Allen.

Miller, J. (2016). *Audrey Hepburn Reveals Heartbreak and Discusses Secret Wedding in Never-Before-Seen Letters.* Article. 14 June 2016. New York, NY: Vanity Fair, vanityfair.com

Morrow, E. *Born This Day: A Daily Celebration of Famous Beginnings.* Citadel Press.

Paris, B. (2014). *Audrey Hepburn.* New York, NY: Berkley Books.

Payne, C. (2018). *Beyonce & JAY-Z Dedicate Brooklyn Park Bench to Rapper's 93-Year-Old Grandmother.* Article. 27 December 2018. New York, NY: billboard.com

Razzetti, G. (2018). *Resilience: How to Rescue Yourself from Adversity.* Article. 29 July 2018. medium.com

Riding, A. (1991). *25 Years Later, Honour for Audrey Hepburn.* Article. 22 April. New York, NY: The New York Times, nytimes.com

Sheridan, J. (2010). *Fashion, Media, Promotion: The New Black Magic.* Hoboken, NJ: Wiley, wiley.com

Tenorio, R. (2019). *How Hollywood idol Audrey Hepburn Helped save Dutch Jews during the Holocaust.* Article. 12 June 2019. Jerusalem, Israel: The Times of Israel, timesofisrael.com

Unicef Profile of Audrey Hepburn. unicef.org

Ward, M. (2016). *5 Things You Didn't Know About Audrey Hepburn.* Article. 1 October 2016. New York, NY: Vogue Magazine, vogue.com

Weatherhogg, N. (2016). *Living with Depression.* Milton Keynes: AuthorHouseUK.

Werner, E. (2005). *Focal Point Research, Policy and Practice in Children's Mental Health Summer 2004, Vol 19, No 1, pages 11-14.* Portland State University. pathwaysrtc.pdx.edu

Wigley, S. (2017). *The Letter That Made Audrey Hepburn A Star.* Article. 9 February 2017. London: bfi.com.

Zinneman, F. (1992). *A Life in the Movies: An Autobiography*. London: Macmillan Books.

Chapter Nineteen - Bruce Lee

Bruce Lee (2002). *The Immortal Dragon*. Documentary. 29 January 2002. New York, NY: A&E Television Networks.

Burrows, A. (2002). *Bruce Lee*. Article. 21 October 2002. historylink.org

Day, M. & Gu, J. (2019). *The Enormous Numbers Behind Amazon's Market Reach*. Article. 27 March 2019. New York, NY: bloomberg.com

Editors. (2009). *Actor and Martial-arts Expert Bruce Lee Dies at Age 32*. A&E Television Networks. history.com

Editors of Black Belt Magazine. (1993). *Black Belt: Bruce Lee Collector's Edition, Vol.1 No.1*. Summer 1993. Oklahoma City, OK: Rainbow Publishing.

Harms, W. (2011). *Writing About Worries Eases Anxiety and Improves Test Performance*. Article. 13 January 2011. Chicago, IL: UChicago News, news.uchicago.edu

Hill, J. (2020). *A 'CURA' for COVID-19*. Article. 25 March 2020. world-architects.com

Kayvan K. (2020). *How Bruce Lee Can Help Young Leaders Adapt and Overcome Obstacles*. Article. 7 May 2020. Jersey City, NJ: forbes.com

Kelly, T. (2013). *So You Want To Be A Spaceman? 12 Days On The Seabed, A Week In A Cave, Lessons In Russian (And The Didgeridoo) ... The Gruelling Training Of Britain's New Astronaut*. Article. 20 May 2013. London: The Daily Mail, dailymail.co.uk

Kennedy, J.F.K. (1963). *Address in the Assembly Hall at the Paulskirche, Frankfurt*. 25 June 1963. Boston, MA: JFK Library.

Kramer, P. (2017). *A More Elite Man*. Bloomington, IN: WestBow Press.

Lee, B. *Be As Water, My Friend*. youtube.com

Lee, B. (2016). *Bruce Lee Letters of the Dragon, Edited by John Little*. Clarendon, VT: Tuttle Publishing, tuttlepublishing.com

Lee, B. (2017). *Bruce Lee: Words of the Dragon. Edited by John Little.* Clarendon, VT: Tuttle Publishing, tuttlepublishing.com

Lee, B. (2018). Valencia, CA: Black Belt Books.

Lee, L. (2003). *The Bruce Lee Story.* Santa Clarita, CA: Ohara Publications.

Little, J. (1996). *The Warrior Within. The Philosophies of Bruce Lee for Better Understanding the World Around You & Achieving a Rewarding Life.* New York, NY: McGraw-Hill.

Macdonald, S. (2019). *Think Like a Dog: How Dogs Teach us to be Happy in Life and Successful at Work.* Bloomington, IN: Indiana University Press.

Mosley, T. Hagan, A. (2020). *Be Water Explores Life and Legacy of Martial Arts Star Bruce Lee.* Article. 4 June 2020. wbur.org

Newspapers.com/clip/38977251/colour-him-green

Ostlere, L. (2018). *A Walking Miracle: How Tiger Woods Came Back To Be In Master's Contention Happy, Healthy And With A New Swing.* Article. 5 April 2018. London: The Independent. Independent.co.uk

Putranto, L. (2015). *The Inspirational Life of Bruce Lee.* Article. 3 April 2015. bookmartialarts.com

Rafiq, F. (2020). *Bruce Lee: The Life Of A Legend.* Edinburgh: Arena Sport.

Robertson, R. B. (2007). *The Dictionary for Life: A Practical Guide to Improving the Essence of Life.* Bloomington, IN: iUniverse.

Rufino dos Santos, N. *Calmness is the Greatest Expression of Psychological Security and Self-Control.* medium.com

Thomas, B. (1994). *Bruce Lee, Fighting Spirit.* Berkeley, CA: Frog, Ltd.

Various Articles and Podcasts.Brucelee.com

Zahid, A. (2017). *Secrets of Becoming World Class. Live Your Dream Life.* Guaranteed. Independently Published.

Chapter Twenty - Ella Fitzgerald

BBC. *6 Modern Artists we Wouldn't Have without Ella Fitzgerald.* London: bbc.co.uk

Clause, G. (2018) *Remembering Riverdale Roots of 'Queen of Jazz'.* Article. 2 September 2018. New York, NY: The Riverdale Press, riverdalepress.com

CNN. (1996). *Ella Fitzgerald Dies, June 15, 1996.* New York, NY: cnn.com

EllaFitzgerald.com

Grammy.com

Grammymuseum.org

Havers, R. (2020). *Norman Granz: The Man Who Helps Create the Music Biz.* Article. 6 August 2020. udiscovermusic.com

Henry, A. & Fishbein, R. (2019). *The Science of Breaking out of Your Comfort Zone (and Why You Should).* Article. 26 September 2019. lifehacker.com

Hershorn, T. (2011). *Norman Granz: The Man Who Used Jazz for Justice.* Berkeley, CA: University of California Press.

Hershorn, T. (2019). *Ella Fitzgerald & Norman Granz: She was His Star.* Article. 26 April 2019. Braintree, MA: Jazz Times.

Holden, S. (1996). *Ella Fitzgerald, the Voice of Jazz, Dies at 79.* Article. 19 June 1996. New York, NY: The New York Times, nytimes.com

HoustonSymphony.org

Hollins, P. (2019). *The Science of Breaking Out of Your Comfort Zone.* San Francisco, CA: PKCS Media, Inc.

Irishtimes.com/blogs/ontherecord/2015/10/27/the-adele-effect/

Kaufman, S. B. (2011). *Why Inspiration Matters.* Article. 8 November 2011. Brighton, MA: Harvard Business Review. hbr.org

Kettler, S. (2019). *Ella Fitzgerald and Marilyn Monroe: Inside Their Surprising Friendship.* Article. 24 June 2019. biography.com

Lady Gaga Singing Along w/ Ella Fitzgerald – My Romance by Rodgers & Hart. theglobalherald.com

Mark, G. (2018). *Ella: A Biography of the Legendary Ella Fitzgerald.* New York, NY: Ultimate Symbol Inc.

Nytimes.com/1996/06/19/opinion/journal-how-high-the-moon.html

Nicholson, S. (2004). *Ella Fitzgerald: A Biography of the First Lady of Jazz (Updated ed.).* London: Routledge.

Piper, A. (2018). *Norman Granz: Revolutionizing Jazz for Social Justice.* Article. 2 April 2018. National Museum of American History. americanhistory.si.edu

Robbins, T. *How to Surround Yourself with Good People.* San Diego, CA: tonyrobbins.com

Roman, J. (2015). *Chronicles of Old Los Angeles: Exploring the Devilish History of the City of Angels.* New York, NY: Museyon Guides.

Stamberg, S. (2010). *Ella Fitzgerald: America's First Lady of Song.* Article. 29 March 2010. Washington, DC: npr.org

Stamberg, S. (2017). *Early Hardship Couldn't Muffle Ella Fitzgerald's Joy.* Article. 25 April 2017. Washington, DC: npr.org

Thompkins, G. (2019). *The World of Ella Fitzgerald: A Turning the Tables Playlist.* Article. 3 September 2019. Washington, DC: npr.org

Voce, S. (1996). *Obituary: Ella Fitzgerald.* Article. 17 June 1996. London: The Independent. independent.co.uk

Washingtonpost.com/archive/lifestyle/1983/06/04/ella-the-lady-be-good/c1236c19-ae85-42c3-af6e-bdf88ebad243/

Chapter Twenty-One - Amelia Earhart

Backus, J. L. (1982). *Letters from Amelia, 1901–1937.* Boston, MA: Beacon Press.

Branson, R. (2016). *My Top 10 Quotes On Pushing Boundaries.* Article. 15 February 2016. London: virgin.com

Connor, R. (2013). *Amelia Earhart and the Profession of Air Navigation.* Article. 12 February 2013. Washington, DC: Smithsonian National Air and Space Museum, airndspace.ie.edu

Curnock, D. (2015). *History's Greatest Pilots Close Up (War Chronicles)*. New York, NY: Rosen Publishing. issuu.com

Crouch, T. D. (2007). *Searching for Amelia Earhart. Invention & Technology*. Article. Summer 2007. Rockville, MD: americanheritage.com

Editorial. (2012). *Opinion Malala Yousafzai's Courage*. Article. 10 October 2012. New York, NY: The New York Times, nytimes.com

Edwins, L. (2012). *Amelia Earhart: Pilot and Feminist*. Article 24 July 2012. csmonitor.com

Forney Museum of Transport, forneymuseum.org

Garrett Jones, V. (2009). *Amelia Earhart: A Life in Flight*. New York, NY: Sterling.

Haugen, B. (2006). *Amelia Earhart: Legendary Aviator*. Minneapolis, MN: Compass Point Books.

Karbo, K. (2019). *Excerpt: How Amelia Earhart Navigated The Skies And Society*. Article. 28 January 2019. Washington, DC: National Geographic. nationalgeographic.com

Lovell, M. (2009). *The Sound of Wings: The Life of Amelia Earhart*. London: St. Martin's Griffin.

Pal, M. (2012). *Amelia Earhart Exhibit Honours History, Legacy*. Article.26 June 2012. Washington, DC: wtopnews.com

Pearce, C. A. (1988). *Amelia Earhart*. New York, NY: Facts on File.

Purdue University. (2008). *Amelia Earhart Biographical Sketch. George Palmer Putnam Collection of Amelia Earhart Papers*. Article. 1 April 2008. collections.lib.purdue.edu

Rousell, M. (2017). *Amelia Earhart and Neta Snook: Pioneering Aviators*. Article. Cheltenham: thehistorypress.co.uk

Schifrin, N. (2013). *How Malala Yousafzai's Courage Inspired a Nation: 'We are No Longer Afraid'*. Article. 7 October 2013. New York, NY: ABCNEWS 7

Sherman, S. (2012). *Amelia Earhart Aviatrix Lost Over the Pacific*. Article. 26 September 2012. acepilots.com

Taylor, S. (2013). *Self-Sufficiency: An Essential Aspect of Well-Being.* Article. 25 March 2013. New York, NY: Psychology Today, psychologytoday.com

Trussell, D. (2012). *Amelia Earhart: What Happened.* Article. 20 July 2012. Washington, DC: The Washington Post, washingtonpost.com

Waxman, O. B. (2019). *Amelia Earhart Was Declared Dead 80 Years Ago. Here's What to Know About What Actually Happened to Her.* Article. 4 January 2019. New York, NY: Time Magazine, time.com

Chapter Twenty-Two - Muhammad Ali

Assael, S. (2016). *Reliving the Rivalry Between the Late Muhammad Ali and Sonny Liston.* Article. 4 June 2016. Bristol, CT: espn.co.uk

Brown, D. (2018). *Shoot Them for What? How Muhammad Ali won his Greatest Fight.* Article. 16 June 2018. Washington, DC: The Washington Post, washingtonpost.com

Calamur, K. (2016). *Muhammad Ali and Vietnam.* Article. 4 June 2016. Washington, DC: theatlantic.com

Callahan, M. (2015). *How Muhammad Ali Secured the Release of 15 US Hostages in Iraq.* Article. 29 November 2015. New York, NY: New York Post, nypost.com

Cooper, C. (2016). *Muhammad Ali Dead: Boxing Legend was a Great Warrior in the Battle against Parkinson's Disease.* Article. 4 June 2016. London: The Independent, independent.co.uk

Davis, V. (2016). *Ali Beyond the Ropes: Muhammad Ali's Philanthropy Efforts Accompany his Golden Gloves.* Article. 9 June 2016. Indianapolis, IN: Indianapolis Record.

Davies, D. (2017). *New Muhammad Ali Biography Reveals A Flawed Rebel Who Loved Attention.* Article. 4 October 2017. Washington, DC: npr.org

Detroit Free Press. 8 March 1971. newspapers.com

Dodd, J. (2017). *Boxing Great Muhammad Ali's 'Sad Decline' from Brain Damage Explored in New Biography.* Article. 13 October 2017. Des Moines, IA: people.com

Doeden, M. (2017). *Muhammad Ali: The Greatest.* Minneapolis, MN: Lerner Publishing.

Editorial. (2016). *Our View: Why do we Love Muhammad Ali? Because we Hated Him First.* Article. 6 June 2016. Phoenix, AZ: The Republic Arizona Central. eu.azcentral.com

Espncricinfo.com

Eig, J. (2017). *Ali: A life.* New York, NY: Houghton Mifflin Harcourt.

Hobbs, A. (2016). *Muhammad Ali and His Audience.* Article. 10 June 2016. New York, NY: The New Yorker, newyorker.com

Izenberg, J. (2020). *Once They Were Giants: The Golden Age of Heavyweight Boxing.* New York, NY: W. Norton.

Jones, G. (2010). *Developing Mental Toughness.* New Delhi: Viva Books.

Myers, W. D. (2018). *The Greatest: Muhammad Ali.* New York, NY: Scholastic USA.

Kang, J. C. (2013). *The End and Don King: The Crumbling of an American icon.* grantland.com/story/_/id/9123674/don-king-faces-end-career

Keating, F. (2016). *Muhammad Ali Obituary.* Article. 4 June 2016. London: The Guardian, theguardian.com

Morella, C. (2020). *Near-Death Experience in 'Thrilla' Changed Ali, Frazier Forever.* Article. 6 November 2020. Manila: The Manila Standard.

Peter, J. (2014). *Revisiting The Rumble in the Jungle 40 Years Later.* Article. 30 October 2014. McLean, VA: eu.usatoday.com

Rodriguez, F. M. (2009). *Dad, Me, and Muhammad Ali: A Father-And-Son Story.* New York, NY: iUniverse

Rosenbaum, D. E. (1971). *Ali Wins to Draft Case Appeal.* Article. New York, NY: The New York Times, nytimes.com

Savory, T. (2017). *Muhammad Ali: The Greatest.* West Berlin, NJ: Townsend Press, townsendpress.com

Seward, J. (2020). *As Mike Tyson, 53, Eyes a Return to the Boxing Ring, a Word of Warning.* Article. 20 May 2020. London: The Guardian, the guardian.com

Velin, B. (2016). *Fight by Fight: Muhammad Ali's Legendary Career.* Article. 4 June 2016. McLean, VA: USA Today, usatoday.com

Westheider, J. (2007). *The African American Experience in Vietnam: Brothers in Arms.* Lanham, MD: Rowman & Littlefield.

Wolfson, A. (2019). *Muhammad Ali Lost Everything in Opposing the Vietnam War. But in 1968, He Triumphed.* Mclean, VA: eu.usatoday.com

Chapter Twenty-Three - Wilma Rudolph

Anderson, J. J. (2011). *Wilma Rudolph: Track & Field Inspiration.* Abdo Publishing Edina, Minn.: ABDO Publishing Company.

Bagchi, R. (2012). *50 Stunning Olympic Moments No. 35: Wilma Rudolph's Triple Gold In 1960.* Article. 1 June 2012. London: The Guardian, the guardian.com

Biracree, T. (1988). *Wilma Rudolph: Champion Athlete (American Women of Achievement Series).* New York, NY: Chelsea House Publishing.

Geggel, L. (2016). *Closeness to Family, Not Friends, Helps You Live Longer.* Article. 25 August 2016. livescience.com

Gora, S. (2012). *Michael J. Fox Brings Hope to People with Parkinson's.* Article. December 2011 / January 2012. brainandlife.org

Flanagan, A. K. (1999). *Wilma Rudolph.* Chicago: Ferguson Publishing Company.

Haney, J. E. (1992). *Notable Black American Women.* Detroit, MI: Gale Research.

Hecht, A. (2009). *Polio.* New York, NY: Infobase Publishing.

Hine, D. C. Barkley Brown, E. & Terborg-Penn, R., eds. (1993). *Black Women in America: A Historical Encyclopaedia II.* Bloomington, IN: IU Press.

Honouring a Legendary Coach: Ed Temple. Article. Nashville, TN: The Community Foundation of Middle Tennessee. cmft.org

Johnson, A. J. (1996). *Great Women in Sports*. Detroit, MI: Visible Ink Press.

Keenan, R. (1989). *Wilma Rudolph Marney Rich. Keenan*. Article. 8 January 1989. Chicago: IL: Chicago Tribune, chicagotribune.com

Liberti, R. & Smith, M. (2015). *(Re) Presenting Wilma Rudolph*. Syracuse, NY: Syracuse University Press, press.syr.edu

McMillen, M. *Denzel Washington's Greatest Role: Mentor*. Article. webmd.com

Reid, H. & Austin, M. (2012). *The Olympics and Philosophy (The Philosophy of Popular Culture)*. Lexington, KY: University Press of Kentucky.

Roberts M. B. *Rudolph Ran and the World Went Wild Special*. Bristol, CT: espn.com

Ruth, A. (2000). *Wilma Rudolph by Amy Ruth*. Minneapolis, MN: Lerner Publications Company.

Smith, J. C. ed. (1992). *Notable Black American Women*. Detroit, MI: Gale Research. historyofjesuschrist.org

Thompson, S. (2012). *Wilma Rudolph: An American Hero's Lasting Example of Triumph Under Pressure*. Article. 16 May 2012. San Fransisco, CA: bleacherreport.com

Williams, R. (2016). *Temple and his Tigerbelles: The Brilliant Sprint Queens of Tennessee*. Article. 30 September 2016. London: The Guardian, the guardian.com

Chapter Twenty-Four - Jesse Owens

Angel, R., Bottomley, P. & Doyle, J. (2016) *Leicester City FC and the Benefits of an Underdog Brand*. Article 12 August 2016. Brighton, MA: Harvard Business Review, hbr.org

Ashdown, J. (2011). *50 Stunning Olympic Moments No 6: Jesse Owens' Four Gold Medals, 1936*. Article. 21 December 2011. London: The Guardian, theguardian.com

Baker, W. (2006). *Jesse Owens: An American Life*. Champaign, Il: United States.

Best, T. (2016). *Obituary Jesse Owens: A Chilly Reception in Nazi Germany, Then Olympic Glory.* Article. 8 August 2016. New York, NY: The New York Times, nytimes.com

Folsom, B. W. (2009). *New Deal or Raw Deal? How FDR's Economic Legacy Has Damaged America.* New York, NY: Threshold Editions.

Gentry, T. (1990). *Jesse Owens: Champion Athlete.* Danbury, CT: Grolier Incorporated.

Gitlin, M. (2018). *The 100 Greatest American Athletes.* Lanham, MD: Rowman & Littlefield Publisher.

Litsky, F. (1980). *Jesse Owens Dies of Cancer at 66; Hero of the 1936 Berlin Olympics.* Article. 1 April 1980. New York, NY: The New York Times, nytimes.com

Kim, L. *3 Ways to Discover Your Hidden Natural Talent.* Article. New York, NY: inc.com

McRae, D. (2000). *How Did it Come to This?* Article. 3 September 2000. London: The Observer Sport Sunday, theguardian.com

McDougall, C. (2011). *Jesse Owens: Trailblazing Sprinter.* Edina, MN: ABDO Publishing Company.

Nurmohamed, S. (2020). *The Upside of Being an Underdog.* Article. 14 January 2020. Brighton, MA: Harvard Business Review, hbr.org

Personality v. Character. psychologytoday.com/gb/blog/happiness-in-world

Posner, M. *15 Factors about Reb Zusha of Anipoli.* Article. New York, NY: chabad.org

Schaap, J. (2016). *How Jesse Owens' Childhood Made Him the Champion Seen in Race.* Article. 19 February 2016. New York, NY: Time Magazine, time.org

Schwartz, L. *Owens Pierced a Myth.* Article. Bristol, CT: espn.com

Sports Illustrated. (2010). *Greatest 45 Minutes Ever in Sports.* Article. 24 May 2010. New York, NY: si.com

Schaap, J. (2008). *Triumph: The Untold Story of Jesse Owens and Hitler's Olympics.* Boston, MA: Houghton Mifflin Harcourt USA

Schaap, J. (2016). *How Jesse Owens' Childhood Made Him the Champion Seen in Race.* Article. 19 February 2016. New York, NT: Time Magazine, time.com

Smith, A. (2016). *Leicester City's Soccer Underdog Story Rivals Miracle on Ice.* Article. 30 April 2016. New York, NY: nbcnnews.com

Smith, S. (2014). *Jesse Owens Defied Nazis as Star of the 1936 Olympics.* investors.com/news/management/leaders-and-success/jesse-owens-won-four-olmypic-golds/

Streissguth, T. (2005). *Jesse Owens: Just the Facts Biographies.* Minneapolis, MN: Lerner Publications Company.

Susman, W. (2003). *Culture as History: The Transformation of American Society in the Twentieth Century.* 1st Edition. New York, NY: Pantheon Books.

StrengthsLauncher.com

Taha, L. (2020). *Jesse Owens: Olympic Triumphs and Olympic-Sized Struggles.* Article. 23 January 2020. biography.com

The Christian Science Monitor. (1980). *Jesse Owens: His Place in History.* csmonitor.com/1980/0401/040128

The International Olympic Committee. *Jesse Owens and The Greatest 45 Minutes in Sport.* Article. olympic.org.

Chapter Twenty-Five - Althea Gibson

American Lawn Tennis: Illustrated Magazine of the Game. cdn0.scrvt.com/c2465e9022ba946df66d1244a69b1c75/a20d82cad29e73bb/c30905d4c41e/Alice-Marble---Althea-Gibson-Letters.pdf

Afremow, J. (2014). *The Champion's Mind How Great Athletes Think, Train and Thrive.* Danvers, MA: Rodale Books

Alvarez, A. (2017). *At the Height of Her Tennis Career, Althea Gibson Turned to Golf.* Article. 22 December 2017. wbur.org

Baker, W. (2020). *Science Agrees You Should Stop Being Afraid to Ask for Help. An Expert Debunks 2 Big Myths About Why People Don't.* Article. 14 January 2020. New York, NY: businessinsider.com

Clear, J. *Rome Wasn't Built in a Day, But They Were Laying Bricks Every Hour.* jamesclear.com

ESPN (2003). *Althea Gibson Obituary.* Article. 28 September 2003. Bristol, CT: espn.com

Eubanks, S. (2020). *Pioneer Althea Gibson: An Almost Forgotten Figure in Two Sports.* Article. 19 February 2020. lpga.com

Cass. (2019). *Harlem's Althea Gibson First Black Woman to Win A Championship at Wimbledon.* Article. 16 May 2009. New York, NY: Harlem World, harlemworldmagazine.com

Drucker, J. (2018). *Courage in Action: Althea Gibson Shatters the Race Barrier.* Article. 7 July 2018. International Hall of Fame. tennisfame.com

Harvard Health Publishing. *Giving Thanks Can Make You Happier.* Article. Brighton, MA: health.harvard.edu

Gibson, A. & Fitzgerald, E. (1958). *I Always Wanted to Be Somebody.* New York, NY: HarperCollins.

Gray, F. C. & Lamb, Y. R. (2004). *Born to Win: The Authorized Biography of Althea Gibson.* Hoboken, NJ: John Wiley & Sons.

Isaacson, M. (2003). *Althea Gibson.* Article. 29 September 2003. Chicago, IL: Chicago Tribune, chicagotribune.com

Jacobs, S. (2019). *Althea Gibson, Tennis Star Ahead of Her Time, Gets Her Due at Last.* Article. 26 August 2019. New York, NY: The New York Times, nytimes.com

Jurejko, J. (2019). *Althea Gibson: The Pioneering Champion America Forgot.* Article. 23 August 2019. London: BBC Sport, bbc.co.uk

Macguire, E. (2014). *Althea Gibson: The 'She-Ro' Who Inspired Tennis.* Article. 2 September 2014. New York, NY: edition.cnn.com

Maxwell, J. (2003). *Developing the Leaders Around You.* Nashville, TN: T. Nelson.

McG. Thomas Jr, R. (2003). *Althea Gibson, First Black Wimbledon Champion, Dies at 76.* Article. 28 September 2003. New York, NY: The New York Times, nytimes.com

McG. Thomas Jr, R. (2003). *An Unlikely Champion.* Article. 29 September 2003. New York, NY: The New York Times, nytimes.com

Newman, P. (2017). *The Story of Althea Gibson: The First African American to Win the US Open and How She Changed the Game Forever.* Article. 7 September 2017. London: independent.co.uk

Sokolowski, A. (2020). *The Day Althea Gibson Became the First Black Player to Win a Grand Slam.* Article. 26 May 2020. tennismajors.com

Stanmyre, J. (2016). *Althea Gibson and Arthur Ashe: Breaking Down Tennis' Colour Barrier.* New York, NY: Cavendish Square Publishing.

Tennisfame.com/blog/2018/7/tennis-worthy-althea-gibson

The Story of Althea Gibson.nypost.com/2001/07/12/new-york-post-from-july-12-1957/

Time Magazine. (1957). *That Gibson Girl.* Article. content.time.com/time/magazine/article

Wiggins, D. (2008). *Out of the Shadows: A Biographical History of African American Athletes.* Fayetteville, AR: University of Arkansas Press.

Chapter Twenty-Six - Ben Hogan

Barton, J. (2019). *The Problem with Hogan: Revisiting the Hogan Mystique and What it Means to be a Man.* Article. 24 May 2019. New York, NY: Golf Digest.

Benhoganfoundation.org

Benhogangolf.org

Bonfield, N. (2018). *Ben Hogan Golf's Greatest Comeback.* Article. 5 April 2018. Farnborough: Golf Monthly, golfmonthly.co.uk

Chicagotribune.com/news/ct-xpm-1997-07-26-9707260145-story

CPD Training Accreditation. cpduk.co.uk

Diaz, J. (2009). *Tiger Woods: What Happened?* Article. 28 December 2009. New York, NY: Golf Digest, golfdigest.com

Corrigan, J. (2008). *Tommy Bolt: Golf Champion Prone to Tantrums.* Article. 9 September 2008. London: The Independent, independent.co.uk

Diaz, J. (1997). *One of a Kind Ben Hogan was Often Imitated, but There Will Never be Another Like Him.* Article. 4 August 197. Sports Illustrated, vault.si.com

Dorman, L. (1997). *Ben Hogan, Golf's Iron-Willed Legend, Dies at 84.* Article. 26 July 1997. New York, NY: The New York Times, nytimes.com

Gladwell, M. (2009). *Outliers: The Story of Success.* London: Penguin Books.

Hess, E. (2014). *Learn or Die: Using Science to Build a Leading-Edge Learning Organization.* New York, NY: Columbia Business School Publishing.

Hogan, B. (2006). *Wind, Herbert Warren, Ravielli, Anthony Five Lessons: The Modern Fundamentals of Golf.* London: Simon & Schuster.

Levin, M. (2017). *The One Thing You Need for Success, According to Michael Jordan and Tony Robbins.* Article. 24 July 2017. New York, NY: inc.com

Oats, B. (1988). *Ben Hogan Became a Champion by Practicing 12 Hours a Day: Master of the Game.* Article. 19 June 1988. Los Angeles, CA: Los Angeles Times, latimes.com

Patton, D. *Ben Hogan's Five Rules for Golf.* Article. Orlando, FL: Golfweek, golftips.golfweek.com

Peterson, T. (2004). *The Hard Life of a Golfing Great.* Article. 18 June 2004. New York, NY: Bloomberg Businessweek.

Sportsandspiritualityblogspot.com

Tampabay.com/archive/1999/07/15/wee-ice-mon-made-lasting-impression/

Thoughts on Ben Hogan *Tommy Bolt and Being Cool.* Article. 19 January 1975. New York, NY: The New York Times, nytimes.com

Winters, R. (2004). *The Ten Commandments of Mindpower Golf: No-Nonsense Strategies for Mastering Your Mental Game.* New York, NY: McGraw-Hill Education.

Chapter Twenty-Seven - Fanny Blankers-Koen

Associated Press. (2012). *At '48 London Games, Blankers-Koen's Will to Win Captivated London.* Article. 7 April 2012. New York, NY: The New York Times, nytimes.com

Bagchi, R. (2012). *50 Stunning Olympic Moments No 10: Fanny Blankers-Koen Wins Four Golds.* Article. 18 January 2012. London: The Guardian, theguardian.com

Bijkerk, A. (2004). *Fanny Blankers-Koen A Biography.* Article. Found in Journal of Olympic History 12 (2) 12 May 2004. isoh.org

Coe, S. (2018). *The Olympian Who Changed the Face of Athletics for Women.* Article. London: Country and Townhouse Magazine.

Commire, A. & Klezmer, D. (2000) *Women in World History.* Detroit, MI: Gale Group.

Independent.co.uk/sport/olympics/blankers-jnr-my-mother-only-enjoyed-herself-when-she-was-being-worshipped.

King, G. (2012). *'The Flying Housewife' of the 1948 London Games.* Article. 31 July 2012. Washington, DC: Smithsonianmag.com

Mason, N. (2004*). Fanny Blankers-Koen Obituary.* Article. 26 January 2004. London: The Guardian, theguardian.com

Manchester Guardian. (1948). *Two Women Break World's Record.* Article. 5 August 1948. Manchester: The Manchester Guardian, theguardian.com

Mott, S. (2016). *Jessica Ennis-Hill Urges Sporting Mums to Speak Out.* espn.co.uk/athletics/story/_/id/14922938/jessica-ennis-hill-urges-sporting-mums-speak-out.

New York Times. (1982). *Players: Olympian Ahead of Her Time.* Article. 2 October 1982. New York, NY: The New York Times, nytimes.com

Olympics Website. (2019): *Snapped: The Day Fanny Blankers-Koen Ripped up the Rulebook.* Article. 15 June 2019. olympics.org

Sommerlad, J. (2018). *Fanny Blankers-Koen: Who was the Dutch 'Flying Housewife' and How Did She Change Life for Women in Sport Forever?* Article. 26 April 2018. London: The Independent, independent.co.uk

Vanacker, H. & Kooman, K. (2004). *Sprinting between Kitchen, Children and Podium: The Life and Times of Fanny Blankers-Koen - Found in The Low Countries.* Jaargang 12. dbnl.org

Woolum, J. (1998). *Outstanding Women Athletes: Who They are and How They Influenced Sports in America.* Westport, CT: Greenwood Publishing.

Wharton School: University of Pennsylvania. (2007). *Workplace Loyalties Change, but the Value of Mentoring Doesn't.* Article. 16 May 2007. knowledge.wharton.upenn.edu

Chapter Twenty-Eight - Virginia Hall

Branson, R. (2020). *My to-do list in 1972.* Article. 6 November 2020. London: virgin.com

CIA (2015). *Virginia Hall: The Courage and Daring of The Limping Lad.* Article. Langley, VA: Central Intelligence Agency.

Foot, M. R. D. (1966). *SOE in France,* London: Her Majesty's Stationery Office.

Gralley, C. R. (2017). *A Climb to Freedom: A Personal Journey in Virginia Hall's Steps in Studies in Intelligence.* Vol 61 No 1. March 2017. Langley, VN: cia.gov

Gralley, C. R. (2019). *Hall of Mirrors: Virginia Hall: America's Greatest Spy of WWII.* Chrysalis Books, LLC.

Elder, H. (2016). *Faces of Defense Intelligence: Virginia Hall - The Limping Lady.* Article. 27 October 2016. Defence Intelligence Agency.

Grey, M. (2019). *A Woman of No Importance Finally Gers Her Due.* Article. 18 April 2019. nrp.org

Mind Tools Website Creative Problem Solving. Article. Edinburgh: mindtools.com

Pearson, J. (2009). *The Wolves at the Door: The True Story of America's Greatest Female Spy.* New York, NY: The Lyons Press.

Purnell, S. (2019). *A Woman of No Importance: The Untold Story of Virginia Hall: WWII's Most Dangerous Spy.* London: Virago Press.

Purnell, S. (2019). *Virginia Hall was America's most Successful Female WWII Spy. But She was Almost Kept from Serving.* Article. 9 April 2019. New York, NY: Time Magazine.

Ruiz, G. (2018). *Why the Nazis Called Virginia Hall "The Most Dangerous of All Allied Spies.* Article. 27 June 2018. allthatsinteresting.com

State.Gov *Not Bad for a Girl from Baltimore: The Story of Virginia Hall.* PDF

Topham, G. & Kollewe, J. (2019). *Richard Branson's Virgin Galactic Prepares to go Public.* Article. 9 July 2019. London: The Guardian, theguardian.com

Viewpoint: *How Creativity is Helped by Failure.* Article. 14 November 2015. London: bbc.co.uk

Warren, J. (2019). *Virgina Hall: The Spy the Nazis Could Never Catch.* Article. 30 May 2019. London: The Daily Express.

Chapter Twenty-Nine - John McCain

Alexander, P. (2002). *Man of the People: The Life of John McCain.* Hoboken, NJ: John Wiley & Sons.

Archives.Gov: *Executive Order 10631--Code of Conduct for members of the Armed Forces of the United States.*

Bowdon, C. (2014). *John McCain: I Was Lying.* 7 May 2014. gq.com/story/i-was-lying

Carroll, J. (2017). *The True Nature of John McCain's Heroism.* Article. 21 July 2017. New York, NY: The New Yorker, newyorker.com

Elkins, K. (2018). *Mark Cuban Wakes Up Every Morning at 6:30 - Here's the First Thing He Does.* Article. 22 October 2018. Englewood Cliffs, NY: CNBC.com

Eu.usatoday.com/story/news/politics/2018/08/26/six-times-sen-john-mccain-earned-title-maverick/1104737002/

Gambino, L. (2018). *It's Going to be Difficult to Fill His Shoes: Arizona Remembers John McCain.* Article. 27 August 2018. London: The Guardian, theguardian.com

Green, M. (2020). *McCain's Reset: US Vietnam Relations Going Strong after 25 Years.* Article. 11 July 2020. Washington, DC: The Hill.

Kabaservice, G. (2018). *John McCain was a Paradox. There's No-one Like Him Left in Congress.* Article. 27 August 2018. London: The Guardian, theguardian.com

Keiningham, T. L., Aksoy, L. & Williams, L. (2009). Why Loyalty Matters. Dallas, TX: Benbella Books.

Knowledge@Wharton (2012). *Seems Awkward, Ignores the Rules, But Brilliant: Meet the Maverick Job Candidate.* Article. 29 August 2012. New York, NY: Time Magazine.

Kuhnhenn, J. (2008). *Navy Releases McCain's Military Record.* Article. 7 May 2008. New York, NY: Associated Press.

Linden, M. (2008). *Posttraumatic Embitterment Disorder and Wisdom Therapy.* Journal of Cognitive Psychotherapy. 22. 4-14. 10.1891/0889.8391.22.1.4. Berlin: reserachgate.net

McCain, J. & Salter, M. (2003). *Worth the Fighting for: The Education of an American Maverick and the Heroes Who Inspired Him.* New York, NY: Random House.

McCain, J. & Salter, M. (2007). *Character is Destiny.* New York, NY: Random House Paperbacks.

McCain, J. & Salter, M. (2009). *Faith of My Fathers: A Family Memoir.* New York, NY: Perennial.

Nytimes.com/2000/04/27/world/mccain-in-vietnam-finds-the-past-isn-t-really-past.

O'Dowd, N. (2018). *Duty, Honour, Country, Heritage: Our 2006 interview with John McCain.* Article. 26 August 2018. Irish Central, irishcentral.com

Povich, E. S. (2019). *John McCain: A Biography.* Westport, Conn: Greenwood Press.

Purdum, T. S. (2018). *John McCain and the Lost Art of Decency.* Article. 25 August 2018. Washington, DC: theatlantic.com

Purdy, E. R. (2020). *Charles H. Keating.* Article. 27 March 2020. Encyclopaedia Britannica.

Schleifer, T. (2016). *McCain to Trump: A Concession Isn't Just An Exercise In Graciousness - It Is An Act Of Respect.* edition.cnn.com/2016/10/20/politics/john-mccain-donald-trump-concession/index.html

Seltzer, L. (2015). *Don't Let Your Anger Mature into Bitterness.* Article. 14 January 2015. New York, NY: Psychology Today, psychologytoday.com

Start of Tragedy: Pilot Hears a Blast as He Checks Plane. nytimes.com/1967/07/31/archives/start-of-tragedy-pilot-hears-a-blast-as-he-checks-plane-tragedys.

Timberg, R. (1996). *The Nightingale's Song.* New York, NY: Simon & Schuster.

Urbaniak, G. C. & Kilmann, P. R. (2003). *Physical Attractiveness and the "Nice Guy Paradox": Do Nice Guys Really Finish Last?* Sex Roles, Vol 49, No 9/10: 413-426. Columbia, SC: drpeterkilmann.com

Chapter Thirty - Irena Sendler

Atwood, K. (2011). *Women Heroes of World War II.* Chicago, IL: Chicago Review Press.

Biography.com (2016). *Irena Sendler Biography.* A&E Television Networks.

Campbell, S. (2018). *7 Ways Modest Leadership Increases Team Success.* entrepreneur.com

Campbell, S. (2016). *6 Characteristics of Resourceful People that Bring them Success.* Article. 10 March 2010. Irvine, CA: Entrepreneur.com

De Quetteville, H. (2008). *'Female Schindler' Irena Sendler, Who Saved Thousands of Jewish Children from the Nazis has Died Aged 98.* Article. 11 May 2008. London: The Daily Telegraph, telegraph.co.uk

Fox, M. (2011). *Modesty is the M.O. for Polish Heroine Irena Sendler.* jweekly.com/2011/04/22/modesty-is-the-m-o-for-polish-heroine-irena-sendler/

Halter, M. (1998). *Stories of Deliverance: Speaking with Men and Women Who Rescued Jews from the Holocaust.* Chicago, IL: Open Court.

Harding, L. (2008). *Irena Sendler: A Holocaust Heroine*. Article. 1 August 2008. London: The Daily Mail.

Horan, G (2007) *Irena's Children*. aish.com

Imperial War Museum. *Daily Life in the Warsaw Ghetto*. London: iwm.org.uk

Jewish Virtual Library. *Irena Sendler*. Article. American Israeli Cooperative Enterprise (AICE). Chevy Chase, MD: jewishvirtuallibrary.org

Kroll, C. *Irena Sendler: Rescuer of the Children of Warsaw*. thejewishwoman.org. Article. New York, NY: chabad.org

Lerski, J. J. (1996). *Historical Dictionary of Poland 966-1945*. Westport, CT: Greenwood Press.

Lopez, S. J., Teramoto Pedrotti, J. & Snyder, C. R. (2015). *Positive Psychology*. Thousand Oaks, CA: Sage Publications.

Marytrimblebooks.com/book-review-life-in-a-jar-the-irena-sendler-project.

Nazar, J. (2013). *The 21 Principles of Persuasion*. Article. 26 March 2013. Jersey City, NJ: forbes.com

NHS. (2020). *Over 400,000 People Join NHS Army of Volunteers in One Day*. 25 March 2000. england.nhs.uk

Sciutto, J. (2007). *Holocaust Hero Turns 97*. Article. 2 November 2007. New York, NY: ABC News.

The Wiener Holocaust Library. *Warsaw Ghetto*. Article. theholocaustexplained.org.

The Daily Telegraph. (2008). *Irena Sendler Obituary*. 12 May 2008. London: telegraph.co.uk

The Irena Sendler Project. *Life in a Jar - The Courageous Story of Irena Sendler*. Article. irenasendler.com

Usatoday30.usatoday.com/news/world/2008-05-12-1916156174_x.

Vance, Sandra S. & Scott, Roy V. (1994). *Wal-Mart: A History of Sam Walton's Retail Phenomenon*. New York, NY: Twayne Publishers.

Yad Vashem Women of Valor - *Stories of Women Who Rescued Jews During the Holocaust*. Article. Yadvashem.org

Walton, S. with Huey, J. (1992). *Sam Walton, Made in America*. New York, NY: Doubleday.

Washingtonpost.com/wp-srv/aponline/20010526/aponline091226_000

Zamoyski, A. (2009). *Poland: A History*. New York, NY: Harper Press.

Woo, E. (2008). *WWII Saviour of Young Jews*. Article. 13 May 2008. Los Angeles, CA: Los Angeles Times, latimes.com

Conclusion

Churchill, W. S. (2013). *Never Give In! Winston Churchill's Speeches*. Selected and Edited by his Grandson. London: Bloomsbury Academic.

Esfahani Smith, E. (2013). *There's More to Life Than Being Happy: Meaning Comes from the Pursuit of more Complex Things than Happiness*. Article. 9 January 2013. Washington, DC: theatlantic.com/health/archive/2013/01/theres-more-to-life-than-being-happy/266805/

Frankl, V. (2006). *Man's Search for Meaning*. London: Beacon Press, beacon.org

Gerver, R. (2019). *Education: A Manifesto for Change*. London: Bloomsbury.

Greenfield, S (2018). *Stephen Hawking Remembered: Beyond His Towering Intellect was a Passion for Sharing with Everyone the Wonder of Science*. Article. 14 March 2018. London: The Independent, independent.co.uk

Lowry, B. (2003). *Her Dream of Dreams: The Rise and Triumph of Madam C. J. Walker*. New York, NY: Vintage Books

Mandela, N. (1995). *Long Walk to Freedom: The Autobiography of Nelson Mandela*. London: Abacus.

Myre, G. (2013). *Nelson Mandela and the Virtue of Compromise*. Article. 8 December 2013. Npr.org

Oxford Dictionary of English. (2020). Oxford: oed.com

Sazegar, N. (2017). *Irena Sendler's Quotes Show Us What it Means to Help Others.* Article. 2 October 2017. Entitymag.com

Schuller, R. H. (1988). *Tough Times Never Last, But Tough People Do.* New Delhi: Orient Paperbacks.